Social Patterns
in Australian Literature

BY THE SAME AUTHOR

T. Inglis Moore

SOCIAL
PATTERNS
IN
AUSTRALIAN
LITERATURE

 ANGUS AND ROBERTSON

1.

First published in 1971 by
ANGUS AND ROBERTSON (PUBLISHERS) PTY LTD
221 George Street, Sydney
54 Bartholomew Close, London
107 Elizabeth Street, Melbourne
89 Anson Road, Singapore

National Library of Australia
card number and ISBN 0 207 12174 5

Published with the assistance of the Commonwealth Literary Fund

Registered in Australia for transmission by post as a book
PRINTED IN AUSTRALIA BY HALSTEAD PRESS, SYDNEY

To my wife, Peace,
whose devoted and understanding support
has made this book possible,
and to my daughter, Pacita Alexander,
who helped in times of need.

Preface

THIS study examines Australian literature, not as literature, but as Australian—as the expression of significant patterns of thought, feeling, and behaviour distinguishing the Australian society.

Whilst it recognizes the existence of other social patterns in our writing, it is concerned especially with the major ones, and it naturally concentrates on their most representative writers rather than on those authors who have deviated from the main literary traditions.

As a socio-literary interpretation it attempts to define and analyse the major social patterns, to trace their origins, and to explore their interrelations. The first, introductory chapter clears the ground by a discussion of the aims, problems, and limits of this complex task.

The second chapter follows on with the integrating principle that brings the diversity of the patterns into an ecological unity, since the shaping of the society is seen as the interaction between the People and the Place. It is not a case of geographical determinism alone, because at times the nature of the People—which included, of course, the cultural forms and national traditions brought here from England, Scotland, and Ireland—was the stronger force in moulding the patterns. Events of history, such as the establishment of the convict system, also played their considerable parts. Often, however, the Place was the primary determinant of the social patterns. They were largely born of the land, epiphanies of the *genius loci*, the spirit of the country. To some extent, therefore, this study is an essay in human ecology, and chapter III surveys the environmental and historical factors at work. The separate patterns are then analysed and illustrated in the remaining chapters.

The literary evidence indicates that the major patterns were largely formed during the first half of the nineteenth century, and arose among the bushmen, comprising the settlers, squatters, selectors, and bush workers. Behind them lay the fundamental factor of the bush itself, not because of any fanciful mystique of the soil, but simply because of the hard, practical fact that during the pastoral age the character of the land determined so emphatically, so inevitably, the kind of economy, the way of living, and the distinctive outlook on life.

Since the second world war, however, the original influence of the bush has been modified substantially by the stronger contemporary influences exerted by our highly urbanized and industrialized society. The social patterns have been visibly changing, and the changes are reflected in the literature. The old values of Lawson and Furphy, of Katharine Prichard, Vance Palmer, and Mary Gilmore have often been replaced by the very different values of such writers as Patrick White, Christina Stead, and A. D. Hope.

This study was begun in the 1930s, and some of its themes formed the subject of Commonwealth Literary Fund Lectures I gave at the universities of Sydney and Queensland in the forties. In 1951 a first draft of some 70,000 words entitled "The Social Mirror" shared the first prize for a work of non-fiction in the Commonwealth Jubilee Literary Competition. At that stage it was a completely pioneering venture, since there were then no books whatever dealing directly with such social interpretation. Circumstances, however, prevented the final shaping and publication of the draft, although the concentration on Australian literature through the teaching of the first University degree course in the subject from 1954 to 1966, at the Canberra University College and then at the Australian National University, provided intensive research and further ideas. The early draft was therefore rewritten, brought up to date, and expanded to almost twice the original length.

I am indebted for valuable advice and criticism to friends and colleagues, especially the late Gavin Long, Mr A. E. Mander, Professor A. D. Hope, Professor Manning Clark, Mr D. W. A. Baker, Professor Robert L. McDougall of Carleton University, Ottawa, Professor Geoffrey Blainey, and Mr Douglas Stewart.

I wish to express my thanks also to the staffs of the Australian National Library, the Mitchell Library, and the La Trobe Library; to the writers whose work has been quoted in extracts (to whom acknowledgment is made in the footnotes) and to Angus and Robertson (Publishers) Pty Ltd for permission to quote the following complete poems: "Nationality" by Mary Gilmore, "During Drouth" by Ernest G. Moll, "Emus" by "E" (Mary Fullerton), "O desolate eves" by Christopher Brennan, and "Woman to Man" by Judith Wright; to the Australian Research Grants Committee for a research grant and the Australian National University for its administration; and to Mrs A. Guenot for her expertise with the typescript.

T. Inglis Moore

Canberra
1970

Contents

I

The Social Element
in Literature

Confucius said: Truth does not depart from human nature. If what is regarded as truth departs from human nature, it may not be regarded as truth. The Book of Songs says: "In hewing an axe handle, the pattern is not far off."

TSESZE[1]

A work of literature is not a mere individual play of imagination, the isolated caprice of an excited brain, but a transcript of contemporary manners, a manifestation of a certain kind of mind.

TAINE[2]

Our literature precisely has the merit that, almost without any exception, its best representatives, ahead of our intelligentsia—please note this point— bowed before the popular truth, and recognized the people's ideals as genuinely beautiful. In fact, literature was compelled to adopt them as standards, almost involuntarily.

DOSTOIEVSKY[3]

> She is the scroll on which we are to write
>   Mythologies our own and epics new ...
> Yet she shall be, as we, the Potter, mould:
>   Altar or tomb, as we aspire, despair:
> What wine we bring shall she, the chalice, hold:
>   What word we write shall she, the script, declare: ...

O'DOWD[4]

[1] The Golden Mean of Tsesze in Lin Yutang, *The Wisdom of China* (London 1944), p.276.
[2] H. A. Taine, *History of English Literature*, trans. from the French by H. van Laun (Edinburgh 1873), 4 vols, vol.I, p.1.
[3] F. M. Dostoievsky, *The Diary of a Writer*, trans. by Boris Brasol (London 1949 ed., first publ. 1873-81), p.203.
[4] Bernard O'Dowd, from "The Bush", *Collected Poems* (Melbourne 1941), pp.208-9.

A Story and a Search

This study originated, aptly enough, in "the *Bulletin* pub", the hotel near the *Bulletin* office in George Street, Sydney, whose bar had been the happy rendezvous of Australian writers for decades. There Roderic Quinn, Frank Davison and I were drinking and yarning one day when we were joined by the late Percy Lindsay. Beer in hand, radiating his genial charm, Percy told a story of the days when he, his brother Norman, and other artists were painting in a small settlement outside Melbourne. On Saturday nights they forgathered at the local pub and were good friends with the pubkeeper and his daughter Molly. One night when they were engaged as usual in drinking, singing, and arguing over art, life, and women, Molly came over to them and said, "I'm sorry, boys, but would you mind breaking it down a bit."

They were taken aback at this unusual request, and at their look of surprise she explained, apologetically, "Dad's gone and hanged himself in the woodshed."

"And sure enough," said Percy, "there was the poor bastard hanging from a rafter, dead as a doornail. He had his mouth half open in a funny way, and looked a bit grim. We had quite a job getting him down."

This story struck me as peculiarly Australian in many ways: in its matter-of-fact realism, with a dash of hardness, hinting at the callous; its sombreness, with a touch of the macabre; its stoic lack of emotion or melodrama, shown in the girl's laconic announcement of her father's suicide; the understatement, both emotional and verbal, with the meiosis of the idiomatic "a bit" used by both Molly and Percy; the easy, friendly democratic equality with which she treated the artists in her "I'm sorry, boys"; the kindly, almost "matey" consideration in her apology for disturbing them; and the ironic contrast between the revelling of the artists in the bar and the grimness of their host's body suspended in the woodshed, suggesting the harsh irony familiar to a people living in a land where the bounty of a good season is soon mocked by the death and desolation of the drought. Australian, too, is the conjunction of care-free pleasure and calm endurance, the hedonism of the artists complementing the stoicism of the pubkeeper's daughter.

This story, with its distinctive combination of characteristics, could not have occurred in any other country than Australia. In England, for instance, the daughter of a local innkeeper would not have treated a group of professional men with such egalitarian camaraderie. An American account of the suicide would have been marked by over-statement rather than under-statement. In any

European country Dad could not have hanged himself in the wood-shed without arousing emotion and drama.

Listening to Percy Lindsay's story, I was immediately reminded of certain tales and sketches of Henry Lawson that embodied the same qualities—"The Union Buries its Dead", "The Bush Undertaker", "In a Dry Season", and "The Drover's Wife". Afterwards I looked them up, and was impressed by their strong and unmistakable rendering of basic Australian ideas and sentiments. So I began a general search into our literature to see how far, as a body of national writing, it expressed distinctive ways of life and thought and feeling, working inductively to discover what the literature itself revealed to an objective analysis.

This book, then, is the result of that search. It is a sociological study, although its primary source material is Australian creative and critical writing, reinforced by some relevant historical work. It has a double concern, first with *what* the social patterns are, and then with *why* they developed as they did. The exploration of their origins goes beyond the literature to draw on biology, geography, and history in presenting an ecological synthesis.

In the first concern the literature is taken as a social mirror reflecting those traits of sentiment and outlook distinguishing a particular society which are best called *social patterns*. These are associated as a complex in which a common home in a country, common blood, a common language and literature, a common system of government, education and religion, all serve to unite the members of a society, make it a community, and give it a collective spirit that differentiates it from other societies. Although various societies have similar social patterns, each has a special combination of them which is distinctive.

Since societies are organized in a national framework, it is said that national literatures reflect national characteristics. In his ingenious and often penetrating study, *Englishmen, Frenchmen, Spaniards*, Salvador de Madariaga contends that

However hasty these sketches of national types may be, they have the merit of establishing beyond doubt the great fact which many a dogmatic internationalist would have us forget. There *is* such a thing as national character. Opinions may differ as to the influences which create or alter it. Race, climate, economic conditions, may enter for a greater or a lesser part in its inception and development. But the fact is there and stares us in the face. History, geography, religion, language, even the common will are not enough to define a nation. A nation is a fact of psychology. It is that which is *na*tural or *na*tive in it which gives its force to the word *na*tion. A nation is a character.[5]

[5] Salvador de Madariaga, *Englishmen, Frenchmen, Spaniards* (London 1931), p.xi.

Even granting that there is such a thing as "national character", the fact remains that the word "national" today carries many confusing connotations, whilst the term "national characteristics" often implies unscientific assumptions of racial psychology and inherited group qualities. If a nation is a fact, sometimes an elusive and ambiguous one, a race is frequently only an ancillary myth employed for political ends. A society, however, is a concrete fact which is clear and definite. The term "social", moreover, is wider than "national", whilst it retains a more objective character, free of the restrictive sentiments and confusing prejudices evoked by "national". Historically it is more precise here, since Australia developed a distinctive society with its own *mores* long before it evolved into the further stage of nation-hood. Where "national characteristics" may be suspect, therefore, "social patterns" can be used objectively and with historical aptness.

At the same time, most, if not all, of the social patterns discussed have become accepted over the years by Australians generally, so that they have finally developed into national traditions. Indeed, I might well have used the term "national traditions" correctly in a broad sense, and it was tempting to adopt such a popular usage. The temptation was resisted, however, for the sake of exactness, since a tradition connotes a general conscious acceptance of it by society, whereas several of the patterns have not yet gained this explicit recognition, even if they are recognized unconsciously and implicitly.

The Three Elements of Literature

Moreover, the term "social patterns" is more suitable to a consideration of the social element in literature and its relation to the other two elements contained in literature as a work of art, the personal and the universal. In this triad of art the personal element is the one most easily apparent in every literary work, which is *sui generis*, an individuation as a specific utterance of the writer's personality, unique as embodying the flesh, blood, and mind of its creator. It is determined by his special beliefs—a complex which has never occurred before in exactly the same shape and will never happen again. None of us can ever escape from the irrevocable fate of always being ourselves. We are all bound to the Promethean rock of our ego by unbreakable chains. All writing, even the most imaginative, is ultimately autobiographical, spun with thread drawn, like a spider's web, from the body of the writer's perceptions and thoughts, dreams and desires and memories.

Every great work also contains a universal element that goes beyond person, time and place. It is shaped into a form that expresses the thoughts and feelings common to mankind and recognizable as such. Without abdicating personality, it also transcends it to reach the plane of the universal. The writer can then proclaim with Walt Whitman: "I pass death with the dying and birth with the new-wash'd babe, and am not contain'd between my hat and boots."[6] With such a passing into the universal the poet can sound his "barbaric yawp", not merely to himself or a shocked, unbelieving America, but "over the roofs of the world". He creates, in Shelley's phrasing of the poet's task, "Forms more real than living man, Nurslings of Immortality". Whether a writer has created such forms is determined by the judgement of time and men.

This power of endurance, bred of a happy marriage between artistic form and significant content, is the specific literary quality in any writing. It is more important, of course, than any personal or social element since it alone connotes survival, whether in a limited degree within a national literature or in full-blown universality as a work of world literature.

The Social Element

Here, for the special purpose of this study, our concern is concentrated on the third element in literature, the social one. Whatever his personal or universal character, every writer is also a part of his society, his country, and his century. As Sir Leslie Stephen pointed out in his *English Literature and Society in the Eighteenth Century*:

Every writer may be regarded in various aspects. He is, of course, an individual, and the critic may endeavour to give a psychological analysis of him. ... But every man is also an organ of the society in which he has been brought up. The material upon which he works is the whole complex of conceptions, religious, imaginative, and ethical, which forms his mental atmosphere. Fully to appreciate any great writer, therefore, it is necessary to distinguish between the characteristics due to the individual with certain idiosyncrasies and the characteristics due to his special modification by the existing stage of social and intellectual development.[7]

Thus Dante and Shakespeare were social writers who reflected their times: "The *Divina Commedia* also reveals in the completest way the essential spirit of the Middle Ages", whilst "If any man ever initiated and gave full utterance to the characteristic ideas of his contemporaries it was Shakespeare, and nobody ever accepted more thoroughly the forms of art which they worked out".[8] Indeed, it is impossible to imagine Shakespeare writing characteristically as a Frenchman, a contemporary of Pope, or a mid-Victorian. Despite his universality he is nothing if not an Englishman and an Elizabethan.

The social element is naturally marked in literature since of all the

---

[6] Walt Whitman, "Song of Myself", *Leaves of Grass* (Philadelphia 1884), p.34.
[7] Leslie Stephen, *English Literature and Society in the Eighteenth Century* (London 1904), pp.8-9.
[8] Ibid., p.16.

arts it contains the greatest conceptual content. It is more concrete than such arts as painting, sculpture and music, which contain more of the abstract and approach closer to pure form, a point illustrated by the masterly discussion of the abstract and concrete elements in music by Albert Schweitzer in his illuminating *J. S. Bach*. A sonata or a statue may contain little but the pure formal beauty of sound or shape, but a novel or short story, drama or epic, even a lyrical poem, has a content which naturally tends to hold some social significance as it describes humanity or nature, tells a story, fashions a character, depicts human action, or voices feelings and ideas.

Literature, although it exists primarily for its own sake, is also a function of its society. It fulfils the purpose of acting, as defined by Hamlet to the players: "to hold, as 'twere, the mirror up to nature; to show virtue her own feature, scorn her own image, and the very age and body of the time his form and pressure". Hence literature becomes, in Taine's phrase, "a transcript of contemporary manners, a manifestation of a certain kind of mind". This manifestation may be made in two different ways: through the content of the work, with its scene, action, and characters, or through the writer, expressing his personal outlook and sympathies.

Similarly, the social element with its patterns may be expressed either implicitly or explicitly. It is usually implicit in the attitude of the writer to his subject, and even non-social poets like Neilson and McCrae express it unconsciously in this way. On the whole, however, the social patterns find a conscious articulation in Australian writing, just as they do with the majority of modern writers in England, Europe, and America—with Shaw, Wells, and Joyce, T. S. Eliot and Greene; with Toller, Thomas Mann, Sartre, and Pirandello; with Hemingway, Steinbeck, and Faulkner. In contemporary American writing the strength of the social element has been well described in an article in *The Times Literary Supplement* on the "American Way":

It is the commitment of every American writer to express and explore something of the American identity, the American way of life, of that elusive state of mind which makes an American an American, which makes all Americans, whatever clothes they wear, or jobs they hold, equal, which is symbolized not by a queen, not even by a President, but by an abstract flag, the Stars and Stripes.[9]

Australian writers, especially the novelists and short story writers, are similarly committed to exploration of their own world and its way of life, creating a *littérature engagée*.

---

[9] *The Times Literary Supplement*, 16 Aug. 1957, p.iii.

Relation of the Social to the Personal and
Universal Elements

In any literature this social element is generally mingled with the personal one without any contradiction, since the writer is a social being as well as an individual. Part of his personality, at least, is determined by his environment, including the cultural matrix in which he is embedded. Thus the great majority of Australian writers express some of the prevailing social patterns. The strongest representations of the national traditions come from such writers of fiction as Henry Lawson, Joseph Furphy, and Katharine Susannah Prichard, and such poets as O'Dowd, Mary Gilmore, and Judith Wright, who are especially social and national in outlook. In their case the personal and social elements are closely identified with each other.

At the same time the social element, like the personal and universal elements, varies considerably in character and degree with each writer. It is negligible in a few writers who live in their own imaginative worlds and seem to owe little to the world around them. This occurs with poets rather than novelists and dramatists. Walter de la Mare offers a fit example in modern English writing, Christopher Brennan in Australian literature. Only a few poems of Brennan's deal with the local scene or contain such images drawn from his native background as "My days of azure have forgotten me". His true skies, however, were not Australian but European, in which shone his guiding lights of French symbolism and German romanticism. His poetry, as he himself said, might as well have been written in China as in his own country. He was never happily at home here, remaining, as Hugh McCrae put it inimitably, "a star in exile, unconstellated at the south".[10] Yet even he expressed, as we shall see, some Australian qualities.

So, too, in fiction Henry Handel Richardson drew upon European naturalism for her outlook and technique. As an expatriate she wavered in her attitude towards her homeland: she stated in one letter that she had always considered herself a good Australian; in another she wrote, "Hartley Grattan is beginning to think that I am not a good enough Australian. God forbid that I ever should be!"[11] Yet she confessed in *Myself when Young* that she was strongly influenced by the Australian environment of her youth, she drew her themes largely from her experiences within it, and she became the most powerful exponent of the realistic spirit common to most Australian novelists. Richardson fits into our scope, therefore, whilst writers like Brennan find a relatively small place in a study of social patterns in Australian literature for the same reason that Professor

[10] Hugh McCrae, *Story Book Only* (Sydney 1948), p.92.
[11] Henry Handel Richardson, Letter to Mr Schwartz, MS in J. K. Moir collection.

B

Parrington gives scant consideration in his *Main Currents in American Thought* to Edgar Allan Poe, who stood apart from such currents.

Any disregard of non-social writers here does not, of course, reflect in any way upon their artistic merit, since the social and universal elements are distinct. There is no necessary correlation between them. The folk ballads and Henry Lawson, for example, are both rich in social significance, but the ballads lack literary form whilst Lawson is an original artist in the short story. Brennan is a fine poet who has little Australian content, but his compeers in Neilson, FitzGerald, Slessor, and Judith Wright are deeply concerned with their Australian earth and society. Usually the Australianity of a writer and his literary quality are commingled and unified; sometimes they bear no relation to each other.

Indeed, the distinction between the social and universal elements, or, to use the more common phrasing, between national and literary values, is a clear and elementary one which should not need discussion. Yet the failure to make this fundamental distinction has caused considerable confusion in Australian literary criticism. On the one hand the two elements have often been fallaciously equated, on the other they have been opposed in a false contradiction.

The confusion is common amongst nationalist critics who tend to assume that if a work is strongly Australian in subject and outlook it is *ipso facto* a good one; if it is not Australian it is bad. The more national a work is, the better it is. A nationalist inflation was displayed in the worship of Gordon by his devotees, the idolizing of Lawson as a poet by his old mates, and Miles Franklin's claim that Furphy is superior to Henry James, Proust, and Joyce.

The bias of an ardent nationalism produced in turn an equally unbalanced reaction from critics who tended, in their eagerness to affirm literary standards, to go to the other extreme and fall into the fallacy of assuming that if a work was wholeheartedly Australian it must be bad. They assumed, implicitly as a rule, that to be universal a writer should be un-Australian or even anti-Australian.

In both of these cases an irrelevant non-literary criterion—the presence or the absence of national values—was used to make judgements on literature. In particular the anti-nationalist bias has had a curious, anachronistic revival since the last world war. The flogging of the dead nationalist horse has persisted long after the writers themselves, both in prose and in poetry, have passed beyond nationalism to a natural, mature acceptance of the world they live in.

A rootless cosmopolitanism, furthermore, is as shallow as the sentimental nationalism of the past. Nor should this be confused with a true universality, which arises out of the particular. The anti-nationalist of today shudders at the mention of an unabashed gum-tree, that crude Australian object of the bush which comes between the wind and his sophisticated, urban nobility. Then Judith Wright disposes of this attitude convincingly by her "Gum-trees Stripping", a beautiful lyric that combines a universality of concept with concrete, imaginative particulars:

> *Wisdom can see the red, the rose,*
> *the stained and sculptured curve of grey,*
> *the charcoal scars of fire, and see*
> *around that living tower of tree*
> *the hermit tatters of old bark*
> *split down and strip to end the season;*
> *and can be quiet and not look*
> *for reasons past the edge of reason.*[12]

Thus Judith Wright shows that the despised tree can call forth, no less than a classical myth, lyrical power and depth of vision, with "this fountain slowed in air" turned into a universal symbol of the "silent rituals" of seasonal earth. The fault, dear Brutus, is not in our gum-trees, but in ourselves if we are underlings unable to create high poetry out of them, or, indeed, to create enduring literature out of the Australian world we live in. Shaw Neilson, who joins Judith Wright as one of the two finest Australian lyrists, can similarly make a subtle, intangible magic out of a common orange-tree or transmute a mushroom into autumnal enchantment. In fact, the best of Australian writing in poetry and prose alike, with only a few exceptions, strikes its roots deep into its own earth and its own people.

This leads to the fundamental point that the social and universal elements, the national and the literary, are not in themselves opposed or contradictory. They may be dissociated, but in general they join harmoniously in the work of literature. The great writers are usually both national and international. Louis Esson, whose ideal was the building up in Australia of an indigenous theatre expressing the national spirit, has drawn attention to the sound comments of a leading French author on this precise point:

The position of the writer in relationship to his country and to humanity in general has been stated clearly and justly by André Gide. In an address given in Paris to an international group of writers, Gide declared that no one was more specifically Spanish than Cervantes, more English than Shakespeare, more Russian than Gogol, more French than Rabelais or Voltaire, and at the same time more universal and more profoundly human, his contention being that it is precisely in literature that this triumph of the general in the particular and of the human in the individual is most fully realised.[13]

[12] Judith Wright, "Gum-trees Stripping" in *The Two Fires* (Sydney 1955), p.21.
[13] Louis Esson, in *Australian Writers Speak*, a series of talks arranged by the Fellowship of Australian Writers for the Australian Broadcasting Commission (Sydney 1942), pp.9-10.

It might be added that in Australian literature no one is more specifically Australian than Lawson, and at the same time "more universal and more profoundly human". Thus Mitchell is both swaggie and sardonic Hamlet of the bush. Joe Wilson, the struggling selector, is also the lover and the father. Australian to the core, he is also Everyman.

Esson also drives home his point where he says sensibly:

The Australian writer asks no more than is taken for granted by the writers of every other country.

No one would accuse Balzac, Dickens, or Tolstoy of being local or provincial, lacking in universal appeal, because their subject comprised characters and themes typical of their own country and period. As Havelock Ellis once put it, "the paradox of literature is that only the writer who is first truly national can later become international."[14]

The Social Element in Australian Literature

The great majority of Australian writers are certainly "truly national", since here the literature, like the society it mirrors, developed a distinctive character of its own. Again, the national or social element is especially strong in Australian literature for several reasons. To begin with, it is stronger than in some other literatures simply because Australian writing, being younger than they are, is more concerned with exploring its environment. Older literatures, having already made this exploration and arrived at definitions of their societies as geographical and national entities, have often passed on to more universal concerns, such as metaphysical issues and the intimate processes of the mind. Australian literature is still highly localized, particularly in its fiction; over-busied with description of its external surroundings. Whilst this local exploring places limits on fiction's literary value, since it conduces at times to a superficial concentration on externals and results in reportage instead of creative imagination, it produces, on the other hand, a richness of social content.

A strong social consciousness, moreover, has always been a characteristic of Australian writing. This finds expression not only in an exploration of its environment but also in two other forms: the depiction of social groups rather than of individuals, and a criticism of society which springs from the characteristically Australian demands for democratic equality and social justice.

The social group has always been particularly stressed in Australian writing. From the beginning, when Kingsley, Clarke, and Boldrewood concentrated on such social themes as the life of the pastoralists, the convict system, and bushranging, the novelists have been concerned with depicting communities and occupational groups. Their approach

[14] Ibid., p.9.

has been communal, not individual, whether it was Furphy rendering the Riverina world of teamsters and squatters, the host of historical novelists tracing the fortunes of the pioneers, the social realists giving critical accounts of contemporary society, or the reformers attacking the social problem of the aborigines. A representative novelist like Katharine Prichard describes such groups as timber-workers, pioneers, squatters and aborigines in the north-west, opal miners and gold miners. Another, like Kylie Tennant, ranges from the country town, bagmen on the dole, and city slum-dwellers to coastal villagers, juvenile delinquents, and travelling bee-keepers. The result of this dominant trend is that fiction has often lacked the depth and universality of individual character, but shown abundance of social description and criticism. Some novelists such as Prichard, Vance Palmer, and M. Barnard Eldershaw combine character and environment, but relatively few novelists—with exceptions like Richardson, Eleanor Dark, and Christina Stead—concentrated on the psychology of the individual until the last two decades, which has been marked by the psychological novels of such writers as White, Stow, Astley, Harrower, and Keneally.

So, too, the lively social conscience which flourishes in the Australian society appears in its writing as an important aspect of the pattern of radicalism. This radical strain has produced a wealth of social criticism from the folk ballads through the poems, novels, and short stories of the nationalist period down to the contemporary fiction of social realists and the verse of the left-wing poets.

The poetry, however, has been more universal in character and less highly localized than the fiction, since it is predominantly lyrical and so concerned with the emotions common to all mankind. Love and hate, anger and grief transcend all national frontiers. The poets, moreover, have often been preoccupied with universal concepts and metaphysical questions such as the nature of the universe, the meaning of life, and the problem of time. A tradition of philosophical poets has been established, running from Brennan and O'Dowd to Wilmot and Baylebridge, FitzGerald, Mary Gilmore and Judith Wright. Just as the poets have produced more universal thinking than have the novelists until the coming of Patrick White, so they have become more advanced in completing their assimilation to the environment. This advance has enabled them to use their country as a natural background, not to keep it in the foreground as the novelists tend to do, but to pass on to wider fields of thought and feeling. The advance in assimilation has been aptly phrased by "a distinguished Australian poet and critic" in an article in a *Current Affairs Bulletin*: "The best Australian poetry today gives the impression of poets who start *from* the local scene as something given, rather than the impression the older poetry gave of poets who aimed *at* the local scene as something to be domesticated in literature."[15]

On the other hand, there has also been a strong social strain amongst the poets, occurring even in such lyrists as McCrae and Neilson. The bulk of the lyrical poetry has been descriptive, limning the country and the feelings it has inspired. In contemporary poetry there has been a development of other forms than the lyric, such as satire, drama, and the narrative. These forms naturally contain more of the social element than the pure or descriptive lyric. Thus Paul Grano, A. D. Hope, James McAuley and Bruce Dawe offer satirical comments on the national society. Douglas Stewart deals with history in his drama *Shipwreck* and with a national tradition in his *Ned Kelly*. Stewart, FitzGerald, Slessor, Francis Webb, and Judith Wright have given tales and pictures of the explorers, adventurers, and pioneers, creating a new significance out of the nation's past. They are myth-makers building up from history and legend viable concepts of the Australian heritage. They are fulfilling the ideal of the Jindyworobak movement of the 1930s in creating new "environmental values", although they stand apart from the Jindyworobak poets, who voiced their fervent nationalism in a cult of the aborigine and a mystique of the soil.

The social approach of many contemporary poets only follows, however, a social tradition in poetry going back to the folk ballads. Whatever their crudeness of literary form, the old bush songs and ballads gave a clear and often forceful articulation to the people's ideas and feelings, offering a wealth of social history and repository of Australian social patterns. This tradition was continued by the *Bulletin* literary balladists of the nineties, so that Lawson and Paterson, Dyson, Ogilvie and a host of other bush balladists gave graphic accounts of bush life and formulated as a permanent, seminal tradition of Australian literature and society the indigenous social patterns which had gradually evolved, decades before, in the pastoral age. This formulation was particularly effective as a social force because the balladists spoke the language of the people and expressed popular sentiments so that they found their audience not in a few literary readers but in a whole nation. A further formulation, more conscious, more intellectual, and more purposive, was provided by poets who were also thinkers and social reformers—Bernard O'Dowd, Frank Wilmot as "Furnley Maurice", and Mary Gilmore.

The Zeitgeist

This development of the social tradition moves in the dimension of

[15] Anon., "Standards in Australian Literature", anonymous article (by A. D. Hope) in *Current Affairs Bulletin* (University of Sydney), vol.19, no.3, 26 Nov. 1956.

time. Each age will have its own spirit, its *Zeitgeist*, mirrored in its literature. Hence there are, in a very real sense, as many literatures as times. If, for example, we try to generalize about the social patterns of English literature, do we mean Elizabethan, Restoration, Augustan, Romantic Revival, Victorian or modern literature? The writing of each period varies sharply in character, just as each succeeding form of society differs in economic structure, social classification, intellectual currents, religious and ethical beliefs, and prevailing temper. French literature, for instance, shows marked variations in the ages of Corneille and Racine, Mallarmé and Baudelaire, Camus and Anouilh. Is there, indeed, any common factor in the spirit of the times reflected in American literature by Longfellow and Lowell, Mark Twain and Whitman, John Dos Passos and Tennessee Williams? What of the operation of the *Zeitgeist* in Australian literature?

The spirit of the age manifests itself, in fact, in Australian as in all other literatures. Times have changed, the society has evolved, and the writing expresses the changes. It is a far cry from Barron Field to Kenneth Slessor, from *Quintus Servinton* to *Riders in the Chariot*. Each writer reflects, in general, the climate of his own day. Kendall, writing in the sixties and seventies, was as much a product of a society that was only starting to move away from the old colonial complex as Paterson was of the nationalist period, or as Judith Wright is of the atomic age. Thus Kendall, "a singer of the dawn", as he called himself, invoked the Muse of Australia with an image of sunlight, "A lyre-bird lit on a shimmering space", whilst Judith Wright, preoccupied with the darkness of war-threatened times, takes a blind man as her symbol. A. G. Stephens wrote in 1900 in a spirit impossible in 1850 or 1950, since his exuberant nationalism could not have been socially developed at the earlier period, whilst his optimistic utopianism could hardly have been preserved undimmed if he had experienced two world wars.

On the whole, however, Australian literature has had too short a life to cover, like the literatures of the older nations, a great variety of ages and societies. It includes, broadly, three main periods: the colonial, nationalist, and modern. The colonial period runs from the beginnings of settlement to 1880, when the *Bulletin* was founded to usher in and dominate the nationalist period. The latter may be taken to conclude in 1918, after the first world war had broken down the Australian dream of a self-contained community developing in isolation from the rest of the world, and taken Australia willy-nilly into the modern age with all its problems and complexities. The war itself, of course, intensified national sentiment and created the Anzac tradition, but in literature the nationalist fervour of the nineties, which had been cooling down during the first decade of the twentieth century, was replaced by internationalist movements and a drift into individual writing.

The writing during the colonial period came mainly from English, Scottish, and Irish immigrants who preserved quite naturally their old outlook when describing the new environment. It has been a common error to condemn this writing as the nostalgic literature of exiles. In fact, the note of yearning for the homeland is only struck occasionally, and in fiction such novelists as Charles Rowcroft, Catherine Spence, Henry Kingsley, and Marcus Clarke were interested in the strange, difficult, or exciting life of this antipodean land, its problems and possibilities, the adventures of the immigrants and the horrors of the convict system. Although Gordon, the only migrant poet of significance, wrote largely on oversea themes, he also identified himself sufficiently with the country and its people in his galloping balladry of action for Marcus Clarke to say with justice that the reader of Gordon's poems would "find in them something very like the beginnings of a national school of Australian poetry".[16]

The native-born writers were also "colonial" in that they followed English models. But also, even the earliest of the poets, such as the nationalist Wentworth and the pensive Charles Tompson, cherished pride in their homeland and love of its beauties. Australian sentiment became a passion with Charles Harpur and Henry Kendall. Indeed, Kendall, who signed himself on occasion as "N.A.P."—Native Australian Poet—earned his title.

Rolf Boldrewood also made the country more familiar in *Robbery Under Arms*, with its national scene, character, and idiom. He stands out as the first genuine *Australian* novelist just as Kendall was the first truly Australian poet. These two are transitional figures coming at the close of the colonial period and opening the way to the succeeding stage of nationalist writing. They begin to embody more fully the social patterns of the people which had only been expressed in part and occasionally by earlier literary writers, although the popular ballads and old bush songs had been a rich repository of them.

This embodiment became complete in the writing of the nationalist period. By the 1890s the native-born, who had been a rebellious minority in earlier decades, were emerging as an assured majority of the adult population in the Australian colonies, a majority which kept increasing. This change in the composition of the Australian people was accompanied by a corresponding change in the literature from a colonial to a national character. The nationalist sentiment which had been accumulating slowly during the nineteenth century now swelled to full volume and flooded into national utterance. In the *Bulletin*

[16] Marcus Clarke, Preface to Adam Lindsay Gordon's *Sea Spray and Smoke Drift* (Melbourne 1876), p.1.

and other popular magazines writers who came from the people wrote of the people and for them. Where Kendall had found a few hundreds of cultivated readers, Lawson and Paterson were read by thousands all over Australia, and were recited in city and shearing shed and by the camp-fires of a continent. Steele Rudd created bush characters who became living portraits in the national mind. Furphy and O'Dowd, more intellectual and less popular, formulated the nationalist values, with their revolt against colonialism, their ardent democratic spirit, republican sentiment and socialist faith, radical criticisms of the present society, and utopian dreams for its future.

Some of the ideas and sentiments expressed in the nationalist period, such as republican tenets, were peculiar to the time, but in general, as will be seen more fully later, this period crystallized and made explicit the pioneering patterns evolved during the first half of the nineteenth century. These were now acclaimed as the national *ethos*, since the writers made writing in Australia fully Australian in theme and spirit and language. In doing so they fixed a humanist, democratic, radical, and realistic mould for Australian literature.

During the modern period after 1914 this mould endured, even if it became chipped, battered, and changed in some ways as a result of the different nature of the modern age. The nationalist sentiment itself weakened after the establishment of the Commonwealth, blazed forth most strongly during the first world war, then was dimmed in the disillusionment of the 1920s, only to find a fresh renaissance during the thirties and forties. After 1918 there was a slight break with the past as literary trends swung towards either individual writing, apart from the people, like that of Henry Handel Richardson and Baylebridge, or to international attitudes, such as that of the *Vision* group led by Jack Lindsay. Where the nineties were centripetal, the twenties were centrifugal. The unity of the nationalist period, with the *Bulletin* as a central integrating influence, dissolved into separate, unrelated efforts. Simplicity was replaced by complexity. Literature lost its popular character, its close touch with the people.

The thirties and forties, however, linked up again with the nineties. The times, indeed, exerted a sobering and maturing influence. The youthful ebullience had gone. The national feeling in literature moved more quietly, but it ran deeply. It ran, for instance, in a strong stream of historical novels and pioneering sagas. These two decades were marked especially by the growth of the novel, and such novelists as Katharine Susannah Prichard, Vance Palmer, Miles Franklin, M. Barnard Eldershaw, Frank Dalby Davison, Leonard Mann, Xavier Herbert, and Kylie Tennant continued the basic traditions of the nationalist period. The old note of radical criticism, with its implication of an idealist faith, was strengthened by the economic depression of the thirties, and the contemporary school of "social realists" in fiction has sought to widen the appeal of its Leftism by claiming kinship with the radical nationalism of the nineties as well as by finding historical continuity with such earlier events as the Eureka Stockade.

The short story, developing fresh vigour in the forties, showed the same trends as the novel. From the thirties and the appearance of Ion L. Idriess's *Lasseter's Last Ride* (1931) a spate of travel writers made descriptive prose a popular medium for fresh discoveries of the Australian scene, even if none of the later writers had the interpretative penetration shown earlier in Dr C. E. W. Bean's brilliant travel books *On the Wool Track* (1910) and *The Dreadnought of the Darling* (1911). Although the lack of an indigenous theatre and lack of support from either commercial entrepreneurs or public stifled efforts, like those of the Pioneer Players, to found a national drama, Australian plays have slowly fought their way to acceptance. Early playwrights such as Esson, Palmer, Tomholt, and Dann were followed by Douglas Stewart and Locke-Elliott. Lawler's success with *Summer of the Seventeenth Doll* marked a temporary break-through of local drama. With the partial exception of Tomholt, all these playwrights had given dramatic shape to the social patterns of a common national tradition. With Lawler's *The Piccadilly Bushman* and the plays of Beynon and Seymour came, however, a more critical questioning of aspects of this tradition, together with an extension of theme and outlook. A further expansion of the drama was given by Patrick White's plays in their expressionist revolt against the current realism and their introduction of symbolism and satire.

In fiction, too, White's three later novels—*The Tree of Man* (1955), *Voss* (1957) and *Riders in the Chariot* (1961)—came as a revolutionary phenomenon. They went far beyond the work of the social realists to new dimensions of imaginative depth, psychological insight, and spiritual issues. White's influence has already been exerted on younger novelists, notably Randolph Stow. Like the fiction, the poetry has experienced a new movement in the post-war period and expansion into fresh modes. A. D. Hope has proved, like White in fiction, a brilliant and significant revolutionary figure. He has led the way to an intellectualist approach, a neo-classical style, the symbolist use of classical myth, and witty, mordant satire. His influence is seen in the work of McAuley and Buckley, who have also written a religious poetry hitherto alien to the literary tradition. All these modernist developments have cut across the traditional social and literary patterns, making the post-war writing richer and more complex than that of previous periods.

On the other hand, the growth of enthusiastic interest in the old bush songs and folk ballads from the fifties onwards offers a striking example of the way in which the sentiment of today, in search of a national heritage, has gone back to the past and the patterns shaped in pioneering times.

Despite the complexity of the modern period, therefore, and the growth of conflicting movements, there remains a broad continuity of the literary tradition. This continuity, although challenged, is still stronger than the instances of revolutionary change. The persistence of the dominant traditions means that Australian literature can be viewed validly as one consistent, developing body of writing. Changes wrought by the *Zeitgeist* are subordinate, so far, to the general unity. The social patterns can still be caught and described effectively.

Limitations of a Looking-glass

Before defining them, however, some preliminary qualifications must be made, some warnings issued. It must be recognized at the outset that a society and its literature by no means form a perfect equation. The literary looking-glass has its limitations as well as its powers of significant reflection of prevailing patterns. The glass distorts as well as reflects. On the one hand, it contains personal elements belonging to the writer which are not characteristic of the society at large, such as the spiritual hunger of a Brennan or Patrick White, the fantasy of McCrae, or the old-world elegance of Ethel Anderson. On the other hand, it does not contain some patterns typical of the community. Sport, for instance, is a dominant interest of the Australian people, but its expression in literature is negligible. Religion, too, has played an important part in the community life but has been largely disregarded by writers until its recent emergence in the novels of White and the poetry of McAuley, Buckley and Francis Webb. Religious poems had been written earlier by Ada Cambridge, William Gay, and Bishop Gilbert White, but these had been exceptional.

Whilst some social elements have been thus neglected, others have been exaggerated in relation to their actual role in the society. Most Australians today, for example, accept the general *status quo* of society even when they desire specific changes for their own economic or social benefit, whereas Australian writers, like writers in most other countries, naturally question the existing order more critically. They tend to be more radical than the majority of their comfortable fellow citizens. Thus radicalism, which has been a feature of Australian society in the past, today appears more strongly in literature than in ordinary life. So, too, there is a deeper stress on utopianism, since writers usually cherish ideals, including those for the future of their country, more deeply than the average Australian concerned with his material present, his work, family, and sport. He does not enter fully into the passionate idealism of such patriots as Lawson, Furphy, and O'Dowd, Miles Franklin or Katharine Prichard. Our myths and ideals are far larger in our literature than in our life.

Indeed, one of the most striking facts to emerge from an objective study of the social patterns in the literature is the occasional disparity between these and the contemporary reality. This is due mainly, of course, to the fact that the prevailing patterns pictured came from a pioneering past which was vastly different in many respects from the industrialized, urban, atomic present. Other differences arise from a particular emphasis made by the writers. They have largely concentrated, for example, on the working class as a subject. The large middle class of business and professional groups has received comparatively little representation in literature. Again, through their selection of themes the writers have also exercised a further kind of literary gerrymandering by largely disfranchising the cities as against the country. Ever since the earliest days the population has been concentrated in the coastal cities, and today Australia is the most highly urbanized country in the world. Yet its literature has always been predominantly rural. It is a phenomenal case of the literary tail wagging the demographic dog.

A few of the earlier novelists, such as Catherine Helen Spence, Caroline Leakey, and Mrs Campbell Praed, wrote of the cities. Then the country took over, with only a trickle of urban fiction until after the second world war when the trickle swelled into a vigorous stream with such contributaries as Patrick White, Judah Waten, Elizabeth Harrower, Thea Astley, and Thomas Keneally. Fiction is now coming to close grips with the contemporary city realities, just as it is turning away from the reporting of the external world by social realism to a more imaginative, more creative, probing of the inner world of the mind.

The new impulses of the last two decades in both prose and poetry have compelled comment on the disparity often occurring between the traditional literary picture and the contemporary actuality. It may be argued, with some truth, that our literature in general presents many scenes, characters, and ideas of the past that have been transformed into myths, legends, and dreams remote from the present.

Yet the social patterns discussed here are still powerful as national traditions, operating as forces conditioning our contemporary ways of thought, feeling, and behaviour. As such they are not mythical or legendary but factual, current realities to be reckoned with. Furthermore, their representation in our literature is also an undeniable fact; and when I set out here that fact of representation, with all the weight of the evidence, I am dealing with entities, not as mythical as the Jack of Spades, but as real as yesterday's strike and today's drought in the wheat belt.

The Patterns Defined

As I worked through our literature a number of social patterns became patent, but it seemed to me that ten of these emerged as major ones of national significance. They may be described in different phrases or placed in varying orders, of course, but I shall discuss the following as the major patterns.

1. *The Spell of the Bush*, that has been dominant in Australian society and literature alike as the primary force, since the social patterns as a whole were born of the land itself and bred in the bush. This dominance runs throughout our writing, from the old bush songs down to *The Tree of Man* and *Voss*. The bush has been the matrix of our sentiments and ideals, symbol of a distinctive national character, and a religious mystique invoking salvation for the spirit. It still holds the people's imagination.

2. *The Clash of Cultures* as the established colonialism, based on the imported British way of life, was challenged by the growing indigenous ethos, creating a long-drawn-out conflict between their contrasting values, until the two cultures became integrated finally in an independent Australian culture, even if in a few cases the old struggle between colonialism and nationalism is still not entirely resolved. In general the organism was forced to adapt itself to the environment by means of a new culture: the people who came to change and subdue the land were themselves changed by it in the end, and compelled to submit to its demands.

3. *Realism*, the outlook inevitably developed amongst the pioneer pragmatists by a hard land which brooked no romantic emotion or false illusion but demanded acceptance of reality for survival, so that the writers in turn grew realists and developed a creed of integrity to the truth of life. This realism achieves honesty and power, but often falls into reportage of externals, uses observation rather than the creative imagination, and misses the wonder and mystery of life.

4. *Sombreness*, discussed under the title of "The Cry of the Crow". Its main causes were the unpredictable onslaught of drought, flood, and fire, the struggle with an arid and recalcitrant land, the loneliness of a harsh bush life, and the tragic death of explorers. Like the realism with which it is interlinked, it also had the convict system as an historical determinant. In the literature the social realists became professional specialists in sombreness as they concentrated on the ills of society.

5. *The Keynote of Irony*, hard and realistic, sardonic and sansculottist, which is dominant in Australian humour, more significant, more distinctive, and also more subtle than such other forms of humour as broad farce, tall stories, trickster tales, satire, and comedy of character. Arising, like the sombreness, out of the land's vicissitudes, it has been used as a self-protective device to stave the sombreness off, a kind of philosophic whistling to keep one's courage up in facing disaster. Lawson employs it in masterly suggestiveness, sometimes drily, sometimes bitterly. It is acidly incisive in Lennie Lower, satirical in Kylie Tennant, and savage in Xavier Herbert. Upon it Furphy bases the whole intricate, ingenious design of *Such is Life* and his concept of Tom Collins.

6. *The Creed of Mateship*, the loyalty of man to man in a special relationship, born of the land as a practical necessity for bushmen living in a vast, lonely, and often dangerous environment, and hence, like irony, a defensive mechanism against the land; strengthened by the lack of women and religion in the outback; widening into a national convention in alliance with the democratic pattern; strongest amongst bushmen, workers in hazardous occupations, and the men of the fighting services in wartime; varying from a superficial friendliness to a religious depth of self-sacrifice.

7. *Radical Democracy*, the combination of the two patterns of radicalism and democratic belief, so closely interwoven that they are best treated as two aspects of the one embracing social pattern emphasizing equality and its consequent demand for social justice. Ecologically this was drawn mainly from the organism, not the environment, from the kind of people rather than the type of place, with a background of historical factors such as the French Revolution, English liberalism, Scottish independence, the rebel Irish, the emancipists, and the struggle for the land. Ultimately, however, the pattern only operated effectively because the workers enjoyed independence on account of the strong demand for their labour, which in turn resulted from the smallness of the population and the largeness of the land with all its undeveloped resources.

8. *The Great Australian Dream*, a utopian vision which was, like the creed of mateship, a form of idealism that complemented the common realism. The greatness of the land and its potentialities were joined with such forces as nationalism and socialism to stimulate the dream of a paradise on Australian earth, an Eden of prosperity, freedom, equality, and justice. Australia was to be a Commonwealth devoted to serving the common weal. This social pattern arose early and its expression has persisted through all the periods of the literature.

9. *Earth-vigour*, a physical vitality grown into a national tradition of sporting prowess, generated by the environment of a temperate climate and favorable living conditions, and developed by a pioneering life on the land. So, too, whatever the shortcomings of the literature in artistic form, it is marked by vigour. Despite the strain of sombreness, there is a positive affirmation of life, of courage and endurance, of human endeavour and the individual will, an affirmation expressed powerfully in FitzGerald's poem "Essay on Memory" and Douglas Stewart's verse play *The Fire on the Snow*. In poetry this earth-vigour is also symbolized by a celebration of Pan, the earth-god, patron of shepherds and herdsmen.

10. *Humanism*, the faith in the human spirit, with man as the measure of values, is so closely allied with the pagan earth-vigour that the two patterns are taken together in a chapter entitled "The Palingenesis of Pan". Whereas the Christian religions have played a significant part in the history of Australian society, it is a striking fact that the Australian literature, from the old bush songs and the balladists, through the socialists like Lawson, Furphy, and O'Dowd, down to the more modern writers like the poets McCrae and Neilson and novelists of social realism, has shown itself as either completely indifferent to religion or highly critical of it. In general the writers, like the society, turn, not to God, but to man; not to Heaven but to a utopia for men on earth. The writing is nothing if not humanist in its outlook and sympathies, hedonistic in its enjoyment of life, and stoic in its facing of adversity.

Since the last world war this humanism has been challenged by a new strain of religious feeling voiced by Patrick White and some Roman Catholic poets. The humanist tradition, however, still remains in the ascendant. Few writers would wish to follow White's Voss into a journey towards God and humility, but most would have a fellow feeling for Brennan when, facing misery, he found a humanist salvation in the friendly sky and wind, his own manhood, and man's "note of living will":

> I said, this misery must end:
> shall I, that am a man and know
> that sky and wind are yet my friend,
> sit huddled under any blow?
> so speaking left the dismal room
> and stept into the mother-night
> all fill'd with sacred quickening gloom
> where the few stars burn'd low and bright,
> and darkling on my darkling hill
> heard thro' the beaches' sullen boom

heroic note of living will
rung trumpet-clear against the fight;
so stood and heard, and rais'd my eyes
erect, that they might drink of space,
and took the night upon my face.[17]

[17] A. R. Chisholm and J. J. Quinn (ed.), *The Verse of Christopher Brennan* (Sydney 1960), p.168.

II

The Ecology of an Ethos

There were begetters, there were mighty forces, free action here and energy up yonder.

Who verily knows and who can declare it, whence it was born and whence comes this creation?

THE RIGVEDA[1]

Australian history is almost always picturesque and, indeed, it is so curious and strange, that it is itself the chiefest novelty the country has to offer... It does not read like history, but like the most beautiful lies. And all of a fresh, new sort; no mouldy old stale ones. It is full of surprises, adventures and incongruities, and contradictions, and incredibilities; but they are all true; they all happened.

MARK TWAIN[2]

I wonder whether there was any difference whatever between Noah, his lions and his sheep towards the end of their journey during the flood?—Each individual as a phenomenon is only as much as he is able to express, and he becomes greater or lesser, thus or different in accordance with the traits which are accepted by his surroundings; this explains the immense power of milieu.

KEYSERLING[3]

The Anglo-Australian has perished or is absorbed in the Interiors much more rapidly than on the sea-slope and in the towns. . . .

Where the marine rainfall flags out and is lost, a new climate, and, in a certain sense, a new race begin to unfold themselves . . . .

The one powerful and unique national type yet produced in Australia is... that of the Bushman.

FRANCIS ADAMS[4]

---

[1] Hymn XXVIII from the Rigveda, in N. Macnicol (ed.), *Hindu Scriptures* (London 1938), p.37.
[2] Mark Twain, *Following the Equator* (New York 1897), p.168.
[3] Count Hermann Keyserling, *The Travel Diary of a Philosopher* (New York 1925), p.32.
[4] Francis Adams, *The Australians* (London 1893), pp.166, 144, 165.

C

A Lawson Exemplar

The social patterns just defined do not stand apart as simple and separate attitudes but emerge as strands which criss-cross with one another in a fascinating complexity of interrelationships. The task of examining them, therefore, is not a simple chronological one with the line of events running directly from past to present, but rather the unravelling of an intricate design interwoven as in a Persian carpet, with motifs constantly repeating themselves, the same yet different because they change shape and colour, even if subtly, when they reappear in fresh contexts or make new associations with allied or contrasting patterns.

No better example of the way they can combine in cross-patterning could be found than Henry Lawson's short story "The Drover's Wife" which also illustrates an effective blending of the three elements in a work of art, since it is at once personal, universal, and social. This is a plain, realistic tale of a bush mother protecting her children from a snake lurking under the slab floor of her lonely home in the bush. It is characteristic of Lawson himself in its integrity to the truth of life, its depth of sympathy, and its skilful balancing of pathos by strokes of humour. "We have many clever writers," A. G. Stephens observed, "but we do not know another than Lawson who could write the sketch 'The Drover's Wife'. You may ransack the realm of Australian prose without finding a mate for that sketch."[5]

Only Lawson could have made the direct, laconic style, seeming so homespun, even artless, fitting its subject as smoothly as an old glove, become so vivid, flexible, and imaginative. Its surface simplicity is deceptive, since it evokes a richness of significance. A casual phrase turns out to be surprisingly reverberant, beating back into poignancy, as a whole world of hard, courageous living in the isolation of the outback is opened up to the mind by a couple of simple statements: "One of the children died while she was here alone. She rode nineteen miles for assistance, carrying the dead child."[6]

Characteristic, too, of Lawson is the penetrating treatment which uses only a slight narrative to achieve his real purpose, which is not to tell a story but to evoke the character of a bush woman and her way of living. In her night vigil the drover's wife thinks as she watches for the snake to appear: "She thinks of things in her own life, for there is little else to think about."[7] In her memories she relives a past in which she had fought a bush-fire, a flood, the pleuro-pneumonia killing the few remaining cattle, a mad bullock, crows and

---

[5] A. G. Stephens, "Henry Lawson" in *The Bookfellow*, 28 Feb. 1922, p.21.
[6] Henry Lawson, "The Drover's Wife" in *While the Billy Boils* (Sydney 1898), p.132.
[7] Ibid.

eagles, and threatening strangers. So the story spreads out in reminiscent ripples till it is no longer a small billabong but a spacious lake. It expands from a factual sketch into a moving epic of human courage constantly exerted in a patient, never-ending battle with threatening forces of life and death. The story grows into a miniature *Iliad* of the bush. The drover's wife emerges as a battler no less brave in her struggles than Achilles in his.

This capacity to focus life by an insight interpreting the human spirit gives "The Drover's Wife" a universal quality. An English critic, Edward Garnett, recognized the story's universality when he wrote of it: "If this artless sketch be taken as a summary of a woman's life, giving its significance in ten short pages, even Tolstoy has never done better."[8] So, too, the French critic Professor Emile Saillens found in Lawson's work "abundant evidence of the spirit that makes the classics, a genuine comprehension of what is deeply and eternally human".[9] In fact, the universal element in Lawson's stories has been given a wide international recognition by publication in England, the United States, France, Germany, Hungary, Israel, the Soviet Union, and Japan.

"The Drover's Wife", then, is characteristic Lawson. It is world literature. It is also Australian. Indeed, the social element not only blends with the personal and the universal, but is also especially notable, since Lawson remains the most representative Australian writer. His work bears the distinctive colouration of his country and its society. His identification with the Australian social patterns is so close and intimate that "The Drover's Wife" embodies no less than eight out of our ten patterns.

Thus its setting is the bush, its theme is bush life, and its heroine a bush woman. The clash of cultures enters in a curious yet unmistakable way, when the drover's wife persists in retaining the English tradition of keeping Sunday as a special day and dressing up for it:

All days are much the same to her; but on Sunday afternoon she dresses herself, tidies the children, smartens-up baby, and goes for a lonely walk along the bush-track, pushing an old perambulator in front of her. She does this every Sunday. She takes as much care to make herself and the children look smart as if she were going to do the block in the city. There is nothing to see, however, and not a soul to meet.[10]

Here the incongruity between the inherited sabbatarian custom and

[8] Edward Garnett, "Henry Lawson and the Democracy", *Friday Nights* (London 1922), p.184.
[9] Emile Saillens, "The Discovery of Australia by France" in *The Lone Hand*, 1 June 1909, p.239.
[10] Henry Lawson, op. cit., p.135.

the environment of the lonely, monotonous bush is painfully sharp, and the woman's gesture is at once pathetic and gallant.

An uncompromising realism sets its stamp on the story throughout, whilst the picture of dangers, hardships, and misfortunes in the lonely bush is full of sombreness. When Lawson relieves this by humour, it comes in the keynote of irony. This holds a wry bitterness in the incident of the stray blackfellow whom the drover's wife engaged to bring her some wood whilst she went in search of a missing cow:

On her return she was so astonished to see a good heap of wood by the chimney, that she gave him an extra fig of tobacco, and praised him for not being lazy. He thanked her, and left with head erect and chest well out. He was the last of his tribe and a King; *but he had built that wood-heap hollow.*[11]

When she pulls out a piece of wood for the fire the wood-heap collapses. Disillusioned and hurt by this shabby deception, she cries. When she takes up a handkerchief to wipe the tears away, she pokes her eyes with her bare fingers instead, since the handkerchief is full of holes. So Lawson introduces a second ironical touch, but this a gentler one at which the drover's wife herself can laugh.

Completely Australian is the democratic spirit of Lawson which assumes, as an unquestioned matter of course, that a plain working woman, with no pretensions to beauty or romance, is a fit and proper heroine for literature. This aspect of Lawson, so natural to Australians that it passes unnoticed by them, impressed Edward Garnett, accustomed to the contrary tradition of English middle-class writers treating the working class from outside, rather self-consciously and often condescendingly. He writes in praise:

Lawson, however, has the great strength of the writer writing simply as one of the democracy, and of the man who does not have to climb down from a class fence in order to understand the human nature of the majority of his fellow men. I have never read anything in modern English literature that is so absolutely democratic in tone, so much the real thing, as "Joe Wilson's Courtship". And so with all Lawson's tales and sketches.[12]

Finally, the drover's wife, living close to earth, embodies in herself the pattern of earth-vigour, attacking the snake as vigorously as she has battled over the years with drought and flood, with bush-fire and loneliness. Her fighting spirit remains strong. She has vitality, pluck and endurance. It is in these human qualities, too, that she trusts in her struggles with death and disasters, not in any God. In her review of her life, religion never comes into her reckoning. The bush life has simply turned her into a fatalist and stoic. So, too, Lawson is a fellow humanist with her in the telling of her story: humanist in his under-

[11] Ibid., p.136.
[12] E. Garnett, op. cit., p.181.

standing of her life, his sympathy with her troubles, and his tribute to her courage.

The Ecological Unity

"The Drover's Wife" gives, even in a brief sketch, some hint of the complexity of the social patterns in respect to their qualities and their inter-connections. When we go further, however, to explore their origins and try to find out why they developed as they did, we discover a still greater complexity, with a number of factors interacting in a system of multiple causation. Yet, paradoxically, it is in the analysis of this causation that I have found a method of synthesis by going to science and applying an ecological approach. For some years the complex of social patterns seemed to me to present only diversity. True, they had numerous associations with each other and inter-relationships, but there appeared to be no single unifying element to bring them together into a significant design. Then a comparative study of Australian and some parallel literatures brought out, first, the differences between them, including the varying outlooks they expressed, and, secondly, the revealing fact that their literary and social differences could be traced primarily to their respective environments. Australian, Canadian, and New Zealand literatures differ because they embody three different societies, and the societies differ simply because Australia, Canada, and New Zealand are distinctive lands. It is the country that counts.

A new light was thus thrown upon our own social patterns when I saw them integrated within an ecological unity as forms of response made by the organism to the environment, adaptations of Australians to Australia.

The overall Pattern of our patterns, therefore, is the interaction between the people and the place in which each plays a part. As General Smuts put it:

The organism is not itself alone and in isolation. As a unit it is a mere static abstraction. The real dynamic unit is the organism functioning in its environment. This complex concept is the real biological unit and starting point. Life is living, and living is an active reciprocal relation between organism and environment. This is the central concept in ecology, and it has already led to a revolution of our biological sciences. It enables us not only to account for the existence and development of communities, societies, their histories, phases, and climaxes and all the complexes we find in the living nature. In the end they all follow certain large rhythms which prevail in nature.[13]

"The Drover's Wife" offers an authentic illustration of this account of human ecology, since it shows the organism functioning in its environment, the bush woman living out a life determined almost

[13] J. C. Smuts, Introduction to J. W. Bews, *Human Ecology* (London 1953), p.xi.

wholly by the bush, adapting herself to the demands of the land, and following the rhythms of nature prevailing in the Australian outback. Lawson's story also fulfils exactly, in a concrete literary form, the definition, given by a British scientist, of ecology as "the study of living things in relation to their surroundings and to one another".[14]

Whilst such an ecological approach to the social patterns embodied in our literature may seem novel and perhaps debatable to the literary critic, the ecologists themselves stress its validity firmly. Thus a South African one declares:

The value of human ecology, as in the case of ecology generally, lies in its synthesizing effect. It not only provides a pattern into which may be fitted all the separate human sciences, but it affords a means of testing the relative value of each method of approach to the all important, all embracing, question of how and why man is as he is, and behaves as he does... His functional relationship to his environment is not merely physiological but psychological as well. Human ecology, therefore, has to include the study of man's mental processes and their results as well as his physiological responses.... The biological triad (of environment, function, and organism) is just as true for man's mental life as it is for his life as a whole.[15]

In applying the biological triad to man's mental life as represented here by the social patterns, it is important to note that in this case the organism consists of the Australian people with its characteristics of race, nationality, class, occupation, and culture. The environment in turn consists of the social environment as well as the basic physical one of soil, climate, and other geographical factors. The Australian society represents, as its most distinguished geographer phrased it, "an interesting experiment in anthropo-geography where Man is 97.8 'British' and the Environment is perhaps 87 per cent 'warm and dry' ".[16]

In respect to the social environment a significant point has been made by a British biologist who applied the methods of ecology to a study over many years of the West Highland people among whom he lived, and was struck by the importance to the individual of the community's *ethos*, or characteristic spirit and tone:

Tradition and accumulated experience are part of man's environment, and for all the importance of the physical and biological factors I have mentioned, the *ethos* is still the biggest ecological factor of all on the life of the individual.[17]

Since the *ethos* comprises, in fact, a community's social patterns, this study presents the reverse side of the biologist's coin: it shows the

[14] Leslie Reed, *The Sociology of Nature* (London 1962), pp.14-15.

[15] J. W. Bews, op. cit., pp.9, 13, 15.

[16] Griffith Taylor, *Australia* (London 1940), p.3.

[17] F. Fraser Darling, "The Ecological Approach to the Social Sciences" in *American Scientist*, 1951, vol.39, p.254.

environment as the biggest factor in the development of the patterns, giving the ecology of the Australian *ethos*.

The Early Shaping of the Patterns

Human ecology, however, differs strikingly from the ecology of plants and animals in that man, alone of the living organisms, possesses the power to change his physical environment. He can circumvent nature, and alter his surroundings to suit himself, especially in societies highly developed technically. In the modern urban and industrial centres man largely creates his own environment. On the other hand, in more primitive societies, such as those of foodgatherers, like the Australian aborigines, or of herdsmen and pastoral nomads, like the squatters and bush workers, man is especially dependent on his physical environment. He can alter it slightly, but in general is forced to adapt himself to his local conditions of soil and climate and topography, just as plants and animals accept their given surroundings and function within them.

This brings us to the fundamental point that our main social patterns were developed within the first half century or so of Australian history. The evidence of this early shaping of the patterns is given in the chapters following which discuss them individually. The evidence is clear and definite, whether it comes from the creative literature of the first half of the nineteenth century, including the folk songs and ballads, or from the historical writing of such contemporary observers as Alexander Harris, P. Cunningham, and Gerstaecker, or the diaries and reminiscences of the early settlers. Although the analogy between a community and an individual is not always valid, it does emerge that, just as the decisive formative stage of an individual's character lies, according to modern psychology, in his earliest years, so, too, the chief shaping of the Australian people's outlook and attitudes occurred in the first half-century of its growth. Inevitably, therefore, the values that developed were those of the pioneering pastoral age; they arose in the outback, usually termed "the bush", as adaptations to the bush environment, and were especially determined by it.

At the same time the organism also played its part in the ecological interaction between it and the environment, with the character of the people also making its contribution to the formation of the social patterns. As British the newcomers to the land brought with them as characteristics the language, customs, ideas, and beliefs of their homeland. They did this, of course, from the beginnings of the settlement of the convict colony in New South Wales, so that once again we see the early shaping of the patterns. Strong testimony to this is given by a leading historian when Professor Manning Clark writes:

By 1817, too, the main ideas which were to mould the minds of Australians
in the nineteenth and twentieth centuries had been transplanted from Europe.
The early Church of England chaplains, Johnson and Marsden, had sowed the
seeds of the Protestant view of the world—the connexion in their minds
between liberty, material well-being, and the Protestant religion, the Bible
and sabbatarian values. With the Irish convicts in 1791 came the Catholic view
of the world as moulded to meet conditions in Ireland. Thus even before 1800,
the contenders in the great conflict in the nineteenth century on religion,
education, and politics had arrived on the shores of Australia. So, indeed, had
the third force—the ideas of the Enlightenment on liberty, equality, happiness,
and progress. And though the men on the front of the stage in our documents
speak of food, of shelter, of loneliness and isolation, and squabble of trifles,
this is the period in which the shape of things to come is first formed.[18]

The Shaping in Time and Space

After considering this early shaping of the patterns, two further
points should be noted as complementary: its extension in time and
space.

Whilst the patterns were formed by 1850, they were not fully
formulated until the 1890s when, as we have seen, Lawson and
Paterson on the popular level, Furphy and O'Dowd on the philosophical one, elevated them into national traditions, with their writings
as cultural dynamics. Paterson spread the pastoral *ethos* by direct
appeal to the people through his balladry, an appeal which still
maintains its vigour. Lawson, embodying the patterns most richly of
all our writers, has had a slightly less popular appeal in his short
stories, but exerted a profound influence on a generation of prose
writers. Thus the first volume of an anthology of Australian short
stories published in 1967 is subtitled *the Lawson Tradition*. The
extent of Lawson's influence is shown by the roll call of writers
selected, and by the fact that some of them did not have a first book
of their stories published until after 1940, over half a century after
Lawson contributed his first story to the *Bulletin* in 1888. The editor
of the anthology, Douglas Stewart, in his Introduction states, aptly for
our theme:

Since the anthology was to be based on Lawson and his school it would have,
necessarily, a certain unity of style and flavour... The stories would chiefly
and essentially be concerned, like their contemporary bush ballads, with the
conquest of the land. They would be a sort of reconcilement with its
harshness.[19]

The stories chosen, therefore, not only illustrate in general the social
patterns quite clearly, but they also confirm the dependence of the
literature on the land.

---

[18] M. Clark (ed.), *Sources of Australian History* (London 1957), pp.60-1.
[19] Douglas Stewart (ed.), *Short Stories of Australia: the Lawson Tradition* (Sydney
1967), p.xiii.

It is equally significant that the second volume of the anthology, chosen by Beatrice Davis, reveals substantial developments away from the traditional patterns. As Miss Davis points out:

Preoccupation with the conquest of the earth has given way to a study of personal relationships and a more searching exploration of character; the simple and direct tale has been replaced by something more subtle and more complex.... But once the conquest of the land had been achieved, once the stories of the conquest had been written, there had to be a change. Writers could not go on dealing with problems and situations that had ceased to exist, except to look back and re-create them as part of their heritage.[20]

The same kind of changes have been taking place in the poetry written during and after the second world war. Some of the poetry, too, has become more complex, more subtle, and more introspective. It has lost assurance and become more questioning, more critical and even sceptical. It is concerned with present realities, and often displays towards the past the disillusioned detachment voiced by the young poet Thomas W. Shapcott in his "Time on Fire":

> *The past leers gaunt*
> *as sapless trees which take the white-boned airs*
> *of death on the vast burnt paddocks where these fires*
> *have gorged.*[21]

The new generation of poets already regard the modern but older poets like Slessor, FitzGerald, Hope, and Judith Wright as "The Establishment" from which they want to break away, finding fresh themes, attitudes, and forms.

On the other hand, as indicated earlier, there is continuity as well as change and conflict in the post-war developments. Both poets and prose writers, for instance, still re-create the past and give fresh interpretations of the old traditions. Whilst some of the social patterns have become outmoded, others have persisted in modified forms. The utopian ideal has retreated in the unpropitious environment of an urban, industrialized community, an atomic age, and an interrelated shrunken world where an isolated Australian Eden grows ghostly. Whilst the democratic spirit remains pervasive, its radical aspect, although still championed by the forces of the Left, has generally had its edge blunted by an affluent society and the hire purchase system of credit, the two factors making the working class merge into the middle class. Mateship is still an operative tradition, but has been receiving a sharp critical scrutiny from some writers.

On the other hand, some patterns remain strong, if modified to suit the temper of the times. The clash of cultures may still be seen in

---

[20] Beatrice Davis (ed.), *Short Stories of Australia: the Moderns* (Sydney 1967), p.viii.
[21] Thomas W. Shapcott, *Time on Fire* (Brisbane 1961), p.24.

different aspects, such as the analysis of expatriates by Ray Lawler in *The Piccadilly Bushman.* The roles of realism have been reversed. Once dominant in fiction, it has been weakened there by the new imaginative, introvert writing, but it has passed over into poetry, a field in which it was formerly minor except for the folk and bush balladry. Sombreness is now stronger than ever and is deepening into a genuinely tragic expression in both prose and poetry, with the shadow cast, not by drought on the land, but by the fear, violence, and individual alienation pervading the "civilization" of today.

So, too, the keynote of irony, whilst flourishing in prose as satire, has invaded our contemporary poetry and stands out as one of its distinctive characteristics. The vigour remains in the society, but is increasingly mental rather than physical, moving especially over to the arts and the sciences, displaying creative power in painting, music, and literature or in such new fields as radio astronomy. Australian scientists, for instance, have been winners of Nobel Prizes.

Finally, although the literature as a whole is less secular than before as religious feeling finds increased expression, both the society and its writing continue to be humanist, with the essential humanism growing wider and deeper with the development of greater tolerance and a stronger sense of compassion. Thus the ecological unity of the patterns is preserved, but the literature now reflects the dominant influence on Australian society, not of the physical environment, but of the social environment. The land counts for less, and the society itself, with all its changes, problems, and perplexities, now presses more heavily on the thinking individual and the interpretative writer.

Just as the shaping of the patterns has been thus extended in time, so there has been a two-fold extension in space. The first spatial widening of the patterns came when they spread from the mother colony of New South Wales to all the colonies. For the existence of aberrancies and some imbalances in the Australian society has not prevented it from developing a working cohesion and unity. Despite wide differences of climate and topography, it is remarkably homogeneous. Queensland and Western Australia today may be closer to pioneering life and values than other States, Tasmania may be more English in environment and tradition, South Australia may be proud of its convict-less "Paradise of Dissent", or Sydney and Melbourne cherish their particular traits. Yet when the citizens of the various States come together in an Australian fighting force or sporting team or professional conference, the differences between them are minor if at all distinguishable, whilst their common national character is unquestionable. Australian writing, in turn, has not developed regional literatures such as we find in Europe or America, but only a common national literature which embodies common social patterns.

In the more recent embodiment the literature has reflected the changing society in a second extension of the patterns in space. In the post-war period the most striking development has been the wave of immigration which has resulted in one-sixth of the Australian population being migrants, and roughly about two-thirds of these being European by birth. The influx of Italians, Dutch, Germans, Greeks, Poles and other Continental peoples has affected our *ethos* as well as our economy. Another social feature has been the extent to which Australians of many occupations have travelled or lived overseas. The combination of this travel with the coming of the "New Australians" has produced a marked enlargement of the provincial Australian outlook, greater tolerance and understanding, a partial breaking down of racial prejudice and xenophobia. The society has grown more cosmopolitan, and the literature, in turn, mirrors this by an extension of theme and attitude beyond the Australian continent. Miss Beatrice Davis has noted that the contemporary short story has grown more cosmopolitan, and to that extent less distinctively Australian. Thus we find stories in her anthology set in Greece and Finland. A glance at our fiction written during the last few decades shows novels set in England, Germany, Italy, Russia, Greece, Crete, the United States, Japan, the Philippines, Vietnam, and Tibet. So, too, in poetry the use of oversea themes, seen earlier in Brennan and O'Dowd, McCrae and Slessor, has increased. We can pick up volumes of contemporary verse and see in Vincent Buckley's *Masters in Israel* pieces dealing with England, Ireland, and the Hungarian Cardinal Mindszenty; in *No Fixed Address* by Bruce Dawe, poems entitled "A Traveller in Eastern Europe, 1960", "Hungary: 1956-7", and "Poznan: July 1956"; in Rodney Hall's *Eyewitness* sections headed "Nine Poems from England" and "Six Poems from Greece" and in a later work of his "Poems of Many Places", which contains 32 poems set in 14 lands and oceans. Thus Australian writing in both prose and poetry is expanding spatially in its themes and backgrounds, leaving the bush and local city to go out into a wider world, gaining a new maturity, richness, and universality but losing in the process something of the old national flavour and tang of the social patterns.

The Shaping Forces

Contemporary developments in the literature illustrate, therefore, changes in the society and the forces determining them. At this stage it will be valuable, before discussing the individual patterns, to give a brief survey of the forces which have determined the original growth of the patterns.

There were four main sets of these forces: the outside pressures from the world, the internal history, the people, and the physical environment. Within them worked, of course, the influence of significant individuals. Although distinct, these four factors were intimately related and to a large degree interdependent, like the patterns they helped to create. Varying weight can be given to each, but undoubtedly the last two were the most important, and of these, in the end the environment was the most decisive. Whatever colonial settlement might have been made, whatever its vicissitudes, whatever people had come to Australia—British, Spanish, Malaysian, or Chinese—the land itself would have demanded certain types of economy, made certain occupations prevail, and so determined basically the way of life. The land was the constant factor amongst many variables, a datum that had to be accepted on its own terms, even if it was the unique combination of the four main sets of forces that forged the special amalgam of the Australians.

It is important to distinguish, however, those historical events and movements which directly influenced the growth and development of the social patterns, and those which had little or no such direct influence, however important they may have been in Australia's economic and political history. Of the outside pressures, for example, Australia became one of the heirs of the French Revolution and was influenced by its dynamic ideas of liberty, equality, and fraternity, especially through English liberalism. On the other hand, whilst the American Revolution was partly responsible for the founding of Australia as a colonial receptacle for the English convicts who could no longer be transported to the former American colonies, and later the anti-transportation movement in protesting against the cargo of the convict ship *Hashemy* in 1849 drew a revolutionary warning paralleled from the Boston Tea Party, the American Revolution in itself had little, if any, direct effect on the shaping of the patterns, even if some American authors influenced a few Australian writers.

So, too, there was little such effect from the world economic depression of the 1890s, although it led to large-scale conflict between organized capital and labour in the maritime and shearing industries, whereas the second great depression in the thirties of this century not only caused wide suffering and demoralized a generation of youth deprived of work and training in a skilled trade, but also engendered a sense of disillusionment and uncertainty amongst the people as a whole. Both the political and economic systems, it was generally felt, had failed to meet the crisis adequately. As Paul Hasluck put it discerningly,

Probably no more potent influence than the economic depression has shaped and directed Australian political thought and attitudes.... It left a heritage of distrust, bitterness and resentment—perhaps, too, a feeling of loneliness....

The ideal of "mateship" was dimmed in the new meaning being given to the "class struggle".[22]

Both the political and economic systems were criticized bitterly in literature, especially in the upsurge of fiction during the thirties which expressed a renaissance of radicalism. Old concepts of the social patterns were revised in a new spirit of realism.

The Outside Pressures

It was an accident of history that the Australian society began as one of transplanted Britons, not one of Malayan, Spanish, Dutch or French settlers. Australia might even have become Chinese, since it is possible, as one historian suggests, that a Taoist image found near Darwin is a relic left by a Chinese maritime expedition sent southward by the Emperor Yung Lo in the early fifteenth century.[23] Brown sailors from Macassar touched perhaps on Australia's shores in the north, as they did on New Guinea before Torres. Long before 1770 the Dutch were familiar with the northern, western, and southwestern coasts of the continent, but the barren sand-dunes of New Holland repelled all possible boarders, so that the character of the land influenced even the earliest Australian history.

The ocean winds, too, were winds of destiny, determining the choice of routes that left the eastern coast unseen until Cook chose a passage that ultimately led, as Kenneth Slessor has pointed out vividly, to the making of our literature:

> So Cook made choice, so Cook sailed westabout,
> So men write poems in Australia.[24]

Our history took a new turn when the British Government chose Botany Bay as the site for a new antipodean jail. The Industrial Revolution in England played its part by producing an excess of convicts through stimulus to unemployment, poverty, and crime, and later by forcing its dispossessed to emigrate to New South Wales. Poverty, famine, and political conflict in Ireland brought thousands of Irish here as prisoners, paupers, and settlers, so that they and their descendants played a distinctive part in the shaping of the Australian society.

The first world war broke the dream of an isolated utopia, woke a new consciousness of nationality, blooded the young nation, and gave it a legend to live by through the exploits of the Anzacs and the first

[22] Paul Hasluck, *The Government and the People 1939-41*, vol.1 of Series 4 (Civil) in the official history, *Australia in the War of 1939-1945* (Canberra 1952), pp.5-8.
[23] C. P. Fitzgerald, "A Chinese Discovery of Australia?" in T. Inglis Moore (ed.), *Australia Writes* (Melbourne 1953), pp.74-86.
[24] Kenneth Slessor, "Five Visions of Captain Cook", *Cuckooz Contrey* (Sydney 1932), p.32.

A.I.F. in Palestine and France. It also strengthened such patterns as the democratic spirit, mateship, and sardonic humour. Later the Russian Revolution produced organized Communism, which sharpened the edge of the existing class warfare here, and created a number of communist or "fellow-traveller" writers who have notably increased the radical pattern in the literature, even if such factors as the comfortable living standard, the interest in sport, the Roman Catholic element in the Labour movement, and the democratic tradition have all discouraged revolutionary communism in politics.

The second world war weakened considerably the British element in the already diminished clash of cultures in two ways: it taught Australians a hitherto neglected lesson in geography by making them aware that they lived in the Pacific and Indian oceans close to Asian neighbours and must reckon with Asia; it drove home the harsh fact that their survival as a free people depended upon aid, not from London, but from Washington.

Intellectually the outside pressures had only a limited force, since three factors militated against the import of cultural ideas into colonial Australia: its comparative isolation from Europe and America, the aggressive nationalism which distrusted philosophies and movements coming from an old world regarded as alien and effete, and the indifference of almost all classes to the things of the intellect. Even from earliest days there have been groups of intelligentsia, but they formed only a very small minority. The Australian community, busied in struggling with a difficult environment, earning a livelihood, and enjoying its pleasures, has rarely shown any intimate concern with general ideas. Many observers from overseas have commented, at different times, on this obvious and continuing feature of the Australian society. Even that sympathetic observer, Dr Thomas Wood, was forced to remark:

this country of great distances does not necessarily breed great minds. It tends, on the contrary, to breed narrow ones.... . I have met throughout Australia men who were as well-informed and as imaginative as any one could wish for; but they are not typical. A great many of their countrymen made me feel that I was talking to precociously alert and self-satisfied children; and that I was an old, old man.[25]

On the other hand, the Australian colonies were never so isolated that they were completely insulated against contact with the ideas and movements stirring the outside world, even if these came in the form of general diffusion or influences upon individuals rather than as main currents of thought. Only occasionally did ideas from the outside world gain some general currency for a period, like the single tax on

[25] Thomas Wood, *Cobbers* (Melbourne 1948), p.155.

land proposed by Henry George in his *Progress and Poverty*, which was championed by such writers as John Farrell and Catherine Helen Spence, and the vision of a socialist utopia presented by Edward Bellamy in his *Looking Backward*, a book which was published serially in William Lane's Queensland *Worker*, inspired Bellamy Clubs, and was discussed hopefully in city and bush alike. Henry Lawson, as realistic in his prose as he was often idealistic in his verse, satirizes a shiftless selector arguing with a neighbour about the respective merits of Henry George and Bellamy, but these reformers made a genuine, if temporary, appeal in the 1890s because they offered versions of the Great Australian Dream.

In literature the outside pressures were evident, but it is difficult to estimate how deeply or widely their diffusion went. Who can calculate, for instance, how far the clamant, democratic voice of Whitman echoed through his mouthpiece Bernard O'Dowd, who furnished inspiration to many thinkers and writers of his time? What were the reverberations of Wordsworth's pantheism sounding in the efforts of Harpur and Kendall to assimilate Australian nature, thus heralding that sacerdotal approach to the land which, developed further by O'Dowd, Wilmot and other poets, helped to bring about a revolutionary change in the attitude of Australians to their country? How can we gauge the impact of Nietzsche's philosophy through its championship by Norman Lindsay, whose protean genius has been one of our cultural dynamics?

From Europe and America came a number of influences upon our writers. Nietzsche's ideas, for example, reappeared not only in the Lindsay-inspired *Vision* school of poets but also in Baylebridge and Hope, and in the novels of Henry Handel Richardson and Patrick White. Richardson took her outlook and methods from Bjornson, Jacobsen, Flaubert, and Dostoievsky, so that her adoption of European naturalism strengthened the pattern of realism in our fiction. In drama the Irish nationalism of Yeats and Synge moved Louis Esson by personal association with them to apply their nationalist spirit and naturalist treatment to local themes. Whitman inspired William Gay and J. Le Gay Brereton as well as O'Dowd by his fervent belief in democracy and human brotherhood.

Thus, although Australian writing developed along its own lines, it also owed much to writers and movements overseas. Most of such influences were confined, however, to purely literary themes and techniques, which do not concern us here.

Internal History

More important than the outside pressures as determinants of our social patterns were the forces working in Australia's internal history.

The most significant of these were the convict system, the pastoral age, the gold discoveries, the struggle for the land, nationalism (discussion of which will be reserved for the chapter on the clash of cultures), and the Labour movement.

In respect to the convict system historians have tended to disagree about the character of the convicts and to preserve a wary reticence about their social influence. Were the influences of convictism, however, actually vague or negligible? It may be true that the convicts left few descendants owing to the scarcity of women, the prevalence of prostitution in the early days, and the high infant mortality rate, but this is irrelevant, since the issue is one of social, not physical, inheritance. It seems extremely unlikely that convictism, which dominated more than one-third of the total life of the Australian society, could have softly and silently vanished away, like Carroll's Snark, without leaving any trace or making any social impress. It was the very *raison d'être* of the colonies, it produced the main political issues of its day, it laid the economic foundations of the country, and it affected all activities and all individuals during its regime. The 160,000 convicts who came to Australia must have left their mark upon the community during its formative stages. In 1821 the convicts formed 43 per cent of the population of New South Wales and Van Diemen's Land. As late as 1840 there were 56,000 convicts in servitude, apart from the thousands of emancipists.

The penal system with its savagery of the lash certainly tended to brutalize the whole community of officers, clergy, officials, settlers, and labourers as well as the convicts themselves. As Colonel Arthur pointed out, it was impossible for "such a class of persons" as the convicts to be "residents in any community without the most polluting consequences"[26] and the demoralization of the whole community. That penetrating observer, Alexander Harris, considered that the free were infected by the bond, that laxity of life was no less rife in the middle and upper classes of the population as in the lower, whilst the labouring class had deplorable habits:

Drunkenness, profanity, dishonesty, and unchastity are the prevalent habits which the class has acquired. What else indeed could be expected? The original stock is the very lowest; the blood-stained hand and ruthless heart from the most barbarian parts of Ireland; the professional depredator from the vilest haunts of London; the lowest slaves of profligacy, inebriation, violence, and lust; men who have sought and found the very abysses of crime.[27]

[26] Report from the Select Committee on Transportation, *British Parliamentary Papers*, 1837, XIX, 518, p.313.
[27] "An Emigrant Mechanic" (Alexander Harris), *Settlers and Convicts*, ed. C. M. H. Clark (Melbourne 1953 ed., first published 1847), referred to in succeeding references as A. Harris, *Settlers and Convicts*, p.230.

Did not this general coarsening of the social fibre contribute towards such cruder elements, persisting throughout the Australian society until the present day, as lawlessness, larrikinism, drunkenness, vandalism, hostility towards the courtesies of civilized life, suspicion of anyone or anything revealing qualities of refinement, and that "lowbrowism" which Sidney J. Baker found to be such a marked characteristic of Australian speech?

Australia has been pictured so often as a fair and youthful princess that it is forgotten that she was born and bred as an ill-favoured by-blow of the squalor and criminality of eighteenth century industrial England and the poverty of Ireland. For her first decades she was little more than a dirty little Cinderella, smudged with ashes and cinders. Would it be surprising if a few of her early slatternly habits have survived?

A closer examination suggests that the convict legacy is not negligible but, on the contrary, that most of the social patterns described here often show some trace, however small, of convict ancestry, and this heritage will be considered later, in the discussions of the individual patterns.

In general it must be noted that the convict outlook contributed especially to the traditions of the outback bushmen during the early pastoral age. In the outer districts of New South Wales in 1841, for example, there were 5,388 convicts and emancipists as against only 2,557 persons "arrived free". The squatters naturally preferred the assigned convicts to free labourers: the convicts were cheaper, tougher, more adventurous, and more adaptable than the ordinary immigrant labourer. For their part the convicts made their way out-back since they found more freedom there than in the cities. Thus they became the "old hands" of the bush and exercised a dominating influence upon the "new chum" immigrants, who absorbed their values.

On the other hand, two offsetting factors are important and must be taken into account: the gradual swamping of the convicts by the free immigrants, and the changes in the character of the convicts produced by association with them as well as by the new environment.

Recent research into the composition of the convicts has exploded the favorable views of them expressed by such earlier social historians as Hammond, Wood, and Vance Palmer. The number of political offenders, Irish peasantry, and poachers amongst them was negligible. "Most of them were from the towns and Ireland; most of them were

D

workers, the unskilled outnumbering the skilled; most of them were transported for theft."[28]

Their criminality may often have come, however, from their environment of poverty, squalor, and vice rather than from any inherent depravity. The typical convict was an Artful Dodger or a Bill Sykes, not a cousin of the Jukes family. This is shown not only by the good records of many convicts as assignees and emancipists, but also by the physical and moral healthiness of their offspring, the Currency lads and lasses.

The new land gave the convicts in many cases a new life and character. There is abundant evidence of this transformation. One judicious observer, for example, wrote:

Even in the class of the more depraved convicts transported for serious crime, the instances of a reformed character were numerous and gratifying. London pickpockets and convicts from Dublin, Liverpool, and the large towns of the United Kingdom, who, from their childhood upwards, had been brought up in ignorance, and had led lives of habitual crime, if not from principle, from obvious motives of interest in the prospect of becoming independent in a land of abundance, altered their course of conduct and became industrious members of society.[29]

This change was facilitated, of course, by the skills learnt during periods of assignment and the better living conditions in the colonies.

Convict reform, if by no means universal, was especially common under the conditions provided by the land in the outback. Thus a Victorian squatter tells of reform amongst his men, who "were an average lot of ruffians, who had all shortly before been convicts",[30] and explains that "station life not only put a stop to drunkenness and theft by the absence of grog and anything worth stealing, but the constant absence of temptation had a tendency to throw the convict's mind into a better groove."[31] A visitor records that "the best and most honest servants in the interior, as I have been told by a great many old inhabitants, are convicts."[32] This fact is confirmed by many other writers. Rolf Boldrewood tells how his father's convict servants, being well treated at Enmore House in Sydney, were generally well behaved. They accompanied his father when he overlanded to Port Phillip in 1838, and remained happily on his Victorian cattle and sheep stations as efficient and trustworthy workers.

[28] M. Clark, "The Origins of the Convicts Transported to Eastern Australia, 1787-1852", *Historical Studies: Australia and New Zealand*, vol.7, no.26, p.132.
[29] R. Therry, *Reminiscences of Thirty Years' Residence in New South Wales and Victoria* (London 1863), p.18.
[30] Edward M. Curr, *Recollections of Squatting Life in Victoria*, etc. (Melbourne 1883), p.437.
[31] Ibid., p.439.
[32] F. Gerstaecker, *Narrative of a Journey Round the World*, etc., 3 vols (London 1853), vol.2, p.271.

The outback convicts who contributed to the shaping of the social patterns did so, in effect, not as convicts but as bushmen. Most of them had, in a very real sense of the biblical term, been born again as new men, with fresh characters and characteristics born of the land.

The Pastoral Age

The bush was an ecological determinant profoundly affecting all people living within it, squatters as well as convicts, bond and free alike. But the character of a community as a whole is inevitably bound up with its chief occupation, and its way of living determines its way of thinking. As wool-growing dominated the economy it produced traditional values which permeated the whole society, urban as well as rural.

It might seem, of course, that the sharp demarcation between the squatter and his workers represented the very antithesis of the democratic spirit which became a fundamental Australian characteristic. Many squatters belonged to the upper or middle classes of England and Scotland, whilst their employees were almost entirely drawn from the working class. Between them lay a social as well as economic gulf, a gulf widened by the conscious effort of many squatters to establish an aristocracy along hierarchical English lines. Tom Collins commented on Runnymede station: "In the accurately-graded society of a proper station you have a reproduction of the Temple economy under the old Jewish ritual . . . . And the restrictions of the temple were never more rigid than those of a self-respecting station."[33]

The early squatter, Furphy suggests, ruled his convict servants by physical force and his immigrant servants by moral force, but times had changed. Furphy goes to the core of the matter when he observes that the only reserve-force of the station aristocracy was the manager's power to "sack", and this force had little power when the sacked worker could secure another job without difficulty. This was the strongest reason why the monism of the democratic spirit proved stronger than the old dualism of squattocracy.

This reason was reinforced, of course, by other factors. There was, for instance, no fixed aristocratic order, stabilized by centuried usage, as in England, since the pastoral age was a fluid one in which the station owner of one day might himself be "sacked" the next day by those two great levellers, drought and the banks, and descend to the ranks of the drovers, whilst the thrifty or enterprising bush worker might rise to station manager and squatter, like James Tyson

[33] Tom Collins (Joseph Furphy), *Such is Life* (Melbourne 1917 edition, originally published 1903), pp.204-5.

or Lawson's Andy (Middleton's rouseabout). The environment put a natural premium, again, on individual strength and resourcefulness that weakened the more artificial divisions of class. The bush worker rose to a status of sturdy independence unknown to the rural or industrial workers in England. The squatter, in turn, was also a robust individualist. He belonged, too, in the early days to the freemasonry of the bushmen no less than the workers, sharing the bush skills and work. This freemasonry was quickened, too, by the variety of types found among the squatters and workers. Thus one discerning observer declared:

Few places can show so strange a mixture, and yet so complete a "fusion", of the heterogeneous materials of its society as "the Bush" of Australia. It is curious to see men differing so entirely in birth, education, and habits, and in their whole moral and intellectual nature, thrown into such close contact, united by common interests, engaged under circumstances of perfect equality in the same pursuits.[34]

This evidence discredits the radical picture of an early class war in the bush. Indeed, in the literature dealing with the pastoral age the general note struck is one of democratic independence shown by the workers towards the squatters as individuals rather than of popular hostility towards the squatting class. The accounts of pioneering days relate many instances of the mutual respect squatter and bush worker developed for each other in their common fight against the dangers and hardships of life in the outback. The old bush songs, which reflect the social attitudes of the people, are sometimes critical of the squatter for taking the land, impounding the drover's cattle, or over-working his men; yet other songs, like "The Squatter of the Olden Time", treat the squatter in a friendly fashion, or recount his troubles with sympathy, as in "The Broken-down Squatter". Paterson, the bush balladist who reflected the spirit of the folk most intimately, praises the old-time squatter in his ballad "On Kiley's Run".

The key to this sympathetic attitude is perhaps given in the old bush song "The Sheep-washer's Lament", which laments the good old days when

The master was a worker then,
The servant was a man.[35]

Squatter and worker, in effect, during the early pastoral age, before the struggle for the land sharpened antagonism, were allied in a double camaraderie of hard work and individual independence which tended to offset the class barrier.

[34] H. W. Haygarth, *Recollections of Bush Life in Australia during a Residence of Eight Years in the Interior* (London 1848), p.22.
[35] A. B. Paterson (ed.), *Old Bush Songs* (Sydney 1905), p.53.

The Gold Discoveries

Since the main social patterns had become well established during the pastoral age before the 1850s, the gold discoveries, spectacular as they were, did not effect revolutionary changes in the existing social patterns, even if they served to strengthen or modify them. As a contemporary observer, William Westgarth, put it at the time:

Victoria's democracy has been most conspicuous since the sudden accession of popular strength from the immigrating masses brought by the discovery of gold. But it would be an error to infer that the colony was not democratic previously.[36]

The legend that democracy arose on the gold diggings or was born as a fully-panoplied Minerva on the Eureka Stockade is more myth than historical fact. The gold discoveries, in fact, did not immediately usher in a democratic golden age for two sound reasons: a substantial measure of democracy already existed before them, and the measure after them, if increased, still fell far short of the radical ideal.

On the other hand, gold not only increased the population and wealth of the eastern colonies remarkably, but also deepened and widened the existing social patterns of the democratic spirit and radicalism. The diggers in general stood strongly for independence and equality. Their influence probably helped to speed up considerably the liberal reforms which were to make the colonies advanced democracies by the end of the century.

The Struggle for the Land

One important effect of the gold discoveries was the new turn they gave to the struggle for the land. As alluvial diggings declined, thousands of diggers, disappointed in the search for gold, sought the land already occupied by the squatters. The squatter was often a well-to-do English immigrant and the would-be selector often a native-born colonial—perhaps the son of a convict or emancipist—who resented *his* land being occupied by an alien. The gold-digger, who had been his own master, also naturally wanted to preserve his independence, and was reluctant to decline into an employee working for a boss. The frustration of the landless bred a sense of injustice which had not been prevalent in the earlier days of the pastoral age when land was available to any who had enough capital for stock and working expenses.

The demand to "unlock the land" in the fifties and sixties strengthened the social pattern of radicalism, the sense of class warfare, and the literature of social protest. The popular sympathy with

36 William Westgarth, *Victoria and the Gold Mines in 1857* (London 1857), p.270.

the bushrangers formed one expression of this anti-squatter radicalism, as in the old ballad of "The Wild Colonial Boy":

> *He robbed those wealthy squatters, their stock he did destroy,*
> *And a terror to Australia was the wild Colonial boy.*[37]

It was one thing, however, for the colonial legislature to "open up the land", but quite another to make farming pay. The soil and the climate, which favoured the large pastoral holding rather than the small farm, proved stronger than all the varied selection laws, just as Macarthur with his flocks had been economically right as against Macquarie with his vision of a sturdy yeomanry. Except in South Australia, inland agriculture rarely flourished until the eighties, and by then prices were falling everywhere. The environment dictated its own terms.

The Labour Movement

The original development of the social patterns proceeded without influence from a labour movement as such, since trade unionism did not become influential until the seventies and eighties, and it was not until 1899 that the short-lived Dawson Ministry in Queensland became the first Labour government in Australia. On the other hand, the working class had already exerted a powerful influence in moulding the national traditions. On the industrial side, moreover, as early as 1856-8, when working hours were excessively long in Britain and throughout Europe, many workers of the building trades, starting with the stonemasons, secured the eight hour day and so set up an inspiring goal for other artisans. Later a new and significant development in trade unionism was introduced when the formation of the Amalgamated Miners' Association was followed by the organization of the bush workers, especially the shearers, by W. G. Spence in inter-colonial unions. This was a distinctive Australian development for which there was then no adequate parallel in oversea unionism. This mobilization of the bush workers reinforced the bush-bred social patterns and helped to incorporate them into the philosophy of Australian trade unionism, which grew to be one of the most powerful social and political, as well as economic, forces in the national society.

The bush cult of mateship, in particular, was taken over and expanded into the class loyalty of trade union solidarity. Such democratic and radical principles as equality, the demand for social justice, and the utopian ideal of a new and juster world for the workers, all became woven into the tradition, first, of unionism, and then of the Australian Labour Party. Thus the labour movement stabilized these particular patterns, and helped to popularize them and

---

[37] A. B. Paterson, op. cit., p.33.

make them widely accepted. Its socialist enthusiasm brought to them an emotional, even a religious, fervour which transformed familiar ideas into a faith to be fought for.

Furthermore, the nationalist writers who formulated and idealized these patterns during the nationalist period from 1880 to the first world war were mainly socialists or supporters, at least, of the Labour movement. John Farrell, William Lane, Lawson, Furphy, O'Dowd, the Victor Daley who wrote as "Creeve Roe", Mary Gilmore, and Miles Franklin all voiced Labour sympathies, protests, and aspirations. Most of them were intimately associated with Labour journalism for many years. Indeed, it was the Labour journals, such as the Queensland *Worker*, the Sydney *Worker*, the *Boomerang*, the *Republican*, and the *Tocsin*, along with the *Bulletin*, then a radical paper championing most of the Labour programme, which provided the writers with the media for building up a national tradition. It was among their working class readers, including the bush workers, that the writers found their most responsive audience.

Thus the shaping of the social patterns in literary form was carried out by the writers in a fruitful alliance with the labour movement and the expanding national sentiment.

III

The People and the Land

The striking thing about the first squatters was how many of them were men of good birth, education and capital.... The average squatter was more likely to be an educated member of the middle class than a self-made bushman.

STEPHEN H. ROBERTS[1]

Then hurl me to crime and brand me with shame,
But think not to baulk me, my spirit to tame,
For I'll fight to the last in old Ireland's name,
Though I be a bushranger,
You still are the stranger,
And I'm Donahue.

JACK DONAHUE (?)[2]

It is a strange thing, but the more desolate and cruel is the land, the finer, in their simple way, are the people. I defy anyone to move among the folk in the Australian interior and come away without an unshakable belief in the fundamental decency and kindness of the human race.

FRANCIS RATCLIFFE[3]

Every man has a genius, though it is not always discoverable. Least of all when choked by the trivialities of daily existence. But in this disturbing country...it is possible more easily to discard the inessential and to attempt the infinite.

PATRICK WHITE[4]

[1] Stephen H. Roberts, *The Squatting Age in Australia, 1835-1847* (Melbourne 1935), pp.371-2.
[2] Douglas Stewart and Nancy Keesing (ed.), *Old Bush Songs* (Sydney 1955), p.38, "Jack Donahue and His Gang".
[3] Francis Ratcliffe, *Flying Fox and Drifting Sand* (Sydney 1947), p.278.
[4] Patrick White, *Voss* (London 1957), p.38.

The People: a Common Characteristic

Whilst outside pressures and internal history were important in shaping the Australian society, the chief forces were the people and the land. What kind of people, then, adapted themselves to the environment?

All colonists, to begin with, shared a common characteristic: the fundamental urge to better their economic conditions. It was the one driving force which propelled almost all the voluntary migrants to the remote antipodes. The desire to improve their fortunes was the one touch of nature that made the colonists akin. They were predominantly people "on the make", and they formed a strongly acquisitive society. The prevailing acquisitiveness was only emphasized by the fortune-seekers of the gold-rushes. Henry Handel Richardson, with her limpet-like fidelity to fact, seized on this basic feature when she entitled her trilogy *The Fortunes of Richard Mahony*. Money, she herself declared, was as much a protagonist in the book as Mahony himself.

So, too, the stress on money-making struck an oversea visitor to Sydney in 1851, who observed:

Sydney has, in fact, little or nothing to do with romance; for there is hardly a place in the world—even the Yankee States, or California not excepted—where you would find a more thoroughly business-life than here. Pounds and shillings are the only musical words to enliven the features of all who surround the stranger.[5]

Again, the impulse behind the English settlers was expressed bluntly, without making any bones about it, by the successful Mr Buffray of Bandra: "England's the best country in the world when a man has made his money, but there's no place like Australia for making it. It's the place for a young fellow to go that has all the world before him."[6]

This dominant economic drive of the colonists made the colonial society eminently utilitarian, materialistic and realistic in temper. The realism became a main pattern, reinforced by the pioneering conditions on the land and the prevailing practicality of the contemporary Englishman. Inevitably the English settlers made many mistakes in trying to subdue the baffling, resistant country. Yet they persisted and prospered with that capacity celebrated neatly by a modern American poet:

    ... *The English are sweet,*
And we might as well get used to them because when they slip and fall
They always land on their own or somebody else's feet.[7]

[5] F. Gerstaecker, *Narrative of a Journey Round the World*, etc., 3 vols (London 1853), vol.2, p.269.
[6] Rolf Boldrewood, *A Sydney-side Saxon* (Sydney 1925 ed., first publ. 1891), p.41.
[7] Ogden Nash, quoted in D. Brogan, *The English People* (Melbourne 1945), p.14.

The English Dominance

More striking than any common characteristics of the colonists, however, were the distinctive peculiarities of the different national groups and class sections. There were four main national groups: English, Irish, Scottish, and non-British. Of these the various foreign migrants exerted minor influences as individuals, not as a group. Each of the three British elements of the people, on the other hand, including a minor Welsh group, brought its own national character, religion, politics, outlook, and habits, whilst each displayed special traits as the country itself brought its pressure to bear on them.

There was far less homogeneity and a far greater diversity in the English national group than in the Irish and Scottish ones. Not only did the English stock cover a far broader cross-section of classes, but religion, divided between the established Church and the various non-conformist sects, exerted less unifying power than Roman Catholicism exerted among the Irish or Presbyterianism among the Scots.

The English, nevertheless, as the majority, exercised a dominance. The colonies, after all, were English colonies. They used the English language, thought in English, spoke in English, and wrote in English. They were nurtured in English literature, and imported English books, magazines, and plays which helped to maintain the old culture. The system of government, political institutions, and common law were all English as well as the social traditions and cultural background of the majority of the people. Although the new land forced profound changes and a gradual evolution of Australian social patterns, these grew out of the English ones and were based on them. There was no sudden break but a line of continuity in the gradual development. This continuity was preserved partly by the continuing maintenance of the economic, political, and cultural bonds between Australia and England.

The Australian social pattern of radical democracy, for instance, was based on an original liberalism brought from England. A Catholic historian has said: "Politically, Australia developed under the influence of English liberalism and largely reflected its fortunes from the thirties until the eighties."[8] The Australian colonies developed, in fact, under the dominant idea of liberalism prevailing in the England of the nineteenth century in the same way that the American colonies earlier had developed under the dominant puritanism of seventeenth century England.

Behind the new liberalism in England, however, lay the older tradition of individual freedom that had flourished there for centuries.

---

[8] James G. Murtagh, *Australia: the Catholic Chapter* (New York 1946), p.xv.

England did not practise equality, but it believed in liberty. Magna Carta, trial by jury and the Habeas Corpus Act were a fundamental part of the English heritage transplanted to the colonies. When the colonial editors fought governors for the freedom of the press they quoted Milton's *Areopagitica*. When colonial politicians struggled for wider freedoms, for representative institutions and self-government, they invoked the name of John Hampden and the principles of John Stuart Mill. Australian radicalism was sired by English liberalism.

On the other hand, the English dominance came into conflict with the developing Australian attitudes, thus creating the fundamental social pattern of the clash of the two opposing cultures, a clash sharpened by the national pride of the English. This had already developed vigorously before the foundation of the Australian settlement. During its growth in the nineteenth century England advanced to defeat the all-conquering Napoleon, to extend its empire, and to become the forge, the workshop, the carrier, and the financier of the world. It enjoyed the prestige of the world's greatest power. Inevitably the countrymen of Clive and Hastings, of Wellington and Nelson, brought a national self-confidence to their enterprise in subduing the Australian continent. Kingsley has pictured this English pride clearly in his portraits of such settlers as Geoffry Hamlyn and Major Buckley.

If the Hamlyns merely wished to use Australia as a place to make money to be spent later in England, the majority of the English settlers with capital were content to remain in the colonies so long as they could make them over, as far as possible, in the English image and bestow on them the goodly heritage of England. The best illustration of this determination to Anglicize the colonial wilderness is found in William Hyde's declaration to his wife Adela:

"I have striven to reproduce our English life as far as possible," said William with pride and complacency. "I think it is the duty of every Englishman to reproduce English conditions as far as possible wherever he may be. The man who does not is, I don't scruple to say it, a renegade.... . What finer thing can we do for Australia than make it another England? ... Who are we to edit the greatest civilization the world has known? ... Ours is a race of empire-builders because no Englishman worthy of the name ever yields to climate or environment."[9]

In the end, of course, William was wrong. His ideal of Englishry yielded, in time, to the climate and the environment, which remained stubbornly, invincibly Australian. The endeavours to transplant the English modes of life and thought gradually met with increasing opposition as the native-born, shaped by the land, developed their own

[9] M. Barnard Eldershaw, *A House is Built* (London 1929), pp.152-3.

modes of thought and their own national pride. So the clash of cultures entered on its long career.

The Irish and the Scots

Whilst the Australian colonial society was dominated by the English element, it was a British community, after all, not merely an English one. The Celtic element of the Irish and the Scots formed an important minority qualifying the English ascendancy, a minority which became relatively stronger in numbers in the Australian population than in the population of the United Kingdom. In this sense, it has been claimed, the Australian people is more British than the people of Great Britain.

Both the Irish and Scottish arrivals in Australia brought with them their own national traditions in ways of life, religion, and politics, traditions which often differed fundamentally from the English ones. Between the Irish and the English, indeed, there was an ancient hostility. Once in Australia, however, the Irish and Scottish did not form separate national groups gathered together in closed communities, as the Irish migrants did in parts of America, but became assimilated into the new national amalgam of the Australians. As Dr Madgwick pointed out:

The Irish immigrants had no difficulty in finding employment and were soon merged into the colonial population. Like the English, Scotch, and Welsh, they lost many of the national characteristics which may have distinguished them from the rest of the population...it was not long before English, Scotch and Irish forgot national antipathies and settled down as a united people in a new land.[10]

In this process of assimilation, nevertheless, the Irish and Scots did not just abandon their national characteristics but fused them with the developing social patterns of the Australian people. Some of the distinctiveness of these patterns derives, therefore, from the important contributions made by them.

The more important minority influence was exerted by the Irish because of their numbers, since before 1851 they seem to have formed about one-third of the population in the Eastern colonies. Famine and destitution in Ireland, together with political strife, swelled the numbers of Irish transportees. One historian estimates that from 1791 to 1802 about 40 per cent of the convicts transported from the United Kingdom were Irish,[11] whilst another historian considers that the proportion of Irish convicts was between 30 and 40 per cent

[10] R. B. Madgwick, *Immigration into Eastern Australia, 1788-1851* (London 1937), pp.235-6.
[11] E. O'Brien, *The Foundation of Australia, 1786-1800* (Sydney, 2nd ed., 1950), p.21n.

for the period 1802 to 1847.[12] Similarly the Irish supplied a large proportion of the immigrants to eastern Australia. Between 1839 and 1851—the only years for which detailed figures are available—of the assisted migrants 37,306 came from Ireland, as against 30,471 from England and 10,066 from Scotland. During this period, in fact, the Irish supplied almost half (48 per cent) of assisted migrants, and in the year 1850 they supplied 79 per cent of them.[13] Such figures indicate how substantial the Irish element was in immigration, even if it provided few amongst the unassisted immigrants.

This Irish stock and its descendants affected the shaping of the Australian society at many points. They brought Irish words into the language and a dash of the Irish imagination, wit, humour, and colour into the literature. They gave the prevailing realism touches of romantic feeling, especially in poetry. In politics they supplied a large part of the leadership in the Australian Labour Party, and no less than five Prime Ministers.

The Roman Catholic priesthood was almost an exclusive Irish preserve during the nineteenth century, and it is difficult to estimate the influence wielded by the Irish through their Church not only in religion but also in education, politics, and social behaviour. This influence was deepened by the insistence of the Church in maintaining its own schools.

The notable contribution of the Irish element to the Australian pattern of radicalism was stimulated, moreover, by the special character of the Roman Catholic Church in Ireland in the eighteenth and nineteenth centuries. In the Catholic countries of Europe, such as Italy and Spain, the Church has been traditionally conservative and associated closely with the political ruling class. In Ireland there was no such association. On the contrary, the Church there was in bitter opposition to the English Protestant rulers, who were regarded as heretics as well as alien tyrants. Thus the Roman Catholic Church became closely associated with the Irish people in a common struggle for freedom. It grew radical in outlook, with a philosophy of revolt against the heretical, foreign oppressor. This outlook and philosophy were preserved in Australia, especially as the great majority of the Church's Irish adherents were members of the working class, a class inevitably radical as a result of a long history of poverty, oppression, and suffering. A significant illustration of this radical link between the Church and the workers was the stand taken by a Catholic prelate, Cardinal Moran, in support of the strikers in the great maritime strike of 1890.

[12] M. Clark, "The Origins of the Convicts Transported to Eastern Australia, 1787-1852", *Historical Studies: Australia and New Zealand*, vol.7, no.26, p.132.
[13] R. B. Madgwick, op. cit., p.234.

Not only did the Irish element make a marked contribution to Australian radicalism, but it also added a special strain of lawlessness which qualified the prevailing English respect for law and order. The Irish, whether convicts or immigrants, brought with them a long tradition of revolt against authority. Conditions in Ireland had made them rebels, continually "agin the government". Denied constitutional remedies for their ills in Ireland, they had been driven to use violence as their political weapon.

In Australia the habit of lawlessness lingered on among some sections of the Irish. It was Irish prisoners, including "United Irishmen", who took up arms in rebellion at Vinegar Hill, near Windsor, in 1804. Half a century later, at Eureka, the Irish were again prominent in another instance of armed resistance to authority. The password for the stockade was "Vinegar Hill". "The evidence we have been vouchsafed," writes Dr Currey, "does abundantly support the conclusion that, had it not been for Peter Lalor and the Tipperary Boys, there would have been no stockade at Ballarat."[14] The Irish element figured largely, moreover, in the lawlessness of the bush-rangers, from Jack Donahue to Ned Kelly. The rebellious chip on the Irish-Australian shoulder has been a significant factor promoting social protest.

Irish opposition to Britain also stimulated Australian nationalism. Thus the three early native-born poets who championed the then fledgeling cause of local patriotism—Wentworth, Harpur, and Kendall—were all of Irish descent. It was a natural step for the anti-British sentiment of the Irish element to express itself in a pro-Australian form. Such an expression was the most effective way of carrying on the traditional struggle against the hated English. How effective it could be was proved most strikingly by the anti-British J. F. Archibald, the son of an Irish police sergeant, who used the nationalist *Bulletin* to attack Britain by advocating an independent republic of Australia and ridiculing British institutions. So, too, the Irish background of Furphy, free of any allegiance to England, enabled him to satirize the English concept of gentility, to defend his Australian isocracy, and proclaim *"Aut Australia, aut nihil"*.

The Scottish element in the population of the colonies also played its part in developing Australian nationalism. If it had no bitter hostility to the English, such as the Irish cherished, it was untrammelled by old loyalties to England. Its own sturdy independence naturally entered into the sentiment for an independent Australia. For this ideal there was no doughtier champion than that bellicose and tenacious Scot, John Dunmore Lang.

If Archibald was the founder and style-maker of the *Bulletin*, that

14 C. H. Currey, *The Irish at Eureka* (Sydney 1954), p.87.

uninhibited organ of nationalism could never have survived and become a patriotic power in the land if it had not been for the band of Scotsmen who devoted their varying talents to its gospel. It was that "huge Highlander", W. H. Traill, who consolidated the paper decisively as a national forum during his dynamic editorship from 1881 to 1887. James Edmond largely formulated its political policies. William McLeod kept the *Bulletin* on an even business keel during his forty years in the manager's chair. Finally, its literary reputation was created with nationalist fervour by another Celt in A. G. Stephens, son of a Welsh father and Scottish mother.

The Scots also brought to the colonies a robust individualism and sense of individual worth that contributed to the growth of an Australian democratic spirit. In this spirit the stress on human equality only echoed the tradition of a people nourished on Bobbie Burns and his warm faith that "A man's a man for a' that". Whilst the English educational system was based on class distinctions, the sons of laird and crofter sat together under the parish dominie in Scotland. There was no need for local conditions to exert their democratic influence on the Scots—they were vigorous democrats already.

On the cultural side the Scottish element, usually better educated than the Irish or English working class immigrants, provided leaders in our educational development. It also made a distinguished contribution to the growth of indigenous writing. Take away the Celtic muster of Irish and Scottish names and there would be little left of Australian literature.

The Importance of Class

In the making of the Australian society, however, the class to which the immigrants, bond or free, belonged proved at least as important as the national composition of the people. The English worker had stronger ties with his fellow workers, Irish or Scottish, than with the English gentlemen. Disraeli's dictum that there were two nations in England, the rich and the poor, illustrated the gulf between the upper class and the working class. Moreover, the emphasis upon the economic aspect, already noted as a dominant feature of the colonial society, inevitably tended to make the class grouping based on an economic division particularly important.

There were three main sources of immigration: the penal settlement, comprising the civil administration, military garrison, and convicts; the immigrant settlers, independent or assisted; and the miners of the gold-rushes. In each case the majority element was the working class. This was true of all the colonies except South Australia, with its independent middle-class settlers and strong dissenting element of the lower middle class. It was this latter element, with its Puritans, Quakers, and other Dissenters, which was most heavily represented in the early American colonies, so that an American sociologist claimed that "America is the one country whose whole tradition grew out of an unadulterated petty bourgeois psychology. It is the one country which the petty bourgeois was able to control from the very beginning and shape in terms of its own destiny."[15] In Australia, on the other hand, the working class has been the class contributing most to the shaping of the social patterns. Thus some of the differences between the Australian and the American outlooks may perhaps be reasonably traced back to the differences between the psychology of the working class and that of the lower middle class.

Australian democracy represents to a large extent a social as well as ideological assertion of the working class in that from an inferior position it secured a balance with the other classes in the community. This balance was only won after struggle, since various bids were made to establish in the colonies an aristocracy on the English model, the most important being that made by the squatters. The bids failed because an aristocracy cannot exist on aristocrats alone, but requires a submissive "lower" class as complement and basis. As Miles Franklin put it forcibly:

No section of society can maintain aristocratic amenities and elegancies without a submerged race, whether slaves of another breed or the unprivileged of its own, to do the hard and menial labour. Australia began with manacled slaves... but many factors operated against the continuance of this ancient social composition.[16]

Probably the main factor here was the levelling nature of pioneering conditions, but another factor was the refusal of the working class to submit to any aristocratic dominance, and a third was the demand for labour that made the refusal possible. Thus the claims, first, of the exclusivist "pure merinos", and then of the squatters, to aristocratic ascendancy never obtained general acceptance. Wentworth's proposals of 1853 for an Upper House of hereditary peers, to be drawn mainly from the squatters, received short shrift. The popular reaction against them was eloquently expressed by "Little Dan" Deniehy when he ridiculed the prospect of "these harlequin aristocrats, these Botany Bay magnificos, these Australian mandarins". The people would have no truck with "a bunyip aristocracy", and the concept was fairly laughed out of court.

So, too, the claims of the middle class of wealthier commercial and

[15] V. F. Calverton, *The Liberation of American Literature* (New York 1932), p.55.
[16] Miles Franklin, *All That Swagger* (Sydney 1936), p.98.

professional classes of the cities of Sydney and Melbourne to constitute an upper class failed to impress the people, since these claims were mainly based on the acquisition of wealth. In England wealth often commanded popular prestige because it was associated with birth and rank. In America it is looked up to as the success won by the superior ability and enterprise of outstanding individuals. It thus embodies one of the American ideals. In Australia, on the contrary, respect has not been popularly accorded to wealth as such. Indeed, at the best it is regarded as the product, not of superior abilities, but of good luck, whilst at the worst it is regarded with cynical suspicion as the result of close dealing or profiteering. Hence no genuine aristocracy could be founded here by a mere plutocracy. Higinbotham's derisive phrase "the wealthy lower orders" typifies a characteristic national attitude, and many Australians would agree with the implication of the *Bulletin's* former title for its financial column, "Business, Robbery, Etc."

The Working Class

This rejection of a traditional aristocracy illustrated an outstanding phenomenon in the development of the Australian society—the influence wielded by the working class in the shaping of the social patterns. The workers were democratic in spirit, often radical. They held the utopian dream of social justice, being the class in the community which would gain most from its realization. Mateship was their special custom, and their experience of life inevitably made them more realistic in temper than the well-to-do. They shared the ironic humour and the earth-vigour of the society. In the clash of cultures they contributed greatly to the growth of a nationalist sentiment, since it was they who identified themselves with the country closely in the early days when the immigrant upper classes often clung to the British way of life.

This identification of the working class with its adopted country was, indeed, one of the chief factors why it was so influential in forming the Australian outlook. In the first formative half century of the colonies some migrants of the British upper and middle classes either returned home after bettering their fortunes or retained links with it, sometimes visiting it, sometimes sending their sons and daughters back to the old land for education. Some families, like the Montforts pictured by Martin Boyd, developed a curious Anglo-Australian ambivalence. The members of the working class, on the other hand, had no choice but to remain in the colonies, whilst they had only limited opportunities of maintaining old associations with the homeland, especially as many of them could not read or write. Thus the new land became their home, claiming their future aspira-

E

tions as well as present energies. Even the convicts, predominantly members of the working class, often regarded the land as theirs, as "the prisoners' country". This feeling of identity with the country was even stronger, of course, amongst the "natives", the colonial-born who had never known any other home.

The working class, moreover, formed the great majority of the population. Its numbers helped to develop a democracy, and as the community became more democratic so it benefited by the rule of the majority. To this class belonged most of the convicts, colonial-born, and assisted migrants, whilst it was reinforced strongly by the gold-diggers. Although these were a varied assortment comprising men of different classes, as diggers they all became manual workers and so enlisted in the ranks of the working class. The gold-fields, in any case, acted as an equalizing force. The few Englishmen of birth and breeding among the diggers, Trollope observed, came to adopt the common proletarian digger dress, language and behaviour. This illustrated the truth of Wakefield's sapient observation: "Whilst in old countries modes and manners flow downward from the higher classes, they must, in new countries, ascend from the lowest class."[17] In the Australian colonies the environment brought some, at least, of the upper class down just as it lifted the working class up to a position of independence and a standard of living far beyond proletarian conditions in England or Europe. The gold-fields created a levelling towards a certain common denominator of vigorous, independent worker.

It was this same type of independent worker which had developed already in the bush. As the shepherd gave way to the shearer, drover, and station hand, the bush worker evolved into a special type, a member of the working class marked by a vigour and independence that made him a symbolic figure, first for the workers, and then for the whole people as the embodiment of the "true Australia". Francis Adams saluted the bushman as "the one powerful and unique type yet produced in Australia".[18] Thus the values of the working class prevailed to a significant extent in shaping the social patterns through its special exemplar of the bushman as the ideal national type.

When these values were voiced as national traditions by the writers of the nineties they usually adopted a working-class point of view. Most of these writers had, at some period of their lives, been workers in the bush, the mines, or the city. Others, like Mary Gilmore, O'Dowd, and Miles Franklin, had worked professionally, but almost all the writers had strong working-class sympathies and a radical outlook. "Banjo" Paterson, although squatter, solicitor, and journalist,

---

[17] E. G. Wakefield, *A Letter from Sydney* (London 1829), p.51.
[18] Francis Adams, op. cit., p.165.

expressed the point of view of the bush worker in his ballads, and the hero of his national song "Waltzing Matilda" was not the squatter or the troopers, but the swagman.

So, too, although later writers have rarely been members of the working class themselves, they have largely continued the tradition of Lawson and the nineties in celebrating the values of the worker, using proletarian themes, and adopting a proletarian outlook. Hence the hero-cult of the bushman in Australian literature was turned into an apotheosis of the working class by radical writers and historians, so that an American observer concluded that "glorification of the common man"[19] was a basic element in the Australian literary tradition.

Who Were the Bushmen?

The apotheosis of the bush worker has been elaborated, with a persuasive wealth of historical evidence, by Professor Russel Ward in his important study, *The Australian Legend*. Starting with a list of characteristics popularly embodied in a stereotype of the "typical Australian", he claims:

all these characteristics were widely attributed to the bushmen of last century, not, primarily, to Australians in general or even to country people in general, so much as to the outback employees, the semi-nomadic drovers, shepherds, shearers, bullock-drivers, stockmen, boundary-riders, station-hands and others of the pastoral industry.[20]

This pastoral proletariat, which Trollope called "the nomad tribe of pastoral labourer", is considered to be a unique social group especially influenced by its convict and Irish elements. Its bush *ethos* became the strongest force in the creation of a national tradition:

From the beginning, then, outback manners and *mores*, working upwards from the lowest strata of society and outwards from the interior, subtly influenced those of the whole population... the attitudes and values of the nomad tribe were made the principal ingredient of a national *mystique*.[21]

Professor Ward's seminal book brings forward many valuable illuminations of our social history. I agree completely that the origins of our social patterns lie in the formative period before the gold-rushes and began in the bush with the bushmen. On the other hand, when Professor Ward, following Francis Adams, restricts his "bush-men" to the single group of the nomad tribe of the pastoral proletariat, Australian history and literature both demur. His thesis is bold, positive, and clear-cut. It looks attractively democratic. Its very

[19] C. Hartley Grattan, *Australian Literature* (University of Washington Chapbooks, no.29, Seattle 1929), p.29.
[20] Russel Ward, *The Australian Legend* (Melbourne 1958), p.2.
[21] Ibid., p.12.

simplicity is cajoling. Yet surely this simplicity also means an undue narrowing of all types of bushmen to a single group? Is not the problem of origins over-simplified? The social patterns, we have seen, are not simple but highly complex, and the forces that shaped them also had more complexity than was contained in the shearers, drovers, and other "outback employees". Emphasis is laid on such bush workers by the old bush songs, or folk ballads, of course, because they were the expression of the working folk's outlook. But this is only one source of origins, with a particular bias. A different picture emerges when we examine three other relevant sources: the literature of the squatters, whether in their own journals and reminiscences or in the historical works written on them; the school of bush balladists, led by Paterson and Lawson; and, finally, the fiction dealing with the various types of bushmen.

In all these other sources the squatter and the selector are represented as important types of bushmen who cannot be cut summarily out of the bush reckoning. It might be mentioned, too, that many, perhaps most, bushmen did not belong to "the nomad tribe" but were settled as station hands, and sometimes worked on the one station most of their lives. Again, if to be nomadic is a virtue, who wandered further and wider than many of the pioneer settlers, adventurous spirits like Patsy Durack, of whom Mary Durack, his grand-daughter, recorded:

And so he rode on and on, hungry for land and more land and the security that seemed always just out of reach. Land hunger was a disease of his time, leading many besides himself on pastoral trails that ran out as often as not into sand and ruin. Will Landsborough, Nat Buchanan, John Costello, the brothers Prout, Patsy Durack...riding, riding.... Cattle, horses, country.[22]

The Squatters

The squatters, as Furphy pointed out in *Such is Life*, comprised a wide variety of types. Many of the later ones, like the squatter in the old bush song "The Broken-down Squatter", were native-born. Born and bred in the bush, they enjoyed the bush *ethos* as a birthright. Of the earlier emigrant squatters from England and Scotland, some maintained, as far as practicable, their old associations and ideas. Thus they largely dissociated themselves from the developing Australian social patterns. This was mainly true of "those men of passion and power, the Scottish squatters" who settled in the Western District of Victoria. Their historian Margaret Kiddle recognized of the typical Scots squatter there that "In the broadest sense he had little influence on the social and spiritual 'ideal' Australian who had evolved by the

[22] Mary Durack, *Kings in Grass Castles* (London 1959), p.161.

end of the century."[23] At the same time she also gave the other side of the picture when she wrote of these squatters:

They had sought only to exploit the land they took possession of, but as the years passed, they found that man cannot live by profit alone. They became rooted in the new country. In it they tried to recreate the Old World they had lost, but despite themselves, they founded and helped to build a new society.[24]

Most of the emigrant squatters, in fact, particularly those in the outback of New South Wales and Queensland, made Australia their home, developed a skill in bushcraft at least the equal, if not the superior, of the skill possessed by bush workers, and thoroughly identified themselves with the country and its outlook. Hamilton Hume, Charles Throsby, "O'Brien of the River", James Chisholm of Kippilaw, Tyson, Kidman, the Hentys, Manifolds, Learmonths, and Niel Black, Patrick Leslie, Patsy Durack, John Costello, and Christison of Lammermoor, not to mention the fictional Stewart of Kooltopa, Mazeres and Pooles, and Danny Delacey—squatters all, how can such pioneers be possibly denied the title of true bushmen? Or be strangely excluded as making no significant contribution to the shaping of a national tradition? Is not the omission of the squatter from the pattern-making bushmen the playing of Hamlet without the Prince?

The pioneer squatters were, in many respects, "the men who made Australia". They provided the capital, the character, the leadership and the dynamic enterprise which built up the great wool industry. Of all groups in the colonies they made the largest contribution to the development of the country's economic resources. Their courage and determination laid the foundations for a prosperous society, opening up the vast hinterland, pushing the frontiers back, fighting hazards of the climate and the loneliness of isolation. While the weaker went to the wall the strong survived, developing the tough strength of pioneering virtues.

The historical and literary evidence shows that, whilst some squatters preserved the old-world class distinctions, others treated their workers with what might be called an Australian camaraderie in the early formative stages of the pastoral age. Good treatment of his men was, of course, a virtue that was largely a necessity for the squatter, since bad treatment meant that he suffered from resentful workers or was unable to secure workers at all. There was often hostility between the squatter and workers as classes, yet one is constantly struck in the literature about the squatting age with the

[23] Margaret Kiddle, *Men of Yesterday: a Social History of the Western District of Victoria 1834-1890* (Melbourne 1961), p.480.
[24] Ibid., p.511.

good relations depicted between the individual squatter and his men, the way he treated them democratically as fellow individuals, and the frequency with which he praised them.

Thus James Chisholm of Kippilaw did all he could to aid his namesake but no relation, Caroline Chisholm, in her work for the immigrants, and denounced flogging of convicts for minor offences. "Fortunate indeed had been the bond men and women assigned to Kippilaw, for Mr Chisholm and his good wife had helped many a lost soul to a new start in life. No bushranger ever molested his property or those belonging to it."[25] So, too, Patsy Durack, the king in his grass castle, treated men on their merits and the aborigine Pumpkin as a friend:

Servants he always regarded and treated as members of the family, and if they left for any reason he kept in touch with them wherever they were, worried about them if he heard they had struck bad times and remembered their children's birthdays. This human attitude he had to all men may explain his wonderful tact and unusual success in dealing with the aborigines. Dear old Pumpkin always regarded himself as one of the family, referred to Father as his "brother" and would have given his life for any one of us.[26]

Outstanding in the fiction are the portraits of Stewart of Kooltopa in *Such is Life*, of Danny Delacey in *All That Swagger*, and of individual squatters in Lawson's short stories. No writers could be more Australian in outlook, more staunchly democratic and egalitarian, than Furphy, Miles Franklin, and Henry Lawson, yet all unite in giving admiring or affectionate pictures of squatters. Stewart is shown as giving a swaggie a lift, helping the misanthropic bullock-driver Alf Cooper, and even letting "nearly all the uncircumcised of Riverina, with their homeless bullocks and horses", settle in his Mia-Mia Paddock during the 1883 drought. No wonder Tom Collins proclaimed, in his peculiar style:

Stewart, it must be admitted, was no gentleman. Starting with a generous handicap, as the younger son of a wealthy and aristocratic Scottish laird, he had, during a Colonial race of forty years, daily committed himself to actions which shut him out from the fine old title. He was in the gall of altruism, and in the bond of democracy.[27]

Danny Delacey, fearless and independent, was a pioneer of democratic equality as well as of the Australian Alps. When a stray frost-bitten Chinaman struggled through the snow to him for rescue, Danny took him to his homestead and bandaged the nipped feet and fingers.

[25] Mary Durack, op. cit., p.20.
[26] Ibid., p.153.
[27] Tom Collins, *Such is Life*, p.164.

He placed Wong in his own berth, and laid himself on the floor.
"What else would a man do, and calling himself a Christian? No man has the
rights of neighborliness if he balks at color, class, or even character."[28]

Danny lived up to his beliefs: "I'm free meself and would wish every
man-jack, black and white, to be the same—aquil before his Maker."[29]

In "Telling Mrs. Baker" Lawson tells how the drovers Andy and
Jack looked after Bob Baker, a squatter who had turned boss drover
when he went broke, after he was sacked and the drovers paid off,
because, Jack explains, "the boss was a mate of ours; so we stuck to
him."[30] So, too, in the bush ballads Paterson gives a similar account of
mateship between squatter and station hands:

> *The station hands were friends, I wot,*
> > *On Kiley's Run,*
> *A reckless, merry-hearted lot—*
> *All splendid riders, and they knew*
> *The boss was kindness through and through.*
> *Old Kiley always stood their friend,*
> *And so they served him to the end*
> > *On Kiley's Run.*

And when the droughts had ruined the squatter and his bankers took
the stock away,

> *Old Kiley stood and saw them go*
> > *From Kiley's Run.*
> *The well-bred cattle marching slow;*
> *His stockmen, mates for many a day,*
> *They wrung his hand and went away.*
> *Too old to make another start,*
> *Old Kiley died—of broken heart,*
> > *On Kiley's Run.*[31]

Thus any attempt to ostracize the squatters as a class apart, alien to
their Australian homes, hostile to their workers, outside the charmed
circle of bushmen, must be regarded as invalid. Not only is it refuted
by the historical documents, but it is also disproved by the very
writers who did most to create a literary expression of the Australian
social patterns. The class bias of the folk songs is discounted by the
weightier testimony of such true democrats and humanists as Lawson
and Paterson, Furphy and Miles Franklin.

Settlers and Selectors

Like the squatters, the settlers and selectors form another considerable class of bushmen who contributed to the bush way of life and

[28] Miles Franklin, op. cit., p.110.
[29] Ibid., p.78.
[30] Henry Lawson, *Prose Works* (Sydney 1935), p.162.
[31] A. B. Paterson, *Collected Verse* (Sydney 1921), pp.58-9.

thinking. Early in the First Settlement farming began at Sydney Cove, Parramatta, and Toongabbe, and soon extended into what was then wild bushland. It might be claimed with justice that the settlers around the Nepean and Hawkesbury rivers were actually the first group of bushmen, although earlier individual "bolters"—escaped convicts—had taken to the bush. They had struggled with the land, with floods, droughts, and bushfires, and had developed characteristics as bush groups for several decades before the nomadic old lag had made his exodus to the outback.

The pioneer settlers formed a numerous class in all the colonies, and they made invaluable contributions to their development. Their character and conditions, together with their skill in bushcraft and the changes made in their outlook by their environment, may be seen admirably, for example, in the books dealing with the Bussells and Molloys in Western Australia and the Skemps in Tasmania.[32] Charles Rowcroft has also given a vivid account of Tasmanian settlers in his lively *Tales of the Colonies*. Later, when the grant system had given way to free selection, the small settlers were established in the form of selectors and became an important subject in the literature, both prose and verse.

Nor was there any strict line of demarcation between the selectors and the shearers or drovers as between opposed groups. On the contrary, many shearers and drovers also became selectors, whilst it was customary for selectors in hard times to become bush workers of one sort or another, including shearers. A North Queensland pioneer, for instance, records: "Amongst the shearers will be found many respectable men, who have homes or selections of their own on which their families reside, and who travel round a few sheds to earn enough money to carry on with and support their homes."[33]

The old bush songs deal with the selectors in many aspects. A few, like "The Stringy-bark Cockatoo" and "Cockies of Bungaree", criticize them for the low wages and hard conditions of their labourers. Most of the songs, however, are favorable to the selectors, expressing their delight in independence in "Then Give Me a Hut in My Own Native Land", showing sympathy for their tribulations in "An Old Hand's Chaunt", "The Cocky Farmer", and "Stir the Wallaby Stew", and telling of their cheerful duffing in "The Eumerella Shore". A cheery note is also struck in the earlier celebration of the Henty pioneer settlers in "The Henty Song":

[32] See E. O. G. Shann, *Cattle Chosen* (London 1926); Alexandra Hasluck, *Portrait with Background* (Melbourne 1955); J. Rowland Skemp, *Memories of Myrtle Bank, 1883-1948* (Melbourne 1952).

[33] Edward Palmer, *Early Days in North Queensland* (Sydney 1903), p.190.

Come join along with Henty and all his joiful crew
For a Set of better fellows in this world you never knew.[34]

Most important of all, the writers of the nineties who were the literary creators of "the Australian legend"—bush balladists, novelists, and short story writers—all pictured the selectors as true bushmen, the battlers on the land, full members of the Australian brotherhood. Many ballads to this effect could be quoted from Lawson, Paterson, Ogilvie, Dyson, Brady, "Jim Grahame" and others. Charles Souter and "John O'Brien" concentrated on bush ballads dealing sympathetically with South Australian settlers and the predominantly Irish selectors of New South Wales respectively. The hero of the most popular of all bush recitations, "How McDougall Topped the Score", is a Scottish selector.

In fiction, "Steele Rudd" (A. H. Davis) created a folk saga with Dad as a folk hero. There was later burlesquing of Dad, partly encouraged by Davis himself when he found that his gift of humour was so popular that he fatally resorted to farce in his later books of the *Selection* series. Originally, however, Dad, Mother, Dave and the other members of the Rudd family were presented partly with infectious humour but essentially as warm, human, friendly figures and brave battlers. The spirit of *On Our Selection* is indicated unmistakably in the dedication by Steele Rudd to "The Pioneers of Australia":

... to You who strove through the silences of the Bushlands
and made them ours.
to You who have done MOST for this Land ...
and to you particularly,
GOOD OLD DAD,
This Book
is most affectionately dedicated.[35]

Again, Lawson, the most representative Australian writer, chose as the character whom he was to develop most intimately, with sympathetic understanding, not Mitchell the shearer, but Joe Wilson, a selector. In both Dad and Joe the chief characteristic is the determination "never to submit or yield", but to battle on whatever the odds. Lawson's friendly portrayal of the selector has been carried on by such modern short story writers as Brian James and E. O. Schlunke.

The Land

The bushman, however, whether squatter, selector, or bush

34 Douglas Stewart and Nancy Keesing (ed.), op. cit., p.88.
35 Steele Rudd, *On our Selection* (Sydney 1899), Dedication.

worker, was only the natural product of the bush, a unique type because moulded by the inexorable creative force of the land, which thus triumphed, slowly, insensibly, and subtly, over the men engaged in subduing its resources for their own ends. The people of variant stock and differing classes who came voluntarily to Australia to wrest a fortune from it exploited the land greedily, without care for the soil or thought for the morrow. They changed the face of the country, turning forests to grasslands, pastures into ploughed fields, and fertile areas into eroded deserts. They destroyed the natural beauty of the countryside by pockmarking it with unlovely towns and settlements. Yet, in the end, it was the country which conquered the people, forcing them to adapt themselves to its climate and physiography.

To begin with, the land seems to have developed a distinctive physical type marked by certain characteristics of physique and features, such as relative tallness of stature, leanness of build, and narrowness of face, with the nose also narrow, the lips thin, and the eyes blue or grey. This type began to manifest itself even in the very first generation of the native born, and was noted by such diverse observers as Commissioner Bigge, Alexander Harris, and William Westgarth.[36]

The psychology was influenced just as strongly by the land as the physique, and this change in character is indicated by the ironic meditation of Tom Collins upon the teamster Alf Morris after the stolid, stupid English migrant Sollicker had declared that the English stock deteriorated in Australia:

Without being aggressively handsome, like Dixon or Willoughby, Alf, in his normal state, was a decidedly noble looking man, of the so-called Anglo-Saxon type, modified by sixty or eighty years of Australian deterioration. His grandfather had probably been something like Sollicker; and the apprehensions of that discomfortable cousin were being fulfilled only too ruthlessly. The climate had played Old Gooseberry with the fine primordial stock. Physically, the Suffolk Punch had degenerated into the steeplechaser; psychologically, the chasm between the stolid English peasant and the saturnine, sensitive Australian had been spanned with that facilis which marks the decensus Averni.[37]

This shaping by the environment did not have to wait, however, for a generation, since its changes took place with the British settlers. In the historical documents, nowhere is this development illustrated more clearly than in the delightful letters written by Rachel Henning, the English gentlewoman who found Australia distasteful on her first visit but later learnt to enjoy its delights, to relish roughing it in the

[36] See J. T. Bigge, *Report on the State of Agriculture in N.S.W.*, etc. (London 1823), p.81; A. Harris, *Settlers and Convicts*, pp.71, 89; W. Westgarth, op. cit., p.282.
[37] Tom Collins, op. cit., p.161.

Queensland wilds with her brother Biddulph, and finally to make her home in them quite happily. We have already, too, seen how the land changed the character of many convicts.

In fiction Brian Penton has traced convincingly the transformation of Derek Cabell from a shy, delicate English youth to a dominating, hard-bitten Australian squatter. Eleanor Dark has depicted the staunchest of conservatives, her Mr Stephen Mannion, an Irish aristocrat who considered such a powerful parvenu as John Macarthur his social inferior, as disturbed by a comment of Governor Phillip:

For the Governor, looking at him with an offensive amusement (Mr Mannion was not accustomed to being regarded as comical) had said: "You intend to exploit this land. Have a care, Sir, that it does not end by exploiting you!"

Mr Mannion had thought it a ridiculous remark. Yet when he returned to Ireland, he found himself drawn back to the colony. He felt this had something to do with a change in himself, and began to wonder if

there might have been, after all, some sense in Phillip's cryptic observation. For if the land were dragging out of him some qualities which had hitherto lain dormant, was not the land exploiting him? Was not the mark which he laid upon it, whatever it might be, ultimately its own mark?[38]

Such examples of individual character change illustrate the agreement of these novelists with the claim of the ecologist that

From the beginning of his history, his living environment has profoundly affected man's feelings and emotions and general psychological outlook. A proper understanding of the literature, art, music, religion, and indeed all the work of men's minds, can only be attained if this simple ecological fact is definitely recognized and appreciated.[39]

The environmental impress was stamped deeply, of course, upon the culture of our early society as a whole as well as upon the individuals who composed it. The social patterns became the embodiment of the *genius loci*, since every culture is a distinctively local culture. Every god is ultimately a local god, a true spirit of the place. Even universal religions inevitably became localized, adapted to the particular environment. The law of Mahomet gets variant readings in the stern deserts of Arabia and the tropical isles of Indonesia. An English Anglican, a German Lutheran and a Spanish Roman Catholic may all be nominally "Christians" along with a Copt of Abyssinia, a Greek Orthodox Russian, and a native pastor of Papua, but their varying concepts of Christianity would have puzzled Paul and astonished Aquinas. Jack McLaren's *Songs of a Fuzzy-top* illustrate how Christian mission teaching may suffer a sea-change into some-

[38] Eleanor Dark, *Storm of Time* (Sydney 1948), pp.46-7.
[39] J. W. Bews, op. cit., p.35.

thing rich and strange when translated into the environmental terms of the South Sea Islands.

So, too, the mark of the land was placed on the culture brought by the British migrants and transformed it into an Australian one. The place-spirit has been so strong that the People are often seen as part of the Place, and less important than it. In most literatures the environment is the background to man, merely the setting for his action and thought, but in Australian writing it is frequently moved forward to become the foreground. Even if it remains ostensibly in the background, it is made the true centre of interest. This phenomenon is paralleled by a similar development in the impressionist school of Australian landscape painters, where the focus of interest shifted from the foreground, where it was usually placed in European art, to the background of blue-hazed horizons. This is particularly true of the landscapes of Streeton and Gruner, as well as the earlier art of Tom Roberts before he became interested in using human figures such as shearers and bushrangers to give dramatic effect. Even with the contemporary figurative painters like Nolan and Drysdale, Boyd and Tucker, the landscape is as important as the figures, and sometimes more memorable.

Both Nolan and Drysdale probe into the essential qualities of the land, stressing its harshness, immensity, and loneliness, trying to capture its uniqueness. Long before them Mark Twain wrote of it:

the exterior aspects and character of Australia are fascinating things to look at and think about, they are so strange, so weird, so new, so uncommonplace, such a startling and interesting contrast to the other sections of the planet.[40]

Another visitor, D. H. Lawrence, was deeply impressed by the "weirdness" of the land itself and made many references to its uniqueness in his letters and his novel *Kangaroo*, where Harriet Somers is entranced by the beauty of the bush: "The bush! The wonderful Australia!"[41] Lawrence thought he saw, too, the influence of the bush on the people in creating what he termed "the profound Australian indifference".[42] A similar thought was expressed by the native-born critic A. G. Stephens when he suggested that the chief cause of bushmen writing so much verse was

the dominance in Australia of Space and Time ... the Universe presses very closely upon a solitary or semi-solitary dweller in the bush. He loses pride of humanity in the sense that he is but an atom in the grand scale of Nature moving grandly about him.[43]

Certainly the power of the bush was cast like a spell upon the Australian imagination and the Australian literature.

[40] Mark Twain, *Following the Equator* (New York 1897), p.118.
[41] D. H. Lawrence, *Kangaroo* (Penguin ed. 1950, first publ. London 1923), p.391.
[42] Ibid., p.379.   [43] A. G. Stephens in *The Bookfellow*, 28 Apr. 1899.

IV

The Spell of the Bush

Le bush a son histoire, qui est celle de l'Australie . . . le bush n'est pas un lieu fixe, un pays que l'on puisse inscrire sur une carte; c'est un lieu en mouvement, presque un état de choses: le terrain de rencontre de la nature intacte et des hommes modernes. Et les bushmen sont donc l'avant-garde de l'Australie . . . . C'est dans le bush aussi que la vie individuelle de l'Australien a le plus le caractère, et se prête le mieux à l'interprétation littéraire.

(The bush has its history, which is that of Australia . . . the bush is not a fixed place, a country that one can inscribe on a map; it is a place in movement, almost a state of things: the meeting ground of unspoilt nature and modern men. And the bushmen are therefore the vanguard of Australia. . . . It is in the bush, too, that the individual life of the Australian is most characteristic, and lends itself best to literary interpretation.)

EMILE SAILLENS[1]

I cry to my country for she is woman,
The water and the soil of life,
That her voice shall sing in his blood
And her strong loins hold him.

MARY DURACK[2]

The weird silent timelessness of the bush impressed him as nothing else ever did, in its motionless aloofness. "What would my father mean, out here?" he said to himself. And it seemed as if his father and his father's world and his father's gods withered and went to dust at the thought of this bush . . . he felt as if the old world had given him up from the womb, and put him into a new weird grey-blue paradise, where man has to begin all over again.

D. H. LAWRENCE AND M. L. SKINNER[3]

Nor need we dread the fogs that round us thicken
Questing the Bush for Grails decreed for man,
When Powers our fathers saw unseen still quicken ·
Eyes that were ours before the world began.

BERNARD O'DOWD[4]

[1] Emile Saillens, "Le Bush Australien et Son Poète" in *Mercure de France*, 1 octobre 1910 (Paris), pp.431, 434, 442.
[2] Mary Durack, *Keep Him My Country* (London 1955), p.71.
[3] D. H. Lawrence and M. L. Skinner, *The Boy in the Bush* (London 1924), p.95.
[4] Bernard O'Dowd, from "The Bush", *Collected Poems* (Melbourne 1941), p.201.

A Literature of the Land

If the land itself was the strongest single determinant in shaping the forms of the society, making Australians out of colonials, it was also the dominant influence in our writing. Australian literature is essentially a literature of the land. In it we see the land, under the broad, familiar symbol of the Bush, casting a potent spell, becoming a pervasive force closely interlinked with the main social patterns, helping to create the people's democratic spirit, inspiring its utopian dreams and the creed of mateship, flavouring its realism, hardening its humour, and providing its earthy vitality.

The bush has given us our folk lore and balladry, our epics and sagas of action, our historical novels, and the bulk of our short stories and descriptive prose, together with most of our poetry and drama. It has not only been the background of the nation's story, but also the home of its heroes, the maker of its ideals, and the breeding ground of its myths. It has even developed, amongst a people eminently secular and pragmatic, an unexpected strain of mysticism that has produced a mystique of the bush.

A comparison with other literatures soon reveals how distinctively Australian literature has been dominated by the presence and the imaginative stimulus of its vast hinterland. Although English literature, for instance, has expressed the traditional English love of the countryside by means of its pastoral poetry and fiction of regional novelists from George Eliot and Hardy to Mary Webb and H. E. Bates, London and the provincial cities have always held their own. In modern English novels, plays, and poetry the countryside has played only a minor part. There has been in English literature as a whole a balance between rural and urban themes, with an increasing emphasis on the latter. This is also true, in general, of European literatures. In French writing Paris has been a national centre far more than the provinces. Only in Scandinavia, perhaps, has there been a strong feeling for the soil which brings literature closer to the Australian mode.

Even American literature, which dealt at first with the New England country and the frontier lands of the Middle West, became strongly urban in all its forms. When not concerned with the social and industrial life of the cities, it is regional, as with Frost and Faulkner, rather than rural only.

Only with those countries which are still close, like Australia, to their pioneering days, such as New Zealand, South Africa, and the Argentine, do we find literatures still dominated by the land.

What is perhaps most striking is the fact that the spell of the bush in our literature, far from becoming an historical tradition as the society grows more and more heavily urbanized, flourishes in contemporary writing more potently than ever. Whilst the novel has shown an increasing treatment of the comparatively neglected cities, the majority of fiction still "goes bush". This is true not only of the straightforward descriptive novels, such as *Vision Splendid* and *Brigalow*, the frequent novels on the aborigines, and historical fiction, but also of the two extreme ends of fiction in the imaginative and the commercial writers. The bush claims both the poetic novels of Patrick White and Randolph Stow as well as the best-sellers of E. V. Timms, D'Arcy Niland, and Jon Cleary.

Professional short story writers like Dal Stivens and Alan Marshall have revived the ancient bush cult of the tall story, whilst the bush is a setting for the short stories of Katharine Prichard, Vance Palmer, Brian James, Gavin Casey, Schlunke, and David Campbell. When the Canberra Fellowship of Australian Writers produced an anthology of contemporary prose and verse in 1953, it chose its selections from a mass of writing published in periodicals over the previous five years and more than a thousand manuscripts submitted to it, but it could not find more than a single story of merit dealing expressly with life in the cities. Later, as we have already seen, the trend towards more urban and more cosmopolitan writing accelerated.

Yet, the fifties witnessed the phenomenon of a popular return to the bush in the form of a folklore movement. Historians, scholars (American as well as Australian), and writers began to collect the folk ballads and old bush songs. The Australian Folklore Society and Bush Music Club sprang up and flourished. The old songs were sung by the Bush-whackers' Band, broadcast over the air as popular items, and put on to gramophone records by the Wattle Recording Company. In 1954 appeared the first substantial anthology of folk lore, *The Australian*, described as "Yarns, Ballads, Legends and Traditions of the Australian People", gathered together by Bill Wannan. The same year saw the publication of *Australian Bush Ballads*, a very substantial collection edited by Douglas Stewart and Nancy Keesing, to be followed three years later by their companion volume, *Old Bush Songs*. Based upon the original collection made by Paterson, it also drew upon the researches made by such collectors of folk balladry as Dr Percy Jones, Russel Ward, and John Meredith. Hugh Anderson embodied his research in his *Colonial Ballads*, 1955, which gave not only the words of the ballads but also their music and annotations. Thus the decade of the fifties witnessed a remarkable enlargement of the lore, legends, and mythology of the bush.

Meanwhile the great majority of the poets continued to find fresh interpretations of the country in lyrics and narratives, building up traditions, discovering symbols, and creating myths. A further proof of the continuing strength of the bush's appeal was provided by

Gwen Meredith's popular radio serials, "The Lawsons" and "Blue Hills", in which Gwen Meredith, whilst detailing domestic incidents of love and marriage as a radio Jane Austen, placed her characters in a bush setting. Publishers found, moreover, that fiction was not as popular as the travel and descriptive books which dealt mainly with the outback. Ion L. Idriess, who largely initiated the popularity of this genre in the thirties and remained its most successful practitioner, captured his audience by bringing out the romantic colour of the remoter frontier areas, telling glamourized yarns of the bush, and giving a popular folklore flavour to such characters as Lasseter, Kidman, and "Flynn of the Inland". Following the earlier trails blazed by Mrs Aeneas Gunn, Dr Bean, E. J. Brady, Randolph Bedford, Jack McLaren, and John Armour, a host of travel writers in the thirties and onwards explored the landscape of the outback—Myrtle White, R. B. Plowman, William Hatfield, Francis Ratcliffe, Fred Blakely, and Ernestine Hill, for example.

Flora Eldershaw, discussing the modern landscape writers as part of the continuance and renewal of the folklore element, said truly of them:

Varied though their approach may be, together they give a romantic vision of a world with which many men secretly or openly want to identify themselves, the unique Australian world that is the possession and kingdom of our imagination. We, a small people, can say: "We have this strange, this antique, still virgin world; it is ours." They are wonder books . . . . They are about *us*, even if we are townsmen.[5]

This exploitation of the more picturesque aspects of the bush in a spirit of wonder shows a significant contrast to the writers of the nineties who had pictured the bush in realistic, sombre terms. Like the revival of the bush ballads and bush folklore, it forms part of the contemporary glorification of the land as the basis of a national tradition.

The Paradox of Bush and City

Although the dominance of the bush in our literature is accepted by us as a mere matter of course, it presents, as mentioned earlier, a striking paradox in face of the great importance of the capital cities as the centres of Australian life.

The majority of the population, in fact, has always tended to live in the urban areas, despite the tremendous size of the hinterland. From the earliest days the people clustered in the coastal cities and towns. In the colony of New South Wales when Governor Macquarie took his census of 1816, Sydney held 6,695 of the 15,175

[5] Flora Eldershaw, "The Landscape Writers" in *Meanjin*, vol. XI, no.3, 1952, p.219.

persons in the colony.[6] The census of 1828 showed that the urbanized county of Cumberland held 31,042 of the total population of 35,596 —"excluding the Runaway Convicts in the Bush and Persons who have no fixed Place of Residence". In the county, Sydney alone accounted for 10,815, and the two towns of Parramatta and Windsor for another 9,172.[7]

Despite the opening up of the country in the pastoral age, in 1851 there were 159,546 persons in the urban settled districts as against only 27,697 in the outer squatting districts—the real bush. Again the county of Cumberland held the greatest concentration of population, its 81,114 contrasting with the 4,671 of the largest squatting district, the "Morumbidgee".[8]

When the Commonwealth was founded, its first official year book was moved to comment that "A feature of the distribution of population in Australia is the tendency to accumulate in the capital cities ... .That this metropolitan concentration is phenomenal, may be readily seen by comparing the percentage of the total population with the similar figure for the principal cities of Europe."[9] Figures tabled show that in 1906, whereas in Australia the six capital cities contained 35.49 per cent of the total population, London, Paris, and Rome contained only 20.59, 6.97, and 1.42 per cent respectively of the populations of England, France and Italy.

During the twentieth century the urban concentration has further increased, so that the capital cities now hold over one-half of the Australian population and four of them more than half the people of their respective States. The 1961 census gives the urban population as 81.94 per cent and the rural population only 17.82 per cent of the total population.[10]

An economist friend has worked out for me the relative proportion of people living in cities of 100,000 and over to the total population in ten countries. The results will astonish many Australians as well as observers abroad. The five highest urban scores, given in percentages of the total population, run: Australia 60.1, U.S.A., 54.6, Japan 50.4, United Kingdom 48.5, and Canada 45.3.[11]

Australia, therefore, is easily and most unmistakably the most highly urbanized country in the world. In fact, we are more urbanized than

[6] From *A General Statement of the Inhabitants of New South Wales* (undated extract in the National Library).
[7] *The Colony of New South Wales for the Year* 1828.
[8] *Census of the Colony of New South Wales*, etc. (Sydney 1851).
[9] *Official Year Book of the Commonwealth of Australia, 1901-7* (Melbourne 1908), p.158.
[10] *Year Book of the Commonwealth of Australia*, No.51, 1965, pp.260-7.
[11] Taken from analysis of statistics in the *United Nations Demographic Yearbook* 1965, and the *Commonwealth Year Book* 1965.

F

this comparison reveals, since the figure given does not take in—as our census quoted above does—the thousands living in our numerous small towns.

As well as being sparsely populated, the land, moreover, has been subsidiary in the national economy for some time, since secondary industry has long outstripped primary industry in the national production, whilst there has been a vast expansion of the tertiary industries in the cities.

The cities have been the citadels of politics and the seats of government, the centres of learning and culture as well as of industry and commerce. Most Australian writers have always lived in the cities, and have written about the bush as "city bushmen".

Reasons for the Paradox

Why, then, has the bush become such a prevailing force in our literature and cast such a potent spell over the national imagination? How explain the paradox? The answer must be complex, since a number of reasons join together to make a complete explanation.

Firstly, there is the economic importance of the land in the nineteenth century when the primary industries, including mining, produced the wealth of the colonies, and the parasitic cities lived upon this production, themselves producing little in the form of secondary industries. The latter developed late, attaining importance only during the first world war. The colonies grew up with the country as the great source of wealth, first with wool, then gold, then wheat, meat, and dairy products. The Australian people lived under the dominating shadow of the land.

Secondly, there is the continuing importance of the primary industries for the nation's export trade. Although the secondary industries have outstripped the primary ones in the production of the nation's wealth, this fact has been obscured by the more obvious one that primary produce supplies the great majority of our exports, with wool in the lead.[12] Australia is still the leading wool-growing country in the world. It is only natural, therefore, that Australians themselves, as well as the rest of the world, think of the country as essentially pastoral, as the land of "the bush".

The third reason for the dominance of the bush then follows: the lag of literature behind life. Economic and social conditions change more rapidly than cultural ones. It took time for the writers to adapt themselves to such changes, to express the evolution which had taken place from a primitive pastoral society to a highly industrialized urban one. It was not until the forties and fifties of this century that the writers as a body began to develop urban themes.

---

[12] See *Commonwealth Year Book*, 1965, pp.501-21.

Fourthly, the transition was made more difficult for the writers by the historical fact that the growth of an indigenous literature, largely under the stimulus of the *Bulletin*, came in the nationalist eighties and nineties in the form of a massive exploitation of the bush as theme and inspiration. Not only did the bush become identified with the national spirit and outlook, but Lawson and Paterson, Miles Franklin, Furphy, O'Dowd, and others established a literary tradition of bush subjects and bushmen values. Both national sentiment and literary convention, therefore, encouraged the writers to continue the dominance of the bush, sometimes giving it fresh interpretations, at other times merely imitating its earlier expression in stereotyped forms to exploit commercially the heritage of the nineties.

The "Real Australia"

It is the fifth and final reason for the paradox, however, that is most powerful: the national psychology which prizes the bush as the creator and the home of a distinctively Australian way of life. This feeling has been shared by observers of other nationalities. Thus Francis Adams, as an English observer, stated of the bush in 1893: "I find not only all that is genuinely characteristic in Australia and the Australians springing from this heart of the land, but also all that is noblest, kindliest, and best."[13] In the bushmen he found, as we have seen, "the one powerful and unique national type yet produced in Australia".[14]

The French critic Professor Emile Saillens wrote of Henry Lawson in 1910 that he expressed the bush completely, and it was understanding of the bush life that gave the key to the rest of Australia:

Lawson incarne en sa personne le bush australien tout entier, et la meilleure part de son oeuvre en est une émanation directe. Or, la connaissance de la vie du bush est précisément la seule donnée qui nous manque pour comprendre le reste de l'Australie.[15]

There is a general feeling amongst Australians themselves, even amongst the city-dwellers, that cities, after all, are much the same all the world over in modern civilization, whereas the bush and its bushmen are not only unique but also typify the "real Australia" and the "real Australian".

This view has been put strongly by Dr C. E. W. Bean, and there was no one more highly qualified to judge than this great Australian with his penetrating judgment and his wide experience of the country and the people. After he had travelled out west in New South Wales in 1909 he declared: "out here you have reached the core of Aus-

13 Francis Adams, *The Australians* (London 1893), p.154.
14 Ibid., p.165.
15 Emile Saillens, op. cit., p.429.

tralia, the real red Australia of the ages."[16] After moving along the Darling, he recorded his belief in the importance of the outback to the Australian people:

In guessing at the future of Australia—which of course is still a guess—it seems essential to remember that the Australian, one hundred or two hundred years hence, will still live with the consciousness that, if he only goes far enough back over the hills and across the plains, he comes in the end to the mysterious half-desert country where men have to live the lives of strong men. And the life of that mysterious country will affect Australian imagination much as the life of the sea has affected that of the English.[17]

Years later, when Dr Bean came to write the history of the first A.I.F., he pointed out that the training of the A.I.F. was made easier by the fact that behind it was the experience and tradition of the bush life: "The bush still sets the standard of personal efficiency even in the Australian cities. The bushman is the hero of the Australian boy; the arts of the bush life are his ambition."[18]

Marjorie Barnard summed the matter up well when, after recognizing that most Australians are city-dwellers, she said: "But our literature is bush born and bred. We think of the typical Australian as a bushman . . . . It is the bush which feeds and stimulates the national imagination, even sight unseen."[19]

The literature expresses, therefore, a distinctive social pattern which is widely recognized as such. Cynics can easily point out, of course, some sharp discrepancies between the contemporary realities of our urbanized people and the belief in the bushman as a national prototype from the past. What is important, however, is the undoubted fact of the belief itself, which presents a valid reason for the spell of the bush prevailing in the literature. Several writers have recently explored the historical factors behind this belief. For example, A. E. Mander, in his suggestive and often penetrating study *The Making of the Australians*, has traced various "Australian characteristics" to the conditions of inland settlement. Effects both good and bad are seen as derived from the harshness and loneliness of the life of the early sheep and cattle men, from the individual character of the settling as contrasted with the community character of American settlement of the Middle West and Far West, and from the need for the pioneers to turn their hands to doing a great variety of jobs on their own:

Very few of them knew how to do any of those things when they started out. But they learned, or they perished. Each man who survives must have learned

[16] C. E. W. Bean, *On the Wool Track* (Sydney 1925), p.72.
[17] C. E. W. Bean, *The Dreadnought of the Darling* (Sydney 1956), p.222.
[18] C. E. W. Bean, *The Official History of Australia in the War of 1914-18*, vol.I (Sydney 1937), p.46.
[19] Marjorie Barnard, "Our Literature" in *Australian Writers Speak* (Sydney 1942), p.104.

to do everything for himself, to cope with every sort of emergency, to battle through every sort of difficulty—alone. So they are bound to become *self-contained, self-sufficient, self-reliant, extraordinarily independent and resourceful* ... as no townspeople, and no village people, anywhere in the world, ever could be.[20]

At the same time this sociologist gives impartially other aspects:

But there must be also some very serious defects—defects of mind and character—produced by those *same* conditions.... Social morals and manners alike can be the products only of community living. And so from the kind of life we have seen in the Australian Inland, we must expect to find men growing up *uncouth in manners*, and *without any sense of responsibility*, and *self-centred* and *ruthlessly hard*.[21]

Mr Mander's analysis opens up a wide field of discussion extending beyond our purpose at this stage. It would be easy, for instance, to quote illustrations of Australian irresponsibility in social matters or in the errors scattered so freely in Australian literary criticism, history, and bibliography. Casualness has its drawbacks. On the other hand, in the first world war Australia maintained the A.I.F. throughout by voluntary enlistment. So, too, in the second world war Australian volunteers maintained as many divisions, in proportion to population, as the United States maintained with conscription. These facts indicate a strong sense of responsibility among Australians in times of national crisis.

At this stage we are concerned with the bush rather than the bushmen, but the two are inextricably linked. Since the social patterns were chiefly bush-bred, their literary expression formed one way in which the dominance of the bush exerted itself, if indirectly, in Australian writing. Furthermore, it is certainly true that, as Professor Ward phrased it aptly: "The extinct bushman of Lawson and Furphy became the national culture-hero on whose supposed characteristics many Australians tend, consciously or unconsciously, to model their attitude to life."[22] Thus the bush cast, it might be said, a triple spell: from its vast crucible came the patterns embodied in the bushmen; these were articulated by the writers of the nineties and their followers; and this articulation, in turn, helped to mould the Australian way of life and thought.

The Bush in Colonial Literature

In what other and more direct ways has the spell of the bush shown itself in our literature? Three chief ways can be discerned clearly, although each of these has its different aspects. The bush appears as

[20] A. E. Mander, *The Making of the Australians* (Melbourne 1958), pp.25, 26.
[21] Ibid., p.27.
[22] Russel Ward, *The Australian Legend* (Melbourne 1958), p.196.

a dominant subject matter, either as theme or as background. It appears in varying concepts of the land, concepts changing with the times. Finally it emerges as a mystique in which the bush is invested with sacred and even redemptive powers. A complete treatment of the bush in Australian literature in these three forms would require, of course, a whole book to itself. Here we can only indicate the salient features.

Let us look first at the bush as subject matter, beginning with colonial literature.

In colonial poetry the bush was the outstanding theme, from the days when Barron Field was stirred to eulogy of the epacris (a heath) down to the bush lyrics and narratives of Harpur and Kendall. The literary drama mainly went overseas for its heroics, but early exceptions were the plays of Harpur and Burn about bushrangers and James Tucker's *Jemmy Green in Australia*. Later when the commercial theatre exploited the possibilities of Australian themes in the eighties, it was mainly in bush-based plays like *The Breaking of the Drought*, *The Sunny South*, or a dramatization of *Robbery Under Arms*.

In colonial fiction, however, the odds were more evenly divided between the bush and the city, since the time had not yet come for the apotheosis of the bushmen. Naturally, however, the bush was the background for the novels dealing with the excitements and hardships of pioneering, the problems of the immigrant, and the adventures of bushranging. Lively incidents, realistic description of the bush, and solid information were combined in Rowcroft's entertaining *Tales of the Colonies*; in Howitt's melodramatic and discursive *Tallangetta*, and in *The Emigrant Family*—later titled *Martin Beck*—in which the "emigrant mechanic" Harris showed his usual acumen in discerning the growth of a bush *ethos*. Caroline Atkinson gave intimate glimpses of the bush trees, flowers, and animals in her two novels of station life. In *The Recollections of Geoffry Hamlyn* Kingsley not only produced the most workmanlike novel of the colonial era, despite its Victorian melodramatic claptrap and its superficial view of station life, but he also described the bush landscape with gusto.

Of the women novelists who were partly colonial in period and wholly colonial in outlook, Ada Cambridge began her career with *Up the Murray*, Tasma dealt with station life lightly in several novels, and Rosa Campbell Praed used her native Queensland bush background for various early novels, notably *The Head Station*. Despite her escape from her "eucalyptic cloisterdom" to the elegancies of England, she looked back to the bush with affection in later days:

It is an odd, but very real thing—the nostalgia of the gum-trees.... I never smell the pungent, aromatic scent, which for twenty-two years was the breath of my nostrils, without being carried back to the old, vivid world of untrodden pastures and lonely forests, without falling again under the grim spell of the bush.[23]

On the other hand, these three novelists all did their best work in novels with the backgrounds of Sydney, Melbourne, and Brisbane, such as *A Marked Man, Uncle Piper of Piper's Hill*, and *Policy and Passion*. Ada Cambridge, who came to Australia knowing nothing of "the mysterious Bush" which she thought of as "a vast shrubbery, with occasional spears hurtling through it",[24] was mainly interested in criticizing social orthodoxy. Tasma and Mrs Praed were concerned mainly with social relationships. So, too, was Catherine Spence, who passed shrewd comments on Adelaide's colonial customs in *Clara Morison*.

The city background was also prominent in such novels of convictism as *Quintus Servinton*, John Lang's *Assigned to His Wife*, and Caroline Leakey's *The Broad Arrow*. These novels, moreover, like *Geoffry Hamlyn* and Marcus Clarke's *For the Term of His Natural Life*, were set in England as well as in Australia.

In colonial fiction, therefore, the bush played an important but by no means a dominating role, sharing the honours with such other interests of the times as convictism, the gold-fields, and city life.

The Bush v. the Bushmen

In the nationalist period (1880-1914), the bush found a strong articulation, and its voice overwhelmed all other subjects. Certainly Brennan stood outside the general movement; Daley was either immersed in his Celtic twilight or striking out vigorously in radical verse; and Brady sang his salt-water ballads. A few writers like Dyson, James Edmonds, and Dowell O'Reilly wrote short stories about city life in factories, lodging houses, and suburbia. Louis Stone pictured the larrikin pushes of Sydney in *Jonah*, creating the character of Mrs Yabsley for enduring delight. But these were the exceptions that proved the rule of the bush in the nationalist period. It was the bush which was celebrated in the vast majority of the balladry, the short stories, and in the novels of Steele Rudd, Miles Franklin, and Joseph Furphy.

To be more exact, it was not the bush itself that was celebrated, but the bushmen. Contrary to popular opinion, the writing of the nineties does *not* glorify the bush. Rather it is a glorification of the bushmen versus the bush environment. What had been a picturesque setting for the earlier colonial novelist and an idyllic background for Kingsley now emerges, realistically and sombrely, as a force affecting

[23] Mrs Campbell Praed, *My Australian Girlhood* (London 1902), pp.1-2.
[24] Ada Cambridge, *Thirty Years in Australia* (London 1903), p.2.

the lives of men profoundly, sometimes as a companion or solace, but most frequently as a constant enemy giving no quarter, a capricious fate, or a creator of loneliness and despair. In the *Bulletin* writers the bush is largely the means whereby the noble qualities of the bushmen are brought out—their courage and endurance in fighting the bush, their generosity and loyalty to a mate. It is the black shadow which throws up, in a simple, stark chiaroscuro, the light of the bush hero.

Thus Lawson shows the finer qualities of Joe Wilson being brought out in his struggles on his selection, or the courage of the drover's wife among loneliness, danger, and hardship. Steele Rudd's Dad is an heroic as well as a comic figure, a folk hero, a battler against the odds of the bush. With Miles Franklin the rebel spirit of Sybylla triumphs over the drab bush setting in *My Brilliant Career*, just as later in *All That Swagger* the bush is the dangerous unknown conquered by the indomitable Danny. In *Such is Life* the land is described with sympathy and understanding, but it is the human drama which counts most, and the staple of the book is the vicissitudes of the teamsters in their fight for the squatters' grass.

Life, then, was viewed as an unremitting struggle against the bush, and when Paterson gives a contrary view in "Clancy of the Over-flow", painting the romantic pleasures of the bush, Lawson protests cynically:[25]

> *Ah! we read about the drovers and the shearers and the like*
> *Till we wonder why such happy and romantic fellows strike.*
> *Don't you fancy that the poets ought to give the bush a rest*
> *Ere they raise a just rebellion in the over-written West?*

Indeed, despite the romance of Ogilvie and the cheerful humour of Paterson, Thomas E. Spencer, Goodge, and "John O'Brien", many of the bush balladists take a realistic, often gloomy view of the bush itself. With Boake it is the place "out where the dead men lie". Lawson's savage description of the bush is given resoundingly, with all stops out, in his verse "Up the Country".

In his stories Lawson treats the bush harshly, giving a depressing one-sided picture. In his sketch "In a Dry Season", for instance, he describes the barrenness along the western railway line from Bathurst, and adds: "Somebody said to me, 'You wanter go out back, young man, if you wanter see the country. You wanter get away from the line.' I don't wanter; I've been there."[26] The most powerful short story writer of the *Bulletin* period after Lawson, Barbara Baynton, out-does Lawson himself in attacking the bush. She finds the language of the

[25] Henry Lawson, "The City Bushman" in *Poetical Works* (Sydney 1956 ed., first publ. 1925), p.228.
[26] Henry Lawson, *Prose Works* (Sydney 1935), p.62.

crude rouseabout Billy Skywonkie suitable for the bush scene: " 'Damned' the wretched, starving, and starved sheep looked and were; 'bloody' the beaks of the glutted crows; 'blarsted' the whole of the plain they drove through."[27] She is exceptional, however, in finding the bushmen and women as barbarous and revolting as she finds their environment.

Bush and City in Modern Fiction

In the period from 1914 to 1950 the bush is still dominant in all literary forms, but more attention is paid to the cities, especially in fiction. Sydney is treated in widely different aspects by a number of novelists. It is the setting for Chester Cobb's experiment in the stream-of-consciousness technique, John Dalley's social satire, the humours of Lennie Lower, and the study of pathological characters by Christina Stead. M. Barnard Eldershaw treated its early growth in *A House is Built* and its disintegration during the depression in *Tomorrow and Tomorrow*. Leonard Mann and Eleanor Dark used it as background for psychological studies and human dramas, and Dark also recreated its early days. Kylie Tennant turned her spotlight on to its slums. In the forties and fifties the "low life" of Sydney was explored by *The Harp in the South, You Can't See Round Corners, Come in Spinner*, and *Jimmy Brockett*. Later, Patrick White, George Johnston, Keneally and other novelists used the Sydney background.

The earlier history of Melbourne was described in *The Fortunes of Richard Mahony, The Montforts*, and *Lucinda Brayford*, in all cases with a strong dash of satire. This appears, too, in *The Getting of Wisdom*. Serious studies of character against the Melbourne background are presented in *The Swayne Family* and *The Go-Getter*, whilst *Power Without Glory* takes a wide social sweep. Judah Waten treats of immigrant problems and the criminal underworld, and John Morrison covers the waterfront in vivid stories. David Martin uses Melbourne for his novel of Greek migrants.

Other cities, too, have provided settings for the novelists—early Adelaide for Phyllis Somerville, colonial Hobart for William Hay and Roy Bridges, Perth for Judah Waten and G. M. Glaskin, Newcastle for Dymphna Cusack, Hobart for Christopher Koch, and Brisbane for David Forrest. Thus urban society has not been as neglected in our fiction as is frequently charged, and from the 1940s onward writers turned increasingly to the cities.

On the other hand, it remains true that the majority of modern novelists have gone to the bush for their inspiration. In particular, the outstanding novels which followed one another with the renaissance

27 Barbara Baynton, *Bush Studies* (London 1902), p.96.

of fiction in the late twenties and thirties almost all continued the bush tradition. To it belong *Working Bullocks* and *Coonardoo*, *Up the Country* and its Brent of Bin Bin sequels, together with *All That Swagger*, *The Passage*, *Man-Shy*, *Capricornia*, and coming over into the forties, *The Timeless Land*, *The Battlers*, and *The Pea Pickers*. These titles indicate clearly enough that much of the best fiction is bush-bred; and it is a fact that when leading novelists like Prichard, Palmer, Dark, and Tennant have used both bush and urban themes, they have drawn more strength and inspiration from the land than from the cities. The bush had the richer tradition and the greater power to stimulate the creative imagination until the advent of Patrick White.

Nor did the stream of bush novels slacken in the fifties, but rather it broadened out as it flowed strongly, bearing the novels of Ronan, Porteous, Xavier Herbert, and H. D. Williamson, the popular work of Timms, Niland, and Cleary, and the imaginative creations of Mary Durack, White and Stow, as well as being fed by a full tributary of novels dealing with the land and the aborigine.

Two contrasting features in the treatment of the bush are marked in our modern fiction. On the one hand, in the commercial novels the bush tradition often runs very thinly, the characterization is shallow, and the writing is cheapened by sentimentalism and melodrama. There is an inherent falsity in such work, as can be seen by comparing such a brummagem imitation as *The Shiralee* with the genuine original article in *Coonardoo* and *The Battlers*.

On the other hand, the most imaginative novelists have also been returning to the bush—using the term in its widest sense of the land—in order to create fresh spiritual interpretations. Patrick White, for example, goes to the soil and the pioneers in *The Tree of Man* in an attempt to make a universal allegory. The experiment, despite its brilliancies and its moments of sensitive beauty, does not quite come off. The bush is curiously un-Australian. Richness of individuality and intimacy of place are sacrificed at times for the bloodless absolute of the universal. Stan Parker, the pioneer made Everyman, remains inarticulate, solitary and shadowy. He never drinks with a mate, and he spits mystically. He is a ghost beside Joe Wilson. Yet the concept informing the novel is significant, and in *Voss* a further essay in spirituality is remarkably successful.

Some of the best short stories, like those of Casey, Morrison, and Waten deal with social and industrial conflicts in city or town, whilst Ethel Anderson stands apart in her elegant tales of old Parramatta. Until the sixties the majority of our short stories, however, gave a varied treatment of the bush background. In the last decade the urban stories are growing dominant. Yet few can challenge in quality such bush evocations as Frank Dalby Davison's "The Road to Yesterday" and "The Good Herdsman".

Modern Drama and Poetry

In modern drama and poetry the spell of the bush has been pervasive. When the Pioneer Players tried to found a national drama in the twenties, the chief playwright was Louis Esson. He had been impressed in Ireland by Synge, who had urged him to write plays about his own country, saying "You ought to have plenty of material for drama in Australia. All those outback stations with shepherds going mad in lonely huts".[28] Esson himself had a strong feeling for the bush, and he wrote to Vance Palmer: "London has a lot of interests, but we do miss the Bush. The English country has a character of its own, but it is not the same. Our own means more to us."[29] And so, although he used Melbourne settings in several plays, he was most effective in *The Drovers*, with its classic economy, laconic bush idiom, and true poignance. The more melodramatic *Dead Timber* and poetic *Mother and Son* also used bush settings.

The more tragic aspect of life on the land, mooted by Synge and developed by Esson, reappeared in a number of outstanding plays such as Vance Palmer's *The Black Horse*, Sydney Tomholt's *Anoli the Blind*, Betty Roland's *The Touch of Silk*, and Millicent Armstrong's *Drought*. An anthology of one-act plays revealed the same trend.[30] Alexander Turner used the countryside of Western Australia skilfully for stage and radio plays. In his *Ned Kelly* Douglas Stewart developed a philosophical interpretation of a legendary bushranger hero. Sumner Locke-Elliott's documentary comedy of army life, *Rusty Bugles*, was laid in the remote outback. Even Ray Lawler's *Summer of the Seventeenth Doll*, despite its Melbourne setting, derived much of its strength from the characters and background of the Queensland canefields. Although there have been plays of merit on subjects far from the bush by Tomholt, G. L. Dann, Dymphna Cusack, Max Afford, Beynon, Seymour and Patrick White, the bush has provided the widest inspiration for the drama.

This inspiration is perhaps even more notable in modern Australian poetry. Of course, much of the work is purely lyrical, dealing with personal emotions of a universal kind. Some of it is metaphysical or broadly philosophical. Some, like that of McCrae, Neilson, and Hopegood, contains its own imaginative worlds. The work of Hope and McAuley is intellectual and detached from the local scene, except

---

[28] Vance Palmer, *Louis Esson and the Australian Theatre* (Melbourne 1948), p.3.
[29] Ibid., p.14.
[30] See William Moore and T. Inglis Moore (ed.), *Best Australian One-Act Plays* (Sydney 1937).

when they satirize it. A few poets only have turned to the cities: Wilmot created a Melbourne of the mind effectively in his *Melbourne Odes*; Slessor celebrated Sydney streets, whilst the Sydney Harbour is the setting for his magnificent elegy *Five Bells*; and Nancy Keesing has also sung of Sydney effectively. A few poets have ranged beyond Australia, like FitzGerald in his Tongan narrative and his dramatic sketch of Warren Hastings, or Douglas Stewart in his Antarctic theme of *The Fire on the Snow*, the finest poetic drama yet written here. The poetic trend towards re-creation of the Australian past has also led away from the land to the sea and the exploits of Cook, De Quiros, and Tasman.

Our modern poetry presents, therefore, a considerable variety of themes. Yet the call of the bush is as strong as ever. Different poets treat the land individually, so that the various Australias of Slessor and FitzGerald, Judith Wright and Douglas Stewart, David Campbell and Roland Robinson, for instance, are as unlike each other as the personalities, interests, and styles of the poets. The contemporary poets do not merely describe the land, but find in it many significances, giving it a richer fertility of meaning.

These poets are endeavouring to create four different forms of meaning for the land: historical, national, philosophical, and spiritual. There is, to begin with, a consciousness of Australia as an historical fact, and an effort to realize this by recreating the past of the explorers, the pioneers, and the aborigines. At the same time the history is turned into a national tradition, the figures of the past becoming mythical prototypes of such qualities as

> *Honor, ambition, courage, rearing from madness*
> *Three tablets for all to read.*

So Francis Webb interprets Leichhardt,[31] and pictures him as the land's explorer:

> *Southward the new, the visionary!*
> *This is a land where man becomes a myth;*
> *Naked, his feet tread embers for the truth:*
> *Desert will claim him, mountain, precipice,*
> *(Larger than life's their terror, lovelier*
> *Than forms of mere life their forms of peril); beauty*
> *Shed league by league disfigurements of living,*
> *The past, dishonour. No famished eyes save his*
> *Shall know her radiant body; for the dark hunters*
> *Are eyeless and incurious as death,*
> *Mountain, or precipice.*[32]

[31] Francis Webb, *Leichhardt in Theatre* (Sydney 1952), p.2.
[32] Ibid., pp.3-4.

So the poets become myth-makers, with their figures, like Leich-hardt's, larger than life, since the past has now become usable by the imagination and can furnish symbols by which the people can live. Earlier the utopian writers, feeling the lack of tradition and the inadequacy of their history, had looked to the future. Today the process is reversed, as Mary Gilmore proclaims the riches of our heritage:

> *Never allow the thoughtless to declare*
> *That we have no tradition here!*
> *... Australia's wells are deep and full.*[33]

She takes the ringer of the shearing shed as a symbol for the courage and enterprise which built up national achievements in many fields. So, too, Judith Wright goes to the bush for another symbolic figure in her "Bullocky", and Ian Mudie links the land with the swagman in "The Australian Dream" (a title afterwards to be used, for very different purposes, by David Campbell).

The poets go to the bush, moreover, for symbols of universal as well as national significance in poems essentially philosophical in character. Judith Wright, for example, draws an understanding of wisdom from gum-trees stripping their bark, or uses the blind man Delaney as an image of the Eros principle. Douglas Stewart finds the music of silence sounding in a helmet orchid, and David Campbell visions a stockman as an image of time.

Some of these interpretations drawn from the land, stressing spiritual elements, become religious in feeling. Mary Gilmore discerns a guiding Power in the trackless flight of swans at night, Nancy Cato sees a lonely swagman as an image of "Man and his independent spirit", and Judith Wright pictures a flame-tree as "this living ghost of death" or the wattle-tree making its immortality as it breaks "into a million images of the Sun", its God. Gradually the land, with its plains and deserts, its trees and flowers and animals, together with its human associations, is invested by the imagination of the poets with wider and deeper meanings.

Concepts of the Land

It is fascinating, indeed, to follow the changes in the concepts of the land as expressed in the writings about it from the first settlement to the present day.

To the first English arrivals this curious country of the antipodes was romantically picturesque. That genial observer Captain Watkin Tench delighted in the abundance of flowering shrubs, "surpassing in beauty and fragrance, and number all that I ever saw in an unculti-

[33] Mary Gilmore, "The Ringer" in *Selected Verse* (Sydney 1948), pp.161-2.

vated state".[34] Soon, however, this first pleasure changed to complaints about the sombreness of the bush and the monotony of its ubiquitous gum-trees. This was not merely the nostalgia of English and Irish exiles longing for the green fields of home, since even the native-born Wentworth, fiercely patriotic, pictured the desolation of the Blue Mountains.

This gloomy concept was strengthened by the tragedies that befell the early pioneers and the explorers. Bernard Smith comments:

These disastrous expeditions and the gloomy accounts which followed added a deeper, more tragic strain to the melancholy interpretation of Australian nature. There was no need after Leichhardt's death to talk of the desolation and monotony of Australian nature as though it were an aesthetic opinion.[35]

Both Harpur and Kendall expressed this gloom in poems based on actual tragedies, such as "The Creek of the Four Graves", "The Glen of Arrawatta", and "Cooranbeen". Death and violence, horror and terror, became associated with the bush as well as desolation. Marcus Clarke only voiced a general view in his vivid preface to Gordon's poems:

What is the dominant note of Australian scenery? That which is the dominant note of Edgar Allan Poe's poetry—Weird Melancholy. . . . The Australian forests are funereal, secret, stern. Their solitude is desolation. They seem to stifle in their black gorges a story of sullen despair.[36]

This land of gloom still persisted, as we have seen, in much of the writing during the *Bulletin* period, both in the bush ballads and the short stories of Lawson, Baynton, and others. It was revived later by D. H. Lawrence, when he describes Harriet Somers as torn between attraction and repulsion in her feeling towards the bush: "Sometimes a heavy, reptile-hostility came off the sombre land, something grue-some and infinitely repulsive."[37]

On the other hand, side by side with this sombre concept ran its opposite, the idea of a land inspiring by its varied beauties. Kingsley was impressed by the grandeur of the Australian Alps:

A new heaven and a new earth! Tier beyond tier, height above height, the great wooded ranges go rolling away westward, till on the lofty sky-line they are crowned with a gleam of everlasting snow.[38]

[34] Captain Watkin Tench, *A Narrative of the Expedition to Botany Bay* (London 1789), p.119.

[35] Bernard Smith, "The Interpretation of Australian Nature During the Nineteenth Century", unpublished thesis, University of Sydney.

[36] Marcus Clarke, "Australian Scenery" from the preface to Gordon's poems, *The Marcus Clarke Memorial Volume* (Melbourne 1884), pp.114-15.

[37] D. H. Lawrence, *Kangaroo* (Penguin ed. 1950), p.385.

[38] Henry Kingsley, *The Recollections of Geoffry Hamlyn* (Sydney 1935 ed., first publ. 1859), p.135.

So, too, Harpur also gave, despite his usual sombreness, glimpses of the bright loveliness of his land, and asked whether it was a "felt happiness"

> *When the woods are whitened over by the jolly cockatoo,*
> *And swarm with birds as beautiful as ever gladdened through*
> *The shining hours of Time when the golden year was new?*[39]

With Kendall a personal melancholy did not prevent him finding in his coastal bush a radiant loveliness that flashed and dazzled, gleamed and glowed, in his lyrics. The cheerful tone of his bush ballads captured a welcome from youth, since Frank Dalby Davison has related to the writer in a letter how as a boy he and his school mates read "The Song of the Shingle Splitters" in their State school paper, and he remembers "three or four of us lads chanting it together as we marched home from school with our bags on our backs". Gordon, again, pictured the bush as both beautiful and inspiring happiness: his stockman was "merry 'mid the blackwoods". Later McCrae brought his gaiety to his vignettes of Camden, Neilson invested nature with his own delicate joy, and Dorothea Mackellar expressed her love for her native land with a rich warmth in the familiar "My Country". So, too, many contemporary poets, thoroughly at home with the land, sing of it with delight. The terror and sombreness of the colonial concept have virtually disappeared.

In most of the modern novels the same attitude of pleasure occurs. A deep feeling for the bush, an affection quick to stir at its beauty, is vibrant in *Working Bullocks* and *Coonardoo, Man-Shy, The Passage, Capricornia, Up the Country, All That Swagger, The Timeless Land*, and *The Pea-pickers*, to mention only a few instances. In such works, moreover, there is also a constant sense of close harmony between man and his country, a new sense of the intimate relationship between them.

After the land had changed from a sombre alien enemy to a beautiful and beloved country, a further step was taken when it became so intimately associated with the lover that they are bound together in an indivisible significance. Thus a number of our modern novels are concerned with characters who have achieved such a harmonious affinity, even an identity, with their environment that they have become the communal spirits of the place. The most numinous of such figures is Coonardoo. Katharine Prichard shows that to the aborigines on Wytaliba station she is its very soul, and its fortunes are hers:

Coonardoo's spirit had withered and died when she went away from Wytaliba . . . . And that withering and dying of Coonardoo's spirit had caused

[39] Charles Harpur, "Early Summer" in *Poems* (Melbourne 1883), p.434.

a blight on the place. She had loved Wytaliba and been bound up with the source of its life. Was she not the well in the shadow? Had she not some mysterious affinity with that ancestral female spirit which was responsible for fertility, generation, the growth of everything?[40]

So, too, Vance Palmer represents Lew Callaway in *The Passage* as a symbolic figure, the leader of his community because he alone is fully integrated with the Passage, moving in harmony with its tides, sharing its fortunes. Kylie Tennant creates a similar affinity between Alec Suderman and Lost Haven, so that the settlement's "decayed amoral animalism" finds fit expression in Alec's despairing view of humanity. In *Keep Him My Country*, too, Mary Durack makes Dalgerie the spirit of the country.

The Mystique of the Bush

A further development created a special mystique in which the bush took three forms: first as a sacred place with spiritual powers, then as Alcheringa, and finally as the desert offering salvation.

In the development of the concept of the land as something sacred the forerunner was Kendall. In "To a Mountain" he identifies the mountain with deity, hears from it "God's grand authentic gospel", and addresses it as his Bible:

> *In the psalm*
> *Of thy grave winds, and in the liturgy*
> *Of singing waters, lo! my soul has heard*
> *The higher worship.*[41]

He feels the ecstasy of revelation when he walks "in exalted woods of naked glory". Although he expresses the pantheistic ideas then current from Wordsworth and Emerson, his passion for nature was felt in his pulse, and so was his feeling for its sanctity.

Voiced in Kendall, this feeling was developed explicitly into a complex mystique by O'Dowd in "The Bush".[42] A later poet, John Thompson, writes of "this wary gaunt oracular bush";[43] and O'Dowd was the seer proclaiming its oracles. Equating the bush with Australia, he sees it as both the rich legatee of past civilizations and the matrix forming its own destiny with infinite possibilities of future creation.

It is also a sacred place, with all its leaves as symbols, serving a Shape of God, holding ancient, invisible presences, and creating rapture:

[40] Katharine Susannah Prichard, *Coonardoo* (London 1943 ed., first publ. 1929), p.266.

[41] Kendall, "To a Mountain", *Selected Poems* (Sydney 1957), p.21.

[42] For a fine interpretation of this mystique see E. Morris Miller, "O'Dowd's *The Bush:* an Exposition" in *Diogenes* (University of Tasmania, 1957), pp.18-40.

[43] John Thompson, "The Traveller" in *Thirty Poems* (Sydney 1954), p.45.

We marvel not, who hear your undersong
And catch a glimpse in rare exalted hours
Of Something like a Being gleam along
Festooned arcades of flossie creeper flowers,
Or, toward the mirk, seem privileged to share
The silent rapture of the trees at prayer.[44]

The same mystical feeling informs Wilmot's poem "The Gully", when he finds solace in the bush since

There is a spirit bound
Within this holy ground.[45]

It recurs with a number of later poets, such as Neilson, Douglas Stewart, and Roland Robinson.

Alcheringa

The hallowing of the land received a new extension when it was linked with the aboriginal religion as the sacred place of the tribe, associated with the great creative powers of the universe, made holy by the spirits of the Dream Time. Indeed, place and spirit are so interwoven that they can be merged into one another, since, as Dr Stanner points out, "A blackfellow may call his totem, or the place from which his spirit came, his Dreaming."[46] For centuries its inhabitants had regarded the land as holy, inspiring awe and reverence, a source of spiritual strength flowing to the worshipper.

O'Dowd already had "In Alcheringa found the Golden Age", but it was the Jindyworobak movement, led by Rex Ingamells, which adopted the idea of Alcheringa, the Dreaming, as a symbol denoting a mystique of the land, with "environmental values" that could be of service and significance to us as people of the aborigines' country. Thus Rex Ingamells asserted:

Alcheringa is this Land's very soul,
its bold and subtle essences imbue
Australian scenes forever, constitute
a bright allure and stern hypnotic power:
it is the breath of sacred Yesterday,
with import for Today and Tomorrow.[47]

Other poets drew imaginatively from the concept, like Ian Mudie:

Deep flows the stream,
feeding the totem-roots,
deep through the time of dream
in Alcheringa.[48]

[44] O'Dowd, "The Bush", op. cit., p.198.
[45] Furnley Maurice, *Poems* (Melbourne 1944), p.62.
[46] W. E. H. Stanner, "The Dreaming" in T. A. G. Hungerford (ed.), *Australian Signpost* (Melbourne 1956), p.51.
[47] Rex Ingamells, *The Great South Land* (Melbourne 1951), p.50.
[48] Ian Mudie, "Underground" in *Poems 1934-44* (Melbourne 1945), p.19.

G

Many critics, especially those who were Europo-centric in outlook, ridiculed the Alcheringa symbol as an impossible going back to the gunyah. By the fifties, however, the attitude of the intelligent Australian towards the aborigines had changed greatly. Anthropologists such as Professor Elkin, Strehlow, and the Berndts enlarged our understanding of aborginal culture, whilst writers like Bill Harney, Alan Marshall, and Roland Robinson brought the aboriginal myths, legends, and way of life into our literature as a fertilizing element. Novels like *Coonardoo*, *Capricornia*, *The Timeless Land*, and *Keep Him My Country* created a new consciousness of the aborigine's intimate relationship with his land and a new sympathy with him as an individual. Novelists and dramatists dealt sympathetically with the social problem of the aborigine and the half-caste. In *Corroboree* and *Dalgerie* the aboriginal theme has inspired ballet and opera. Fresh enrichment of aboriginal culture will come with the publication of Strehlow's important translation of aboriginal songs and legends.

Thus we have arrived at a deeper, closer knowledge of the complexity of aboriginal culture. Above all, there has grown a sense of the richness of spiritual meaning with which the aborigine invested his sacred land. Thus Eleanor Dark writes:

Silence ruled this land. Out of silence mystery comes, and magic, and the delicate awareness of unreasoning things. The black men learned from it, having no other teacher . . . . Thought made man one with his environment . . . Eternity was ever-present to him, past and future interwoven with his own life by legend and unvarying tradition, so that all time was the frame for his mortality, and contentment his heritage.[49]

Drawing a contrast between black and white civilizations in *The Timeless Land*, Eleanor Dark suggests that it is the aborigine who is often the spiritual superior. We, the poor whites, she implies, are spiritually impoverished beside the blacks who are rich in their beliefs and ritual. It is significant that in recent novels concerned with spiritual values the aborigine plays an important part. Thus Dalgerie is invested with a haunting spell of beauty in *Keep Him My Country*. In *Voss* the explorer forbids his party to fire on the blacks, "For they were his", whilst it is the black boy Jackie who completes the sacrifice of Voss by killing him. In Stow's *To the Islands* the missionary Heriot flees the mission because he thinks he has killed the aborigine Rex, whilst it is the faithful Justin who accompanies him. In Lyndon Rose's *Country of the Dead* the half-caste boy Nugget chooses the blackfellow way of life as more spiritually satisfying than white civilization.

[49] Eleanor Dark, *The Timeless Land* (London 1942), pp.24-5.

Salvation in the Desert

In these novels the concepts of the land and the mystique of the bush receive a further spiritual extension, since the desert country becomes a place of redemptive power offering salvation to the seeking soul. This concept was first adumbrated by Marcus Clarke in his Preface to Gordon's *Poems* when he found that "that wild dream-land termed the Bush interprets itself". Later, Ernest Favenc, explorer and writer, also stressed the mysterious character of the Australian desert:

There is a wondrous fascination in it, in its strange loneliness and the hidden mysteries it might contain. To pass a night alone in the desert spinifex country, is to feel as much cut off from the ordinary life of the world as one could feel if transplanted to another sphere .... A land such as this, with its great loneliness, its dearth of life, and its enshrouding atmosphere of awe and mystery, has a voice of its own.[50]

A. G. Stephens, too, noted its power:

Sometimes the Bush is an ecstasy and an inspiration .... And sometimes the Bush is a desolation and a despair .... Human forces seem puny in face of the Bush; they are extinguished where the Bush joins hands with her terrible sister the Desert.[51]

O'Dowd's fertile imagination visioned the bush as a virginal wilderness that might produce its own evangel for the spirit: with it before us

> *We marvel not that seers in other ages,*
> *With eyes unstrained by peering logic, saw*
> *The desolation glow with Koran pages,*
> *Or Sinai stones with Tables of the Law.*[52]

This idea of the possible thaumaturgic value in our desert has appealed to modern Australian poets and novelists who have suffered from the malaise of Western civilization, felt a hunger for God or some fresh symbol for the spirit, and turned to the desert to allay their theozetesis.

Thus A. D. Hope, after satirizing his country savagely in his "Australia", ends, somewhat surprisingly, by echoing O'Dowd:

> *Yet there are some like me turn gladly home*
> *From the lush jungle of modern thought, to find*
> *The Arabian desert of the human mind,*
> *Hoping, if still from the deserts the prophets come,*

---

[50] Ernest Favenc, *Voices of the Desert* (London 1905), pp.xii-xiii.
[51] A. G. Stephens, "Says and Hearsays" in *The Bookfellow*, 29 April 1899.
[52] O'Dowd, "The Bush", op. cit., p.198.

> *Such savage and scarlet as no green hills dare*
> *Springs in that waste, some spirit which escapes*
> *The learned doubt, the chatter of cultured apes*
> *Which is called civilisation over there.*[53]

Judith Wright, seeking some reconciliation of the world's fears and conflicts, ends one of her books with the same idea:

> *Wounded we cross the desert's emptiness,*
> *and must be false to what would make us whole.*
> *For only change and distance shape for us*
> *some new tremendous symbol for the soul.*[54]

So, too, John Thompson returns from European civilization to find solace in the bush, and his pining "vanishes in this wise wilderness", whilst James McAuley out of his discontent writes of

> *that deep longing for an exorciser,*
> *For Christ descending as a thaumaturge*
> *Into his saints, as formerly in the desert,*
> *Warring with demons on the outer verge.*[55]

Enunciated in poetry, the redemptive desert is explored more fully in contemporary fiction. Lyndon Rose, tracing the quest of the half-caste boy Nugget for a faith to live by, shows him killing his white father and joining his blackfellow uncle in a return to the aboriginal culture: "Together they would go back to the desert."[56] Randolph Stow tells how the missionary Heriot goes out into the desert and finds salvation there, losing hate and finding a forgiving love, ending with the old man content by the sea after his pilgrimage: " 'My soul,' he whispered, over the sea-surge, 'my soul is a strange country.' "[57]

It is in Patrick White's *Voss*, however, that the pilgrimage into the redemptive desert is presented most strikingly as it attempts to find Judith Wright's "new tremendous symbol for the soul". On the mundane level the expedition, with the incompetent band chosen by Voss and his fanatical, inept leadership, cannot be taken seriously—and it is not intended to be, since it is a spiritual exploration with a religious theme of suffering man finding, like the saints, salvation in the wilderness. Voss is more than a grotesque moving angularly in a nightmarish fantasy. He is a Petroushka alive with a passionate aspiration, since he yearns to conquer the country by the triumph of his will. In the end he achieves the humility desired by his Laura. When all the other members of the expedition had died or deserted,

---

[53] A. D. Hope, "Australia" in *Poems* (London 1960), p.100.

[54] Judith Wright, *The Two Fires* (Sydney 1955), p.51.

[55] James McAuley, "New Guinea" in *A Vision of Ceremony* (Sydney 1956), p.19.

[56] Lyndon Rose, *Country of the Dead* (Sydney 1959), p.188.

[57] Randolph Stow, *To the Islands* (London 1958), p.204.

"Only he was left, only he could endure it, and that because at last he was truly humbled. So saints acquire sanctity who are only bones."[58] And Laura, mystically sharing his agony, concurs: "When man is truly humbled, when he has learnt that he is not God, then he is nearest to becoming so. In the end, he may ascend."[59] So Voss, transposed into a Christ-like figure, ascends into both legendary lore and godhead. In his ascension he is borne aloft not on the wings of will or courage but, true to the Christian paradox, on the pinions of humility.

The journey of Voss into the purifying agonies of the wilderness is painted in the morbid, macabre style of early Italian paintings depicting the crucifixion. It is a *pietà* in which Laura, the Virgin, clasps the spirit of Voss in a telepathic embrace. It is a personal vision continuing Patrick White's preoccupation throughout his novels with pain and suffering, but deepening it into a redemptive humility, thus expressing an attitude quite alien to Australian humanism. Yet *Voss* also forms part of the contemporary movement towards a religious mystique of the desert, standing out as its most powerful parable.

[58] Patrick White, *Voss* (London 1957), p.414.
[59] Ibid., p.411.

V

The Clash of Cultures

Meanwhile indoors we were studying the Victorians and Victorian society. Party followed party, and it was English life over again; nothing strange, nothing exotic, nothing new or original, save perhaps in greater animation of spirits. The leaves that grow on one branch of an oak are not more like the leaves that grow upon another, than the Australian swarm is like the hive it sprung from. All was the same—dress, manners, talk, appearance.

FROUDE[1]

"To be *colonial* is to talk Australian slang; to be badly dressed, vulgar, everything that is abominable," replied Honoria with grave simplicity; "at least that is the general opinion. I have seen Englishwomen who talked slang, only in a different way; nevertheless we all tried to imitate them, just as we copy Paris models for our gowns. You will see that it is the fashion out here to be as British as possible."

MRS CAMPBELL PRAED[2]

And aha! . . . Hope! In some recent N.S.W. military manoeuvres "the (Australian) Scotchmen"—not to be targets of opposing marksmen—"adopted the precaution of wearing their hirsute tassel at the rear". A fine symbol. Put Scotland behind, put Ireland behind, put England behind—not as sources of inspiration, but as goals of aspiration—and go forward with Australia!

A. G. STEPHENS[3]

> We whose scope
> clasps the tremendous leagues of summer-south,
> thunder-oppressive with curbed energies,
> least of all folk need question our day's worth
> or think its turmoil twitchings of spent earth.
> Here noon above burnt, bony ridges hung
> nerve tense, is strident with an unheard tongue,
> pregnant with daring and with destinies.

ROBERT D. FITZGERALD[4]

[1] J. A. Froude, *Oceana* (London 1886), p.89.
[2] Mrs Campbell Praed, *Longleat of Kooralbyn* (London 1887), p.154.
[3] A. G. Stephens, *The Red Pagan* (Sydney 1904), p.91.
[4] Robert D. FitzGerald, *Moonlight Acre* (Melbourne 1938), p.70.

The Problem of Colonial Literatures

If the shaping of the Australian social patterns was a complex process involving the action and reaction of many factors, one of the most fundamental was certainly the settlement of Australia as a British colony. In this colonial matrix the Australian nation developed and created its literature. As P. R. Stephensen declared, "Art is internationally appreciated, but all art is nationally created."[5] The social element in literature, as we have seen earlier, expresses the distinctive spirit of a national society functioning within a specific time and place. A special problem arises, however, in the case of nations that have passed through a colonial period, since they have experienced the inevitable clash between two cultures, the imperial and indigenous, and have gone through a struggle, psychological as well as political, to advance from a subduing colonialism to an independent nationalism. The clash between the British and Australian cultures affected the Australian society and its literature profoundly. It took many decades, for instance, for those living in Australia to lose their English vision and look on the country with their own eyes, and various stages before the poets moved forward to what Dr Brian Elliott has termed "a natural revaluation of the environmental image".[6] The psychological effects of the cultural clash even linger on today, as Arthur Phillips has pointed out in his essay on "The Cultural Cringe".[7]

When a colonial people has already enjoyed a traditional culture of its own, the conflict between this and the conquering culture of an alien people is comparatively clear-cut. This can be seen in the Philippines after 1898 when the new Anglo-Saxon culture of the American conqueror was imposed upon the Spanish-Filipino one established during the centuries of Spanish rule, and the Filipinos then struggled to achieve mental independence from colonialism by the creation of a national literature. While political freedom has been won, the cultural struggle still goes on. This is the constant theme of the Filipino literary critics.[8]

The clash of cultures takes on a special complexity when the colony, as in Australia, New Zealand, and America, has been settled by emigrants of the colonizing power. In these cases the British culture was offered no competition by the existing aboriginal, Maori, and Red Indian cultures, but the cultural conflict became a family

[5] P. R. Stephensen, "Book-Publishing in Australia", article in *The Australian Rhodes Review*, March 1934, p.42.
[6] Brian Elliott, *The Landscape of Australian Poetry* (Melbourne 1967), p.xii.
[7] A. A. Phillips, *The Australian Tradition* (Melbourne 1958), pp.89-95.
[8] For example, critics like Maramag, Mangahas, and Yabes in *Filipino Essays in English, 1910-1954* (Quezon City 1954), and in numbers of the *Diliman Review*, 1953 to date.

one in which the colonial offspring gradually developed its own distinctive national ethos until it flung off what had grown into a parental yoke. In each case the conflict has features common to all societies and literatures which have undergone the colonial phase. On the other hand, the literatures have had their own individual modes of interaction between colonialism and nationalism, with varying rates of tempo in the advance towards cultural independence.

In the neighbouring New Zealand, for example, this advance came more slowly than in Australia. There it was never stimulated and hastened by a widespread upsurge of nationalism such as occurred in Australian literature during the 1880s and 1890s. It was probably retarded also by the smallness of the population and the absence of such contentious factors promoting an anti-British, nationalist feeling as the Irish group and the transportation issue in Australia. As late as 1946 a critic discussing the national literature could write: "New Zealand has not yet developed a solidly-based culture of her own, and has almost exhausted the capital of traditional culture she inherited from the pioneers."[9] Another critic stated in 1953 that "The New Zealand literary tradition, in so far as one exists, is still being created and has reached its present development in only two or three generations."[10] A third writer, however, after pointing out the sterility of the earlier colonial period in poetry, considered in 1956 that a change began quietly in the mid-nineteen-twenties when the community had become integrated and by the thirties the poets "took up this function of expressing their land and community without the accompaniment of strident nationalism"[11]—possibly a reference to the Australian nationalism of the nineties. Summing up the country's historical development in poetry, he concludes:

First there was the poetry of Englishmen written in New Zealand. Next came the poetry written about New Zealand produced by men divided between two traditions, one distant and exotic, the other in the making. Finally, in the 'thirties one begins to detect a third and unequivocal answer. For then it became possible to speak of New Zealand poetry as a poetry with which New Zealand patterns of life and thought are fused without effort separate from that of the creative act itself. Time, place and tradition had met.[12]

Certainly the cultural clash has been resolved into national maturity in the work of such poets as Mason, Fairburn, Glover, and Curnow and short story writers like Sargeson and Davin—and that exceptional expatriate Katherine Mansfield.

[9] J. C. Reid, *Creative Writing in New Zealand* (Auckland 1946), p.6. For confirmation of this view, see also E. H. McCormick, *Letters and Art in New Zealand* (1940) and M. H. Holcroft, *The Deepening Stream* (1940) and *The Waiting Hills* (1943).
[10] D. M. Davin (ed.), *New Zealand Short Stories* (O.U.P. 1953), p.6.
[11] Robert Chapman in Introduction to Robert Chapman and Jonathan Bennett (ed.), *An Anthology of New Zealand Verse* (London and Wellington 1956), p.xxv.
[12] Ibid., p.xxiv.

In Canada the French-Canadians built up an indigenous literature rich in folk-song, but the creative writing in English of the British Canadians remained colonial in character and variable in quality until the latter part of the nineteenth century. A. J. M. Smith writes:

It took events like the War of 1812 and the rebellions of 1837 to awaken a lively sense of the need for unity, and it was not until the fifties and sixties that the national ideal began to take shape in reality or to find expression in genuine poetry.[13]

This national idea was retarded and complicated, of course, by the difficulty of welding two peoples with different languages, religions and traditions into one Canadian unity: "Nationalism has had to contend with the instinct or the tradition of racial particularism."[14] The nationalist feeling, however, developed strongly about the same period as it did in Australia, and the ideal of Confederation was expressed by Charles G. D. Roberts in his "Canada":

> *How long the indolence, ere thou dare*
> *Achieve thy destiny, seize thy fame,—*
> *Ere our proud eyes behold thee bear*
> *A nation's franchise, nation's name?*[15]

Roberts and the robust Bliss Carman had to fight for national literary independence until a critic could say: "Their literary conspectus is thoroughly Canadian; and their inspiration and ideals too are Canadian."[16] These two poets joined with Archibald Lampman and D. C. Scott to become leaders in a poetic acclimatization of the Canadian natural scene, making a "Golden Age" of poetry in the nineties. The national past was then explored vigorously by E. J. Pratt, and his interest in people rather than nature is shared by such other contemporary poets as Earle Birney, Irving Layton, and P. K. Page, intellectuals dealing with their own society of today, even if cosmopolitan in their techniques.

In the United States the interaction of British and American cultures presents many parallels to the cultural clash in Australia. There, too, came a slow development from a colonial to a national literature. After the American colonies had fought and won political independence from Britain, it took almost a century for American writers to become fully American. An American critic, after suggesting that it might be said that there was no American literature worth a history in the seventeenth and eighteenth centuries, points out that from the nineteenth century

---

[13] A. J. M. Smith (ed.), *The Book of Canadian Poetry* (Chicago 1943), p.6.
[14] Sir Richard Jebb, *Studies in Colonial Nationalism* (London 1905), p.12.
[15] A. J. M. Smith, op. cit., p.174.
[16] J. D. Logan, *Highways of Canadian Literature* (Toronto 1924), p.106.

almost every history of American literature from the sixties to 1913, when John Macy published his *Spirit of American Literature* and inaugurated the modern interpretation of the subject, not only insisted upon measuring American writers by British standards, but also claimed that American literature was a branch of English letters, a subordinate, if locally interesting, expression of the Anglo-Saxon spirit.[17]

There were aspirations enough for writing of an American character and of universal quality, and as early as 1770 and 1794 such poets of the Connecticut group of "Hartford Wits" as James Trumbull and Timothy Dwight looked forward to American Shakespeares and Miltons in terms almost identical with the hopes for future Australian literary greatness voiced by Wentworth in his *Australasia* ode of 1823.

As in Australia, however, the writers for decades remained colonial and derivative, looking to Britain for inspiration. Thus Robert E. Spiller comments:

Caught between the urge of youth to break all ties with the past and the need of art for a tradition and a model by which to bend the raw material of life to formal expression, our earliest men of letters were at once naive, experimental, conformist, self-conscious, and imitative.[18]

During the nineteenth century the colonial complex still exerted its influence on much of the American writing, especially on the style of expression, even if the topics were specifically American, as when Longfellow and Cooper pictured the Red Indians in poems and novels, when Bryant and Whittier sang the beauties of the New England countryside, or when Hawthorne explored the recesses of the Puritan conscience. Poe and Emily Dickinson, Thoreau and Melville, it is true, were highly independent and original writers. They passed far beyond the limits of colonialism. Yet they remain singular rather than representative of their people and their age. Emerson, too, struck out his own path in poetry when, anticipating *Leaves of Grass*, he experimented with form, rhythm, and symbol. On the whole, however, it may fairly be said that American literature did not become completely indigenous, in idiom and spirit as well as in theme, until the burgeoning in prose and poetry of Mark Twain and Walt Whitman.

In another English-speaking country, South Africa, there was a similar problem of a colonial literature, with a national expression in fiction running from the earlier Olive Schreiner to the contemporary Alan Paton. Although the most important South African poet, Roy Campbell, was a cosmopolite who satirized the more naive forms of nationalist writing and its mystique of the veld, his own work carried characteristics drawn from his country—can one imagine *The Flaming*

---

[17] Howard Mumford Jones, *The Theory of American Literature* (Ithaca 1948), pp.79-80.
[18] Robert E. Spiller, *The Cycle of American Literature* (New York 1955), p.24.

Terrapin coming thunderously, spaciously, from the England of his time?

Finally, the clash of cultures is seen nowhere more picturesquely than in the creative writing of the various republics of Latin America. There the situation has been complicated by the fact that the colonial Hispanic culture, impressed strongly by centuries of rule by Spain and Portugal, passed through a stage of powerful French influence. An American historian writes:

It was not until the latter part of the century that literature began to reach its full stature...as a rule the new writers kept close to the Latin-American soil for their inspiration. The heritage of colonialism had largely worked itself out.[19]

The Mexican writer Alfonso Reyes, in his address to the international meeting of the PEN clubs over which he presided at Buenos Aires in 1936, has described forcefully the colonial problem in Latin America. The previous generation, he said, felt itself within prisoning circles which included

the very specific one of being American, born and rooted in a soil that was not the real centre of civilization, but a branch office. To use the words of our Victoria Ocampo, our grandfathers felt themselves to be the "owners of souls that had no passport"...even within the Hispanic world we were a dialect, a derivation, a second-rate thing, a branch once more: Spanish-American, a name that is joined by a little hyphen like a chain.[20]

There could be no more striking description of the colonial inferiority complex, a complex found in Australia no less than in other countries with a colonial heritage. Señor Reyes ended, however, with pointing out the change that came with the recent development of cultural independence:

For a time now between Spain and us there has existed a feeling of similarity and equality.... In the new literature of (Latin) America there is a marked tendency toward autochthony, which is deserving of the deepest respect especially when it does not stop with the easy achievement of local color but attempts to plumb the depths of our psychological realities.[21]

English and Australian Cultures

In the Australian colonies as the land and its conditions gradually produced a local culture, the differences became more marked between it and the transplanted British culture—particularly the English one held by the upper and middle classes of the dominant group, since the minority groups of the Scots and the Irish fitted

[19] W. L. Schurz, *Latin America* (New York 1941), p.361.
[20] German Arciniegas, *The Green Continent: a Comprehensive View of Latin America by its Leading Writers* (New York 1944), pp.231-2; Alfonso Reyes, "Thoughts on the American Mind".
[21] Ibid.

more easily into the evolving colonial patterns. Thus arose an inevitable clash of two contrasting cultures, paralleling the accompanying conflict in the constitutional field. Just as the colonists battled with the home government for political independence, so another struggle, unorganized and intangible, went on for independence on the broad, shifting cultural front. The differences between the English and Australian senses of values began to be apparent even in the first half of the nineteenth century, and the opposition between them deepened in the last quarter of the century when the native-born, now outnumbering the English immigrants, began to develop a stronger nationalist sentiment and to grow more vocal in its expression. These differences covered marked contrasts between the English and Australian environment, economy, social order, manners, outlook and sentiment.

This opposition in cultures derived basically from the contrast in environments, since the English regarded Australia as the antipodes where everything was topsy-turvy, where the very seasons were reversed and the animals were anachronistic freaks. The scale of sizes, too, was reversed, so that the people of a tight little isle felt lost in a whole continent of interminable space which gave an intoxicating sense of freedom but also intimidated by its vastness and emptiness. The English countryside was mellow and ordered, humanized by centuries of living and associations preserved in songs and poems, but Australia was a new country of grating rawness, sprawling untidily, baffling by its blankness, with "the age-unbroken silence of the Australian bush"[22] reducing man to an intruding cypher and making the traditional English civilization dwindle into an alien far-off insignificance.

Its environment made England an agricultural and industrial country, with an urban culture. In contrast, the Australian environment produced a pastoral economy and occupational values held by a type of individual—the bushman—unknown in England. The bush workers roamed around in a casual freedom for which there was no parallel among England's soil-bound rural labourers or the half-starving helots of the factories.

These workers were symbols of the fundamental disparity between the imperial and the colonial social orders. In the old country there was an established hierarchy of castes, and the lower classes in this system of graded inequalities were generally obedient, despite rebellious minorities of Chartists, Luddites, and trade union agitators. In the colonies, on the other hand, where the evolving social order was relatively amorphous, although the English "gentry" tried to

[22] D. H. Lawrence, *Kangaroo* (Penguin ed. 1950), p.390.

establish the old class distinctions with some success, the working class was insistent on its right to social equality.

There was a sense of freedom in the air antagonistic to the old English inequalities. It has been described aptly by the perceptive D. H. Lawrence, giving the feeling of Somers and Harriet as they lay on the sands of Manly beach:

> Strange it was. And it *had* a sort of fascination. Freedom! That's what they always say. "You feel free in Australia." And so you do. There is a great relief in the atmosphere, a relief from tension, from pressure. An absence of control or will or form. The sky is open above you, and the air is open around you. Not the old closing-in of Europe.... . The sense of irresponsible freedom. The sense of do-as-you-please liberty.[23]

This sense expressed itself in the workers' democratic spirit, based on equality, that stood as the very opposite of the English caste system in which the workers were catalogued as the subservient "lower orders". Observers noted that William Lane's dream of Australia as "The Working Man's Paradise" found some practical realization. Westgarth commented in 1857 that "The phrase that Victoria is the working-man's paradise is true",[24] whilst Mark Twain declared in 1897: "The workingman is a great force everywhere in Australia, but South Australia is his paradise."[25]

The cultural clash was sharpened by the discord between English and Australian manners and speech. The educated English settler was repelled by the colonial informality, crudity, and coarseness. The native colonial in turn usually scorned refinement as an unmanly affectation of the English gentry and preferred to be "rough but honest", illogically equating the two and suspecting the sincerity of anyone refined.

Whereas the English culture cultivated some sensibility to the arts, the Australian colonial culture was notably lacking in "graceful living". Primitiveness was partly inevitable in the bush under pioneering conditions, but in the cities the wealthier native colonists often displayed vulgarity rather than good taste. The tasteless character of Australian architecture, for instance, has been soundly indicted by Robin Boyd in *The Australian Ugliness*. Probably nowhere else in the world has there been a greater insensitivity to beauty, such a tolerance of disorderliness and ugliness as in Australia. Almost any so-called "primitive" people would be superior here to the Australians. This trait, like drinking, cursing and gambling, also goes back to colonial beginnings, perhaps also to convict and working-class influences.

[23] Ibid., pp.32-3.
[24] William Westgarth, *Victoria and the Gold Mines in* 1857 (London 1857), p.5.
[25] Mark Twain, *Following the Equator* (New York 1897), p.193.

The English reaction to this ugliness and disorder is expressed vividly in Henry Handel Richardson's picture of Richard Mahony:

His eyes ached, his brows had grown wrinkled from gazing on iron roofs set against hard blue overhead; on dirty weatherboards innocent of paint; on higgledy-piggledy backyards and ramshackle fences; on the straggling landscape with its untidy trees—all the unrelieved ugliness, in short, of the colonial scene.[26]

The English Attitude of Superiority

The more general attitude of the English to the strain of vulgarity in the Australian people is given by Lawrence in *Kangaroo* when Somers wants to make friends with his Australian neighbours, and Harriet protests : "What are these people, after all? Quite common and—not in your line at all."[27] Another instance is the comment made upon Sim Montfort and his family in England by one of their country cousins: "Young Blair's a nice feller. Wouldn't think he was Australian."[28] And Mary Montfort sums up the situation truly for Raoul Blair:

You know, it is quite a disadvantage being an Australian . . . . In Australia, if you are quiet and don't speak like a servant, you are thought a snob; if you aren't a millionaire you are ignored. If you live in England, wretched middle-class English try to patronise you, expect you to eat like a savage, crack stock-whips and spit on the floor.[29]

This English attitude of superiority galled the colonial deeply. At first this resentment was defensive, but it grew aggressive and counter-attacked with depreciation of everything English as the nationalist spirit deepened. The colonial inferiority complex bedevilled the Australian people and their literature almost from their beginnings right up to the present day. The colonists, especially the emancipated convicts and the native-born, were an un-Christian lot who failed to feel blessed when the Englishman reviled them.

Thus the resentment felt in the colonies was probably not exaggerated by Brian Penton in *Landtakers* when he represented Joe Gursey, the convict blacksmith, showing an insolent anger at the very appearance of the supercilious Derek Cabell and preferring even McGovern the superintendent, the "greedy, swaggering, bloody-minded Currency Lad" who flogged the lags unmercifully. So Gursey cries out to Cabell:

"He's a bastard and nothing's bad enough for him, but you—you'd do anything, anything!" He stopped the grindstone and came nearer as he spoke,

[26] Henry Handel Richardson, *The Fortunes of Richard Mahony* (Melbourne, first Australian ed., 1946; first publ. London 1929), p.362.
[27] D. H. Lawrence, op. cit., p.77.
[28] Martin Mills (Martin Boyd), *The Montforts* (London 1928), p.150.
[29] Ibid., p.319.

waving the axe excitedly over his head. "*He's* one of us, anyway. He doesn't look down on us, whatever he does. But you think we're dirt, don't you? I can see through your aristocratic mug. You think that anything you do to us is right!"[30]

Joe Gursey had already identified himself with the new land, so that his bitterness is a colonial as well as a class one.

The same hostility also moved Furphy, that genial observer and philosopher "whose talk is of bullocks"[31] to lose his geniality for once when he contemplates the English gentleman, especially in fiction. "Go to; I'll no more on't," he cries, "it hath made me mad."[32] So he castigates in a famous passage

the three-penny braggadacio of caste which makes the languid Captain Vernon de Vere (or words to that effect) an overmatch for half-a-dozen hard-muscled white savages, any one of whom would take his lordship by the ankles, and wipe the battlefield with his patrician visage.[33]

This colonial anger was aggravated by the sense of grievance caused by the virtual closing to the native-born of the lands which were granted so freely or later acquired so easily by the wealthier English settlers. The Land Regulations, Alexander Harris points out, locked them out from the land. Hence came "a very bitter and continually deepening feeling of disaffection to the British Government and its Australian employees in the minds of the colonial youth. There is a settled sense among them that they are debarred of their rights."[34] When Australian nationalism later became articulate it often spoke with a republican, anti-British note. "Australian nationalism," Professor Hancock considered, "took definite form in the struggle between the landless majority and the land-monopolising squatters."[35]

The Conflict of Sentiment

Finally, there was the gulf in sentiment between the Englishman devoted to the old country and the native-born colonial developing a love for *his* homeland. This gulf was unbridgable when English patriotism exalted an idealized England at the expense of a disparaged Australia. The classic example of this opposition, of course, was given by Kingsley when he pictured young Sam Buckley describing to his adoring Alice "the magnificent idea" of returning to England to be

[30] Brian Penton, *Landtakers* (Sydney 1934), p.79.
[31] *The Bible*, Ecclesiasticus, XXXVIII, 25.
[32] Tom Collins, *Such is Life* (Melbourne 1917 ed., first publ. Sydney 1903), p.33.
[33] Ibid.
[34] Alexander Harris, *Settlers and Convicts*, ed. C. M. H. Clark (Melbourne 1953 ed.), pp.224-5.
[35] W. K. Hancock, *Australia* (Sydney, first Australian ed., 1945; first publ. London 1930), p.52.

master of his ancestral acres: "I don't want to be young Sam Buckley of Baroona. I want to be the Buckley of Clere. Is that not a noble ambition?"[36]

Sam's insistence reminds one irresistibly of the similar insistence of Charlotte Gilman's new-fledged butterfly who wanted to return to his former state as a caterpillar:

> *"I do not want to fly," said he,*
> *"I only want to squirm!"*
> *And he dropped his wings dejectedly,*
> *But still his voice was firm:*
> *"I do not want to be a fly!*
> *I want to be a worm!"*[37]

And the conservative creature climbed back into his chrysalis like Sam regressing to England.

Young Sam, however, represented only one type of colonist. The native-born were usually content with their own country. Most of the emigrants settled down happily enough. Some were like the old-time squatter Robin Ruff, who returned to England to find that it had grown alien. Back in Melbourne, "he vowed he would go 'home' no more".[38] He had learnt that Australia had become his real home. Many emigrants, from the squatters Alfred Joyce and Niel Black to Alexander Harris, discovered here that they had developed a warm attachment to their new land.

Many also found that there was no necessary opposition between the old love for England and the new love for Australia, but they could be combined happily. Such a one was Henry Parkes. Speaking in 1853 on the New Constitution Bill for New South Wales he declared:

He thought this country was destined to show the spectacle of a great nation perfectly free, profoundly prosperous and glowing with distinctive national aspirations, and yet united in the bonds of affection and political interests to the mother country.[39]

Until this reconciliation occurred within a sentiment of double loyalties, the clash between the English and colonial cultures persisted.

Stages of Liberation

The cultural clash was thus a process complicated by many diverse factors. In Australia as in other colonial countries the evolution

[36] Henry Kingsley, *The Recollections of Geoffry Hamlyn* (Melbourne, Cole's ed., n.d.), p.401.
[37] Charlotte P. S. Gilman, "A Conservative" in Louis Untermeyer (ed.), *Modern American Poetry* (London 1932), p.126.
[38] Marcus Clarke, *Australian Tales and Sketches* (Melbourne 1897), p.123.
[39] Henry Parkes, *Speeches on Various Occasions Connected with Public Affairs*, etc., with introd. by David Blair (Melbourne 1876), p.25.

from colonialism to national maturity moved irregularly and slowly—
far more slowly than the progress from colonial status to political
freedom. It was far more difficult for the colonies to achieve cultural
independence than political freedom, to grow out of a colonial
complex which had pervaded a whole people for a long time. The
people had to be born again psychologically, and the pangs of this
labour were lengthy and arduous.

This struggle for mental and literary freedom paralleled, once again,
the same process at work in the development of American literature.
An early stage of colonial difficulties, for instance, may be seen in the
ambivalence attributed by an American critic to that many-sided
representative American, yet true internationalist, Benjamin Franklin:

The English thought him too American, the Americans thought him too
English.[40]

So, too, the twin recognition of colonial imitativeness and demand
for a national independence of mind are illustrated forcefully in
Emerson's classic address at Dartmouth in 1838 when, after denouncing the failure of America to fulfil the reasonable expectation
of mankind that this land of liberty would produce a brood of Titans,
he issued an eloquent call for a new vigour:

the mark of American merit in painting, in sculpture, in poetry, in fiction, in
eloquence seems to be a certain grace without grandeur, and is itself not new,
but derivative, a vase of fair outline, but empty. . . . The diffidence of mankind in the soul has crept over the American mind. . . . The new man must
feel that he is new, and has not come into the world mortgaged to the opinions
and usages of Europe, and Asia, and Egypt . . . and now we will live,—live
for ourselves,—and not as the pall-bearers of a funeral, but as the upholders
and creators of our age. . . . Now that we are here we will put our own
interpretation on things, and our own things for interpretation.[41]

Similar demands for an original, indigenous literature, free of
colonial influences, were made by other writers, such as Bryant and
Cooper, Lowell and Whitman. Even the aesthetic Poe joined the
national chorus, desiring a Declaration of Independence in letters as
in government. In time the call was amply met by a succession of
masterpieces characterized by abundant originality, and American
writing became a national literature, mature, unique, more than holding its own with other world literatures.

As in Australia, however, the colonial complex died hard, especially
in the academic world. American literature had no recognition in the
universities and colleges until 1872, when the first collegiate course

---

[40] Carl Van Doren, "Benjamin Franklin," in Robert E. Spiller et al. (ed.), *Literary
History of the United States* (New York 1955, first publ. 1946), p.104.
[41] Ralph Waldo Emerson, *Emerson's Complete Works* (London 1903, Riverside ed.),
vol.I, pp.153-155, "Literary Ethics" address.

H

in the subject was taught. As late as 1917 there was only one solitary professor of American literature, although almost all the colleges had professorships in American history.

It was not until the twentieth century, moreover, that the American people appreciated fully the indigenous quality of Walt Whitman. It is perhaps remarkable, therefore, that when the same indigenous quality appeared in Australia with Lawson and Paterson a decade earlier it brought an immediate national response.

Australian literature, we have seen, had three main periods: colonial, nationalist and modern. The resolving of the colonial problem in the literature of different countries, however, has been slightly more complex. It has tended to follow a general pattern of four overlapping stages: (1) the colonial; (2) the semi-colonial; (3) the nationalist; (4) the final stage of national maturity. Australian literature, however, has also added an extra fifth stage between the last two stages: an internationalist interregnum.

The Colonial Stage

In the development of a national literature the colonial stage represented a period of infancy, since usually the only Australian element in the writing was the local scene. The spirit, outlook and style were all English. This was inevitable, of course, in the early decades before the Australian social patterns had time to evolve. It was English writing about Australia, whether written by emigrants or the native-born.

The literary drama, in particular, suffered from the prevailing sense of colonial inferiority, since the playwrights assumed that the crudities of the life around them were quite unfit for treatment in drama with literary pretensions. The novelists and poets at least dealt with the colonial scene, but the playwrights set their plays in every country and century except their own, wandering from ancient Rome to medieval France, from Provence to Asturia.

Two early plays which were exceptional in attempting a local subject illustrated only too sharply the problem of the colonial writer. Charles Harpur and David Burn each wrote a play entitled *The Bushrangers*,[42] and both failed to treat this promising theme effectively. Harpur deserts realities for an artificial imitation of Shakespearean tragedy and comedy. Burn, despite his play's success in Edinburgh in 1829, cannot handle his bushrangers. Both plays

[42] Charles Harpur, *The Bushrangers: a Play in Five Acts, and other Poems* (Sydney 1853). An earlier version entitled *The Tragedy of Donahoo*, which appeared in the *Sydney Monitor* in 1835, seems to have been the first play published in Australia. David Burn's *Plays and Fugitive Pieces in Verse* (Hobart 1842), the first volume of plays published in Australia, did not include his play *The Bushrangers*, but the original manuscript is in the Mitchell Library.

display a striking incongruity between the English and Australian cultures, between the realistic theme and the artificial "literary" treatment of it derived from overseas heroics or melodrama.

The same incongruity prevails in most of the colonial verse. The indigenous and the imported elements proved oil and water, failing to mix into an artistic form. The earliest colonial versifiers, such as Robinson, Barron Field, Wentworth and Tompson, used a polished eighteenth century diction in heroic couplets which ill fitted the raw colonial scene. When the young Charles Tompson entitled his verse *Wild Notes from the Lyre of a Native Minstrel* he only drew attention to the fact that his "wild notes" were extremely tame, and he might well have given his readers the assurance of Bottom the weaver as to how he would play the lion: "I will roar you as gently as any sucking dove."

Later the application of the English romantic diction to the colonial themes resulted in much tepid versifying, exemplified in the anthologies compiled by Sladen and Bertram Stevens. Commenting on the Stevens collection the London *Athenaeum* summed up the colonial verse justly. Quoting Essex Evans's line in respect to Australia, "Her inspiration is her own" it said:

Now this is precisely what is missing. Local colour we find, vivid description, a love of the open air and particularly of horses, a feeling for wild life and wild nature; but all this comes to us, not with an inspiration of its own, but secondhand,—through Thomas Moore and Mrs. Hemans in the earlier pages; through Mr. Swinburne in many of the later pages.... These men in this new world before them, this free life about them...fall back on old times for whatever they have to say.[43]

Although this indictment was true in general, there were, of course, some exceptions. The folk ballads and old bush songs formed a popular, oral literature which took its measures and tunes from the "old country" but also expressed much of the spirit of the new, seeing things as they were without undue sentimentality or rhetoric. So, too, Gordon was popular because some of his ballads described bush life directly and vividly. Charles Harpur leant heavily upon Milton and Wordsworth, but he could also catch the atmosphere of an Australian summer noon, the loneliness of the bush, and the grandeur of its mountain gorges. It is notable, again, that Harpur, like Kendall later, also wrote vigorous satires in colloquial terms, whilst the political satires of Robert Lowe and William Forster dealt with local themes in a popular racy idiom.

The creative prose of the colonial period showed much more vigour than the verse, since it was less derivative in form and less trammelled by the English literary tradition. The colonial novels often

[43] Reprinted in *The Bookfellow*, 14 Feb. 1907.

give, moreover, illuminating glimpses of the emerging social patterns, and the attitude of the writers, mostly English by birth, is usually sympathetic rather than critical. Caroline Leakey may gently satirize the tactlessness of a native-born lady towards her assigned servant in *The Broad Arrow* or Kingsley poke mild fun at a currency lad's ignorance, but Alexander Harris gives an approving account of bush attitudes, Catherine Spence as a sturdy Scotswoman relishes the democratic air of Adelaide, Ada Cambridge delights in showing how the informality of her "Little Minx" shocks the orthodox, whilst both Tasma and Mrs Praed draw a contrast between the rough, honest colonial and the sophisticated but less worthy Englishman. The vulgar, kindly Tom Piper is preferred to the parasitic Cavendish, and the Australian bushman Maddox to Barrington, the villainous English aristocrat.[44] The colonial novelists, therefore, did not suffer unduly in their social description and characterization from the colonial sense of inferiority.

They suffered from it, however, in actual life, and it is significant that both Tasma and Mrs Praed left the colonies for the more cultured Europe and England. The struggles of Harpur and Kendall gave tragic evidence of the obstacles facing the native-born writer trying desperately to secure recognition in his own country. Psychologically, too, the colonial complex often inhibited the writer by prompting an artificial self-consciousness. Practically, the dependence upon English publishers and critics tended to force writers to use English models and appeal to English tastes—to cultivate imitation, in short, rather than a genuine originality. Their writing became, almost inevitably, provincial in character. Local readers found it hard to believe in local talent and gave it virtually no support.

Thus in 1866 G. B. Barton, a serious critic with a balanced judgement, pointed out that in New South Wales all local periodicals had perished and there had been no magazine for seven years. "Why so?" he asked.

Is the community insensible to literature? Is it too small, or too poor, to support it? This is not the character of our community, and consequently another reason must be looked for. It will be found in the fact that it is prejudiced against local productions—or, if not prejudiced, at least unwilling to support them.... The demand for English periodicals is very great.[45]

After deploring the hopeless and tragic plight of the writers, who had starved or fled from the colony, Barton linked this with the attitude of the colonial society and the lack of national feeling:

[44] See Tasma's *Uncle Piper of Piper's Hill* (London 1889) and Mrs Campbell Praed's *Longleat of Kooralbyn* (London 1887).
[45] G. B. Barton, *Literature in New South Wales* (Sydney 1866), p.7.

Unless a radical change takes place in the attitude of the people, the prospects of an independent literature are extremely dim.... . Patriotism has not yet developed itself amongst us; and the history of the world has shown that where there has been no patriotism, there has never been a literature.[46]

The hapless experience of Harpur and Deniehy confirmed Barton's account. The colonial complex was in the ascendant.

The Cult of Local Colour

This position had only improved slightly by the eighties. Nothing is more pathetic in our literary annals than the collection of Kendall letters in the Mitchell Library, a moving testament of the poet's fight against poverty, starvation, and despair. Serious writing still met with an uphill struggle. In the seventies and eighties, however, the first stage of colonial indifference merges into the next stage of an emphasis by some critics of an Australian element in the form of local colour. This was an advance upon the undiluted colonial inferiority complex. Thus it was widely held that one of Kendall's virtues was his intimate and loving picture of the local scene. Where Harpur had been neglected, Kendall was praised as "the first poet in whom, it may be said, Australia speaks".[47] So, too, Gordon was held by others besides Marcus Clarke to have founded an indigenous poetry. Local work was being welcomed, if only by a few, for its native quality.

This quality, nevertheless, was interpreted superficially as a representation of the external scene. In some hands it became exaggerated to an absurd degree. Here the best example is Douglas Sladen, an English visitor who exploited his literary "corner" in Gordon so successfully that he had Gordon's bust placed in Westminster Abbey inscribed "Australia's National Poet". He edited an anthology of *Australian Ballads and Rhymes* which were, in general, neither ballads in form nor Australian in spirit. His aim was "to lay before the English public A SELECTION OF POEMS INSPIRED BY LIFE AND SCENERY IN AUSTRALIA".[48] This cult of inspiration from the local life was later pushed to its extreme when he complained in his preface to Gordon's poems that the poet had missed the wonderful chance to write adequately about the quaint birds, reptiles, and insects around him. This aroused A. G. Stephens to lambast Sladen with a ridicule that reduced the emphasis on a superficial local colour to absurdity.

Echoing Sladen's naive remarks about Gordon, Stephens lets fly:

[46] Ibid., pp.13-14.
[47] Anon. Review of *Leaves from Australian Forests*, *Colonial Monthly*, October 1869, p.148.
[48] Douglas B. W. Sladen, *Australian Ballads and Rhymes* (London 1888), Introduction, p.xv.

"He has very little to say about any lizards!" Now, by the nine-headed Muse, why should a poet say things about lizards? Surely never before in the history of literature was there a preface-writer who complained of his poet's lack of lizards.... Come to think, Gordon says very little about ants either. What palliation can a critic find for such misconduct? None—none at all. "And nothing about the enormous iguana!!!" "Impossible!" you say. Alas! it is true; we have Mr. Sladen's boundless assurance for it. Deaf to the call of conscience, blind to the beacon of duty, Gordon says "nothing about the enormous iguana!" Yet some people pretend that Poetry is not a vain and futile thing. In the name of lizards and the enormous iguana, what are poets for?[49]

The Semi-colonial Stage

This cult of local colour grew more noticeable towards the end of the colonial period when the writers passed into a transitional stage leading to the nationalism of the nineties. Here two significant figures are Henry Kendall and Rolf Boldrewood, already saluted as the first indigenous poet and novelist. Neither, however, was wholly Australian in style, and the English admixture gave them an ambivalence which caused misunderstanding of their true roles in our literary history.

Kendall, for instance has suffered from critics who have not troubled to study his work thoroughly and have thus fallen into such errors as accusing him of being purely English in his outlook and expression, of being incapable of viewing a bush sawmill in local terms, and even of disparaging the bell-bird for being Australian—and all this of the poet who was passionately patriotic, who dedicated his life to the ambition of becoming the national Australian poet, who worked for years in a bush sawmill store and wrote ballads of the local bushmen in a colloquial, realistic idiom, who won the recognition of his contemporaries as the authentic voice of Australia, and was later praised by A. G. Stephens: "There has been no writer more generically Australian than Kendall; the Spirit of the Bush hovers over all his poetry."[50]

The truth is that Kendall is significant historically as the first poet to attempt a thorough assimilation of the Australian environment. At times he succeeded, especially when his language escaped from the Victorian conventions to attain a universal simplicity, as in "Orara" and "The Last of His Tribe". As George Gordon McCrae discerned, he excelled in catching the light and shadow of the coastal scene he knew and loved so well.

On the other hand, he was also a writer of his time. He showed the influences of Wordsworth and Tennyson just as contemporary poets like Slessor, Judith Wright and A. D. Hope show at times the

[49] A. G. Stephens, "Under the Gum-tree", *The Bookfellow*, 1 Nov. 1912.
[50] A. G. Stephens in *The Bookfellow*, 15 Dec. 1919.

influences of Eliot, Yeats and Auden. Although he developed an individual style, he had not the powerful originality of a Whitman to create a new mode of verse expression to suit his new theme. By using the romantic diction current in his day, weighted with its English connotations, he often failed to assimilate his Australian subject, and the clash of the two cultures, English and Australian, each bound up with such widely different environments, produced a falsity of tone. Furthermore, Kendall, steeped in his English poetry, was conscious of the differences, and his self-consciousness at times marred his spontaneity.

This difficulty is seen particularly when he tried to pioneer such purely Australian subjects as shingle-splitters and bullock-drivers, figures so alien to the traditions of English poetry that he could only partly assimilate them. Thus in "Bill the Bullock Driver"[51] he succeeded in such stanzas as this:

> *As straight and as sound as a slab without crack,*
> *Our Bill is a king in his way:*
> *Though he camps by the side of a shingle track,*
> *And sleeps on the bed of his dray.*

This has the true ballad ring and a direct, vigorous idiom. Then sentiment is applied with poetic diction to elevate the theme, but only results in incongruous doggerel:

> *For, rough as he seems, he would shudder to wrong*
> *A dog with the loss of a hair;*
> *And the angels of shine and superlative song*
> *See his heart and the deity there.*

With the entrance of the alliterative angels Kendall loses the ballad naturalness and the authentic touch.

The problem of a truly assimilative language that would render Bill the bullock-driver in Australian terms has here defeated Kendall, to be solved a decade later by the colloquial verse of such balladists as Paterson and Lawson. A further half century was to elapse, however, before Judith Wright's superb lyric "Bullocky" rendered the theme in poetry which was both Australian and universal.

Boldrewood, again, has been represented commonly by critics and historians as a purely colonial writer who wrote for an English audience. In fact, as the researches of Keast Burke have proved conclusively, his novels and short stories were mainly addressed to local readers in the first instance through local periodicals. Of eighteen volumes of fiction no fewer than twelve, including Boldrewood's main writings, were published first in Australia.

Whereas it has been stated that his heroes, like those of Kingsley,

---

[51] T. Inglis Moore (ed.), *Selected Poems of Henry Kendall* (Sydney 1957), pp.147-9.

ended up in the Mecca of England, Mr Burke has pointed out the truth that "the movement of the characters is rather the other way."[52] Thus England is pictured in *A Sydney-Side Saxon* as a country of poverty and ill-rewarded toil for the worker, and Australia as the land of wealth and opportunity. Indeed, Boldrewood's attitude was not English, as often claimed, but that of the experienced Australian squatter, magistrate, and gold commissioner.

As a transitional figure he embodied notably the conflicting elements of the semi-colonial stage. On the one hand, he was truly "colonial" as a political conservative with a distrust of democracy, a respect for the English traditions, and a reverence for aristocracy. On the other hand, in practice he was democratic in his kindliness to all men and in his warm appreciation of the bushmen and the Gulgong miners. He was as fervent a patriot as any nationalist of the nineties. His pride in his country and its people is revealed in his *Old Melbourne Memories, My Run Home*, and various articles. He told an interviewing critic that "the Australian talks better and purer English than the average Englishman . . . and in manners he is above the pure Britisher—except the Irish, whom he equals in generosity."[53]

Robbery Under Arms, Rolf Boldrewood's superb romance of bush-ranging, is thoroughly Australian in theme, setting, and realistic detail. It gives a solid and authentic picture of the bush scene and character, outlook and idiom by one who knew them intimately and relished bush life with unsurpassed gusto. The Marstons are living characters, vital creations.

The novel is "colonial" in only two respects: the character of Starlight as English aristocrat, and part, if not all, of the narrative style. This, taken from Scott and other English writers of romance, changes slightly the tempo and tone of a story told by a bush youth, as can be seen by a comparison with Lawson's bush stories. A. G. Stephens concluded soundly:

The Australian value of this book is that perhaps seven-tenths of it is Australian truth . . . it needed Browne's remarkable knowledge of bush life to harmonize his characters, incidents and scenes. He has had imitators since 1880, but none who comes within a cooee of him.[54]

Nationalism

The problem of assimilating the Australian scene into literature was a double one: it was a matter of finding both the right outlook and

---

[52] Keast Burke, *Thomas Alexander Browne (Rolf Boldrewood): an Annotated Bibliography, Checklist, and Chronology*, no.5 in *Studies in Australian Bibliography*, edited by Walter Stone (Sydney 1956), p.43.

[53] J. Tighe Ryan, "Australasian Character Sketch: an Australian Novelist: Rolf Boldrewood" in *Review of Reviews*, May 1894, p.126.

[54] A. G. Stephens, "Rolf Boldrewood" in *The Bookfellow*, 15 March 1915.

the right language. Of these the technical problem, the development of a diction suitable to the environment, was by far the more difficult. It took just about a century from the First Settlement for writers in Australia to break the colonial mould, made in England, and to evolve a national form of language to express the indigenous culture. The idiom required was only produced slowly after changes in outlook had developed a strong nationalist movement which gathered way in the eighties and flourished in the nineties. A historian comments soundly:

Although in the writings of nationalists, and in the beliefs and ways of life of those who were coming to accept Australia as their homeland, there was the material from which an Australian national concept could be developed, in the period before 1880 it would be truer to say that there were Australian nationalists but that there was not yet an Australian nationalism.[55]

Barton had already recognized in 1866, as we have seen, that this lack of a general national sentiment was the main obstacle to literary development.

There had been ardent patriots in Australia, however, from the very earliest days, including the convicts who spoke possessively of "the prisoner's country".[56] As early as 1823 Wentworth's poem "Australasia" was a remarkably precocious outburst of fervent nationalism by a writer born in the colonies only two years after the First Fleet had landed. No nationalist of the nineties outdid the emigrant John Dunmore Lang in patriotic zeal. From the forties onwards native-born writers like Harpur, Deniehy and Kendall struggled to develop a literature that was national, not colonial. It was their tragedy that they were, like the South American writers already described by Victoria Ocampo, "owners of souls that had no passport"—no valid passport of the right diction to express their national sentiment.

The passport was found and the problem of a suitable form solved when the prose writers of the eighties and nineties wrote of bush life colloquially, and the bush balladists extended the old bush songs to a balladry that gave the authentic voice of the people. In the short stories of Lawson and Dyson, the selection novels of Steele Rudd and the ballads of Paterson, both outlook and idiom were entirely Australian, with nothing English whatever about them. The clash of cultures was resolved when the social patterns were expressed clearly, naturally and maturely. At long last Australian literature, it seemed, was liberated from its colonialism.

The liberation, on the other hand, was only complete in the work

[55] A. G. Thompson, The Bulletin and Australian Nationalism, thesis in Australian National University Library, p.3.
[56] A. Harris, op. cit., p.34.

of some writers. In the work of others full maturity was not attained, since in it ran another strain, a nationalism that was self-conscious, aggressive in its revolt against colonialism and all things English, at times strident in its rebellion. The *Bulletin*, for example, often voiced a chauvinism as narrow as the colonialism it replaced. It was thus a potent force for ill as well as for good. In reaction against the traditional English assumption of superiority, it counter-attacked with assertions of English inferiority. The same spirit moved the youthful A. G. Stephens to proclaim:

Here, away from old world feuds and enmities, we breathe an ampler ether, a diviner air, than the denizens of the old country, steeped in hereditary prejudices. We refuse to be saddled with the antiquated forms and institutions which in England make misery and retard progress.[57]

Thus Miles Franklin in *My Brilliant Career* was also the rambunctious bush girl asserting herself freely in a company unused to such candour. Later she let her patriotism spoil *All That Swagger* by a misguided coda after the death of Danny, which formed its only artistic ending. Randolph Bedford and E. J. Brady on occasion also shouted a little too loudly. The Englishman was a King Charles's head of the nationalists of the nineties, and they saw red whenever the head was raised. Even Lawson grew choleric in his verse, although but rarely in his prose, which was maturely objective.

The nationalist truculence appeared most strikingly in Joseph Furphy, who wrote to Stephens in 1897 that his novel *Such is Life* was "offensively Australian".[58] This is precisely what his hero Tom Collins becomes whenever Englishmen or English values come into the picture. He loses his calm when abusing Kingsley and foregoes his veracity when the English Willoughby is turned to a shallow caricature.

A similar assertiveness marked the revival of nationalism in the 1930s which sprang up partly as a reaction against the survival of colonial attitudes, partly as a counter-movement to the internationalist influences that predominated in the 1920s. P. R. Stephensen, for example, wiped the floor with the English Professor Cowling with the same vigour that Furphy had demolished Kingsley. The Jindyworobak movement, led by Rex Ingamells, crusaded against colonialism in the late thirties and forties.

The movement's demand for "environmental values", if inflated in tone, was sound enough, even truistic. It recognized, too, that the liberation of Australian literature from a derivative colonialism was

[57] A. G. Stephens, Paper read to the Gympie Literary Circle on Seeley's *Colonial Expansion*, 13 March 1889, unpublished MS in the Mitchell Library.
[58] Tom Collins, *Rigby's Romance* (Melbourne 1921) in the Preface by A. G. Stephens, p.vii.

largely the technical problem of form, of finding suitable diction and native imagery. It did useful service in airing this problem and stimulating controversy, as can be seen from the comments of writers in the symposium *Jindyworobak Review 1938-1948*.

The chief weakness of both the more assertive nationalists of the nineties and the Jindyworobaks was self-consciousness. The insistence on "Australia First" formed a stage which, however necessary or useful in its time, was still psychologically adolescent, since maturity means that a writer is national spontaneously and naturally. The assertive fight against colonialism is a recognition of its importance: the colonial complex still exists when it provokes rebellion instead of a former submissiveness. We can apply to the Australian nationalists the words used by an American critic of similar rebels, such as Poe and Emerson, in America:

These very assertions of independence, with their attendant excess of desire to dwell upon American things and American things only, which amounted to an intellectual obsession, were attestations of inferiority rather than of confidence. When writers are certain of themselves, convinced of their national independence, as is the case of American writers to-day, they... accept it as a reality and proceed with their work without giving it further consideration.[59]

Internationalism

Like the modern American writers, some of the nationalist writers here in the nineties maturely accepted their independence as a reality. So did most poets and novelists of the 1930s and onwards. In between, however, there was an interregnum of internationalism, particularly in the twenties. Despite the intense national sentiment aroused during the first world war, international influences became dominant in the literature in the disillusionment after the war. Thus Frank Wilmot protested bitterly to Australia in his poem "Echoes"[60] that she had lost her own inspiration to echo the discontent of Europe:

> *Drowned in echoes of reflected troubles,*
> *Dying amid your groves of golden trees,*
> *Surrounded by the unregarded dawn!*

In literature, like Brennan in the nineties, such writers as Richardson, Stead, and Baylebridge followed European modes of thought and expression. In the twenties the strongest anti-nationalist feeling was voiced by the *Vision* magazine with its aggressive declaration of all art, and especially poetry, as international. Its leader Jack Lindsay sought a Neo-Hellenic renaissance of Beauty through the imagination of the poet, decried nationalism, and proclaimed: "all true poets are

[59] V. F. Calverton, *The Liberation of American Literature* (New York 1932), p.17.
[60] Furnley Maurice, *Poems* (Melbourne 1944), p.44.

really of one stock. If they belong to any nationality, it is one that has no name upon the maps of this world, but lies with Pindar's Hyperboreans."[61] In creating beauty, "A poem in a mediaeval setting like the Eve of Saint Agnes, or Romeo and Juliet, can do this as no poem set in Sydney can."[62] *Vision*, if vitalist in doctrine, was therefore escapist in its exotic romanticism, and it remained for one of its editors, Kenneth Slessor, to disprove Jack Lindsay years later by his *Five Bells*, a poem of rich beauty set in the despised Sydney.

In the thirties a number of literary magazines in Sydney and Melbourne, such as *Stream, Pandemonium, Manuscripts*, and *Point*[63] carried contributions, reprints and translations of oversea writers in America and Europe, showing the internationalist interests of Australian writers. In these cases the oversea cultures acted as a fertilizing stream.

The internationalist influence was revived briefly in the forties when the magazine *Angry Penguins* flared briefly in Adelaide until quenched by the hoaxing of its editor Max Harris by the Ern Malley poems. Its poets followed the oversea movements of surrealism and "The Apocalypse" with work extremely subjectivist, often obscure or pretentious, yet with random flashes of felicity. Like *Vision* the magazine had little general influence, but brought colour and variety to the literary scene as well as experimentation in techniques.

National Maturity

The clash between the English and Australian cultures, already resolved in part by such earlier writers as Lawson, Paterson and Rudd, gradually disappeared during the twentieth century as national maturity advanced. Both the colonial dependence upon England and the nationalist resentment of English attitudes have died out for the Australian people as a whole. For it the colonial and nationalist phases are over, with only a few exceptions.

Some of the older generation, including a few writers, critics, and members of literary groups, still cling to an old-fashioned nationalism of a sentimental, uncritical kind. The colonial inferiority complex, too, still lingers on in a few conservative quarters, such as the churches and universities, and the remnants of academic immaturity remain in the outdated anti-nationalism of an occasional literary critic. Thus a recent collection of critical essays set out to attack any "nationalist

---

[61] Jack Lindsay, "Australian Poetry and Nationalism", *Vision*, no.1, May 1923, p.33.
[62] Ibid., p.34.
[63] Vide John Tregenza, *Australian Literary Magazines of the Last Three Decades*, Paper presented to the Australasian Universities Modern Language Association Conference, Brisbane, 1955.

view of Australian literature".[64] How disastrous this non-literary bias proved to the anthology's literary values was pointed out by discerning critics.[65]

In general, however, Australians have learnt to accept themselves naturally and as a matter of course. This is particularly true of the writers. They have outgrown colonial imitativeness and nationalist aggressiveness. The survival of an Anglo-Australian ambivalence in the family sagas of the expatriate novelist Martin Boyd is a rare exception,[66] and Ray Lawler has also analyzed a special case in his play *The Piccadilly Bushman.*

Australian fiction achieved a general maturity in the late twenties and the thirties when a group of novelists arose, with Katharine Prichard and Vance Palmer in the vanguard, who wrote of their own country naturally and vigorously, catching the rhythms of the people's life and speech. This development marched forward firmly with such novels as *The Fortunes of Richard Mahony, Capricornia, The Battlers* and *The Timeless Land.* In this body of work the Australian values and social patterns are expressed strongly and independently. Whilst the main trends have been towards social realism and the historical novel, there has also been exploration of individual character. From the forties the more imaginative and spiritual elements were developed by a number of novelists of whom Patrick White has been outstanding. The contemporary novel, like the modern Latin American literature described earlier by Alfonso Reyes, "does not stop with the easy achievement of local colour, but attempts to plumb the depths of our psychological realities."

In poetry Slessor and FitzGerald in the thirties led the development of a mature, independent treatment of Australian themes with individual vision and contemporary idiom. Today there is virtually no trace of colonialism or any cultural clash in the poets.

The change from the colonial complex to national maturity can be illustrated clearly by extracts from a poem of the first world war and one of the second. Thus Corporal J. D. Burns, killed on Gallipoli, in "For England"[67] wrote:

[64] Grahame Johnston (ed.), *Australian Literary Criticism* (Melbourne 1962), Introduction, p.viii.

[65] See A. A. Phillips, "Criticising the Critics" in *Meanjin*, no.93, vol.XXII, no.2, 1963, pp.220-5, and Dr Brian Elliott, "Charmed Circle" in *Australian Book Review*, vol.2, no.7, May 1963, p.107.

[66] This point seems to be misunderstood in the otherwise penetrating study by Professor Kathleen Fitzpatrick, *Martin Boyd and the Complex Fate of the Australian Novelist* (Canberra University College 1953).

[67] In Walter Murdoch and Alan Mulgan, *A Book of Australian and New Zealand Verse* (Oxford 1950), p.212.

The bugles of England were blowing o'er the sea,
As they had called a thousand years, calling now to me;
They woke me from dreaming in the dawning of the day,
The bugles of England—and how could I stay?

In "Argument"[68] John Quinn reflects over the body of his mate, killed in the second world war:

You can't argue with a dead man.
. . . You can look at him helplessly,
You can think,
"Once he chattered
And grew indignant over pots of beer,
Grew red in the face,
Or laughed
And said, 'You lovely bastard, you!' "
. . . Lay his head in the mud again,
Wipe the blood from your hands.
You can't argue with a dead man.

Both poems have a moving force and sincerity, but they differ sharply in sentiment and diction. Burns looks to England and expresses a romantic patriotism in traditional terms of bugles and banners. Quinn is grimly realistic and speaks in colloquial Australian. His feeling is deeply individual, but its poignance is universal in quality since here, as Wilfred Owen once said of his war poems, "The poetry is in the pity." "For England" is local in comparison, since its appeal is directed especially to those who hold England dear. "Argument" is more advanced, more mature, in that it reaches for the universal through the individual emotion and vision. This maturity is characteristic of our best contemporary poetry. In drama Ray Lawler's *Summer of the Seventeenth Doll* won international success in England, America and Germany as a play which is not only effective theatre and distinctively Australian in setting and character, but also universal in its theme.

Amongst the writers, then, the national scene is usually treated with a natural acceptance, and the attitude towards their own country, if "nationalist", is the mature one, devoid of chauvinism or provincialism, which has been expressed by Mary Gilmore in her poem "Nationality":[69]

I have grown past hate and bitterness,
I see the world as one;
But though I can no longer hate,
My son is still my son.

All men at God's round table sit,
And all men must be fed;
But this loaf in my hand,
This loaf is my son's bread.

[68] John Quinn, *Battle Stations* (Sydney 1944), pp.17-18.
[69] Mary Gilmore, *Fourteen Men* (Sydney 1954), p.2.

VI

Realism

And of furniture, there's no such thing, 'twas never in the place,
Except the stool I sit upon—and that's an old gin-case.
It does us for a safe as well, but you must keep it shut,
Or the flies would make it canter round the old bark hut.

Chorus In an old bark hut, in an old bark hut.
Or the flies would make it canter round the old bark hut.

OLD BUSH SONG[1]

Draw a wire fence and a few ragged gums, and add some scattered sheep running away from the train, Then you'll have the bush all along the New South Wales western line from Bathurst on . . . .
We crossed the Macquarie—a narrow, muddy gutter with a dog swimming across, and three goats interested . . . .
At 5.30 we saw a long line of camels moving out across the sunset. There's something snaky about camels. They remind me of turtles and goannas.
Somebody said, "Here's Bourke."

HENRY LAWSON[2]

It had always been my wish to write a book about Australia—not a romantic story of the convicts or bushrangers of which we have heard so much, but a plain unvarnished tale of the hard life actually lived, in a new, hard country, by the early settlers . . . . Money is as much the protagonist in the book as Richard Mahony himself.

HENRY HANDEL RICHARDSON[3]

Always something of a frustrated painter, and a composer manqué I wanted to give my book the textures of music, the sensuousness of paint, to convey through the theme and characters of *Voss* what Delacroix and Blake might have seen, what Mahler and Liszt might have heard. Above all I was determined to prove that the Australian novel is not necessarily the dreary, dun-coloured offspring of journalistic realism.

PATRICK WHITE[4]

[1] "The Old Bark Hut", A. B. Paterson (ed.), *Old Bush Songs* (Sydney 1912), p.13.
[2] "In a Dry Season", Henry Lawson, *Prose Works* (Sydney 1935), pp. 61-3.
[3] Henry Handel Richardson, "Notes on My Books", *Virginia Quarterly Review* (Charlottesville), vol.XVI, no.3, June 1940.
[4] Patrick White, "The Prodigal Son", *Australian Letters*, April 1959, p.39.

No Romeos

"Where's your romance?" an Austrian friend asked me after making some researches in Australian literature. Coming from Vienna, the city where love had been the perennial subject of poems and plays, he was especially puzzled by its relative absence from our writing. "Where's your *Romeo and Juliet?*" he inquired earnestly.

I had to explain, apologetically, that we had, with some exceptions, not a great deal of romance; that Australians were practical, realistic people who were lacking in high passion. Even its poets could not rise to the passionate Romeo crying

> *She speaks!*
>
> *O, speak again, bright angel! for thou art*
> *As glorious to this night, being o'er my head,*
> *As is a winged messenger of heaven*
> *Unto the white-upturned wondering eyes*
> *Of mortals that fall back to gaze on him*
> *When he bestrides the lazy-pacing clouds*
> *And sails upon the bosom of the air.*[5]

Its treatment of love, in fact, is a touchstone which shows how Australian writing runs to realism rather than romance, since it is the theme of love that usually evokes most strongly the essential qualities of romanticism: the stress on the personal and the emotional, together with the imaginative concern with beauty and wonder. Realism, on the other hand, contradicts the classic dictum of Keats that "Beauty is truth, truth beauty" and makes a sharp dichotomy. It aims at truth, and tends to find it far from beautiful. Where the romantic imagines the ideal, the realist observes the reality of the hard fact and reports his objective findings. He looks outwards, not inwards, and thus is moved, not to the delight of wonder, but rather to the cynicism of disillusionment or a stoic acceptance that such is life.

Burns is the representative romantic when he glories in his love being like a red, red rose. Furphy is the characteristic Australian realist when he pictures Tom Collins

confiding to Mrs. O'Halloran the high respect which Rory's principles and abilities had always commanded. But she was past all that; and I had to give it up. When a woman can listen with genuine contempt to the spontaneous echo of her husband's popularity, it is a sure sign that she has explored the profound depths of masculine worthlessness; and there is no known antidote to this fatal enlightenment.[6]

Our poetry has some good love poetry, of course, and poems of sentiment such as Kendall's melodious "Rose Lorraine", which his editor, Bishop Reed, has praised as "the most beautiful love lyric ever

---

[5] Shakespeare, *Romeo and Juliet*, Act II, Scene 2.
[6] Tom Collins (Joseph Furphy), *Such is Life* (Sydney 1917), p.74.

written by an Australian".[7] This has its charm, but is unequal, and at its best achieves pathos rather than passion. So, too, the humour is better than the sentiment in the love passages of *The Sentimental Bloke*. Brennan's love poetry, though simple and moving, is below his best work on other themes. Hugh McCrae's delightful "Song of the Rain" is most memorable for its pictorial colouring. So, too, in Kenneth Mackenzie's *The Moonlit Doorway* it is not the emotion itself we remember but the rich sensuousness of its scene, "beautiful in its silky moonlit splendour".[8] Mackenzie, a true romantic in *Our Earth*, became a stronger poet in his later work, such as "The Old Inmate", with its compassionate realism. FitzGerald and Slessor have love poems but no major ones, whilst Hope's erotic pieces are candid celebrations, not of love, but of sex, except his noble "Epistle to Venetia Digby". Douglas Stewart's play *The Golden Lover* has lyrical loveliness, but a New Zealand setting. Such modern anthologies as *Poetry in Australia*, Volume II, *Modern Australian Verse*[9] and *New Impulses in Australian Poetry*[10] contain few love poems. Judith Wright commands a true passion, but her most beautiful work in this genre, "Woman to Man", centres, not on romantic love, but on its realistic issue in the child in the womb.

The poet who comes closest to Shakespeare in his feeling for love's magic, its beauty and wonder, is that gentle romantic, Shaw Neilson. Once again there is no passionate exuberance, no fiery Romeo, but a tender delicacy of generalized feeling, as in "You and Yellow Air":

> *You were of Love's own colour*
> *In eyes and heart and hair;*
> *In the dim place of cherry-trees*
> *Ridden by yellow air . . .*
>
> *Out of your eyes a magic*
> *Fell lazily as dew,*
> *And every lad with lad's eyes*
> *Made summer love to you.*[11]

We have the subtle cadences of that lovely poem, "Love's Coming":

> *Without hail or tempest,*
> *Blue sword or flame,*
> *Love came so lightly*
> *I knew not that he came.*[12]

[7] Thomas Thornton Reed, *Henry Kendall: a Critical Appreciation* (Adelaide 1960), p.24.
[8] Kenneth Mackenzie, *Selected Poems* (Sydney 1961), p.12.
[9] Douglas Stewart (ed.), *Poetry in Australia*, vol.II (Sydney 1964).
[10] Rodney Hall and Thomas W. Shapcott (ed.), *New Impulses in Australian Poetry* (Brisbane 1968).
[11] John Shaw Neilson, *Collected Poems* (Melbourne 1934), pp.46-7.
[12] Ibid., p.36.

I

Or the deep feeling in the simplicity of "The Declaration":

> *And I shall love you till the trees*
> *Know neither sun nor rain;*
> *When morning brings no mysteries,*
> *And love can leave no pain.*[13]

Neilson, however, was exceptional in his treatment of love, just as he was unusual as the half-blind bush labourer with hardly any schooling who wrote some of the loveliest lyrics in the English tongue.

Far more characteristic of the common attitude to love in our verse is the short shrift given to it by the old bush songs. Thus the shearer in "The Banks of the Condamine" is impervious to the appeals of his sweetheart to let her go with him or to stay behind and take up a selection, whilst she as a farmer's wife will help him to husk the corn. Anyone who has husked corn by hand will not be surprised at his answer:

> *Oh, Nancy, dearest Nancy,*
> *Please do not hold me back,*
> *Down there the boys are waiting,*
> *And I must be on the track;*
> *So here's a good-bye kiss, love,*
> *Back home here I'll incline*
> *When we've shore the last of the jumbucks*
> *On the banks of the Condamine.*[14]

And so one more Australian leaves his love to go off with "the boys" in typical off-hand fashion—just as in mixed parties today the men desert their women to join together over the drinks.

The bush balladists, too, with the partial exception of Ogilvie, cherished no Romeos. Theirs was largely a masculine world. They stood in significant contrast to the frontier balladry and films of the American Wild West, replete with romantic sentiment and "love interest". Paterson, the best of them, represented their realism in his ballad "Conroy's Gap". He tells how Ryan, a sheep thief, is caught drunk at the grog-shop under Conroy's Gap by the trooper, and handcuffed. Kate Carew, however, a girl in the shanty bar who loves Ryan, enables him to escape on her wonder horse, the Swagman, the pride of the district, and the trooper fired too late

> *As they raced away, and his shots flew wide,*
> *And Ryan no longer need care a rap,*
> *For never a horse that was lapped in hide*
> *Could catch the Swagman in Conroy's Gap.*

---

[13] James Devaney (ed.), *Unpublished Poems of Shaw Neilson* (Sydney 1947), p.37.
[14] Douglas Stewart and Nancy Keesing (ed.), *Old Bush Songs* (Sydney 1957), pp.257-8.

So far the tale is a straight bush romance. Then Paterson gives the realistic twist at the end:

> *And that's the story. You want to know*
> *If Ryan came back to his Kate Carew;*
> *Of course he should have, as stories go,*
> *But the worst of it is, this story's true:*
> *And in real life it's a certain rule,*
> *Whatever poets and authors say*
> *Of high-toned robbers and all their school,*
> *These horsethief fellows aren't built that way.*
>
> *Come back! Don't hope it—the slinking hound,*
> *He sloped across to the Queensland side,*
> *And sold the Swagman for fifty pound,*
> *And stole the money, and more beside.*
> *And took to drink, and by some good chance*
> *Was killed—thrown out of a stolen trap.*
> *And that was the end of this small romance,*
> *The end of the story of Conroy's Gap.*[15]

In prose, we find, once again, that the treatment of love is realistic rather than romantic or is a blend of the two elements, as in Christina Stead's *For Love Alone* and Eve Langley's *The Pea-pickers*. True, the tremor of youth's first love is suggested effectively in *The Young Desire It* of Seaforth (Kenneth) Mackenzie, with a poetic prose, as when the lad Charles watches the girl Margaret in the bush:

She was very beautiful, he thought. She reminded him, with her effortless stillness, of a sunny day in the hollow valleys of those remote hills hidden now in the rain. Such days were always waiting, still and golden but terribly alert, shining like a girl, but as watchful, and as full of disturbing secrecy.[16]

Henry Lawson, too, has caught love's feeling with understanding in "Joe Wilson's Courtship", whilst the intimacy of married love is evoked with delicate restraint in the later story, "A Double Buggy at Lahey's Creek", with its exquisite ending. Yet here, as always in his best stories, Lawson remains essentially a realist.

We often find love stories treated romantically, of course, in our minor fiction, such as the historical romances of Catherine Gaskin and E. V. Timms, but rarely in the more significant novels. In *Working Bullocks* Katharine Prichard invests the coming together of Red Burke and Deb in the forest with a warm lyricism springing out of her strong feeling for nature and deepened by her Lawrentian belief in the primacy of passion. She gives the union of Hughie and Coonardoo a similar romantic beauty that reminds us that her first book was a volume of poetry. In both novels, however, she develops

[15] A. B. Paterson, *Collected Verse* (Sydney 1921), pp.22-3.
[16] Seaforth (Kenneth) Mackenzie, *The Young Desire It* (London 1937), p.107.

her love theme realistically so that in the end she emerges as a poetic realist rather than a pure romantic. So, too, does Mary Durack in her handling of the relationship between Rolf and Dalgerie in *Keep Him My Country*.

Furphy, the veracious, makes both Tom Collins and Rigby the very reverse of Romeos, and their "love affairs" are marked by irony and indifference. In *Maurice Guest* Richardson deals powerfully with an obsessive passion that holds many elements of nineteenth century romanticism, but she does this by the method of psychological realism. In *The Fortunes of Richard Mahony* the marriage of Richard and Mary begins in an atmosphere of Victorian gentility, sometimes coyly sentimental but never passionate, and it ends with Mary as the protective mother caring for the ruined Richard. In *The Passage* Vance Palmer evokes his setting eloquently but when he arrives at moments of passion, here, as in his other novels, he grows tongue-tied or stammers banalities. Sensitive and perceptive when exploring various human relationships, he is never quite happy with his lovers. Although Eleanor Dark is a romantic in some aspects, when analysing a variety of love's manifestations she employs the surgeon's detachment as well as his skill. There is no room for a Romeo in Xavier Herbert's gusty, turbulent world, nor in the commonplace reportings of the social realists. The cultivated intelligence, satiric wit, and cool urbanity which are Martin Boyd's notable qualities conflict with a romantic view of love, and when he essays this the results, like Lucinda Brayford's experiences, are not felicitous. The love interest turns sentimental or, as in *Outbreak of Love*, grows curiously pallid. Here the author's description of the character Russel might even be applied to himself: "His perfect manners were a gilded cage in which he kept the fluttering bird of his emotions.... The trouble was that when he opened the door of the cage, the bird, confined for so long, was unable to spread its wings."[17] So, too, in *Voss* Patrick White is compellingly successful with the romantic journeyings both outward and inward, of his explorer, but the surrealist union of Voss and Laura is a bloodless nexus, a shadowy intangible.

The Determinants of Realism

What were the forces causing this undeniable dominance of realism seen so strongly even in the treatment of love, the very centre of romanticism? Once again the answer comes clearly as an ecological synthesis combining certain distinctive elements of the People and the Place.

[17] Martin Boyd, *Outbreak of Love* (London 1957), p.66.

With the people, history had ruled that their character should be determined by three factors: their British origin, the convict system, and the relative importance of the working class.

The British settlement, as I have pointed out in Chapter II, brought the heritage of a practical temper to the Australian colonies. A realistic outlook was traditional amongst the English and Scottish immigrants. The Irish cherished a romantic imagination, but this was subdued harshly by the conditions in which the Irish were placed as either convicts or immigrants of the lowest social and economic class. There were few Irish settlers like the Anglo-Irish Samuel Pratt Winter, aristocratic and cultured, with his library and beautifully furnished mansion at Murndal. There was little opportunity for the great mass of poor Irish to be anything but realistic, and often grimly so.

The general temper of the society has been strongly utilitarian, extrovert, with little feeling for the life of the mind and spirit. Observers from overseas and local critics have joined in a consensus of opinion on this point. There is some acid truth in D. H. Lawrence's criticism here through the voice of Somers:

"The Colonies make for *outwardness*. Everything is outward—like hollow stalks of corn. The life makes this inevitable: all that struggle with bush and water and what-not, all the mad struggle with the material necessities and conveniences—the inside soul just withers and goes into the outside, and they're all just lusty robust stalks of people."[18]

This trend to outwardness, this deficiency in the inner life of the emotions and the imagination, this matter-of-factness: all these characteristics of the Australian people are inevitably reflected in the outward-looking realism of the literature—a realism in literary form, opposed to romanticism, and a philosophical realism, opposed to idealism, with stress on things as realities perceived in contrast to the invisible realm of ideas.

For the first half century, the decisive formative period in the development of social and national patterns, furthermore, all colonists, free as well as bond, lived under the dark shadow of the convict system, and no system could have been imagined that would have promoted realism more powerfully and inescapably. Geoffrey C. Ingleton's collection of broadsides, *True Patriots All* alone offers sufficient evidence as to why realism prevailed in the early settlements. The brutal facts of the historical records formed the basis of the penal settlement horrors in *For the Term of His Natural Life* and the grim convict tales of Price Warung. That sober and humane observer Alexander Harris recorded his own experience of the workings of the system for assigned convicts:

[18] D. H. Lawrence, *Kangaroo* (Penguin ed. 1950), p.146.

On many farms it was quite a standing axiom that a prisoner was of no use till he had been twice or thrice flogged.... The slightest occasion, therefore, was laid hold of for sending him to court; and it was generally tolerably well known what would be the result ....

On many farms, ration was so parsimoniously given, and work extorted with such an exorbitant avidity, that no man of an ordinary appetite had anything to eat after Thursday night. There was then Friday and Saturday, till late in the afternoon, to be got over without food.... But all the while the work must be done.[19]

The realism compelled by the convict system was reinforced by that of the working class, who enjoyed a greater importance in shaping social patterns here than in England or Europe, as we have seen, and was far more important in literature here than overseas because of the "proletarian preference" given to it by our writers. Its realistic outlook thus coloured the writing to a special degree.

The Shaping Land

Finally came the determinant of Place, with the hardships and vicissitudes of pioneering forcing all men to be hard-headed, strong-handed realists in order to survive. This struggle is vividly illustrated by Brian Penton in his novel *Landtakers* in many realistic passages, such as the one describing the grog shanty visited by the young Englishman Derek Cabell:

Really the scene was commonplace enough: a number of settlers with unkempt beards and dusty clothes who passed the time drinking while their convict servants were being flogged; a few soldiers, drunk and quarrelsome, and half a dozen bodies stretched out in the dirt, dead-drunk. But for some reason he never forgot it.... In his mind those faces and voices became a symbol, apparently, of all the ruthless, unscrupulous, man-against-man struggle that was the life of this epoch.[20]

Drought, too, often destroyed the patient, determined battling of years. Margaret Kiddle, for instance, has described in a chapter entitled "The Bad Times" the effects of the drought of 1838-40, with squatters boiling down their sheep for tallow or losing their stations; the unemployment, bankruptcies, and bank smashes. One squatter reported: "About twenty of the squatters in the Portland Bay District —were sold off. Three or four I know compromised for less than half with their creditors—there is not one station that I know but my own [and two others] that is occupied by the original squatter."[21]

The tribulations of the selectors have been described by many writers, notably Steele Rudd and Henry Lawson. In *On Our Selection*

---

[19] Alexander Harris, *The Emigrant Family*, ed. by W. S. Ramson (Canberra 1967 ed., first publ. London 1849), p.188.

[20] Brian Penton, *Landtakers* (Sydney 1934), pp.15-16.

[21] Margaret Kiddle, *Men of Yesterday* (Melbourne 1961), pp.135-6.

Rudd describes the tough slogging put in by Dad and his boys to put in a field of corn. The crop turns out a good one, and Dad expected a big cheque when the storekeeper sold the corn. All the family dwelt on what necessities they were going to buy out of the cheque. At last word comes of the sale.

The storekeeper looked at Dad and twirled a piece of string round his first finger, then said—"Twelve pounds your corn cleared, Mr. Rudd; but, of course" (going to a desk), "there's that account of yours which I have credited with the amount of the cheque—that brings it down now to just £3, as you will see by the account."
Dad was speechless, and looked sick.
He went home and sat on a block and stared into the fire with his chin resting in his hands, till Mother laid her hand upon his shoulder and asked him kindly what was the matter. Then he drew the storekeeper's bill from his pocket, and handed it to her, and she too sat down and gazed into the fire. That was *our* first harvest.[22]

Lawson gives many pictures of the harsh, drab, soul-destroying struggle of selectors. They are one-sided, perhaps, yet the truth was often grim enough in poverty, unremitting toil, loneliness, and the disillusionment of a meagre reward or life on a near-starvation level. The sketch "Settling on the Land" is hardly exaggerated as it relates the story of Tom Hopkins and his indomitable fight on a run at Dry Hole Creek, struggling with operations like clearing and grubbing stumps, rust in the wheat, the diseases of "th' ploorer" amongst his milkers and the strangles with his plough-horses, a hailstorm destroying the entire fruit crop, the inevitable drought and flood, and a bitter, losing battle with a neighbouring squatter. The sketch is not only an effective example of realism but also a pointer to the way the environment determined the realistic character of our writing, the ecology shaping the ethos.

Romanticism in Poetry

Let us now examine, in a broader sweep, the various manifestations of romanticism and realism in turn as they occur, first in poetry, then in fiction and drama.

It is in poetry, of course, and especially in the lyric, with its personal and emotional qualities, that we naturally find the commonest expression of the romantic spirit. Again, the English literary history, which influenced the Australian poetry so deeply in the nineteenth century, meant that our poets, after early attempts in the neo-classic modes of the eighteenth century, followed the conventions of the English Romantic Revival until the modernism that began with Slessor in the 1930s. Harpur, Gordon, and Kendall; Brennan,

22 Steele Rudd (Arthur Hoey Davis), *On our Selection* (Sydney 1899), p.13, "Our First Harvest".

O'Dowd, and Baylebridge; Daley and Quinn, McCrae and Neilson; the descriptive poets of nature, such as Dorothea Mackellar: all these were romantics. The romantic element of wonder, for instance, had its finest exponent in Neilson.

Furthermore, from the 1930s onward the romantic impulse found voice in a series of "voyager poems" on the characters and exploits of the explorers on both the sea and the land. Yet the expression of such poems by Slessor, FitzGerald, Stewart, Hart-Smith, Webb, and McAuley was as much realist as romantic in its terms, usually combining both elements in a skilful and forceful balance. They belong only partially to romanticism. This is true also of the modern nature poems by such poets as Judith Wright, Roland Robinson, and David Campbell.

The most complete of the romanticists, the one with the deepest romantic sensibility, was undoubtedly Brennan. His main work belongs to the English romantic movement of the nineties, and was influenced, like it, by developments in Europe. Professor G. A. Wilkes puts this point beyond doubt, and he concludes: "The Edenic vision ruling Brennan's verse ascribes it to a phase of late nineteenth-century romanticism, and his resort to conventions like *ennui*, narcissism, synthaesia and the *femme fatale* makes the ascription more definite."[23]

Indeed, it is fascinating how much of *The Romantic Agony* of Mario Praz, excluding some pathological elements, is applicable to Brennan. Praz opens his chapter on the *femme fatale*, entitled "La Belle Dame Sans Merci", for instance, with a reference to Lilith, the legendary symbol adopted by Brennan. Brennan's pictures of ecstasy, especially in the poem "I saw my life as whitest flame", his constant sense of himself as an exile, and his concept of reality: all these illustrate the statement of Praz in the above chapter:

the exoticist, who is an "ecstatic"—an exile from his present and actual self—is also endowed with a sort of metaphysical intuition which discerns, behind the complex outwards appearances of things, the permanence of a unique essence.[24]

Again, "the tempestuous loveliness of terror" found by Shelley in a painting of the Medusa, explored by Praz as an important element of Romanticism, is also embodied in Brennan's Lilith, particularly in the poem "She is the night: all horror is of her", with its final stanza rising to an apogee of romanticism far beyond the grasp of realism alone:

[23] G. A. Wilkes, "Brennan and His Literary Affinities", *The Australian Quarterly*, vol.XXXI, no.2, June 1959.
[24] Mario Praz, *The Romantic Agony*, trans. from the Italian by Angus Davidson (London 1960 ed., first publ. 1933), pp.227-8.

All mystery, and all love, beyond our ken,
she woos us, mournful till we find her fair:
and gods and stars and songs and souls of men
are the sparse jewels in her scatter'd hair.[25]

So, too, another book dealing acutely, like that of Praz, with certain significances of Romanticism, Frank Kermode's *Romantic Image*, contains much that is relevant to Brennan and helpful to the interpretation of his work, especially in regard to his theory and use of symbolism, one form of nineteenth century neo-romanticism. It quotes, for instance, a statement of Yeats defining his concept of the symbol: "A symbol is indeed the only possible expression of some invisible essence, a transparent lamp about a spiritual flame."[26] This is virtually identical with Brennan's view of the poetic symbol as the embodiment of an ideal reality, expounded in his "Symbolism in Nineteenth Century Literature".[27] Again, in his "Fact and Idea" Brennan holds that we have some indication of a state in which the Ideal, the image of the infinite,

would be given in direct intuition, where thought would be like quivering flame, inseparable from sense, emotion, and imagination. Of such perfect Life all beautiful things by their perfection—limited, 'tis true—are the fitting symbols.[28]

In his paper "Vision, Imagination, and Reality" he declares:

What cannot be described can be adumbrated through symbols, can be hinted at through analogies. The imagination can give us a projection of the reality —our true relation to the spiritual principle of reality—on this life of ours.[29]

In his comprehensive development of the Lilith figure he put his theory into practice and poured into her image a number of the romantic concepts detailed by Mario Praz, with protean changes of her personality as a complex symbol to adumbrate different aspects of reality.

It is ironic, however, that Brennan, for all his learning and his labouring in the steps of Mallarmé, rarely created symbols with the assurance, the originality, and the freshness with which they flowed so freely from Neilson, welling spontaneously up from the intuitive depths of his genius. I have always felt that here he went beyond magic to the miraculous, and was happy when this feeling was confirmed by Professor Chisholm when he declared:

[25] A. R. Chisholm and J. J. Quinn (ed.), *The Verse of Christopher Brennan* (Sydney 1960), p.144, "Lilith" sub-section.
[26] Frank Kermode, *Romantic Image* (London 1961, first publ. 1957), p.113.
[27] A. R. Chisholm and J. J. Quinn (ed.), *The Prose of Christopher Brennan* (Sydney 1962). See pp.54-7, 60, 81, 86-8.
[28] Ibid., p.11.
[29] Ibid., p.38.

For me, it is one of the miracles of poetry that a simple Australian bushman and manual worker like Shaw Neilson should often achieve, without knowing it, some of the effects which French symbolists achieved by years of patient thought and by the elaboration of an extremely subtle technique.[30]

Such lyrics as "Love's Coming", "Song Be Delicate", "Break of Day" and "The Orange Tree" are the very alchemy of romantic poetry, changing ordinary substances into a mysterious golden wonder, glowing with an unexpected beauty. They share an affinity with the ballads of the Spanish poet Lorca. His "Romance Sonámbulo" ("Somnambular Ballad"), for instance, has Neilson's simplicity, sense of the unseen, and love for the colour green, which was one of his favourite symbols:

> Con la sombra en la cinture
> ella sueña en su baranda,
> verde carne, pelo verde,
> con ojos de fría plata.
> Verde que te quiero verde.
> Bajo la luna gitana,
> las cosas la están mirando
> y ella no puede mirarlas.[31]

(With the shadow at her waist she dreams on her balcony, green flesh, green hair, and eyes of cold silver. Green, green, I love you green. Beneath the gipsy moon, things are looking at her, things she cannot see.)

We are reminded here of the poet questioning the girl in "The Orange Tree", of Neilson's green as "a dear colour", of "green joy running out and in", and "the rustling of green girls Under a white sky".

Realism in Poetry

Side by side with the romantic strain, however, has run a notable variety of realistic poetry, expressing itself in three distinct forms: the bush balladry, both folk and literary; humour and satire; and modern intellectualist realism. The first two of these forms demand some special emphasis, since the general anthologies of verse have commonly overlooked them, thus giving a distorted and false view of the verse written in the nineteenth century. Except for a few bush ballads, the anthologists presented nothing but romanticism. The realism was almost completely cut out of the poetic reckoning. Only one general anthology, for example, has given representation to the old bush songs.[32]

[30] A. R. Chisholm (ed.), *The Poems of Shaw Neilson* (Sydney 1965), Introduction, p.15.
[31] *The Penguin Poets: Lorca*, ed. by G. L. Gili (Middlesex 1960), p.39.
[32] *Poetry in Australia*, ed. T. Inglis Moore and Douglas Stewart, vol.1, *From the Ballads to Brennan* (Sydney 1964).

These folk ballads have obvious limitations. Often rough and ready in versecraft, sometimes descending to doggerel, they lack the imagination, dramatic passion, and verbal felicity that make the best English and Scottish Border ballads such stirring poetry. But poetry in the high sense only touches the old bush songs occasionally. We get glimpses of it in the sorrowful cadences of "The Dying Stockman" and the ringing refrain of "The Wild Colonial Boy", in the defiant passion that moves "Jim Jones" and "John Donahue and His Gang". The last songs have something of the dramatic intensity that rises to tragic heights in "Edward, Edward". The supernatural and the world of fantasy, however, are completely missing: there is nothing to suggest such haunting ballads as "Tam Lin" and "The Wife of Usher's Well".

Undiluted realism and earthy humour: these are the two characteristics marking almost all the folk songs. They are often combined, as in the picture by Bob the swagman of "The Old Bark Hut", already quoted.

For pure, sardonic realism it is hard to beat the recital of the woes of a selector's family when the breadwinner was hauled off to jail for following the ancient bush custom of duffing his neighbour's cattle, as related in "Stir the Wallaby Stew":

> *Poor Dad he got five years or more as everybody knows,*
> *And now he lives in Maitland Jail with broad arrows on his clothes,*
> *He branded all of Brown's clean-skins and never left a tail,*
> *So I'll relate the family's woes since Dad got put in jail.*
>
> *Chorus So stir the wallaby stew,*
> *Make soup of the kangaroo tail,*
> *I tell you things is pretty tough*
> *Since Dad got put in jail.*
>
> *Our sheep were dead a month ago, not rot but blooming fluke,*
> *Our cow was boozed last Christmas Day by my big brother Luke,*
> *And Mother has a shearer cove for ever within hail,*
> *The family will have grown a bit since Dad got put in jail.*[33]

The Bush Ballads

Like their prototype, the folk songs, the literary bush ballads are another exercise in realism. This is one main reason why, as Douglas Stewart has rightly claimed, they, "taken as a body, are the most distinctively national statement Australian poetry has yet made".[34] Nor is his comment exaggerated when he states: "What distinguishes these ballads from merely light, merely comic verse is the impression

[33] Douglas Stewart and Nancy Keesing (ed.), *Old Bush Songs* (Sydney 1957), p.195.
[34] Douglas Stewart and Nancy Keesing (ed.), *Australian Bush Ballads* (Sydney 1955), Preface, p.xii.

that they all convey of an underlying reality, a significance. The red earth is in them; the Australian national character."[35]

The bush balladists were not lacking in imagination and feeling: the ring of poetry sounds far more often than in the old bush songs—in Barcroft Boake's "Where the Dead Men Lie", in Paterson's "The Man from Snowy River", in the final memorable stanza of Lawson's "Ballad of the Drover", with its deeply felt image of the riderless packhorse taking home his dumb tidings of the drover's death, and the true Border ballad intensity, simple and sharp, of Ogilvie's finely dramatic ballad "The Death of Ben Hall", with its vivid sketch of the hunted outlaw:

> *But every night when the white stars rose*
> *He crossed by the Gunning Plain*
> *To a stockman's hut where the Gunning flows,*
> *And struck on the door three swift light blows,*
> *And a hand unhooked the chain.*[36]

Ogilvie, it is true, introduced a romantic sentiment into some of his ballads, especially into the old favourite of many bushmen, "The Riding of the Rebel". But this is alien to the true bush ballad, and Ogilvie himself is best in his more realistic pieces, such as "How the Fire Queen Crossed the Swamp", and "From the Gulf". Paterson, the leader of the balladists, has an occasional dash of sentiment for the bush life, as in "Clancy of the Overflow", but he is most himself in his stories of realism and humour. His realistic treatment of the love theme in "Conroy's Gap", discussed earlier, is characteristic both of himself and the bush ballad.

Satire and Humour

The mode of satire and humour joins the folk songs and the bush ballads to strengthen the body of popular, realistic writing, native in character and style, and to disprove the orthodox view of Australian nineteenth century poetry as mainly a local imitation of the English Romantic Movement. This mode began early in the very first verse printed in Australia, a sardonic, realistic *jeu d'esprit* published by the literary-minded convict George Howe, first Australian editor, in the second issue of his weekly paper, the *Sydney Gazette*, in 1803. It dealt with the tragic domestic effects of the period's notorious indulgence in rum:

A RUM EFFECT

> *"My wife's so very bad", cry'd Phil,*
> *"I fear she'll never hold it;*
> *She KEEPS her bed." "Mine's worse," said Will,*
> *"The Jade this morning SOLD it."*[37]

---

[35] Ibid., p.xx.   [36] Ibid., p.5.   [37] Anon., *Sydney Gazette*, 12 March 1803.

In the early days at Sydney satires abounded in the form of "pipes", lampoons, or pasquinades, many extremely libellous, in what one editor called "a most pugnacious colony". Satire in a genuinely literary form flourished during the years 1844 to 1848 in the *Atlas*, founded and largely edited by the brilliant Robert Lowe, afterwards on his return to England to become Viscount Sherbrooke and Chancellor of the Exchequer. The *Atlas*, urbane and cultured, specialized in political satire and raised journalism to literature, especially in the satiric verse of Lowe and William Forster, who afterwards became, for a brief reign, Premier of New South Wales as well as a poetic dramatist. Governor George Gipps was the chief target for the satirical arrows of the *Atlas*, notably in Forster's "The Devil and the Governor", in which the Devil calls on Gipps and warns him to be more moderate in his devilry:

> *You're too violent far,—you rush too madly*
> *At your favourite ends and spoil them sadly.*
> *Already, I warn you, your system totters,*
> *They're a nest of hornets these rascally Squatters,*
> *Especially when you would grasp their cash—*
> *Excuse me, George, but I think you're rash.*[38]

Lowe's "Songs of the Squatters" are lively pieces of realism. The best known of these is an attack on the Commissioner of Lands and the treatment of the squatters by the Gipps administration. Another imagines the squatter addressing his bride before they go up country to his run, telling her of the delights in store:

> *The whizzing mosquito*
> *Shall dance o'er thy head,*
> *And the guana shall squat*
> *At the foot of thy bed ...*
> *So fear not, fair lady,*
> *Your desolate way,*
> *Your clothes will arrive*
> *In three months with my dray.*[39]

Lowe and Forster were professional satirists. What is interesting and significant, however, is the constancy with which the romantic poets of the nineteenth century turned to satiric or humorous writing, so that the parallel streams of literary romanticism and popular realism run in the same poet. This writing will be considered more fully in chapter VIII, but its relevance demands brief mention here. Harpur, Kendall, and Daley, for example, all wrote political satires and realistic bush ballads. Daley, in particular, for long considered

[38] W. Forster, "The Devil and the Governor" in G. B. Barton, *The Poets and Prose Writers of New South Wales* (Sydney 1886), p.52.
[39] Robert Lowe, *Poems of a Life* (London 1885), p.79.

only as a poet of delicate dreaming, was an undiluted realist in his satirical work and his witty epigrams. Brunton Stephens may be remembered for his comic verse rather than his serious poetry. In this century Hugh McCrae in his later work turned increasingly to realistic treatment of local subjects. Even Shaw Neilson wrote a delightful satire in "The Sundowner", ballads, and humorous limericks. James Devaney quotes samples of light verse which Neilson wrote to the girl in charge of the office files of the Country Roads Board where he worked in Melbourne, entitled "To the Angel of the Records on Saturday Morning":

> *Angel whose eyes transport us into Heaven,*
> *May I still trembling fall to earth and speak:*
> *Oh, for that file 3/4/6/stroke/II—*
> *Mud in a Culvert—Urgent—Boggy Creek.*[40]

The verse is light enough, yet it symbolizes, in a single stanza, the significant way in which the romantic and realistic trends come together, as point and counterpoint. We find the same parallelism with such contemporary poets and satirists as Hope and McAuley, Dawe and Stow.

In modern Australian poetry, however, the two elements are usually blended in an imaginative consonance of reality. The change came in 1931 with Kenneth Slessor's "Five Visions of Captain Cook", with its sketch of Cook:

> *Cook was a captain of the sailing days*
> *When sea-captains were kings like this,*
> *Not cold executives of company-rules*
> *Cracking their boilers for a dividend*
> *Or bidding their engineers go wink*
> *At bells and telegraphs, so plates would hold*
> *Another pound.*[41]

This was a new way of writing, with a strength and pungency that made painfully manifest the weakness of the conventional descriptive nature verse, in which, during the first decades of the twentieth century, the romantic convention had run to seed in fanciful sentimentalism.

Frank Wilmot ("Furnley Maurice") protested against such tepid verse, and tried to gain fresh vigour by experimenting with the techniques of the American realistic poets. This could have been stimulating and fruitful if it had been followed up, for Australian poetry at this stage badly needed the kind of vitality found, say, in Carl Sandburg's "Smoke and Steel". Unfortunately Wilmot's

[40] James Devaney (ed.), *Unpublished Poems of Shaw Neilson* (Sydney 1947), p.93.
[41] Kenneth Slessor, *Poems* (Sydney 1944), p.57.

Melbourne Odes (1934) were only successful in passages. Wilmot lacked the sense of form and the original craftsmanship in which Slessor excelled. Thus he became a pioneer without followers, and his example of American realism remained singular, whereas Slessor, by introducing the English intellectual realism of Pound and Eliot, joined with FitzGerald in his realistic reflections to shape our modern poetry.

Whereas their successors in Stewart and Judith Wright, Webb and Hope, blended the romantic and realistic strains, the more recent contemporary poets have grown more realistic still. As Hall and Shapcott have rightly claimed, "The maturity of the new impulses is largely intellectual and is inclined to be dispassionate."[42] Though concerned deeply with social tensions, the younger poets preserve a wry detachment. Suspicious of rhetoric and romanticizing, they adopted the characteristically realist demand for truth. As one of them writes:

> *Our singing was intolerably sober*
> *Mistrusting every trill of artifice . . .*
>
> *Now in the shadows of unfriendly trees*
> *We number leaves, discern faint similes*
> *And learn to praise whatever is imperfect*
> *As the true breeding-ground for honesty.*[43]

Such honesty, for example, gives a dramatic twist to Gwen Harwood's poem describing the woman with her four children in the park meeting by chance a former lover and chatting to him:

> *They stand awhile in flickering light, rehearsing*
> *the children's names and birthdays. "It's so sweet*
> *to hear their chatter, watch them grow and thrive,"*
> *she says to his departing smile. Then, nursing*
> *The youngest child, sits staring at her feet.*
> *To the wind she says, "They have eaten me alive."*[44]

Realism in Fiction

If realism joins romanticism as only one of two trends in our poetry, it has been dominant in fiction until challenged by Patrick White. In the novel and short story it has flowed as the Murray, the main stream, with romance furnishing only the minor tributaries.

Thus the novels of the colonial period were mainly realistic, even although some adopted at times certain melodramatic or sentimental conventions of the English Victorian novel, such as unlikely coincidences, mysteries of birth, aristocratic changelings in the hands of

---

[42] Rodney Hall and Thomas W. Shapcott (ed.), *New Impulses in Australian Poetry* (Brisbane 1968), Introduction, p.4.
[43] Ibid., p.133, Chris Wallace-Crabbe, "A Wintry Manifesto".
[44] Ibid., p.63, Gwen Harwood, "In the Park".

sinister gypsies, sensational incidents, straining of events to meet the exigencies of plots, unconvincing love affairs, and happy endings. Some of these curiosities mar the integrity of *The Recollections of Geoffry Hamlyn, The Broad Arrow, For the Term of His Natural Life* and *The Miner's Right*.

Later, popular fiction, of course, has often been romantic, particularly in historical novels, such as the vigorous *Sara Dane* of Catherine Gaskin, the competent series of chronicles by E. V. Timms, and the Tasmanian stories of Roy Bridges and G. B. Lancaster. There are domestic romances that appeal by their charm and skilful character-drawing, such as Cicely Little's *The Lass with the Delicate Air*, and the gay stories of the West Australian Montgomery family by Dorothy Lucie Sanders. Poetic imagination and verbal richness riot romantically in Christina Stead's *The Salzburg Tales*. Fantasy, however, is rare, although it appears in stories by Hugh McCrae and Les Robinson.

From colonial days then, both the novel and the short story have been, as a rule, thoroughly realistic in content and form. The realism, however, has broadly been of two kinds: objective and purposive. The first is exemplified by Furphy, Lawson, and Richardson; the second by the school of social realists and such individual novelists as Xavier Herbert and Kylie Tennant who are "purposive" in the sense that their realistic descriptions are informed with an ethical commitment.

Both kinds of realism are indigenous developments, with the exception of Richardson, the expatriate influenced by European naturalism. They arose naturally out of the character of the people and the pioneering environment, as we have seen. The ideals of radical democracy and the Great Australian Dream, furthermore, stimulated the social realists to attack the injustices of the society. Both kinds of realists adopted realism because, paradoxically enough, they were genuine idealists, serving the ideal of truth or justice.

Both ideals met in Furphy. In *Such is Life* he subjects everything to the dry light of reason, seeking dispassionately to present the life of the Riverina truly, to show squatters and bullock-drivers with equal honesty, good and bad alike. His attitude here is that of the tolerant, mellow, ironic realist, just as he is also the idealist in preaching his pipe-induced philosophy. Nor does his irony preclude compassion, shown especially in the story of Mary O'Halloran. The child lost in the bush, often fatally, is a favourite theme in Australian fiction, and it has usually been given a sentimental treatment, like Marcus Clarke's in the story "Pretty Dick", with its Dickensian pathos laid on thickly. In contrast, Furphy tells the story with immaculate realism, in authentic bush idiom and thus achieves a genuinely tragic poignance.

Lawson and Richardson

Lawson was not the consistent realist that Furphy was; in a few of his earlier short stories and in many of his later ones he descends to sentimentality. In the best work, on the other hand, he rises to a high artistry of realism, varied with a deeply felt sympathy and a genuine humour. He presents the life he knew with honest objectivity, with a faithfulness to the truth akin to the same fundamental quality in Tolstoy and Tchekhov.

The extracts already quoted from "The Drover's Wife" and "In a Dry Season" illustrate clearly the dry detachment and the clear-eyed realism of Lawson's bush sketches. Typical is the laconic comment in "Settling on the Land" when Lawson tells how Tom Hopkins threw up his city job to go on the land, and arranged with his sweetheart to be true to him and wait whilst he went west and made a home: "She drops out of the story at this point."

Perhaps the most telling example of the realistic outlook and style in Australian writing is Lawson's sketch "The Union Buries Its Dead". This describes the funeral of a young man drowned trying to cross a billabong of the Darling, who was found to be a union man:

The departed was a "Roman", and the majority of the town were otherwise—but Unionism is stronger than creed. Liquor, however, is stronger than Unionism; and when the hearse presently arrived, more than two-thirds of the funeral were unable to follow . . . .

Four or five of the funeral, who were boarders at the pub, borrowed a trap which the landlord used to carry passengers to and from the railway station. They were strangers to us who were on foot, and we to them. We were all strangers to the corpse . . . .

We walked in twos. There were three twos.[45]

This realism speaks for itself. Lawson here holds that integrity to truth which founded a tradition followed by the great majority of the novelists—Prichard, Palmer, Davison, Mann, Xavier Herbert and many others.

Closest to Lawson, perhaps, in his objective realism, is Henry Handel Richardson. Her attitude is given in a letter to Nettie Palmer when she praises the faithfulness of E. F. Benson's biography of Charlotte Bronte: "Myths and exaggerations cleared away, and the real woman shown to us. How I do hate the ordinary sleek biography! I'd have every wart and pimple emphasised, every tricky trait and petty meanness brought out."[46] So in her novels she details unremittingly all the weaknesses of her characters—Maurice Guest, Laura Rambotham, Richard and Mary Mahony. She deliberately set out in *The Fortunes of Richard Mahony* to eschew any romantic or senti-

45 Henry Lawson, op. cit., pp.56-9.
46 Nettie Palmer, *Henry Handel Richardson: A Study* (Sydney 1950), p.196.

K

mental treatment of the Australian pioneers, to give a plain story of the hardships of colonial life, and to treat of an immigrant who was a failure. Her handling of Richard's character is so complete, so intimate, and so ruthless that for adequate comparisons of full characterization we must go to such rounded figures of fiction as Becky Sharp, Anna Karenina, and Madame Bovary.

If Richardson drew her technique from European naturalism, her spirit is completely in accord with the realistic tradition of Australian fiction. She herself said "that fact and fiction were so interwoven in the Mahony chronicle that she herself could not tell where one ended and the other began".[47] Her realism is exceptional in its unswerving toughness and meticulous fidelity to fact. How closely she clung to the factual can be seen in the way she used her notebooks and diary for her descriptions, as shown by the analysis of Leonie J. Gibson (now Professor Kramer).[48]

The Social Realists

Few novelists or short story writers achieved the complete objectivity of Lawson and Richardson, although Barbara Baynton stands out among the short-story writers of the *Bulletin* period on account of the starkness of her *Bush Studies*. Such stories as "Squeaker's Mate", "Scrammy 'And" and "The Chosen Vessel" have an unusual intensity, and they place Baynton as the best of these writers after Lawson. Most of them, in fact, are now badly dated through their sentimentality or melodrama, with Price Warung, Dyson, and Dowell O'Reilly best worth consideration. With Price Warung's tales of the convict days we get a realism that is not objective, but purposive, designed to attack the convict system.

The same purposiveness characterizes the modern school of social realists, since they are usually writers of the Left whose purpose is to indict the evils of the social system. They include a group of able and earnest writers, including Katharine Prichard, Frank Hardy, John Morrison, Judah Waten, and Eric Lambert. They have produced work of considerable vigour and occasional power. All can write well. Yet their realism is often, if by no means invariably, flawed by a propagandist narrowness. Katharine Prichard, the most outstanding of these writers, whose gold-fields trilogy has been widely published in translation in European countries behind the Iron Curtain, presents such a one-sided picture of the Western Australian gold-fields that it falls in literary quality below her earlier works of imaginative realism such as *Working Bullocks* and *Coonardoo*.

[47] Ibid., pp.155-6.
[48] See Leonie J. Gibson, *Henry Handel Richardson and Some of Her Sources* (Melbourne 1954).

Others writers of fiction who fall broadly into the genre of social realism, such as Gavin Casey, Alan Marshall, Kylie Tennant, and the Dal Stivens of *Jimmy Brockett*, are purer realists because they do not let their social sympathies, although these are often strong, distort their renderings of life. Such a fine short story as "Short Shift Saturday", for instance, is moving because Gavin Casey lets his criticism of mining conditions remain largely implicit, and concentrates on the human problems of his characters. Kylie Tennant is convincing in her critiques of society partly because they are so graphic, but also because she gives the sense that she is aiming at the truth rather than delivering a message. The social indictment is there, especially in *Tiburon*, *Foveaux*, and *Tell Morning This*, but its edge is not blunted by didacticism.

The most original writer of all the modern realists is Xavier Herbert, who combines a ruthless realism with imagination and vitality, so that he goes beyond his local scene to create a world of his own. At heart he is a moralist, an idealist with passionate beliefs, whose attacks on the white man's treatment of the aborigines are savage. In *Capricornia*, however, he also indicts the universe for its cruelty, futility, and chaos. His conclusion in the end is really that of Boyle in the final words of Sean O'Casey's *Juno and the Paycock*: "th' whole worl's ... in a terr ... ible state o' ... chassis!" It is the universal concept as well as the superb story-telling and imaginative power of the writing itself that makes *Capricornia* one of our major novels. In *Soldiers' Women* Herbert also displays his characteristic qualities, and the anger of the outraged Puritan lends a savagery to his unbridled descriptions of lust on the loose when the American troops "occupied" Sydney during the last war. There are passages of macabre realism that are strongly akin to the work of Zola: the grim abortion chapter could fit into *Thérèse Raquin* and be at home there.

The Realist Theory of Fiction

Behind the realism of Australian fiction lay the historical and environmental determinants analyzed earlier. In some cases, however, there also lay a definite realist theory of fiction—not only that of the social realists, to whom writing was a weapon in a social and political warfare, but also a doctrine of truth to life held by Miles Franklin and Furphy. Both rejected indignantly the orthodox Victorian romance, with its melodrama, artifices of plot, and sentimentality. To them such work was false and artificial. They looked on the romantic as the opposite of the truthful, just as Pepys recorded of the intrigues of the French kings, "These things are almost romantique and yet true."[49]

49 *The Diary of Samuel Pepys* (first publ. 1825), entry for 10 March 1667.

Miles Franklin was only a bush girl of nineteen when she introduced *My Brilliant Career* with a characteristic blast:

This is not a romance—I have too often faced the music of life to the tune of hardship to waste time in snivelling and gushing over fancies and dreams; neither is it a novel, but simply a yarn—a *real* yarn. Oh! as real, as really real—provided life itself is anything beyond a heartless little chimera—it is as real in its weariness and bitter heartache as the tall gum-trees, among which I first saw the light, are real in their stateliness and substantiality . . . .

There is no plot in this story, because there has been none in my life or in any other life which has come under my notice. I am one of a class, the individuals of which have not time for plots in their life, but have all they can do to get their work done without indulging in such a luxury.[50]

This was in 1899. Then, twenty-eight years later, in 1927, writing in her alternative capacity as "Brent of Bin Bin", she returns to the attack to vindicate her realist methods in her introductory note to *Up the Country*, repeating, first, her denunciation of romanticism, second, her defence of realism:

Research among the printed fiction of the time of the early Australian pioneers—forgotten stories like the unfenced graves, stories lacking sufficient literary value and fact to survive—shows that the writers concocted bloody affrays in an attempt spuriously to supply action, plot, thrill.[51]

She tells how the old hands up the country flock around her, with enough material to fill a three-volume novel. " 'Why not?' they cry, 'many times three volumes are written about the absurdest fancies, and we are real?' "[52]

Furphy equally rejected the orthodox romance, notably in his excoriation of *Geoffry Hamlyn*. At the start of *Such is Life* Tom Collins, in contrast, claims for himself the veracity of the chronicler:

Whilst a peculiar defect—which I should scarcely like to call an oversight in mental construction—shuts me out from the flowery path of the romancer, a co-ordinate requital endows me, I trust, with the more sterling, if less ornamental qualities of the chronicler.[53]

Such is Life, of course, far from being the plain chronicle it pretends to be, is the most subtly designed Australian novel, the most original in form, the most ingeniously devised in its elusive ramifications. It is part of the ironic joke that Tom Collins declares, when he makes a shift in his diary device:

The thread of narrative being thus purposely broken, no one of these short and simple analyses can have any connection with another—a point on which I congratulate the judicious reader and the no less judicious writer; for the

[50] Miles Franklin, *My Brilliant Career* (Edinburgh 1901), pp.1-2.
[51] Brent of Bin Bin (Miles Franklin), *Up the Country* (Edinburgh 1931 ed., first publ. 1928), p.viii, Author's Note.
[52] Ibid., pp.vi, viii.
[53] Tom Collins, op. cit., p.1.

former is thereby tacitly warned against any expectation of plot or denoue-
ment, and so secured against disappointment, whilst the latter is relieved from
the (to him) impossible task of investing prosaic people with romance, and a
generally haphazard economy with poetical justice.[54]

Joseph Furphy himself gives the game away in the synopsis-review of
Such is Life he wrote for the *Bulletin* after its publication:

Underneath this obvious dislocation of anything resembling continuous
narrative, run several undercurrents of plot, manifest to the reader, though
ostensibly unnoticed by the author . . . . In fact, the studied inconsecutiveness
of the "memoirs" is made to mask coincidence and cross-purposes, sometimes
too intricate.[55]

"Too intricate": there is something in the admission, and in Douglas
Stewart's comment on Collins: "His over-subtlety, I think, is a fault.
A novel is not a crossword puzzle, and whimsical fellows have no
right to lead their readers up a gum-tree."[56] Yet the design of *Such is
Life* has interesting parallels, in the use of a narrator, the time-shift,
and the device of multiple angles for revealing significances, with the
construction of *The Ring and the Book* and *Lord Jim*. Both Browning
and Conrad, I feel, would have enjoyed Furphy's effective solution of
the dilemma posed for the realist—to reconcile the maintenance of
that "limpid veracity" which presents life faithfully, on the one hand,
with the shaping, on the other hand, of a reality largely fortuitous
into a planned artistic form.

The Faults and Virtues of Realism

The interesting case of Furphy justifies examination because he is
one of the exceptional realists who has captured the virtues of realism
yet skilfully evaded its pitfalls. Although other Australian realistic
writers have not explicitly proclaimed a literary theory, as Miles
Franklin and Furphy did, they have accepted it implicitly as a rule.
Their primary purpose has been, not to shape a work of art in power
or beauty, but to present life honestly. Conditions of pioneering life in
the new land put a premium on sincerity, translated by the writers as
literary integrity. They render life as they see it, and thus escape the
two weaknesses of the Victorian romantic fiction, sentimentality and
melodrama. Furthermore, they draw strength from keeping close to
life. Katharine Prichard has indicated this when she gave her own
creed through her character Sophie in *Black Opal*: "It's good to keep
close to the earth . . . . In tune with the fundamentals, all the great

[54] Ibid., p.52.
[55] Miles Franklin, in association with Kate Baker, *Joseph Furphy: the Legend of a
Man and His Book* (Sydney 1944), p.87.
[56] Douglas Stewart, *The Flesh and the Spirit: an Outlook on Literature* (Sydney
1948), p.138.

things of loving and working—our eyes on the stars."[57] Many of the realists, of course, have their eyes too angrily fixed on social ills to raise them to the stars, but their concentration on actual life and their sincerity often help to give their writing directness, vitality, and, at their best, a genuine power. When the realism is also combined with other qualities such as imagination, intelligence, or wit we get novels of the calibre of *Such is Life, Coonardoo, The Fortunes of Richard Mahony, Capricornia*, and *The Battlers*.

On the other hand, realism as such often has serious defects, apart from the special case of the social realists whose chief failure lies in not being realistic enough, in failing in fidelity to truth because they distort it for non-literary ends. In general, the stress on the rendering of reality means a stress on subject-matter, with a corresponding neglect of artistic form. Truth is all-important, and Beauty can go hang. Indeed, the worship of sincerity often connotes a distrust of craftsmanship as something artificial. Louis Esson, writing from London to Vance Palmer, put his finger on this weakness whilst affirming his own faith in form:

Literature, finally, never exists for its matter. Form, which must be the spiritual element, alone remains.
... strangely enough people seem to despise in Australia the idea of technique, which seems to them pedantic.[58]

This is not true of such realists as Lawson at his best, Furphy, and Richardson, but it is true of many realist writers. Kylie Tennant, for instance, typifies both the virtues and the defects of realism: sincerity in rendering truth to life, strength of observation, and lucid or vivid portrayal of the external world, together with the deficiencies in passion, imagination, the artistry of form, and the creation of the inward and spiritual qualities of the characters.

Kylie Tennant, however, by means of her vitality, wit, and humour, rises, like Lawson, Furphy, and Herbert, above the chief weakness of an undiluted realism—its depressing dullness. Jacques Barzun has commented that in Europe

For fifty years or more after Flaubert, the novel was to be the plausible and minute recital of commonplace events. More than that, because the setting and routine of life were being made increasingly drab by industry, the contents of the novel became more and more dreary and dull.[59]

Here, too, although the best of the realistic novelists of the thirties were vital and interesting, their minor successors in the forties and fifties grew increasingly dull. Earlier Richardson, as Leonie Kramer

[57] Katharine Susannah Prichard, *Black Opal* (Sydney 1946), p.176.
[58] Vance Palmer, *Louis Esson and the Australian Theatre* (Melbourne 1948), pp.30 and 34.
[59] Jacques Barzun, *Classic, Romantic, and Modern* (New York 1961), p.106.

recognized, had sometimes become "a victim of the dictatorship of facts ... dull and prosy",[60] but this was amply redeemed by her mastery of characterization. Lacking this mastery, the social realists tended to be earnest, dull, and depressing with their chronicling of small beer and their predictable black-and-white versions of the villainous rich and the virtuous poor. They failed to understand that art is creation, not reportage, and that sincerity, like patriotism, is not enough.

Thus Patrick White's personal revolt against the dullness of the prevailing realism in the forties was so timely that it swelled into a general revolution in our contemporary fiction. He had been anticipated earlier in the thirties by Christina Stead with her *Seven Poor Men of Sydney*, with its concentration on the emotions and ideas of her suffering characters, merging of reality and illusion, imaginative creation of Sydney, the exuberant richness of its poetic style, and the brilliance of its imagery. But this novel of an expatriate, published in London, made little impact in Australia. It flashed briefly, a strange meteor, its flight almost forgotten. *The Tree of Man* and *Voss*, in contrast, first aroused puzzlement or hostility—exemplified by A. D. Hope's condemnation of White's prose style as "illiterate verbal sludge"—and then a mounting appreciation. Writers and critics alike realized that White had introduced new dimensions of spiritual depth and complex artistry of music and colour far beyond the drab externalities of the local realism. The thinness of the average realistic novel showed up painfully against the rich, dense texture of his writing. The Australian novel could never be the same again. On the other hand, the vein of realism seen in the satirical parts of *The Tree of Man* and *Voss* has grown stronger at times in White's later novels.

Realism in the Drama

Finally, to round off our analysis of the general dominance of realism, we see this exerted in the drama as in fiction. The heroic verse tragedies of the colonial closet plays died a natural death, and from Louis Esson onwards in this century the playwrights turned increasingly to theatrical realism. Esson himself was a romantic at heart, confessing he liked most "the lyric" and "a glimpse of beauty", but he adopted the realistic mode and gave it an authentic shape in his moving play *The Drovers*. Sydney Tomholt gave his romantic feeling and imagination expression in some of his one-act plays, especially the religious and poetic *The Woman Mary*, but his powerful *Anoli the Blind* combined realism with melodrama, whilst

[60] Leonie J. Gibson, op. cit., p.36.

his exploration of a woman's emotions towards a divorced husband in *Bleak Dawn* was uncompromisingly realistic. Even the poet Douglas Stewart blends his native romantic bent with forceful realism in his verse plays. The Ned Kelly legend, for instance, is analysed with balanced detachment and a perceptive sense of the environmental forces at work. His poetic, imaginative form of realism is also seen in the radio verse plays of Alexander Turner, such as the effective *Australian Stages*.

It is significant that the few plays which won success on the stage were all in the idiom of realism, such as Betty Roland's *The Touch of Silk*, Vance Palmer's *The Black Horse*, Henrietta Drake-Brockman's *Men Without Wives*, George Landen Dann's *Fountains Beyond* and Sumner Locke-Elliott's *Rusty Bugles*.

Realism, reinforced by a professional expertise of playwrights who have enjoyed a larger measure of direct experience of the theatre unavailable to the earlier dramatists, is the mark of the outstanding contemporary plays. These have proved themselves in productions overseas as well as in Australia. Ray Lawler's *Summer of the Seventeenth Doll* made a decisive break-through to the professional stage here and won the critics' verdict as the best play of 1957 in London. Richard Beynon's *The Shifting Heart*, whose ending seemed sentimental in its first production but became, by a change of dramatic emphasis, logical and convincing in a later interpretation in 1962 by the Melbourne Union Repertory Theatre, had success in Olivier's London season. Alan Seymour's *The One Day of the Year* analyzed the Anzac Day mystique with straight-forward naturalism, and it, too, was played effectively in England and won appreciation in the French theatre. Ric Throssell's powerful picture of a world destroyed by atomic warfare, *The Day Before Tomorrow*, with various performances in the United Kingdom, including an Edinburgh Festival production, is imaginative realism. All these plays, nevertheless, go beyond reportage to present themes of a universal character in conflicts between reality and illusion, intolerance and compassion, the older and younger generations, or the destructive and regenerative forces within the human spirit.

In drama as in fiction Patrick White has proved an exception proving the rule of realism, but his plays have not had the influence of his novels—partly, perhaps, because of insufficient production owing to the failure of the promised growth of a vigorous national theatre. *The Ham Funeral*, for instance, was playing to full houses in Sydney when its professional run was cut disappointingly short. This experiment in expressionism, with its symbolism, lyrical rhythm of language, and stylization, cut sharply across the contemporary naturalism. In his later plays, however, such as his satire of suburbia in *The Season at Sarsaparilla*, White has grown more realistic in theme and treatment.

As contemporary fiction has moved away from social realism towards the imagination, inwardness, and artistic design of romanticism, whilst our poetry has turned increasingly towards the sober objectivity and detachment of intellectual realism, the old division between romanticism and realism has tended to become blurred. Out of this development may emerge a clearer recognition that, although both forms of writing in world literature can claim their particular masterpieces, the greatest works are often those which combine the best qualities of each and pass beyond their respective limitations. It is now for the romanticist to admit that beauty's true rose is not just a florist's specimen but a plant rooted in earth and fed by dung, and for the realist to lift his eyes from the dung's drabness to catch the glow of a Super Star bloom or incense of a Crimson Glory.

VII

The Cry of the Crow

To love with the spirit is to pity, and he who pities most loves most. Men aflame with a burning charity towards their neighbours are thus enkindled because they have touched the depth of their own misery, their own apparentiality, their own nothingness, and then, turning their newly opened eyes upon their fellows, they have seen that they also are miserable, apparential, condemned to nothingness, and they have pitied them and loved them.

MIGUEL DE UNAMUNO[1]

There is no stretch of land more ancient than this. And so it is blunt and red and barren, littered with the fragments of broken mountains, flat, waterless. Spinifex grows here, but sere and yellow, and trees are rare, hardly to be called trees, some kind of myall with leaves starved to needles that fans out from the root and gives no shade . . . .

What enormous and desolate landscapes are opened by the voice of a lone crow.

RANDOLPH STOW[2]

This land was last discovered; why? A ghost land, a continent of mystery, the very pole disconcerted the magnetic needle so that ships went astray, ice, fog and storm bound the seas, a horrid destiny in the Abrolhos, in the Philippines, in the Tasman Seas, in the Southern Ocean, all protected the malign and bitter genius of this waste land. Its heart is made of salt: it suddenly oozes from its burning pores, gold which will destroy men in greed, but not water to give them drink. Jealous land! Ravishers overbold! Bitter dilemma! And lost legion! Our land should never have been won.

CHRISTINA STEAD[3]

Hark! there's the wail of a dingo,
　　Watchful and weird—I must go,
For it tolls the death-knell of the stockman
　　From the gloom of the scrub down below.

[1] Miguel de Unamuno, *The Tragic Sense of Life* (Fontana Library 1962, first publ. in English translation 1921), p.143.

[2] Randolph Stow, *Tourmaline* (London 1963), pp.7, 11.

[3] Christina Stead, *Seven Poor Men of Sydney* (Sydney 1965 ed., first publ. 1934), p.309.

Chorus Wrap me up with my stockwhip and blanket,
    And bury me deep down below,
   Where the dingoes and crows can't molest me,
    In the shade where the coolibahs grow.

OLD BUSH SONG[4]

The Sombre Tone

St John Ervine, dramatic critic of the *Observer*, was surprised when his old colleague William Moore sent him in 1937 a copy of the anthology of Australian one-act plays which Moore and I had just edited.[5] "I had always imagined Australia," he wrote from London to Moore in Sydney, "as a free and happy land of eternal sunshine. But what impressed me most about your country's plays is their Greek gloom. They are full of the atmosphere of Greek tragedies. I find this astonishing."

Ervine's comments were valid enough, for my friend "Bill" Moore and I had read almost two hundred manuscript plays searching for some comedies to balance the dominance of tragedies. We found several lighter plays by Henrietta Drake-Brockman, Dora Wilcox, and Miles Franklin, but the great majority of playwrights used murder and violence, drought and fear as their themes. The collection thus began with Esson's *Andeganora*, with an aboriginal holding his spear poised to kill an oppressive white man, and goes on to a morality play with the scene laid in the brain of a man just dead. It ends with a murder in a wheat silo and the death of the terrified murderer. The recurrent motif of death appears in the imaginative treatment of ghosts of dead soldiers in the first world war in plays by Edgar Holt and Sydney Tomholt, in Betty Roland's *Morning* and Millicent Armstrong's tense *At Dusk*, and in plays by Leslie Rees, Charles Porter, and Alexander Turner. The collective death rate would be even higher, I think, than in any proportionate volume of Greek or Elizabethan tragedies. The sombre note also comes into grim reminders of the convict days in dramas written by Katharine Susannah Prichard, Stewart Macky, and Vance Palmer.

The "Greek gloom" of these playwrights, however, is not exceptional in Australian writing, and the death motif is repeated in modern

4 "The Dying Stockman", A. B. Paterson (ed.), *Old Bush Songs* (Sydney 1935), p.67.
5 William Moore and T. Inglis Moore (ed.), *Best Australian One-Act Plays* (Sydney 1937).

plays such as *The Fire on the Snow* and *Ned Kelly, The Shifting Heart, The Ham Funeral*, and *Night on Bald Mountain*.

Indeed, although it has received little recognition in our contemporary criticism, a strong note of sombreness has been a distinctive characteristic of our literature from its beginnings down to the present day. It has, of course, been closely associated with the realism just discussed, but has not been confined to it, and has been a feature of romantic writing in both poetry and prose. Indeed, it was frequently noted by early writers as a distinctive mark of the poets.

Thus William Walker in an address on Australian literature in 1864, after praising Harpur and Kendall, said of the latter, "It is to be regretted that most of his subjects as yet are of a melancholy turn", and added in regard to the verses of the now forgotten Geoffrey Eagar, "They are of a melancholy moralizing cast, as most of the Australian poems are".[6]

S. S. Topp wrote in 1876:

A characteristic which must strike every reader of Mr. Kendall is his extreme melancholy . . . . This vein of sadness is not peculiar to Mr. Kendall, but is apparent in Harpur, Gordon, and indeed, all our poets who have passed much of their time in the bush.[7]

Kendall, indeed, had already referred in his elegy on Gordon to

> *The mournful meaning of the undersong*
> *Which runs through all he wrote, and often takes*
> *The deep autumnal, half-prophetic tone*
> *Of forest winds in March.*[8]

In his poem, "An Australian Symphony", George Essex Evans comments more fully on the mournfulness found in Australian poetry:

> *But undertones, weird, mournful, strong,*
> *Sweep like swift currents thro' the song.*
> *In deepest chords, with passion fraught,*
> *In softest notes of sweetest thought,*
> *This sadness dwells.*
>
> *Is this her song, so weirdly strange,*
> *So mixed with pain,*
> *That whereso'er her poets range*
> *Is heard the strain?*
> *Broods there no spell upon the air*
> *But desolation and despair?*

[6] William Walker, *Australian Literature: A Lecture Deliverd at the Windsor School of Arts, on the evening of Wednesday, the 30th of July, 1864*, etc. (Sydney 1864).
[7] S.S.T., "Australian Poetry", *The Melbourne Review*, vol.I, Jan. to Oct. 1876, p.67.
[8] "The Late Mr A. L. Gordon: in Memoriam" in T. Inglis Moore (ed.), *Selected Poems of Henry Kendall* (Sydney 1957), p.67.

No voice, save Sorrow's, to intrude
Upon her mountain solitude
Or sun-kissed plain?

... The grey gums by the lonely creek,
The star-crowned height,
The wind-swept plain, the dim blue peak,
The cold white light,
The solitude spread near and far
Around the camp-fire's tiny star,
The horse-bell's melody remote,
The curlew's melancholy note
Across the night.

These have their message; yet from these
Our songs have thrown
O'er all our Austral hills and leas
One sombre tone.[9]

Evans, like Topp before him, attributed the sombre tone to the bush solitudes, and this was probably right. The realism of the old bush songs and the bush balladists often took a tragic form, from "The Dying Stockman" and "The Wild Colonial Boy" to Boake's "Where the Dead Men Lie" and Lawson's "Ballad of the Drover". A sombreness came from personal sources in later poets like Brennan and Neilson, Slessor and Webb or from the malaise of our unhappy atomic world in Judith Wright, Hall, Shapcott, and other contemporary poets. Only a few poets, such as Daley, McCrae, and Douglas Stewart, have sung with a spontaneous gaiety. Even a strongly affirmative poet like FitzGerald strikes a tragic note in many poems, especially in the narrative *Between Two Tides* and that grim picture of our convict past, *The Wind at Your Door*.

So, too, in prose the sombre tone came early in the novels and stories exposing the brutalities of the convict days. These were followed by writings depicting the hardships of pioneering, such as Lawson's tales and sketches, especially "Water Them Geraniums", and Barbara Baynton's harsh *Bush Studies*. The sombreness continues as Richardson starts her trilogy with a man buried alive on the gold-fields and ends it with Mahony's insanity and death. Christina Stead finds little but tragedy in the dark lives of her seven poor men in the Sydney of depression times. The social realists, from Frank Hardy's *Power Without Glory* and John Morrison's tales of the waterfront to the novels of Dorothy Hewitt and Ron Tullipan, have concentrated on the poverty, hardships and economic exploitation of the workers, and thus become specialists in sombreness. Like Richardson, Kylie Tennant and Patrick White have been deeply concerned with

[9] Walter Murdoch (ed.), *A Book of Australasian Verse* (Melbourne 1945 ed., first publ. 1918), pp.60-1.

the sufferings of society's misfits and failures, the outsiders and the dispossessed. Amongst other significant novelists Katharine Prichard ends *Coonardoo* with the tragic death of the woman who had once been the life-giving well in the shadows, Eleanor Dark limns insanity and death in *Prelude to Christopher*, whilst Xavier Herbert in *Capricornia* not only welters in death and violence but also indicts society of injustice and the universe of chaos. A tragic vision is frequent in contemporary novelists, such as Stow, Turner, and Keneally. Our fiction of today, like our poetry, has little light-heartedness or joie de vivre. It needs a few writers like Joyce Cary and novels like *The Horse's Mouth* to lighten the shadows of sombreness and give an ampler chiaroscuro to its pictures of the human condition.

The Spirit of Charitas

Our writing, then, has expressed, with undeniable sombreness, many of the darker—and often deeper—aspects of life, of the human spirit, and the nature of the universe. Whatever its faults, it cannot be genuinely charged with being superficial or escapist. In a land of sunlight it has not flinched from darkness. Although it has rarely taken a religious or mystical journey into the dark night of the soul, it is none the less spiritual—not merely materialistic—in its open committal to the facing of the tribulations, the sorrows, and the tragedies afflicting the spirit of man. It might say that this committal, like Sir Thomas Browne explaining his regret for the existence of death and diseases incurable, is "for the general cause and sake of humanity, whose common cause I apprehend as mine own".[10] It is thus linked not only with the social pattern of realism but also with that of radical democracy discussed later, since the radical stresses the plight of the oppressed and the underdog whilst the democratic emphasis on the equality of all men inevitably enlarges the writers' franchise of sympathy as he apprehends the common cause of humanity as his own.

Indeed, we can see here the truth of Unamuno's contention in his *Tragic Sense of Life* that man's consciousness of the misery of his fellow men stimulates his pity and even his love. Pity joins with anger at cruelty, for example, in the convict novels and poems. In his best stories Lawson softens the harshness of his subject by a deep sympathy. Patrick White brings compassion as well as sombreness to *The Tree of Man, Riders in the Chariot* and *The Solid Mandala*, so that these works are more effective than his first novel *Happy Valley*, which directs a tragic focus on the darkness of pain, suffering, and frustration with few redeeming rays of pity or love. It is the strength

---

[10] Sir Thomas Browne, *Religio Medici* (Everyman's Library, London), p.81.

and breadth of her sympathy for her diverse characters that gives a warmth to the novels of Kylie Tennant.

It is with the poets especially that we find Unamuno's "burning charity towards their neighbours" enkindled by misery, pain, or death. "Charity" here, of course, means the true rendering of the original Greek "charitas" as "loving-kindness" or "sympathy", as used by Gwen Harwood in her poem "At the Sea's Edge" where a man and a woman describe a gull for the benefit of their blind and disfigured companion:

> *As the three stand*
> *silent, the blind one smiles. From hand to hand*
>
> *a live hope flows. The wind walks on the sea,*
> *printing the water's face with charity.*[11]

This feeling enters, too, into John Manifold's elegy for his friend killed on Crete:

> *While thus the kind and civilised conceal*
>
> *This spring of unsuspected inward grace*
> *And look on death as equals, I am filled*
> *With queer affection for the human race.*[12]

It comes again and again into the gentle tenderness of Shaw Neilson, giving a depth to such pieces as "The Poor Can Feed the Birds", and is also a recurrent note with the compassionate Mary Gilmore. A similar breadth of sympathy is expressed by Judith Wright as part of her keen sense of the darkness in the world and in mankind. Francis Webb, the poet who voices anguish most intensely today, brings an equal intensity to his pity in such poems as "A Death at Winson Green", "Harry", and "Ward Two: Pneumo-encephalograph":

> *Let me ask, while you are still,*
> *What in you marshalled this improbable will:*
> *Instruments supple as the flute,*
> *Vigilant eyes, mouths that are almost mute,*
> *X-rays scintillant as a flower,*
> *Tossed in a corner the plumes of falsehood, power?*
> *Only your suffering.*
> *Of pain's amalgam with gold let some man sing*
> *While, pale and fluent and rare*
> *As the Holy Spirit, travels the bubble of air.*[13]

Immersed in suffering in his hospital ward, Webb can yet see the courage, the "improbable will" aroused by the suffering, a redeeming

[11] Gwen Harwood, *Poems* (Sydney 1963), p.97.
[12] John Manifold, *Selected Verse* (London 1948), p.85.
[13] Francis Webb, *The Ghost of the Cock* (Sydney 1964), p.45.

spiritual strength blent with the pain. His tragic vision passes over into charitas.

Forms of Sombreness

If such suffering and pity are universal, the sombreness in our literature has taken certain distinctive forms determined mainly by the ecological forces at work in the organism of the Australian people and its responses to its environment, physical and social alike. It seems to me that there are five such forms: the awareness of suffering already discussed, personal melancholy, the loneliness of isolation, fatalism, and the ultimate void of nihilism.

Undoubtedly the sombreness arises mainly in some cases from the personality and temperament of the writer, combined with adverse circumstances. Essentially personal in character, it is revealed in a melancholy tone. This can be seen particularly in the character, life and work of Harpur, Gordon, Kendall, Lawson, Brennan, and Webb. Every one of these writers had a temperamental strain of melancholy, and this was intensified by unhappy experiences. Harpur had a sternness in him which responded to the gloomier features of nature and history: it was characteristic that his best long poem was "The Creek of the Four Graves". Proud, impulsive, and hyper-sensitive, he felt deeply the humiliations suffered through being the son of convict parents as well as being native-born at a time when currency lads were scorned by immigrant critics, of struggling as a poverty-stricken farmer, and of meeting either neglect as a poet or the venomous hostility of such journals as the *Sydney Punch*. His last years were made sorrowful with illness, the death of a son, and disastrous floods. Kendall found him "a noble ruin—one that had been scorched and wasted, as it were, by fire",[14] his face showing the ravages of sorrow and agonies.

Gordon's inheritance of melancholy, aggravated by financial troubles and head injuries from falls in steeplechasing, found a natural outcome in his suicide on Brighton beach. Kendall had a basic reserve of character and a dedication to poetry that enabled him to conquer the drinking habit that was disastrous to him for several years and to win a poetic recognition denied to Harpur, but an inborn tendency to melancholy was deepened by poverty, frustration, illness, despair and even, for a short time, a mental breakdown.

Lawson suffered from an unhappy family life and broken home as a child, from shyness, deafness, a constant struggle to earn a pittance, a shipwrecked marriage, an uncontrollable craving for drink, and an incurable restlessness. He won enough success to have the ball at his

[14] J. Normington-Rawling, *Charles Harpur, an Australian* (Sydney 1962), p.302.

feet when he went to London, but he was so impractical that he could not take advantage of it. But then, if he had been prudently practical he would not have been Henry Lawson. His outlook on the bush was darkened by his father's failure on a wretched selection and by the unlucky chance that his trip to Bourke and Hungerford to get copy for his stories was made desolate by one of the worst droughts in all the continent's history. This shadow of drought, with its associated barrenness and death, hangs gloomily over many of his sketches of the bush.

Brennan was far more fortunate in his circumstances than Lawson, but he knew the disillusionment of his marriage, the loss of his post at the University of Sydney, the accidental death of his beloved "Vi", and his alcoholism. He, too, like Kendall and Lawson before him, wandered the streets of Sydney drunk and destitute. The real sombreness, however, lay deep within the conflicting nature of Brennan himself. It is in the wastes of his own spirit that his poetry becomes a desperate crying, one long autobiographical elegy of lost Edens and hopes denied. The troubled spirit of Francis Webb, grappling with conflicts and fears, has gone beyond the borders of sanity into its own ultima thule.

A personal element of sombreness can be seen or suggested with other writers: Richardson with her self-centredness and ill health; Neilson with his intuitive Celtic perceptiveness of death, "the deep— the dim"; Hope with his childhood's "inner world of panic Nightmares"; Patrick White suffering and introverted by asthmatic pain from his earliest days; and Thomas Keneally, disturbed by religious questionings and the influences indicated in *The Fear*.

The personal melancholy was closely linked in many cases with my third form of sombreness: the sense of loneliness. This was often drawn from what Kendall called "the lot austere" that ever seemed to wait upon the man of letters here, the discouraging lonely isolation of the writer in the midst of an indifferent or hostile community. Such loneliness is, of course, common to writers in other countries and other periods, but it seems to have had special force here right down to recent times.

We have already seen that G. B. Barton pointed out in 1866 this discouragement for native writers.[15] His complaint was echoed in 1894 by Lawson in a bitter preface to his first book. His indictment was still substantially true in 1929 when a visiting American critic described the parlous position of local writers and commented: "Literature is not an intimate concern of the Australian. The whole tenor of society is hostile to it."[16] In 1936 the charge was made again

[15] See pp.106-7.
[16] C. Hartley Grattan, *Australian Literature* (Seattle 1929), pp.37-8.

L

with truth by P. R. Stephensen in his characteristic fashion: "In no other country in the civilised world is literary genius so badly treated, so humiliated and crushed and despised and ignored, as in Australia."[17] As late as the 1950s it was almost, if not quite, impossible for an Australian dramatist to get even a play of distinctive merit given professional production on the local stage, although there was some stage activity earlier.

In modern times the sense of loneliness appears either as the alienation of the artist from the society with which he is at critical odds or as that more universal feeling of the individual's isolation from the rest of humanity which comes, perhaps, to all of us at some moments when we feel terribly alone, the feeling which I once tried to express in "The Inward Eremite":

> *Yet lone as a hawk at noon I came*
> *Out of wild pain to my first light;*
> *I shall still be alone when I go at last*
> *Down to my blind and wordless night.*
>
> *Though I merge with love in imperious fire,*
> *I see, beyond our momentary zone,*
> *The inward eremite in man,*
> *Who moves eternally alone.*[18]

So, too, A. D. Hope has described the same irrevocable isolation, again broken only for the brief moment of love when our "wandering islands" meet but to separate once more:

> *But all that one mind ever knows of another,*
> *Or breaks the long isolation of the heart,*
>
> *Was in that instant.*[19]

Finally, a sombreness came into both our writing and our painting from the general sense of loneliness developed in the isolation of life in the outback. The feeling of Australia as the lonely land has become an integral part of the national imagination, persisting down to the present day and envisaged as a feature of city life as well as of the bush. This loneliness, for instance, is as intense in the city paintings of Dickerson and Brack as in the figurative landscapes of Drysdale, Nolan, and Tucker. It came originally, however, from the bush, and it was sometimes so powerful that it induced strains of madness. There was some sharp truth in Synge's idea of there being plenty of material for drama in Australia with "All those outback stations with shepherds going mad in lonely huts". The bush loneliness did create

[17] P. R. Stephensen, *The Foundations of Culture in Australia* (Sydney 1936), pp.86-7.
[18] T. Inglis Moore, *Bayonet and Grass* (Sydney 1957), p.27.
[19] A. D. Hope, *Collected Poems, 1930-65* (Sydney 1966), p.27, "The Wandering Islands".

its hatters, the classic example being Judith Wright's "Bullocky" in whose brain the years ran widdershins

> *Till the long solitary tracks*
> *etched deeper with each lurching load*
> *were populous before his eyes,*
> *and fiends and angels used his road.*
>
> *All the long straining journey grew*
> *a mad apocalyptic dream,*
> *and he old Moses, and the slaves*
> *his suffering and stubborn team.*[20]

The best expression of what loneliness meant to the bush men and women comes from some of Barbara Baynton's stories and from Lawson in "The Drover's Wife" and in two of the Joe Wilson stories, "Water Them Geraniums" and "A Double Buggy at Lahey's Creek". Joe Wilson stays with Mary for a week or two after he has taken her to their lonely selection to keep her company, and reflects:

The first weeks or few months of loneliness are the worst, as a rule, I believe, as they say the first weeks in jail are—I was never there . . . . But, for my part, I could never get used to loneliness or dullness; the last days used to be the worst with me: then I'd have to make a move, or drink. When you've been too much and too long alone in a lonely place, you begin to do queer things, and think queer thoughts—provided you have any imagination at all . . . . I think that most men who have been alone in the bush for any length of time—and married couples too—are more or less mad.[21]

In the case of their neighbour, Mrs Spicer, Joe and Mary had an ominous warning of the effects of loneliness: the gaunt haggard bush-woman was simply "past carin' ".

Fatalism

Mrs Spicer also provides an instance of our next form of sombreness: fatalism. She is the passive victim of her environment, and she accepts her tragic lot with fatalistic calm, a profound indifference, since she can do nothing to alter her lot. This sombre concept of mankind as the victim of fate is a dark thread running through much of our literature. It is basic, for example, in *For the Term of His Natural Life*, since Rufus Dawes is a helpless sacrifice offered to the convict system. Whatever his struggles, he is bound on its bloodied altar, doomed as irretrievably as a Jewish scapegoat. In *Such is Life*— with an exception provided by the unorthodox Stewart—squatters and teamsters are fated to engage in warfare over the life-giving grass. As Steve Thompson complained to Collins:

[20] Judith Wright, *Five Senses* (Sydney 1963), p.12, "Bullocky".
[21] Henry Lawson, *Prose Works* (Sydney 1935), vol.II, pp.56-7.

mostly every night, we've a choice between two dirty transactions—one is, to let the bullocks starve, and the other is to steal grass for them. For my own part, I'm sick and tired of studying why some people should be in a position where they have to go out of their way to do wrong, and other people are cornered to that extent that they can't live without doing wrong, and can't suicide without jumping out of the frying-pan into the fire. Wonder if any allowance is made for bullock drivers?[22]

Thompson's argument is sound: for him and the other carriers the choice offered to them was no true choice. There was only the primary necessity for them to keep their bullocks alive.

So, too, Richard Mahony's temperament is a compulsion that makes him fated to be a tragic failure, to be always unequal to life's demands. Maurice Guest is helplessly enslaved by Louise. In *Capricornia*, character after character is struck down by a capricious fate, just as the mail-train strikes Ballest and Mick O'Pick, then finally mangles Tim O'Cannon with his Christmas presents—"Oh, death of a kangaroo for a Sergeant Major!" The train is the very symbol of Herbert's macabre orgy of fatalism. Katharine Prichard is an idealist believing that the will of man can change society for the better, yet she also believes in a fated compulsion of the blood drawing together a man and a woman, whilst the loyal Coonardoo is an innocent victim of Hughie's colour prejudice and cruelty. Vance Palmer indicates his philosophy in the title of his novel *Men are Human*: to be human is to suffer from weaknesses and the uncontrollable hazards of life. This aspect of Palmer is rightly summed up by M. Barnard Eldershaw:

This philosophy, or more properly, attitude of mind is sombre to the point of defeatism. It represents man as victim, the victim of casual inconsequent circumstance. His life is made and unmade by events that have little or no logical or emotional connection with it.... Our ends are shaped by a casual unknowing fate.[23]

Eleanor Dark is far from being defeatist in the sense that Vance Palmer can be, and she is hardly a fatalist in her historical novels, but in her other novels accidents often play a decisive role, so that it may be said that they abound in fatalism. This constant employment of accident as a *deus ex machina* has been labelled melodramatic, but I suspect that it is probably a form of realism coming naturally to the wife of a doctor who may be concerned with accidental death and injury day by day. On the other hand, I feel that there is little sombreness of fatalism, little sense of man as victim, since the accident seems created, not by fate, but by the firm shaping hand of

[22] Tom Collins (Joseph Furphy), *Such is Life* (Sydney 1917 ed., first publ. 1903), p.13.
[23] M. Barnard Eldershaw, *Essays in Australian Fiction* (Melbourne 1938), p.99.

Eleanor Dark the skilful craftsman. In contrast, we do find with Kylie Tennant, the faithful observer of life, men and women who are the genuine victims of a society over which they have no control, fated to poverty, depression, or delinquency. The fatalism here is essentially social in character, just as that of Lawson is ecological, concerned with the bush environment, and that of Herbert is metaphysical as embodying his view of the nature of the universe.

The Ultimate Void

It is only one step from fatalism to nihilism, from seeing the universe as the blind workings of a purposeless destiny to finding it completely devoid of meaning, a futile nothingness, the ultimate void. This step is rarely taken by Australian writers, but now and then we come across an echo of Ecclesiastes: "Vanity of vanities: all is vanity . . . . Then I looked on all the works that my hands had wrought, and on the labour that I had laboured to do: and, behold, all was vanity and vexation of spirit, and there was no profit under the sun."[24]

Furphy, of course, is free from such negation. He is a positive idealist as well as a cool, rational ironist, as we can appreciate more fully if we mentally restore to *Such is Life* the deleted *Rigby's Romance*, sliced off the original mammoth manuscript. His philosophy, set out in his analogy of the railway points, is only a semi-fatalism: man's destiny is partly determined, partly a matter of free choice. Despite its ironies and caprices, life is well worth while, and he enjoys its spectacle with a robust relish.

Lawson, apart from his personal melancholy and his atrabilious attacks on the harshness of the bush, has a few black moments of nihilism. In the sketch "Some Day" he shows Mitchell confessing the futility of his life, everlastingly tramping, tramping for tucker, losing ambition and hope, becoming indifferent, "and you go on like this till the spirit of a bullock takes the place of the heart of a man. Who cares?"[25] In "The Union Buries Its Dead" Lawson comments on the funeral procession of fourteen souls: "Perhaps not one of the fourteen possessed a soul any more than the corpse did—but that doesn't matter."[26] And then, when the hard clods rebounded and knocked on the coffin during the burial, he remarks: "It didn't matter much—nothing does."[27]

Brennan's poems often express his frustration and despair in such lines as:

---

24 *The Bible*, Ecclesiastes i, 2; ii, 11.
25 Henry Lawson, op. cit., vol.I, p.101.
26 Ibid., p.56.
27 Ibid., p.58.

In wide revolt and ruin tost
against whatever is or seems
my futile heart still wanders lost
in the same vast and impotent dreams.[28]

or

I know I am
the wanderer of the ways of all the worlds,
to whom the sunshine and the rain are one
and one to stay or hasten, because he knows
no ending of the way, no home, no goal.[29]

Lilith is scornfully nihilistic in her final address to Adam, the Spirit of Man:

the crown that all thy wants confess
is Lilith's own, the round of nothingness ....

Go forth: be great, O nothing. I have said.[30]

Slessor, too, is beset with a feeling of frustration, shown in his recurring symbol of the wan face pressed vainly against the window glass, and of the annihilating dooms wrought on man by time and death. In "Stars" he pictures himself as beating off the stars with their "bottomless, black cups of space between their clusters":

But I could not escape those tunnels of nothingness,
The cracks in the spinning Cross, nor hold my brain
From rushing forever down that terrible lane,
Infinity's trap-door, eternal and merciless.[31]

As I pointed out over twenty years ago in discussing Slessor's philosophy in his poetry:

Each of his main volumes ends in pessimism: *Earth-Visitors*, after all the roistering and wenching, closes with frustration, the dissolution of life, and the passing of the bells of Music; *Cuckooz Contrey* finishes with a desperate appeal to the man-made gods not to leave us "crying in emptiness"; *Five Bells* concludes with the title-poem as an elegy on a drowned friend, gone beyond recall, unable to make himself heard beyond death, with five bells ringing a forlorn evangel of nothingness across the Harbour.

"The true disciple of philosophy," said Socrates in the *Phaedo*, "is likely to be misunderstood by other men; they do not perceive that he is ever pursuing death and dying." This pursuit of death is Ken Slessor's main preoccupation as a poet; it ends in nescience, and he emerges as a grim nihilist.[32]

Just as Slessor's darkness forms the background to the brightness of his poetry's colouring, so, too, Kylie Tennant's liveliness and

[28] A. R. Chisholm and J. J. Quinn (ed.), *The Verse of Christopher Brennan* (Sydney 1960), p.100.
[29] Ibid., p.165.
[30] Ibid., p.140.
[31] Kenneth Slessor, *Poems* (Sydney 1962, Sirius Books), p.26.
[32] T. Inglis Moore, "Kenneth Slessor", *Southerly*, vol.VIII, No.4, 1947, p.205.

humour partly conceal an underlying bitterness at the evils of society and the futility of existence. As I have discussed elsewhere, Kylie Tennant gives many indications of this despair:

All four city novels comment, at times savagely, on the foulness or insanity of Sydney, Bramley Cornish, for example, sees "the running sores of Foveaux slums" unwrapped:

All day long he moved in the sour stench of misery, the dirt, the sweaty, clammy nastiness of diseased people and decayed houses. Sometimes he felt as though he was putting his hand on slime. His gorge rose with it.[33]

The country town is no better. Jessica sees Tiburon despairingly:

The misery, the dirt, the crawling evil, the diseased and festering minds of these people! And Tiburon was the world; and the world was Tiburon . . . .[34]

The coastal village is the worst: a tragic despair broods over the better characters in *Lost Haven*. Bernard Cassels thinks:

It ought to disgust any intelligent and sensitive person to live in Lost Haven and its mental and physical squalor, its decayed amoral animalism.[35]

Len feels that "the game's crook"; Alec sees "no good in the human race"; Orry Mansart kills himself in despair, and Benison agrees with his self-chosen epitaph: "It is hard to say 'Yea Lord' to Nothingness."[36]

The passing of suffering over into despair may be seen also in the novels of Patrick White, especially in the piling up of futilities in *Happy Valley* and *The Living and the Dead* or the madness of Theodora Goodman in *The Aunt's Story*. The same form of sombreness occurs, too, in the fiction of such successors to White as Randolph Stow, Thomas Keneally, and David Ireland, who have followed him to constitute a sombre school of specialists in suffering, violence and the pathological sickness of abnormal characters.

The Answering Affirmation

The strain of sombreness, then, in all the five forms just illustrated, forms a definite social pattern in our literature. Going deeper into its character, we find that it rarely develops into an unmitigated pessimism, as H. A. Kellow has suggested:

Those who imagine that Australia is a land of joyous adventure under bright skies cannot have noted the current of pessimism that runs through Australian literature. All is not devil-may-care in the southern continent. There is a persistent tradition of pessimism which is not merely a poetic pose; it is the natural outcome of life in a new country in which man finds himself discouraged and baffled in the struggle with untamed Nature.[37]

Nor is the sombreness "a sense of the horror of sheer existence",

[33] Kylie Tennant, *Foveaux* (London 1949), p.411.
[34] Kylie Tennant, *Tiburon* (Sydney, Pocket Library, n.d.; first publ. 1935), p.206.
[35] Kylie Tennant, *Lost Haven* (New York 1946), p.287.
[36] T. Inglis Moore, "The Tragi-Comedies of Kylie Tennant", *Southerly*, vol.XVIII, no.1, 1957, p.7.
[37] H. A. Kellow, *Queensland Poets* (London 1930), p.40.

as claimed by another of the few critics who have recognized this element, H. P. Heseltine. His stimulating essay on "The Literary Heritage" in *Meanjin Quarterly* is discerning at many points. Yet his application of a theory of the American critic Lionel Trilling to our creative writing leads, I believe, to a misinterpretation of the sombreness. Dr Heseltine argues that the writer becomes an "outsider" rejecting society, and accepts the Trilling idea that the artist is "the man who goes down into that hell which is the historical beginning of the human soul". He suggests that Lawson and the writers of the nineties expressed "the insane horror of bush life", whilst our Australian writers generally "have had deeply located in their imagination (either consciously or unconsciously) a sense of the horror of sheer existence." Hence "Australia's literary heritage is based on a unique combination of glances into the pit and the erection of safety fences to prevent any toppling in." Finally, Dr Heseltine claims that

The canon of our writing presents a facade of mateship, egalitarian democracy, landscape, nationalism, realistic toughness. But always behind the facade looms the fundamental concern of the Australian literary imagination. That concern, marked out by our national origins and given direction by geographic necessity, is to acknowledge the terror at the basis of being, to explore its uses, and to build defences against its dangers. It is that concern which gives Australia's literary heritage its special force and distinction, which guarantees its continuing modernity.[38]

This thesis is such an interesting one and argued so eloquently at times that it almost seems a pity that it is fundamentally wrong. It just does not work. The literary evidence is heavily against it. Indeed, the weakness of the case is indicated by the fact, pointed out by Arthur Phillips in a penetrating analysis,[39] that Heseltine has to support it by misconstruction of passages from Lawson, Furphy and Slessor.

It seems to me a basic error, of course, to disparage such elements of our writing as mateship, democracy, "landscape" (presumably the bush), and realism in order to exalt a groundless, hypothetic "terror", since these elements, on the solid evidence presented in this whole study of social patterns, are so fundamental and significant that the allegation of them as a mere "façade" is strangely inappropriate. The Trilling concept of a sense of horror, with its accompaniment of nihilism, as being something peculiarly modern seems curious when these go back in history to Taoism and Homer, when they are as old as Agamemnon, Job and Ecclesiastes. What exactly does "that hell

[38] H. P. Heseltine, "Australian Image: (1) The Literary Heritage", *Meanjin Quarterly*, no.88, vol.XXI, no.1, 1962.
[39] A. A. Phillips, "Australian Image: (2) The Literary Heritage Re-assessed", *Meanjin Quarterly*, no.89, vol.XXI, no.2, 1962.

which is the historical beginning of the human soul" mean—if anything? If there ever was such a beginning, why should it be a hell more than a heaven? Why not an initial Eden before a fall of man? The hellish assumption is arbitrary and gratuitous. And why should there be any "terror at the basis of being"?

Like this vague initial hell, "the horror of sheer existence" becomes mythical when applied to the facts of our literature. Dr Heseltine is right in his perception of some forms of what I term sombreness, but misinterprets this when he tries to impose on it a metaphysical notion of horror which would have seemed melodramatic to such clear-eyed realists as Furphy and Lawson, Richardson and Prichard. There were stray hatters in the bush, but they went mad because of the simple fact of loneliness. Moreover, the hatters did not write books. The writers of the nineties, like Lawson and Dyson, Furphy and Miles Franklin, were sane, balanced persons, all with a keen sense of humour, who certainly cherished neither a horror of existence nor an "insane horror of bush life". They would have been very surprised, indeed, if they had been told they nurtured such vipers in their bosoms.

They would have been equally astonished at the charge of being "outsiders" in the European and American sense of this term. Australian writers in general have had a strong social consciousness. Far from rejecting society, they have accepted it even when they have been critical of various aspects of it. Indeed, they have usually been very much an active part of it through their very diverse occupations in a country whose small population has not enabled writers, with only a handful of exceptions, to make a professional living out of creative writing. The only sense in which they have been "outsiders" is that in the past some have felt isolation, not because they rejected society but because society in a sense rejected them.

The pessimist thesis misses, again, what I feel is a central point of the sombreness in our literature, the fact that it has almost always been coupled with an answering affirmation of the value of existence. The sense of life is far stronger than the sense of death in Australian writing, just as the belief in the essential goodness of man predominates over any belief in evil—as shown in the representative traditions of progress and utopianism, mateship, democratic equality, and social justice.

The case of Lawson is especially illuminating. I have quoted two examples of his nihilism, but the rarity of such examples proves the rule of his acceptance of life, his basic belief in positive values. He had deep convictions on the worth of courage and endurance, the loyalty of mateship, the love of man and woman, sympathy, understanding and humour. In the context of his whole body of writing, in prose and verse, his nihilism is only a momentary mood. Indeed, when Mitchell reflects on the futility of his life, he confesses that he is "out of sorts" at the time. So, too, Lawson is "out of sorts"—not himself—when he avers that "It didn't matter much—nothing does" in "The Union Buries Its Dead". He pictures sombrely the loneliness of bush life and its effect in the apathy of a Mrs Spicer, but the true moral of "Water Them Geraniums" is only realized in the following story "A Double Buggy at Lahey's Creek" when Joe Wilson buys the double buggy that rescues his wife Mary from her isolation on their lonely selection. Love triumphs over loneliness, man over the bush. Elsewhere mateship is the victorious reply to loneliness. So, too, "The Drover's Wife" is not a "horror" story because the woman rises superior to all her hardships, including loneliness, by her stoic virtue of courage.

So, once again, the assertion of nothingness in Brennan's "Lilith" is Lilith herself speaking as a character in a dramatic dialogue with the spirit of man rather than Brennan himself, since elsewhere he goes beyond his temperamental gloom and the ultimate void to "take the night upon his face", to "draw courage to front the way", and to proclaim finally his "fidelity to old delight". The stoic will is a significant affirmation. Brennan's night is not without its fields of stars, just as Lilith the all-inclusive holds in herself both horror and beauty.

A similar dualism is also integral to the writing of Slessor and Kylie Tennant. Both can be pessimists at times, yet enjoy life thoroughly as well. Douglas Stewart, after noting how persistent and pervasive the theme of elegy is in Slessor's poetry, points out, rightly, that

The curious thing is that, in spite of the persistence of this theme of elegy in his poetry, Slessor is by no means a melancholy poet to read.... His regret at the brevity of life is, in fact, everywhere counterbalanced by his appreciation of life while we have it. If, as he says, he "won't return", yet still his poetry "lives well, loves well, gives thanks".[40]

The tragic vision of Kylie Tennant is also matched by a zest in what Browning called "the mere living". She affirms a warm idealism in such creations as Sorrell, the Apostle, and David Aumbry, and she explicitly gives the riposte to her more pessimistic view of humanity when she declares: "To be born is to be lucky. Later, life may prove a failure or success, depending on the outlook of whoever is living it;

[40] Douglas Stewart, "Kenneth Slessor's Poetry", *Meanjin Quarterly*, no.117, vol.XXVIII, Winter 1969, p.168.

but that life is there should be a matter of congratulation daily renewed."[41]

Amongst other novelists who express a strong strain of sombreness, Vance Palmer balances his fatalism by a set of positive beliefs, sympathy with his characters, and a poet's appreciation of natural beauty. It is characteristic that he concludes his novel *Golconda* by contrasting pictures of Donovan, the unionist graduated to elected politician, and Neda, the sculptress, as they fly from the mining field to the city. Donovan from the height of the plane sees Golconda dwarfed into insignificance: "A little ant-hill rising out of the hot, crumbly dust". Neda sees the outline of the mountain with the artist's eye and is roused to a feeling "linked with her urge to create, to bring living shapes out of the void".[42] Xavier Herbert deals with horrors in *Capricornia* with a comic gusto that is more powerful than the negations of his turbulent universe. Even Patrick White, obsessed with suffering, affirms "the tree of man" in a continuity of being as in the flashes of beauty and wonder that illuminate the commonplace lives of Stan and Amy Parker; Voss ends his journey into the desert with finding the love of Laura, fulfilment of the spirit in humility, and exaltation into a legend, just as Stow's missionary Heriot finds salvation at the close of his journey in *To the Islands*. The four main characters in *Riders in the Chariot* are spiritually sustained by their mystical faith in their visionary chariots. The novel ends with Mrs Godbold, content in her firm belief in Christ, and blest with a moment of glory:

That evening, as she walked along the road, it was the hour at which the other gold sank its furrows in the softer sky. The lids of her eyes, flickering beneath its glow, were gilded with an identical splendour. But for all its weight, it lay lightly, lifted her, in fact, to where she remained an instant in the company of the Living Creatures she had known, and many others she had not. All was ratified again by hands.[43]

So, too, after Arthur Brown has murdered his brother Waldo, *The Solid Mandala* closes with Mrs Poulter working herself into "a state of exaltation" and affirming her belief in the simple Arthur to the embarrassed sergeant of police: " 'This man would be my saint,' she said, 'if we could still believe in saints. Nowadays,' she said, 'we've only men to believe in. I believe in this man.' "[44] And she proceeds, in typical White fashion, to feed her husband happily with "a real nice loin chop".

White has a far deeper sense than most Australian writers of life's

[41] Kylie Tennant, *Ride On Stranger* (Sydney 1943), p.1.
[42] Vance Palmer, *Golconda* (Sydney 1948), p.287.
[43] Patrick White, *Riders in the Chariot* (London 1961), pp.551-2.
[44] Patrick White, *The Solid Mandala* (London 1966), p.315.

tragedies and futilities, and even goes further to embody a veritable quality of evil in Mrs Jolley and Mrs Flack. Yet, in the end, he joins with the other writers in affirming what Carlyle called the Everlasting Yea.

In addition to those whose sombreness is counterbalanced by their affirmations, there remains, of course, the great majority of Australian writers who stand in the positive, humanist tradition dominating our literature: O'Dowd, Neilson and McCrae, FitzGerald, Hope, McAuley, Wright, Stewart, and Campbell in poetry, for example, or Lawson, Furphy, and Franklin, Prichard, Dark, Davison, and Durack in the novel, and Alan Marshall, Gavin Casey, Morrison, Waten, and Hal Porter in the short story. Here the darkness is often recognized, but the stress is on the light, with the feeling that it must be preserved as in FitzGerald's fine poem "Bog and Candle":

> *So it is body's business and its inborn doom*
> *past will, past hope, past reason and all courage of heart,*
> *still to resist among the roof-beams ripped apart*
> *the putting-out of the candle in the blind man's room.*[45]

The Shadow of Drought

After examining the pattern of sombreness, let us go on to analyse the ecological forces working to create it. Our definition of its various forms has already indicated three different kinds of determinants: the personal, inborn melancholy in the individual organism; the social environment, and the physical environment.

The first of these is an historical fact, a biographical matter which needs no further discussion. The social environment has operated upon the people in three aspects: the convict system, the bush isolation, and the urban, industrialized society of today. Thus the convict system was obviously a potent force in creating both the tragic sense of human suffering and the fatalism that saw man as the helpless victim of the social structure. The novels and short stories of convictism by such writers as Clarke, Leakey, Price Warung, William Hay, and Keneally all abound in these two forms of sombreness. They make black reading.

The social environment of the bush was marked by a lack of community life during its pastoral development and a consequent isolation of individuals that inevitably caused the sombreness of loneliness. This persists in contemporary urban society as the occasional alienation of the writer. The feeling of fatalism also occurs today when man is seen as a predestined cog in the industrial machine, although this is largely offset by the fact that the writers who deal

[45] Robert D. FitzGerald, "Bog and Candle", *Forty Years' Poems* (Sydney 1965), p.216.

particularly with the industrial scene are usually social realists who are militant reformists insisting that conditions can be bettered by collective action.

The most important of the influences exerted here by our troubled atomic society is the sombreness focused on suffering in the more sensational and abnormal features of the social scene. In fiction, for instance, it is perhaps natural that Patrick White and his successors should grow pathological, concentrating on the abnormalities, concerned with the misfits, the fringe-dwellers, and the insane, since we live in a pathological age and a diseased society. " 'Tis a mad world, my masters," and madness or sickness have become the current themes. Our social environment has also deepened the resulting sombreness in two other ways. Urbanization has produced a greater mental and moral complexity, turning writers towards introspection and psychological analysis. Imaginative attention is being directed to the inward life of the individual. At the same time, the mass media of the press, radio and television have brought the world's conflicts and cruelties, its corpses in Vietnam and its starving children in Biafra directly into the daily intimacies of the home, so that we sup on horrors and breakfast on bloodshed in a manner never known before to mankind. The writing thus grows sombre by mirroring the violence thrust before us, whilst the fantasies of fiction are outdone by the fabulous sight of men walking on the moon, talking to us through infinities of space. We turn from White's riders in his Ezekielian chariot to watch the astronauts hurtling through the heavens in their fire-rocketed module. Reality and imagination merge, and traditional norms give place to the bizarre. Patrick White has indicated his consciousness of this when he makes Mrs Poulter in *The Solid Mandala* feel, after discovering the dog-torn body of Waldo Brown, that the films, the papers, and "all the telly" were "turning real".

In the formative stages of the social patterns during last century, however, the strongest single shaping force was undoubtedly the physical environment. It was the land itself, as earlier commentators like Walker and Topp, Essex Evans and Kellow, all clearly recognized, that created the melancholy and pessimism of much Australian writing. The spirit of the Place moulded the minds of the People here, as in other patterns; the spell of the bush has persisted right down to the present day, in both the landscape painting and the literature, and one of the land's most important, pervasive and enduring aspects has been, as pointed out earlier,[46] its influence in fashioning an atmosphere and outlook of sombreness.

[46] See pp.77-9, 84, and 89-91.

To begin with, the land exercised a realistic, sombre effect through much of its landscape. To the English, Scottish, and Irish immigrants, brought up with green fields, purple heather, and "the emerald isle", the Australian scene in the interior was drab, monotonous, and gloomy. Its oppression hung over their spirit. Thus Marcus Clarke declared, in his famous preface to the 1876 edition of Adam Lindsay Gordon's *Sea Spray and Smoke Drift* that the dominant note of Australian scenery was "Weird Melancholy". "All is fear inspiring and gloomy. No bright fancies are linked with the memories of the mountains. Hopeless explorers have named them out of their sufferings—Mount Misery, Mount Dreadful, Mount Despair."[47]

This gloomy concept of the land was a persistent trend, followed by the native-born writers no less than by the immigrants. Thus any nostalgia of the exiles becomes irrelevant. William Charles Wentworth, one of the earliest of the "currency lads" and a devout patriot, describes the Blue Mountains which he had helped to conquer as "one vast forest, uninterrupted except by the cultivated openings which have been made by the axe on the summits of the loftiest hills, and which tend to diminish those melancholy sensations its gloomy monotony would otherwise inspire".[48] In his Cambridge poem "Australasia" he addresses the Blue Mountains again in sombre terms:

> *How mute, how desolate thy stunted woods,*
> *How dread thy chasms, where many an eagle broods,*
> *How dark thy caves, how lone thy torrents' roar,*
> *As down thy cliffs precipitous they pour.*[49]

The sombreness of the land was not just a convention of the poetic imagination, but an actual grim fact attested to by the explorers of the inland in their journals. Some of them were fortunate in finding good country: Mitchell discovered Australia Felix, for example, and Sturt was gladdened by sighting the Darling and the Murray rivers. But it was Sturt also who wrote in his journal on 31 August 1845:

In the afternoon we travelled over large bare plains, of a most difficult and distressing kind, the ground absolutely yawning beneath us, perfectly destitute of vegetation, and denuded of timber, excepting here and there, where a stunted box-tree was to be seen.[50]

Later, he gives a further account of the impression made by the

[47] Marcus Clarke, "Australian Scenery" in *The Marcus Clarke Memorial Volume* (Melbourne 1884), p.115.

[48] W. C. Wentworth, *A Statistical, Historical and Political Description of the Colony of New South Wales, and its Dependent Settlements in Van Diemen's Land* (London 1819), p.14.

[49] W. C. Wentworth, *Australasia*. A Poem. Written for the Chancellor's Medal at the Cambridge Commencement, July 1823 (London 1873 ed., first publ. 1823), p.25.

[50] Kathleen Fitzpatrick (ed.), *Australian Explorers* (London 1958), p.296.

Central Australian scene upon his companion, Mr. Browne, saying that the reader

may form some idea of the one now placed before him, when I state, that, familiar as we had been to such, my companion involuntarily uttered an exclamation of amazement when he first glanced his eye over it. "Good Heavens," said he, "did man ever see such country!" Indeed, if it was not so gloomy, it was more difficult than the Stony Desert itself.[51]

There was the fate of Burke and Wills, and the loss of Leichhardt. There was Gibson riding off to his death in Gibson's Desert, with the vain search made for him by Giles, who himself barely survived. It was Giles who described Buzoe's Grave: "The place might well be termed the centre of silence and solitude; despair and desolation are the only intruders here."[52] There was the indomitable Eyre coming back to camp to find his one white companion Baxter dying, murdered by the two aborigines who had also plundered the precious stores, leaving him to make his historic march to Albany with Wylie, the remaining aborigine, and to record his feeling: "Though years have now passed away since the enactment of this tragedy, the dreadful horrors of that time and scene, are recalled before me with frightful vividness, and make me shudder even now, when I think of them."[53] Such was the country described by the explorers; such was their suffering.

The land thus initiated an awareness of desolation, pain, and suffering. The isolation of its solitudes created an inevitable loneliness. The element of fatalism derived directly and undeniably from the nature of the land and the efforts of the settlers to adapt themselves to its harshness, its unpredictability, and its power of determining human fate by its irresistible weapons of fire, flood, and drought. Against such odds the man on the land has remained relatively helpless, even down to the present day when these ancient weapons still exert their hazardous disastrous power. Drought, in particular, still strikes with death and desolation. It is the great destroyer, the implacable Shiva. Millions of starved sheep and cattle leave their bones on the barren ground. Millions of acres, fertile this season, may be a desert next year. Drought is a despot against whose decrees there is no court of appeal. Man can only confront it with a fatalistic acceptance, the stoic courage enunciated by Gordon as the one creed of the bush, the endurance that calls for the heart of a bullock.

It must be noted, however, that the cruelty has been that of nature, not of man. The struggle has been against the impersonal natural forces, and so in a sense the death by drought has been a simpler,

[51] Ibid., p.305.
[52] Ibid., p.502.
[53] Ibid., p.193.

cleaner thing than the conflict of man against man, with all its complexity, its fears, and its hates. The gloom induced by natural disasters, moreover, has been temporary, since beyond the drought is the perennial promise of rain and the green grass. Thus it has not the passionate depth of that "truceless gloom" of the lost souls described by Dante in the third Canto of the "Inferno".

The Cry of the Crow

The sombreness, however, has its own intensity and its own symbolism. Mario Praz, seeking representative symbols for the beauty, cruelty, and terror of that decadent phase of Romanticism that he calls "The Romantic Agony", finds them in such figures as the Medusa, Cleopatra, Salome, Dolores, and La Belle Dame sans Merci. Frank Kermode, exploring the dynamics of a finer, saner Romanticism as expressed by the creative imagination of Yeats, expounds the significance of the Dancer and the Tree as his central images. What, then, of our sombreness? Have we any symbol to represent it? I suggest that there is one image, recurring in Australian poetry and prose, which expresses this pattern perfectly—the Crow, especially when it is uttering its harsh, penetrating cry that rejoices in its meal of the drought-slain dead, that comes as the triumphant voice of the land itself, evoking its loneliness and death. There is mockery, too, in the morning laughter of the kookaburra, but this is genial, Rabelaisian in its full-blooded gusto, just as its sound at dusk may come weirdly. The crow's cawing is bitter and hostile to man. It is as realistic as the Dancer is romantic, a common daily sound to the bushman, with no trace of beauty or music in it, but carrying always, like Poe's raven, a foreboding or a vindictive "Nevermore!" as it settles by the corpse of its victim.

The recurrence of the crow as an image of death and loneliness has been so frequent in bush literature that G. Herbert Gibson has ridiculed it in his satirical verse entitled "How to Write an Australian Novel". The crow is an essential part of his recipe for the aspiring novelist:

> *Have a drawin' of the station,*
> *And another illustration*
> *Of a carcase, with a crow upon a fence.*
>
> *For—to be a bit digressive—*
> *There is nothing so expressive*
> *Of the sadness of our solitudes immense,*
> *Or so tenderly appealing*
> *To our sympathy and feeling*
> *As a carcass, and a crow upon a fence.*[54]

[54] G. Herbert Gibson ("Ironbark"), *Ironbark Splinters from the Australian Bush* (London 1912), pp.111-12.

"Ironbark" is right when he recognizes, even in satire, the supreme expressiveness of the crow for "the sadness of our solitudes immense".

Thus Lawson uses the crow in "The Drover's Wife" as her enemy, which she combats by a cunning strategem. For the crow, with his custom of picking out the eyes or kidneys of dead or dying lambs, is a villainous bird, as David Campbell declares:

> *The crow throws on his villainous cloak*
> *In the footlights of the sun.*
>
> *And though the lark, the thrush, the wren,*
> *May hiss from stalls of briar,*
> *The black crow looks from lidded eyes,*
> *His voice is colder than the skies,*
> *He pecks a young lamb's kidney out*
> *And throws it to the choir.*[55]

Barcroft Boake links the crows with the dingoes and gives their cries a funeral hoarseness as he pictures them beside the stockman dying of thirst in the Never Never land of the Far West:

> *Gaunt, slinking dingoes snap and snarl,*
> *Watching his slowly-ebbing breath;*
> *Crows are flying, hoarsely crying*
> *Burial service o'er the dying—*
> *Foul harbingers of Death.*[56]

The same association comes in the chorus of the old bush song of "The Dying Stockman", as given in an epigraph earlier, and it is significant that the stockman requests his mates to bury him deep enough to be safe from these two figures of death.

Barbara Baynton, with her feeling for the macabre, uses the crows as images of cruelty in her bush stories. In "Billy Skywonkie", for instance, when the crude rouseabout meets a new housekeeper at the railway, his conversation to her in the buggy as they drive to the station runs:

"No sign er rain! No lambin' this season: soon as they're dropt we'll 'ave ter knock 'em all on ther 'ead!" He shouted an oath of hatred at the crows following after the tottering sheep that made in a straggling line for the water. "Look at 'em!" he said, "Scoffin' out ther eyes!" He pointed to where the crows hovered over the bogged sheep. "They putty well lives on eyes!"[57]

In the grim story, "The Chosen Vessel", a wandering swagman breaks at night into the bush shanty where the woman is alone with

[55] David Campbell, *Speak with the Sun* (London 1949), p.30, "The Kidney and the Wren".
[56] Barcroft Boake, *Where the Dead Men Lie*, ed., with notes and Memoir, by A. G. Stephens (Sydney 1897), p. 3, "From the Far West".
[57] Barbara Baynton, *Bush Studies* (London 1902), p.86.

M

her baby. Terrified, clutching her child to her, she flies out, seeking help from a passing horseman. He gallops away in fear, and the swagman murders her by the creek. Then, at daylight, the crows, linked once again with the dingoes, preside over a scene of Grand Guignol horror as the boundary rider discovers the dead woman, still clutching the living child:

Sleep was nodding its golden head and swaying its small body, and the crows were close, so close, to the mother's wide-open eyes, when the boundary rider galloped down.
"Jesus Christ!" he said, covering his eyes. He told afterwards how the little child held out its arms to him, and how he was forced to cut its gown that the dead hand held.[58]

In *On Our Selection* the crows are used as symbols expressing the stark poverty of the selector and the vainness of his battling against the odds of the land. When Dad brings home a horse, Emmelina is so emaciated that she cannot go anywhere without a flock of crows accompanying her, anticipating the meal that she will soon provide. When Dad rides off on her with his swag to go up country and earn some badly needed cash, the crows follow.

Dad and the Rudd family are slaving on the selection, but Dad promises better times when he gets the deeds of the property from the government. At last the deeds arrive.

Dad said he would ride to town at once, and went for Emmelina.
"Couldn't y' find her, Dad?" Dan said, seeing him return without the mare.
Dad cleared his throat, but didn't answer. Mother asked him.
"Yes, I *found* her," he said slowly, "dead."
The crows had got her at last.
He wrapped the deeds in a piece of rag and walked . . . .
Now Dad regularly curses the deeds every mail-day, and wishes to Heaven he had never got them.[59]

One of the artists who illustrated the book, A. J. Fischer, has given a telling picture of the corpse of Emmelina stretched out on the ground, with sixteen black crows perched on her, using their beaks, or settling down on her for the feast. Nothing could illustrate more graphically the sombre side of life on the land, with the conquest of the crows over Emmelina furnishing a touch of harsh irony, making a mockery of Dad's dreams of prosperity when he got the deeds.

The pattern of sombreness holds more than melancholy or gloom, for it encloses an element of sharp bitterness aroused by the desolation of drought and its destruction of the man on the land's dreams, hopes, and years of hard toil and sheer endurance. Two effective illustrations of this bitterness, this Shadow of Drought, are seen in

[58] Ibid., pp.150-1, "The Chosen Vessel".
[59] Steele Rudd, *On Our Selection* (Sydney 1899), pp.21-2.

Professor Moll's poem "During Drouth" and Dowell O'Reilly's short story "Crows". In each case the crows furnish the significant image. The poem shows the effect of drought on both cattle and man:

> *He said: 'Like flies they die,*
> *Hundreds each day out there*
> *Under the empty sky,*
> *Sprawled in the heat and glare.*
>
> *On dragging hooves they come*
> *Down to the creek and stand*
> *Staring, black-mouthed and dumb,*
> *At the baked mud and sand*
>
> *Day after day until*
> *They drop. With lazy cries*
> *The crows, grown dainty, will*
> *Take nothing but their eyes.'*
>
> *To comfort him I said—*
> *Fearing he felt to blame—*
> *'The beasts have always bled*
> *As their part in the game.*
>
> *Bitter's the role they play*
> *In the world's dismal plan.'*
> *He spat and looked away:*
> *'It's bitterer to be man!'*[60]

Dowell O'Reilly goes further since he makes this bitterness turn into a rejection of God, with the crows as a realistic symbol of triumphant evil. The stockman's rejection is complete, and even the clergyman's faith is shaken. He is a young "Pommy" parson, fresh from Oxford, conscientiously riding his bicycle far out on the drought-stricken plains in "feverish pity and a longing to help".

One day he came upon a stockman stooping over a young ewe, still alive but lying helpless. Her exposed eye was picked out, and her lamb lay near, dead—both eyes gone, the kidneys ripped out. The man lifted her on her legs, but she was too weak to stand.

"Kargh-kargh-kar-r-gh."

"Look," said the stockman.

The parson glanced up.

"No—here!" The man pointed at the ground. The ewe lay in a dusty circle of innumerable hoof-prints. He shook his fist fiercely in the clergyman's face.

"She faced them bloody crows for two days—round and round—her little 'un beside her all the while suckin' her strength—but they got it at last!"

Swete rode on, sick at heart.

"Hey, parson—"

He glanced back over his shoulder. The man was holding up the dead lamb by the tail.

"Feed my lambs!"

---

[60] Ernest G. Moll, *Cut from Mulga: Poems* (Sydney 1940), p.66.

As his head bowed forward the little carcase thudded almost under his wheel and rolled over and over in the dust. He spurted in horror—the insult was not meant for him.[61]

Riding away appalled, Swete hears the cry of the crow, "Kargh-kargh-kar-r-gh!" and "he became conscious of an obscene power of which the evil birds were a manifestation—a power malefic, wide-winged, triumphant, with cruel beak, and tearing talons—'Kar-r-gh'!"[62]

Here the cry of the crow is consciously given as a manifestation of "an obscene power", evil and cruel. The stockman's jeering "Feed my lambs!" is an epitome of bitterness.

In our final illustration, the powerful piece of sombre realism that ends *Capricornia*, Xavier Herbert lets the reader draw his own implications from the event. During the story we develop a strong sympathy for the unfortunate Tocky, the quarter-caste aboriginal girl, who is tossed about helplessly as the victim of the white man's treatment of the aborigines and the mere flotsam of a capricious fate. Her story is invested with Herbert's realistic irony throughout. For instance, Norman Shillingsworth, the "hero", is almost convicted for the murder of Frank McLash, whom Tocky had shot. She lives with Norman as his mistress at his station Red Ochre, and becomes with child by him. When taken by the police to Port Zodiac, she escapes from the aboriginal Compound, and disappears.

The book closes with a grim solution to her mystery, to round off savagely Herbert's interpretation of a fortuitous world. Comedy is placed cheek by jowl with tragedy, since Norman is amused by the absurd efforts of Cho, the Chinese cook, to ride a new donkey.

Norman, spluttering with laughter, went across to the stock-tanks to drink. He was drinking from a trough, when he was startled by the sudden appearance of two crows that swept up from out the broken tank. Then he noticed fluttering from the rim of the tank a piece of dusty blue cloth. He stared. The cloth fell limp, fluttered, fell again. Dry grass rattled against the iron. Dry wind moaned through rust-eaten holes. He stepped up to the tank and peeped through a hole. Nothing to see but the rusty wall beyond. He climbed the ladder, looked inside, saw a skull and a litter of bones. He gasped. A human skull—no—two—a small one and a tiny one. And human hair and rags of clothes and a pair of bone-filled boots. Two skulls, a small one and a tiny one. Tocky and her baby!
The crows alighted in a gnarled dead coolibah near by and cried dismally, "Kah!—Kah!—Kaaaaah!"[63]

"A pair of bone-filled boots": the acme of realism; and the turbulence of a chaotic universe farewelled, tersely, fitly, sombrely by the triumphant Cry of the Crow.

[61] Dowell O'Reilly, *Fivecorners* (Sydney 1920), pp.64-5.
[62] Ibid., pp.67-8.   [63] Xavier Herbert, *Capricornia* (Sydney 1938), p.595.

VIII

The Keynote of Irony

They say you can judge a nation by its jokes. You can, if it tells its own. Australia, however, relies too much and too often on imported ready-mades....

But the native-born is gold, pure gold. It is a joke worth hearing. It comes pat, faintly mocking, hiding a sting in its tail. It is exactly what you might expect from that thin-lipped Australian mouth. Here are two of the right breed.

The first is from Sydney. It is a tale of the Gap, a cliff near the South Head which offers such a deep clean drop from this world into another that all the best suicides give it their patronage.

"And when the policeman got up to the man he was sitting on the edge, all ready.

'What's up, digger?' asked the policeman.

'Everything,' said the man. 'This Depression's got me down. The wife's run off with a cobber o' mine; the shop's gone to the pack; the kid's crook, and I've lost me false teeth.'

'Gow-orn!' said the policeman, sympathetically.

'So I'm going over the Gap,' said the man, and pulled off his coat.

'You may be,' said the policeman, soothing him, 'but we'll have to talk about it first.'

So they had a talk about it first. Then they both went over the Gap."

THOMAS WOOD[1]

He lifted up his hairy paw, with one tremendous clout
He landed on the barber's jaw, and knocked the barber out.
He set to work with tooth and nail, he made the place a wreck;
He grabbed the nearest gilded youth, and tried to break his neck.
And all the while his throat he held to save his vital spark,
And "Murder! Bloody Murder!" yelled the man from Ironbark.

A. B. PATERSON[2]

How many labourers, while wiping the mud off their faces, pause to consider the dignity of labour?

Very few, I am afraid....

This is a wrong attitude, and militates against the workers' own interests.

[1] Thomas Wood, *Cobbers* (London 1948, first publ. 1934), pp.197-8.
[2] A. B. Paterson, *Collected Verse* (Sydney 1921), p.47, "The Man from Ironbark".

How can our employers become sufficiently wealthy to endow public libraries and subscribe to soup kitchens if we don't take an interest in our work?

And in endeavouring to cultivate this assiduity we have countless shining examples to emulate . . . .

Consider Henry Ford. An ordinary man accused of having made thousands of Ford cars, and further burdened with the responsibility of having sold them for the money, would break down. Probably take orders, or confine himself to a monastery.

But our captains of industry are made of different meat. While Rockefeller is toiling on the golf links, Ford is doing the rounds of the factory hospital, inspecting the maimed and injured; giving a kind smile here, and the sack there. Gently chiding a careless workman for having got his legs cut off in the rolling mills, and spreading brightness and cigar-ash all over the hospital.

Then to go off to visit the widows and orphans of men who did not know what a good job they had. Idlers, these men, too tired to keep out of the machinery. Despite the fact that they threw his machinery out of gear and hindered production for five minutes while they were shovelled out of the way, Ford visits the widows and orphans, magnanimously overlooking the faults of their departed breadwinners.

L. W. LOWER[3]

Morning service! parson preaches;
People all confess their sins:
God's domesticated creatures
Twine and rub against his shins;

Tails erect and whiskers pricking,
Sleeking down their Sunday fur,
Though demure, alive and kicking,
All in unison they purr:

"Lord we praise Thee; hear us Master!
Feed and comfort, stroke and bless!
And not too severely cast a
Glance upon our trespasses . . . .

Twice this week a scrap with Rover;
Once, at least, we missed a rat;
And we *do* regret, Jehovah,
Having kittens in Your hat!"

A. D. HOPE[4]

[3] L. W. Lower, *The Bachelor's Guide to the Care of the Young and Other Stories* (Sydney 1941), pp.36-7, "The Dignity of Labour".
[4] A. D. Hope, *The Wandering Islands* (Sydney 1955), p.66, "The House of God".

National Humour

In no fields of literature is the social element stronger than in humour and satire. Each humorist and satirist is, of course, an individual writer, with his own idiosyncrasies, and these may run counter to any general trend. The elegance of an Ethel Anderson, the fantasy of a McCrae, or the sophisticated wit of a Martin Boyd or an A. D. Hope are highly personal, owing more to the writer's individuality than the Australian society. On the other hand, humour is essentially social in nature: a poet may sing to himself of his own joys and sorrows, but a humorist must tell his joke to others, and the satirist must make someone else or an aspect of his society the butt of his mockery.

Thus we find Bergson, for instance, defining laughter as a social gesture designed by society to correct the wayward individual: "Laughter is, above all, a corrective. Being intended to humiliate, it must make a painful impression on the person against whom it is directed. By laughter, society avenges itself for the liberties taken with it."[5] This definition, based largely on the humour of Molière, is too limited. It fails to cover a Panurge or a Falstaff or a Sam Weller, a Dad Rudd or a Mrs Yabsley. Yet Bergson is sound in perceiving the social character of humour as such.

It is but another step to note that humour is also national in type, since societies are organized within national frameworks. In the universality of grief there is no room for nationalism: such things as death are democratic—touches of nature that make mankind akin, so that we all weep alike. But humour is different, and is expressed in national differentiations. Admittedly, certain types of humour, such as farce, have a touch of universality: the Chinese peasants of Manchuria, when the films were shown to them, relished the antics of Charlie Chaplin as keenly as a Western audience. Outside of the broad, human appeal of farce, however, humour tends to speak in different languages. As John Palmer has put it in his brilliant essay on Comedy:

A joke sets all nations by the ears. We laugh in different languages. The Frenchman violently explodes into laughter at something which leaves the Prussian cold as a stone. An Englishman sees very little fun in Alceste. A Frenchman sees in Falstaff no more than a needlessly fat man.... A joke cannot be translated or interpreted.... In the kingdoms of comedy there are no papers of naturalisation.[6]

[5] Henri Bergson, *Laughter*, trans. by Cloudesley Brereton and Fred Rothwell (London 1911), p.197.

[6] John Palmer, *Comedy* (London n.d.), pp. 5-6, in *The Art and Craft of Letters* series.

The Australian Blend

Although overstated, Palmer's contention is broadly true. Certainly the Australian society has developed its own type of humour, with a blend of specific qualities that make it distinctive. This blend is a complex one that mingles elements that seem contradictory, yet become complementary. On the one hand, the humour tends to have a robust crudity, to be simple, direct, and obvious in its humour of action as shown in tall stories, tales of tricksters, and farce. On the other hand, the humour holds as its keynote an irony which demands a sophisticated detachment and an intellectual assessment of conflicting factors calling for some degree of subtlety. This irony usually adopts the method of understatement, moreover, whereas the tall story goes to the extremes of exaggeration. The latter also consists largely in the glorification of fabulous heroes, whilst the more common note in the humour is irreverent, satiric, and sansculottist. So, too, the tall story runs counter to the general trend of realism by its romantic flights of imagination. Whilst there is a popular enjoyment of the purely comic in broad farce, there is also an undercurrent of sombreness, that occasionally delights in death and the macabre, together with a frequent cynicism and wryness.

The literature contains some comedy of character, but this is comparatively minor, especially when we consider how strongly characteristic this element appears in English and Spanish humour. So, too, the wit and play of ideas in which French humour delights has been relatively infrequent in Australian writing until the recent decades after the last world war, when the writers have turned increasingly to urban themes and to satire.

The humour fits in harmoniously with the other social patterns, and reflects some of them directly, such as the dominance of the bush, realism, sombreness, and radical democracy. The unity, of course, is once again an ecological one of the interaction between the people and the land. The realism, crudity, and occasional callousness, for example, derive from both the working-class majority of the people—including the convicts—and the roughness of pioneering conditions in the bush. So, too, the sansculottism was promoted by the people's democratic egalitarianism and radicalism, sharpened probably by the Irish and the convict rebelliousness against authority, and was linked with the way the untamed wildness of the spacious land broke down respect for the old established customs, institutions, and classes. The land's spaciousness and possibilities gave the stimulus for the tall story, just as its harshness produced the wry and sombre notes in the humour.

Above all, the irony was born of the land, even if it drew strength from the working-class realism and was rendered operative to some extent by the democratic independence which enabled individuals of all classes to make their personal assessments of men and events. In the case of the land, it was the unpredictable variability of the seasons that inevitably produced an ironic, sceptical attitude towards life. In such English-speaking countries as the United States, Canada, and New Zealand the climates are both more favourable and more dependable in their regularity, and so the ironic stance has not been developed as strongly as in Australia. The Canadian winter, for instance, has its rigours, and these are just as formidable as the extremities of the Australian summer, but they occur regularly and suitable preparations can be made to deal with the known. In Australia the vagaries of the rainfall are unknown and unpredictable, whilst conditions usually make it impossible to combat a severe drought which may wipe out even millions of sheep and cattle or cause the complete failure of crops, bringing ruin to graziers and farmers.

In fact, the native irony is ultimately one aspect of the Shadow of Drought, and is closely allied to the realism and sombreness which are also induced by it. The insistence upon facing the honest, uncompromising truth of life, stripped of romantic or sentimental trappings, forms the basis of both the ironic and the realistic patterns. Both are chiefly environmental in origin, and the irony, in particular, is fundamentally a climatic phenomenon arising originally from the hazards of heat and rainfall.

Aspects of Hardness

Examining the qualities of the humour and their literary forms, we find, to begin with, there is a general quality of hardness, of which the irony is only one facet. Australia is a hard land, and the hardness has passed over into the humour. Much of it is at bottom a self-defence mechanism used by the Australian to protect himself against the harshness of his environment. Faced by hardship or disaster, the pioneer had either to weep or to laugh. He chose to laugh, since head and will have always been stronger in the society than the heart. His lack of emotion and his pragmatic realism combined to make him reject the tragic mode of grief and choose the comic mode of laughter. *Such is Life* is a striking example of such a choice. So, too, is much of the prose work of Lawson. With Furphy and Lawson alike we see, too, how the awareness of the bush's hardness has coloured their humour with a hard, sceptical, and sombre undertone. There is a disguised wryness of irony in the way Tom Collins tells of how he discovered that his immediate superior in the civil service, on whose death his hopes of promotion hung, was a young and robust athlete. As for Lawson, his sketch "Settling on the Land" is a comedy bitter with the futility of the selector's struggle on the land.

Behind this sketch is the experience of the men who battled, often vainly like Tom Hopkins, with the hardness of the land and who often felt, like John O'Brien's Hanrahan, a disillusioned doubt of the universe: "We'll all be rooned," says Hanrahan, "before the year is out." The epitome of this disillusionment is Lawson's "The Union Buries Its Dead". Its description of the funeral can best be described as sardonic, a term derived from a sort of rictus of the mouth from a poison weed. It fits in with what Dr Wood noted in the quotation used here at the start of the chapter, where he said that the Australian joke comes "faintly mocking, hiding a sting in its tail. It is exactly what you might expect from that thin-lipped Australian mouth". The tale Dr Wood gives as typical has this sardonic touch, as well as being deeply ironic. It is a story of the depression, and behind it is the radical social protest of a people sometimes embittered by injustice, like Lower's ironic comments on Rockefeller and Ford quoted earlier as an epigraph. Here the poison twisting the mouth is social in character, but it carries the same taste as the cynical sombreness pounded by the pestle of the land.

Lawson comments on a practical joke made on the squatter Baldy Thompson that there was something sad and pathetic about it "as indeed there is with all bush jokes. There seems a quiet sort of sadness always running through outback humour—whether alleged or otherwise."[7] This is a recognition of the sombreness, with a last cynical remark. Elsewhere he comments that death is about the only cheerful thing in the bush. In fact, it is curious how often it comes into the humour. "The Union Buries Its Dead" is one instance, and Lawson's "The Bush Undertaker" and Ted Dyson's "The Funerals of Malachi Mooney" are others.

Often this cheery jesting at death, macabre enough, indicates another aspect of the humour's hardness—its callousness. In verse a good contemporary example is Ronald McCuaig's *The Ballad of Bloodthirsty Bessie*. The title verse tells of the farmer near Sydney who secured cheap labour by hiring farmhands, keeping them by the attractions of his daughter Bessie, and then, when they wanted to leave, pushing them off a cliff at the bottom of which Bessie waited to finish them off with an axe. After seventeen farmhands had been buried by the creek, a spying trooper is also dispatched along with nine soldiers whom the farmer makes drunk, pours rum on, and then sets alight:

[7] Henry Lawson, *Prose Works* (Sydney 1934), p.192, "Baldy Thompson".

The soldiers flared up with a crackle,
And over the roar of the flames
Came the farmer's demoniac cackle
And Bessie's recalcitrant screams:
"Oh, father, I say it is cruel,
Oh, father, I say it's unfair:
You're using my sweethearts as fuel
And doing me out of my share!"

For some to be foiled in their passion
Is more than their reason can stand:
The farmer saw firelight flash on
The axe Bessie held in her hand.
He shouted, "No, Bess! You're my daughter!
To threaten your dad is a crime!"
Then he out with a pistol, and shot her
Through the heart, for the first and last time.[8]

The same lighthearted, callous touch is found even in a lyrical and romantic novel like *The Pea-pickers*, where Eve Langley pictures Charl singing

I hadn't much to give her,
So I threw her in the river ... poor thing!
I didn't like to choke her,
So I hit her with the poker ... poor thing![9]

The callous aspect of the humour's hardness also occurs in the old bush songs, occasionally in the bush balladists, in Lawson's verse "The Captain of the Push", and in many novelists. Xavier Herbert, for example, slaughters his characters in both *Capricornia* and *Soldier's Women* as casually as if he were swatting flies.

The callousness, of course, is part of the frequent crudity of the humour, a crudity produced by pioneering conditions and the *mores* of the working class. Thus A. G. Stephens selected Steele Rudd as the representative humorist, saying:

His work stands not for wit, for satire, for irony, but for sheer fun, and the fun is the typical fun of the Bush—obvious, rough, and hearty.... *On Our Selection* is a humorous book; but the humour, possibly, may not appeal to devotees of Charles Lamb, for example. On the other hand, the humour of Charles Lamb does not appeal to the denizens of Bush Australia. To each humorist his audience...Australian humour is rougher, cruder than the humour of "Punch" or "Puck", but it is racier, less attenuated, and to my mind, far more exhilarating.[10]

Sansculottism

Closely linked with the varying aspects of hardness as with such

[8] Ronald McCuaig, *The Ballad of Bloodthirsty Bessie* (Sydney 1961), p.51.
[9] Eve Langley, *The Pea-pickers* (Sydney 1958 ed., first publ. 1942), p.270.
[10] A. G. Stephens in *Review of Reviews*, 20 May 1903, p.447.

social patterns as realism, radicalism, and the democratic spirit is an irreverence to which Australians are accustomed but which strikes the outside observer forcibly. Arnold Haskell as an English visitor commented on this national trait:

Australian humour is crude, it provokes a guffaw rather than a smile; certainly not a snigger. It is primitive, usually irreverent, but humour of an essentially robust, young and healthy type . . . .
A typical example seems to me the following, which actually occurred.
In a country hotel in Queensland the vicar was lunching with his bishop who was undertaking a pastoral tour. The waitress approached and turned to the vicar, "What will you have, Les?" The bishop raises his eyebrows mildly surprised at the familiarity; but it is his turn now. With a beam she says, "And what will little Robin redbreast have?"[11]

This refusal of a Queensland waitress to be impressed by the ecclesiastical status and vestments of the Church is, indeed, quite typical. The irreverence represents the Australian democrat insisting on his (or her) equality with all classes. It also represents, perhaps, the convict mocking at the authorities of the system, the worker asserting his independence, the radical critical of the upper or wealthier classes, the Irishman with a chip on his shoulder defying the establishment, the realist reducing the pretensions of the mighty, and the bushman employing his own new scale of values in a new environment remote from the hierarchies of the old world. It is a young society revolting against parental traditions. Many strains, it seems to me, combine here as determinants of this quality in the national humour.

Symbolic of this irreverence is the incident in *On Our Selection* where the point of the joke is the visiting swagman in a bearskin cap depriving Dad of his pants. Dad is the head of the family, representing parental authority. Thus to "debag" him is to indicate a revolt against the *father* of the type that is analyzed by Freud, since the father represents the old man of the tribe, the established authority. At the same time the revolt of irreverence is symbolized strikingly by stripping humanity of its clothing, just as Carlyle in *Sartor Resartus* illustrates his philosophy of clothes by imagining a "naked Duke of Windlestraws addressing a naked House of Lords". Australian humour, like the society, finds a youthful delight in this radical stripping off the outward conventions of things to lay bare their intrinsic nakedness. Indeed, whilst this national trend is often called *iconoclastic*, the more exact term is really *sansculottist*.

The sansculottism of our humour is, in fact, often a literal one. It actually reduces man to a ridiculous nudity by continually taking

[11] Arnold L. Haskell, *Waltzing Matilda: a Background to Australia* (London 1940), p.37.

off his pants. There is Ernest Favenc's story of how the parson's "blackboy", Charley, removed the pants to go in swimming—and disclosed herself as a gin. There is Dowell O'Reilly's short story "Bull-dogs", in which the new English parson Swete, returning from a Sunday-school picnic, finds bull-dog ants in his pants. In agony from their bites he takes them off, shakes them out of the train window, and loses them, with consequent events. There is Furphy in *Such is Life* expanding the episode where Tom Collins loses his pants and wanders around in breechless absurdity. Lawson saw the pathos as well as the absurdity of the pantless human being when he wrote "When Your Pants Begin to Go". He, too, recognized the pants as the mark of man's self-respect, which went as the pants went.

The Humour of Action: Farce

Australian literature is a popular literature, often plebian in a way not usually found in English and European literatures. Its characters have most often been drawn from the working class. It is natural that its humour should consist largely in the humour of action and situation which has always appealed to the popular taste in every country in all ages. Farce and the practical joke are the earliest and most persistent forms of humour. They form the very stuff of Aesop's *Fables*, of *The Arabian Nights Entertainments*, of the comedies of Aristophanes, of the liveliest stories in the *Canterbury Tales*, of Rabelais and the farces which gave relief in Paris to those grim and sanguinary melodramas staged in the church-like *Grand Guignol*, of the popular comedies in London and New York, of *On Our Selection*. When Dad Rudd rushes after Joe to give him a hiding, or when Paterson's man from Ironbark runs amok in the barber's saloon after the barber has pretended to cut his throat, or when Spencer's Molongo eleven vainly chase the ball in the dog Pincher's mouth while McDougall tops the score, or when O'Ferrall's lioness scares the policeman and the pie-man, or when Lawson's loaded dog causes a scatteration—when you have all this crude, hearty fun, you have the same sort of humour at which Athens split its sides, Chaucer chuckled, and the Elizabethan groundlings roared applause in the Globe. It is the same comic appeal to the people—"who vulgar coarse buffoonery loves".[12]

The tales of the Miller and the Reeve are perhaps a little broader, more vulgar and coarse in their buffoonery, but the antics of Bottom and Malvolio are akin to Australian humour, and there is scant difference between the thrashing given by Dad or the man from Ironbark and the thrashings administered by Oeacus to Dionysus

---

[12] Aristophanes, *The Frogs*, I, 358.

and Xanthias. It happens, of course, that Aristophanes is a better
writer than Steele Rudd or "Banjo" Paterson, but the type of humour
is the same. It is only humbug to pretend otherwise. Only literary
snobbery would laugh at "The Merry Wives of Windsor" and refuse
to see the equally rollicking humour of "The Loaded Dog".

The rough and ready life of the bush gave a robustness to its
humour of the farcical situation, its comedy of action. If we examine
this comedy more closely, we find that it tends to repeat three
patterns of situation: the one of exaggeration, imaginative rather
than realistic, passing into the fantasy or nonsense of the "tall story";
the situation which involves swindling or the outwitting of a trickster, a farce of tricks and counter-tricks, a battle of wits; and thirdly,
incongruities, comic misfortunes, and absurd situations.

The Tall Story

"It will be very strange," wrote Adam McCay, "if Australians do
not develop a bold and generous view of affairs, seeing that life in
this country is of the epic sort."[13] The epic spaciousness did, indeed,
develop something of boldness in humour, just as similar pioneering
conditions in the United States produced a humour of the Middle
West that became characteristically American. There the great
and seemingly immeasurable spaces, with what appeared illimitable
resources, as the pioneers crossed the Alleghanies to the valleys of
the Mississippi and Ohio, found a reflex in a humour of the back-
woodsmen which was full of tall stories, gargantuan exaggeration,
and fantastic nonsense, with situations, ideas, and even language itself
treated with a reckless exuberance as in the folk tales concerning
Davy Crockett, Pecos Bill, and that "helliferocious fellow", Mike
Fink. Josh Billings, Artemus Ward, Petroleum V. Naseby, and Max
Adeler outdid each other in riotous hyperbole, an orgy of bragging.
Mark Twain was the greatest. The New England pundits—except the
far-sighted, democratic Emerson—frowned on this vulgar, crude,
farcical humour of the West—but it established itself as the characteristic American humour. No English writer, for instance, could
have written Mark Twain's "Cannibalism in the Cars", the tale of
the starving Congressmen, snowed up in their mountain train, who
ate each other with full legislative decorum: "The next morning we
had Morgan of Alabama for breakfast, one of the finest men I ever
sat down to—he was a perfect gentleman, and singularly juicy."[14]

Australia had the same spaciousness, the same sort of heroic life,
but not the same richness of resources as America. Hence we only

[13] Adam McCay, "Us Australians" in *Australia To-Day*, Nov. 1913.
[14] Mark Twain (Samuel L. Clemens), *The Complete Short Stories of Mark Twain*,
ed. Charles Neider (New York 1957), pp.14-15.

find a strain of the epic exaggeration, a few trumpet notes—not the whole orchestra blaring as in the American folklore. Yet the notes blare out on occasion. Thus no horsemen ever were seen in Australia like the Snowy River riders, and The Man from Snowy River rode epically. Nor was there ever a polo game like that heroic contest between The Cuff and Collar Team and the Geebung Polo Club, as "they waddied one another till the plain was strewn with dead".[15]

Of the same hyperbolic family, too, was W. T. Goodge's once renowned "The Oozlum Bird" and "Daley's Dorg Wattle", whilst the classic example of the tall story of the bush remains "The Champion Bullock-Driver" by the celebrated Lance Skuthorpe. Furphy joins the fabulists with *The Buln-Buln and the Brolga*, or the lyre-bird and the native companion, a sustained competition in exaggeration between two accomplished liars, Fred Falkland-Pritchard and Barefoot Bob, in contrasting styles and with Furphy's usual disquisitions sandwiched in between the incredibilities.

The post-war awakening of interest in folklore, mostly of the bush, brought about a revival of the tall stories centred on the mythical Speewah station, away out West, over the next range, where everything was on a gargantuan scale, and where such folk heroes as Big Bill, Crooked Mick, and the Boss performed feats as fabulous as those of the American Pecos Bill and Davy Crockett. Alan Marshall has recounted some of the Speewah folk stories with great verve. Dal Stivens, too, has developed the tall story brilliantly in such volumes as *Ironbark Bill* and *The Gambling Ghost*, with exaggerations as far-fetched and original as the folk tales, a remarkable fertility of imagination, and graphic phrasing. One of the best exploitations of the tall story is E. J. Brady's ballad "The Coachman's Yarn", which tells in his vigorous, natural style of the extreme cold on the Monaro, where even the candle-wicks and the sounds froze, and when, as a log began to thaw, they heard the sound of the cross-cut saw thawing out.

Tales of the Trickster

Equally as common as these fantastic flights of imagination are the many instances of the more realistic humour which turns upon some form of trickery. This type of humour seems to be perhaps more common in Australia than in America, although it is also frequent there. Lawson's tales of Steelman, for instance, are paralleled by O. Henry's tales of Jeff Peters. Peters, like Steelman, "was a 'spieler', pure and simple, but did things in humorous style . . . Steelman 'had' you in a fashion that would make your friends laugh." Lawson's tales in this field of humour include "Stiffner and Jim

15 A. B. Paterson, op. cit., p.33, "The Geebung Polo Club".

(Thirdly, Bill)", "The Man Who Forgot", "Mitchell, a Character Sketch", and the Steelman series, in which "The Geological Spieler" is outstanding as an entertaining example of the story in which the fun lies in the way the trickster is himself tricked.

In keeping with the old European picaresque tradition, the roguery is taken light-heartedly and in some cases the reader's sympathy is enlisted for the quick-witted trickster. Paterson's verses show a variety of treatment on the theme of "taking down" people. In "Our New Horse", for example, the biters are bit. In "An Idyll of Dandaloo" it was easy to win sympathy by reversing the usual order to let the bush township take down the smart Sydney stranger. Greek meets Greek in "A Walgett Episode", whilst Saltbush Bill, the travelling drover, varies the trick of fighting to get grass for his sheep. Brunton Stephens brings in an unexpected type of trick in "My Other Chinee Cook"—who used puppy as the chief ingredient in his rabbit pie.

Deservedly famous is one of the best of all the tricks, the highly original device by which McDougall topped the score in a bush cricket match. Here is the raciest humour of action—better, I think, than all the tricks of the horse-racing trade—when McDougall, last man in for Piper's Flat, with fifty runs to make for a win, makes them when his dog Pincher seizes the ball, as he has been trained to do, and runs away with it:

> *He seized the ball like lightning; then he ran behind a log,*
> *And McDougall kept on running, while Molongo chased the dog!*
> *They chased him up, they chased him down, they chased him round,*
> > *and then*
> *He darted through a slip-rail as the scorer shouted "Ten!"*
> *McDougall puffed; Molongo swore; excitement was intense,*
> *As the scorer marked down twenty, Pincher cleared a barbed-wire fence.*
> *"Let us head him!" shrieked Molongo. "Brain the mongrel with a bat!"*
> *"Run it out! Good old McDougall!" yelled the men of Piper's Flat.*[16]

Misadventures

The third category of the humour of action—the farcical adventure or misadventure, with absurd situations—contains a large share of Australian humorous prose and verse. In the verse perhaps the honours should go to Paterson's "A Bush Christening", told with immense verve and a most effective use of double rhyming. In prose Edward Dyson is one of the foremost writers with excellent stories like "The Funerals of Malachi Mooney". "Kodak" (Ernest O'Ferrall) wrote many good pieces, but his short story of "The Lobster

[16] Thomas E. Spencer, *How McDougall Topped the Score* (Sydney 1908), p.25. Originally Spencer spelt the name "M'Dougall" but "McDougall" became the standard form.

and the Lioness" is outstanding. This goes along with Lawson's classic, "The Loaded Dog", to make two of the funniest stories in Australian literature.

Comedy of Character

Sometimes Australian humour rises above farce to a true comedy of character. Joe Wilson, for instance, is not a humorous character, but both he and his story are treated with glimpses of the laughable. Mitchell, on the other hand, is a character who has a keen sense of humour himself—as well as a broad, tolerant sympathy—and whose speech and behaviour are treated in such a way as to present a humorous type—or rather, individual. It is the virtue of Lawson, in fact, that his people are rarely "types"; each has his own individuality; each is a complete human being. Mitchell can tell a joke against himself in his courtship of the ugliest girl he knew; he can "wangle" more than his share as a travelling swaggie who knows his ropes and has plenty of self-confidence; he is shrewd enough to see through Smith, "the man who forgot"; he can be cynical even about the kind-hearted Giraffe; but he also enters with deep understanding into the dark feelings of the Lachlan, the former "hero of Redclay"; he shows a gentle consideration for Peter, the missionary of the bush, and for the digger on the boat whose wife had died; and he is a genial philosopher on such subjects as women, sex, and refusing to take the sack. Bit by bit Lawson builds Mitchell's character up, gives him complexity, and makes him a vital creation. Even Steelman is more than a spieler and sharper, and grows as a likeable trickster.

So, too, Steele Rudd has much the same sympathy as Lawson, coupled with his gift for humour. Dad and Mum, and Dave and Joe, come alive. They are figures in the national gallery of literary creations. Dad Rudd stands out as the most vital person in the Australian comedy of character—and he does so because Steele Rudd had a geniune touch of the Dickensian creativeness.

Such creations are rare here, as elsewhere. The comic gallery is a small one. In it we find Mrs Yabsley, charwoman and personality, genial but decided in opinions, to whom Louis Stone has given a vital gusto in his *Jonah*—Mrs Yabsley who remarks of her husband: "I was his first love, as the saying goes, but beer was his second." Another living character is "The Sentimental Bloke", since C. J. Dennis spins lively narratives which reflect different sides of his character as larrikin, lover, husband, father, and mate—not to mention farmer and son-in-law. The sentimental element has not worn well, and we feel today that it is overdone, too contrived, with the humour also, perhaps, a little synthetic. But it remains amusing still, and such pieces as "The Play" are handled excellently. The reactions of Bill

N

to *Romeo and Juliet* ring true. Once again the humour is sans-culottist, stripping the romance of Shakespeare of its old-world glamour. Bill is in true Australian character when he, a Jacobin of the Melbourne slums, protests:

> *Wot's in a name? Wot's in a string o' words?*
> *They scraps in ole Verona wiv their swords,*
> *An' never give a bloke a stray dog's chance,*
> *An' that's Romance.*
> *But when they deals it out wiv bricks and boots*
> *In Little Lon, they're low degraded broots.*[17]

The essence of both the Bloke and his humour is irreverence: the incongruity between a Shakespearean romance and its treatment in realistic slanguage by a Melbourne larrikin. So, too, Norman Lindsay explores the comedy of adolescence realistically and skilfully in *Redheap* and *Saturdee*, and brings his artists to convincing life in his rollicking *A Curate in Bohemia*.

After these characters who are basically humorous, we find a number who are incidentally humorous. Tom Collins is, of course; but he is more the philosopher, observer, and transcriber, a figure of irony, not of fun—except when he loses his pants. He is an associate rather than a full member of the true comedy club, like Danny Delacey and Old Blastus of Bandicoot, Tilly Beamish, Lawson's Giraffe, Mo Burdekin, and many other characters.

One of the finest pieces of comedy characterization in the drama is Ma Bates, a battler with a rough and candid tongue, in Henrietta Drake-Brockman's play of the north, *Men Without Wives*. There is also true comedy of character in Sumner Locke-Elliott's brilliant play of soldiers being "browned off" in a Northern Territory camp during the war, *Rusty Bugles*, and in Ray Lawler's *Summer of the Seventeenth Doll*.

In the contemporary novel Patrick White's *The Tree of Man* contains two humorous characters in Mr and Mrs O'Dowd, engaged in some amusing farce, but they are rather stock types of the comic Irish. Much more convincing are Kylie Tennant's Ma Jones in the entertaining satires of *Ma Jones and the Little White Cannibals* and her Miss Phipps in *The Battlers*. Phippsy rises above the comic to curious heights when, as the lowliest of "pot-wallopers" on the Hotel Stainford's kitchen staff, she helps the drunken rich grazier's son to bed and he thrusts three crumpled notes into her hand. She discovers she is holding three fifty-pound notes. At first exultant, she finally decides it would be beneath her dignity to keep this wonderful windfall, although she has hardly a penny to her name. Sadly but

---

[17] C. J. Dennis, *The Songs of a Sentimental Bloke* (Sydney 1940 ed., first publ. 1915), p.30.

firmly she goes to the room of the young grazier's father, hands him the money, and bids him a gracious and stately goodnight.

> She had been afraid, but she was afraid no longer. The giving back of that money had freed her from the haunting dread of loneliness and insecurity. She was once again Ruler of the World Feminised State. She decided suddenly she would leave this despicable hotel. It was springtime and she was free, white, and well over twenty-one. She would go cherry-picking. She was not afraid of the road. She was not afraid of anything.[18]

Miss Phipps is a true comic creation with a Dickensian richness.

So, too, is Mr Gudgeon, the boozing hero of Lower's extravaganza *Here's Luck*, a highly original compound of realism, fantasy, absurdity, satire, and sardonic wit. Amidst the hilarious adventures of Gudgeon and his son Stanley their characters emerge clearly, drawn with a sophisticated, cynical pen.

In the short story the comedy of character developed so skilfully by Lawson and Dyson has been followed by a number of later writers. Brian James, for instance, creates his country folk with Lawsonian realism and irony. His gift of easy naturalness is shared by "James Hackston" (Hal Gye), another born humorist with an eye for the idiosyncrasies of personality. Alan Marshall and John Morrison, too, can achieve humour as well as tragedy or pathos in their character sketches. E. O. Schlunke has effective and entertaining character sketches in such stories as "The Enthusiastic Prisoner", "Alfred", and "The Heretic of Isola". In "Fiend and Friend" and "Uncle Foss and Big Bogga" Hal Porter pictures his characters imaginatively and pungently. Thus an Adelaide schoolteacher is described:

> There was a spiritual and a sniffable mustiness about him as though he rarely showered intellectually or actually.[19]

Wit

In Hal Porter's portrait sketch we see, in addition to the sharp probing of character, a lively sense of word values and an urbane wit. These qualities have been emerging more fully in the work of such contemporary writers as Porter, Stow, Thea Astley, Keneally, and Peter Mathers. In the past they were infrequent, since wit requires a keen ear for words, a feeling for style, and an interest in the play of ideas, all of which were generally lacking in a pioneering people. The Australian society was for long too youthful, crude, and energetic as a general rule, to compass the elegant, leisurely wit of a comedy of manners. It would have been impossible to set down Mirabel and Millamant in the outback. Millamant might consent

---

[18] Kylie Tennant, *The Battlers* (Sydney 1945, first publ. 1941), p. 158.
[19] Hal Porter, *A Bachelor's Children* (Sydney 1962), p.244.

"to dwindle into a wife" on a Congreve stage, but she would have dwindled into nothingness once she stepped on colonial soil.

The temper of the society has been aggressively democratic, as we have seen, demanding equality, but wit is by nature more aristo-cratic, since it implies as a rule the superior judgement passing indivi-dual criticism. Often, although not necessarily, it has a satiric edge, as in Heine's comment on de Musset: "Vanity is one of his four heels of Achilles"; or in Rebecca West's on the dandified, Armenian-born Michael Arlen: "He is every other inch a gentleman." Such epi-grammatic condensations of wit have not been common in Australian writing.

Yet there has been a definite strain of wit running through the literature from colonial days, since there was always a cultured minority in the cities. Not only did emigrants like Lowe and Forster, Marcus Clarke and Gordon, Catherine Spence and Ada Cambridge bring with them a cultural background, knowledge of the classics, and a sophisticated, lively intelligence, but the native-born writers like Deniehy, Harpur, Kendall, Tasma and Mrs Campbell Praed also belonged to the cultured few, cultivated the graces of language, and had an interest in ideas.

As early as 1854 Catherine Helen Spence, for long called "the first Australian woman novelist", used satiric wit when she drew the portrait of Miss Withering in Adelaide as the unattractive, super-cilious, genteel Englishwoman declaring: "I have quite made up my mind to remain single unless I could marry a gentleman worth at least eighteen hundred a year—and even then I think I should be thrown away upon such specimens as I have yet seen."[20]

The critical prose of A. G. Stephens abounds in terse, witty judge-ments: "Mr Sladen's work in relation to this country has been characterized by energy and incompetence."[21] And again:

"Geoffry Hamlyn" is a pleasant, rambling story of the old school, patchy in interest, and very patchy in merit. It is never quite dull enough to bore, and rarely bright enough to excite. You put it down without difficulty, and take it up without anticipation.[22]

Here the wit is always to the point, epigrammatic, and illumi-nating. A.G.S. believed in meat off every cut made with his keen critical blade. Hugh McCrae, on the other hand, is whimsical with his wit, as exact as Stephens in his phrasing, but lighter, more dis-cursive. Ethel Anderson is akin to McCrae in the gracefulness of her

[20] Anon. (Catherine Helen Spence), *Clara Morison: a Tale of South Australia during the Gold Fever*, 2 vols (London 1854), p.170.
[21] Vance Palmer (ed.), *A. G. Stephens: His Life and Work* (Melbourne 1941), p.21, "Foreword".
[22] Ibid., p.48.

prose style, her poetic touch, and the polished yet kindly wit that plays over the old-world stories of Parramatta in the 1850s. The style has an elegance that is old-fashioned, in keeping with the period and her upper-class characters. Here, as in McCrae's creation of eighteenth century modes in *The Du Poissey Anecdotes*, we have something exceptional in Australian prose—and all the more valuable for that—a glimpse of the comedy of manners. A delicate and sometimes subtle wit plays over the scene and personae gently, playfully. Take, for example, the chapter in which the venerable vicar of Mallow's Marsh, aged eighty-four, grows concerned over the way the numerous women of the rectory household fondly spoil his fatherless grandson Donalbain. So, the day after Donalbain's fifth birthday, Mr McCree takes him into the orchard, near which Mr Noakes the gardener is working and warns the child against women, to find that the gardener had already given a warning.

"Mr Noakes says I am to avoid women as I would the Devil," said Donalbain....

"Yes," the boy continued, "Mr Noakes says, if you meet a girl and a death-adder, kill the girl and cuddle the adder. He says it's safer."

Sitting in his threadbare black cassock on the grey bole of the fallen tree, Mr McCree, who had served his God devotedly for over sixty years, felt that none of his own experiences had brought him any knowledge so salty. He considered, half astonished, the implications of such an attitude. He was, himself, warning his grandson against the deleterious effects of a woman's love; of a woman's affections. But, need one go so far?[23]

Two more outstanding illustrations of non-satirical wit are Norman Lindsay's book for children, *The Magic Pudding*, and Ray Robinson's *Between Wickets*. The first is deservedly a classic, and its rollicking adventures of Bunyip Bluegum the koala, Bill Barnacle the sailor, and Sam Sawnoff the penguin have such an original combination of wit and humour, in prose and verse, topped off with Norman Lindsay's superb drawings, that *The Magic Pudding* is already occupying in Australia the supreme place in children's books that *Alice in Wonderland* has held for so long in England. It has a final felicity that is lacking in Norman Lindsay's novels, even though these, as we have seen, are entertaining and spirited.

There are a number of excellent writers on cricket, mostly former test players like "Johnny" Moyes and Jack Fingleton, but Ray Robinson is outstanding as the wittiest. He uses simile and metaphor freely, like Neville Cardus, but is superior to Cardus since his style is more spontaneous and flows more naturally. His description of Don Bradman as the Reluctant Dragon, trying to cope uneasily with Larwood's bodyline bowling, retreating to a new line wide of the leg stump, is especially graphic:

23 Ethel Anderson, *At Parramatta* (Melbourne 1956), pp.55-6.

From his remote disadvantage-point Bradman indulged in swishful thinking by attempting slashing square-cuts and cover-hits. His bat, so often described as a flashing broadsword, was used more like a harpoon. If, instead of a body-liner, the ball happened to be straight, Whaler Bradman trusted to luck that it would clear his forsaken stumps....

There was something feverish in Bradman's brilliance. It was as if he had posted up one of those shop placards: *Great Fire Sale. Everything Must Go.*[24]

Of other forms of wit there has been little in parody outside a few skilful verses by A. G. Stephens and Ronald McCuaig. We have been mercifully spared the concept of wit in the shape of mis-spelling which afflicted American humour last century. On the other hand, punning assumed new horrors in the extravaganzas which were popular on the Australian stage in the seventies and eighties of last century; typical examples may be found in Marcus Clarke's *Goody Two Shoes and Little Boy Blue, or Sing a Song of Sixpence: Harlequin Heydiddle-diddle-em and the Kingdom of Coins,* which was produced in Melbourne in 1870. In his far-fetched play on words Clarke showed an assiduous if misplaced ingenuity. The most original punster has been "Lennie" Lower, who, at his best, raised paronomasia to fantastic absurdity, surprising and delighting by unexpected twists of language and thought. His remarks on milk, for instance, are refreshing:

But let us take a look at this milk. It is a thick white substance with rum in it. Or it may be shaken with vanilla in it; it depends on the cow who served you.

There is no udder source of milk than the cow.[25]

Josh Billings, with whom Lower has an occasional affinity, once divided "snaiks into I klass — devlish". Lower discusses several varieties:

The adder is sum snake. It has no eyelids, but sees out of its snaked eye.

The viper is a Jewish snake closely allied to the pen-viper and the dish-viper. It sheds its skin twice a year, but no one can find the shed.

Remember your geometry. A straight line is the shortest distance between a snake and some other place.[26]

In contrast, the worst type of punning and alliteration occurs in the laborious clichés of facetiousness committed by Frank Clune. After reading some of these, Hugh McCrae once observed to me, "A little more of this, and I'll be a complete Clunatic". A study of such afflictions would come, however, into the field, not of literature, but of loimography.

[24] Ray Robinson, *Between Wickets* (London 1958 ed., first publ. 1945), p.133, "The Reluctant Dragon".

[25] L. W. Lower, *Here's Another* (Sydney 1932), p.55.

[26] Ibid., p.43.

Satire

Much of the wit in Australian writing lies in its satire, and can best be considered under this heading. In verse the earliest satirists, Lowe and Forster, were also the wittiest writers of the 1840s. This can not be said of Harpur and Kendall in their satires, which are marked more by vigour than by subtlety, and tend to lose the proper satiric detachment in earnest abuse. Harpur wields a cudgel in his long-unpublished satire "The Temple of Infamy", as can be seen in his hard-hitting attack on Wentworth, the democratic champion of political freedoms who turned to be the spokesman of the wealthy squatters:

> *But now behold him in his native hue,*
> *The bullying, bellowing champion of the Few!*
> *A Patriot?—he who hath not sense nor heed*
> *Of public ends beyond his own mere need!*
> *Whose country's ruin, to his public fear,*
> *Means only this—the loss of Windermere!*
> *And by the same self-legislative rule*
> *Australia's growth the growth of W—tw—th's wool!*[27]

Kendall, too, was liable to be so violently abusive at times that the editors refused to print his verses as too libellous. His publisher originally brought out *Songs from the Mountains* with the satire "The Song of Ninian Melville" included in it, but forced Kendall to withdraw the poem when a reviewer warned that it was ground for a libel suit. Melville was member of the New South Wales Parliament representing Northumberland (which included Newcastle and Lambton) from 1880 to 1894. Kendall attacks him roundly as a politician who had sought popularity among the mob, posing as a freethinker abusing religion:

In the fly-blown village pothouse, where a dribbling bag of beer
Passes for a human being, Nin commenced his new career—
Talked about the "Christian swindle"—cut the Bible into bits—
Shook his fist at Mark and Matthew—gave the twelve Apostles fits;
Slipped into the priests and parsons—hammered at the British Court—
Boozy boobies were astonished: lubbers of the Lambton sort!
Yards of ear were cocked to listen—yards of mouth began to shout,
Here's a cove as is long-headed—Ninny knows his way about![28]

Here are wit and liveliness. They indicate why the editor of the *Freeman's Journal*, in which most of Kendall's satires and lighter verses were published, said to him, "There is nothing the readers of the *Freeman* like so well as your verses."

[27] Charles Harpur, "The Temple of Infamy", unpublished manuscript in Harpur MSS, A87, the Mitchell Library, Sydney, n.p.

[28] T. Inglis Moore (ed.), *Selected Poems of Henry Kendall* (Sydney 1957), p.159.

Victor Daley was unusual in the gaiety he brought to his satires, since most satirical poets were earnest. The satirists closest to him in this respect are two from more recent times, Kylie Tennant and Lower. Typical of Daley's mockery in the social poems he wrote, mostly as "Creeve Roe", is "The Model Journalist":

> Pose as the People's Friend,
> Its candid, calm adviser—
> But never dare offend
> The Lord God Advertiser.[29]

Radical and socialist as well as dreamer of poetic dreams, Daley occasionally is bitter when he satirizes the rich or the office-worker in the straw hat who truckles to them. His wit and satire are at their best, however, in his critique of A. G. Stephens as literary critic in "Narcissus and Some Tadpoles". This is witty and genial, but strikes shrewdly at the foibles of "the three-initialled Terror", as Furphy called him. It says much for A.G.S. that it was he himself who published it.

Kenneth Slessor can also be genially satiric, as in "Country Towns", but there is savagery in other satires such as "An Inscription for Dog River" which comments that the soldiers gave the general everything —"everything but respect", and "Vesper-Song of the Reverend Samuel Marsden", which smites the pastor of convict days who was also such a free dispenser of the lash as a magistrate that he was known as "the flogging parson":

> Lord, I have sung with ceaseless lips
> A tinker's litany of whips,
> Have graved another Testament
> On backs bowed down and bodies bent.
> My stripes of jewelled blood repeat
> A scarlet Grace for holy meat.
>
>> Not mine, the Hand that writes the weal
>> On this, my vellum of puffed veal,
>> Not mine, the glory that endures,
>> But Yours, dear God, entirely Yours.[30]

Beside such scarifying of General Blamey and Marsden, the satirical verses of Paul Grano are mild, and the sharp edge of the laconic satires by E. G. Moll, good as they are, seems relatively to draw little blood.

The political satires of two radical poets, John Manifold and David Martin, are effectively controlled and skilful.

Of all the satirists in verse the most brilliant is A. D. Hope. Etched

---

[29] Muir Holborn and Marjorie Pizer (ed.), *Creeve Roe: Poetry by Victor Daley* (Sydney 1947), pp.70-1.
[30] Kenneth Slessor, *Poems* (Sydney 1944), p.97.

in acid, his lines bite deeply. His wit is cerebral, yet savage, phrased with memorable scorn, sometimes mocking gaily, as in "The House of God", at other times conveying a bitter Swift-like contempt and disgust. He has developed a highly original style despite affinities with Auden in "Toast for a Golden Age" and with Pound and Eliot in "Easter Hymn":

> *The City of God is built like other cities:*
> *Judas negotiates the loans you float;*
> *You will meet Caiaphas upon committees;*
> *You will be glad of Pilate's casting vote.*[31]

In particular, Hope has exploited strikingly a method of his own whereby he pursues a metaphor with penetrating skill throughout a poem so that the imagery is revelatory as well as entertaining. We have seen this method in "The House of God", where the worshippers in church are represented as cats, Jehovah's pets. Love is viewed in sporting images in "Sportsfield", whilst "The Brides" offers (as E. E. Cummings, in a very different style, did earlier) a devastating identification of brides with new cars, mocking the mechanism of modern marriage:

> *Grease to the elbows Mum and Dad enthuse,*
> *Pocket their spanners and survey the bride;*
> *Murmur: "a sweet job! All she needs is juice!*
> *Built for a life-time—sleek as a fish—Inside*
>
> *He will find every comfort: the full set*
> *Of gadgets; knobs that answer to the touch*
> *For light or music, a place for his cigarette;*
> *Room for his knees; a honey of a clutch."* ...
>
> *Her heavenly bowser-boy assumes his seat;*
> *She prints the soft dust with her brand-new treads,*
> *Swings towards the future, purring with a sweet*
> *Concatenation of the poppet heads.*[32]

So Hope flays harshly, bitterly, various aspects of modern society: religion, psychology, love, marriage, suburbia and, above all, the mechanical outlook and the dominance of technocracy. Occasionally the satire weakens as detachment is lost and the scorn plunges into disgust, but usually the keen, penetrating intellect maintains a deliberate, disciplined control, the honesty is unsparing, and the phrasing is powerfully imaginative.

James McAuley, another intellectual, often bracketed with Hope, is a lyrical poet of distinction, but in satire dwindles to a kind of lesser Hope. In "A Letter to John Dryden", as Leonie J. Kramer pointed out, McAuley mixes satirical buffoonery with serious reason-

[31] A. D. Hope, op. cit., p.12.   [32] Ibid., p.58.

ing to produce "an awkward incongruity of tone . . . . McAuley misses the broad-based satirical view of his model; and presents instead rather bad-tempered attacks on secular education and on the substitution of cleanliness for godliness."[33]

Prose Satirists

In prose the satirical note is stronger than usually supposed. Marcus Clarke and Daniel Deniehy in the colonial period were both natural satirists with a command of wit: Clarke in his sketches, essays and the character of Meekin in his novel; Deniehy in his witty, forceful speech on Wentworth's plan for a colonial nobility and his lively, entertaining political satire *How I Became Attorney-General of New Barataria*. The colonial women novelists delighted in satirical touches: Catherine Spence in her character sketch of Miss Withering in *Clara Morison*; Ada Cambridge in her tilts at the narrowness of orthodox religion and morality in *A Marked Man* and the delightful *A Little Minx*; Tasma in her comments in *Uncle Piper of Piper's Hill* on Sara Cavendish and the parasitic, supercilious Mr Cavendish; and Rosa Campbell-Praed in her amusing picture of Brisbane society and politicians in *Politics and Passion*.

In this century Martin Boyd is thoroughly successful in the constant play of a sophisticated, urbane satire in his series of Victorian family novels. Of the religious Susan he tells how she loved her father Sim Montfort but felt that she should not enjoy his malicious comments on men and affairs. "She determined henceforth only to laugh at those of Sim's jokes which were kindly meant, which was not likely to leave her many opportunities for laughter."[34] We may say the same of Boyd's wit, since it is almost always satiric, with a malicious, cynical flavour, often used to garnish the conversations of his characters. Thomas Allman, for instance, whom Sim described as "Bit hairy at the heels", a heavy bourgeois type alien to the aristocratic Montforts, wins the affections of Amy and asks her parents for her hand. Her father Henry was disconcerted, her mother Letitia horrified at the idea of Allman:

> Henry had discussed the proposal with Letitia.
> "But is he a gentleman?" Letitia had cried.
> "Well, in Australia, yes," said Henry . . . "I might confess that he is hardly the young man I had hoped for as a son-in-law, but he is hard-working, sober and industrious."
> "It sounds like a reference for a butler," said Letitia acidly.[35]

[33] Dr Leonie J. Kramer, "James McAuley: Tradition in Australian Poetry", The Canberra University College, *The Commonwealth Literary Fund Lectures 1957* (Canberra 1957), p.4.
[34] Martin Mills (Martin Boyd), *The Montforts* (London 1928), p.128.
[35] Ibid., p.86.

Much of Martin Boyd's success as a satirist comes from the fact that he is a phenomenon now rather rare, a complete Anglo-Australian. Since he is a citizen of two worlds, he can play one off against the other. His ambivalence enables him to see the defects of them both, and to be reasonably impartial in his satiric judgment of each. The ease, polish, and urbanity of his style, like the sophistication of his cultivated wit, make him distinctive in Australian fiction.

Kylie Tennant is just as witty, just as satiric, as Martin Boyd, but they are poles apart because she belongs to the main stream. Her wit has not the polish of his, she eschews his stylistic graces, and her satire is more full-blooded, more masculine than his slightly feminine malice. Where he achieves elegance, she rejoices in a lusty gusto. He has subtlety, but she has strength and colour. Her account of Mrs White in *Tiburon* is characteristic:

Mrs White was a woman contented with very little otherwise she would never have stood Dave, although when she married him he was a good-looking enough chap....
When Mrs White caught a chill waiting for Dave one wet night, the town was divided between the opinion that she ought to have more sense and surprise that anything could kill a White.[36]

Kylie Tennant is notably impartial in her satire. In *Tiburon* she ridicules the snobberies and shams of a country town; in *Foveaux* the dishonesty and greed of politicians, aldermen, and landlords; in *Ride on Stranger* she cracks at every head within reach, with Shannon Hicks rambling around the assorted insanities of Sydney—broadcasting, abortion, the religious Abbey of Human Brotherhood, the Proletarian Club, and the International Peacelovers.

In the post-war years, as the Australian society has grown more self-conscious and critical, the strain of satire has become more noticeable in fiction, so that we have Sutton Woodfield irreverently debunking politics and politicians with an expertise that indicates inside political knowledge in *A for Artemis*, David Forrest pricking the inflated dignity of those august institutions the banks in *The Hollow Woodheap*, and Robert Burns in *Mr Brain Knows Best* subjecting big business, trade union politics, communists, university intellectuals, the public service, and journalism alike to a disillusioned, sardonic wit.

It was surprising when Eleanor Dark, whose novels had been marked by seriousness and dignity, emerged as a genuine humorist with the delightful drollery of *Lantana Lane*, which combined touches of satire and wit with comedy of character and the humour of misadventure. One sketch, "Sweet and Low", as vulgar as Chaucer, triumphs as one of the funniest stories in Australian writing.

[36] Kylie Tennant, *Tiburon* (Sydney 1945 ed., first publ. 1935), pp.8-9.

The strongest and most subtle satire in our contemporary fiction, however, comes from that rich and complex writer Patrick White, although his strength as a satirist has been largely overlooked in the critical attention paid to those more striking and revolutionary aspects of his genius which have made him tower, mountain-like, in our literary landscape. Yet in both *The Tree of Man* and *Voss* the satire runs with greater naturalness and surety than the more ambitious but chequered course of his poetic, imaginative, and symbolic writing. In the latter he is often unequal in treatment and derivative in style, whilst his satirical flair maintains an even pitch and remains all his own.

In *The Tree of Man* he displays brilliantly the hollow efforts of Thelma, that "thin woman of taste", to achieve a brittle gentility:

Presently Thelma Forsdyke opened her crocodile handbag, which she had bought after noticing quietly that such a handbag was carried by those women who frightened her . . . .
She seldom committed herself to emotion, which was bad for her health, or to statement of opinion, for this would have meant her having one.[37]

In *Voss* the mid-Victorian society of Sydney, solid and respectable, is brought to life with a satiric clarity in the shape of the Bonners and their circle, including Lieutenant Radclyffe, who quizzes Laura Trevelyan at the Bonners' dinner party, only to be disturbed by her unconventional reply.

"Dear me, if these educated young ladies are not the deuce," said Tom Radclyffe, whose turn it was to hate.
Ideas disturbed his manliness.[38]

In the later work the satire loses its earlier objectivity at times, and the attacks on the banality of suburbia, like the play *The Season at Sarsaparilla*, are charged with personal bitterness. The portraits sometimes grow savage, so that in the short story "A Cheery Soul" and its dramatization the irritating do-gooder Miss Docker is excoriated ruthlessly. In the novel *Riders in the Chariot* Patrick White passes from satire, which must retain some detachment, into an ethical fierceness when he creates Mrs Jolley and Mrs Flack, not as suburban nonentities, but as living embodiments of almost undiluted evil. The laughter of pure satire is lost as we move from the urbanity of a Pope to the savagery of a Swift.

Satire also mingles with wit in the sketches and articles of such popular humorists as Leon Gellert, Alexander Macdonald, Max Fatchen, Ross Campbell, Cyril Pearl, and Alan FitzGerald. With these writers reaching many readers through the newspaper columns

[37] Patrick White, *The Tree of Man* (London 1958 ed., first publ. 1957), pp.346, 353.
[38] Patrick White, *Voss* (London 1956 ed., first publ. 1955), pp.88-9.

the Australian public is being thoroughly trained to enjoy a humour which has developed, especially since the last war, from the former comedy of action to a sophisticated yet lively play of ideas and a satirical scrutiny of society by keen intelligences. The state of the world today invites criticism—and is getting it plentifully. All our social patterns have come under fire. The spate of satirical and ironical comment shows how the Australian society has to some extent turned inwards to give a long, hard look at itself with a disillusioned, dispassionate eye. Never before has it been so widely self-conscious, critical as it was in the depression years of the thirties. Then the focus was on the economy. Today it has been widened to take in all aspects of the society. Naturally the critics have found abundant scope for satire, whilst the old tradition of irony, which sprang from the land, has been strengthened by its application to the society itself.

Irony

Thus the ironic mode, usually confined to our prose, has invaded the poetry here as it has done elsewhere this century. It is only incidentally satiric, and not quite a full-blown irony. The work of the younger contemporary poets in this mode is ironic chiefly in its understatement, detachment, and intellectual probing of our confused urban life and the many barbarisms of our violent, fear-beset, hate-ridden atomic age. It describes, analyses, and questions, but rarely gives any answers or goes on to any positive affirmation. Its suspension of faith and passion is a direct response, of course, to the disillusioning social environment. It tends to be intelligent, sophisticated, and realistic in mood, precise and often spare in style, and semi-dramatic in its ironic surprise endings.

One critic has drawn perceptive attention to this kind of poetry, characteristic of the fifties and sixties, which he terms "the habit of irony",[39] but several of the poets given as exemplars, like Buckley and Webb, are not essentially ironic at all, whilst better instances are found in such younger poets as Thomas W. Shapcott and Rodney Hall. Shapcott, for example, obtains an ironic shock effect by treating persons and scenes from the New Testament, not in an expected spirit of warm religious feeling, but with a surprisingly cold and dry detachment:

> *Judas has gone, and Peter turns aside*
> *remembering some other topic. The dead*
> *Christ walks among the Chroniclers of his life.*[40]

[39] Chris Wallace-Crabbe, "The Habit of Irony? Australian Poets of the Fifties" in *Meanjin Quarterly*, no.85, vol.xx, no.2, 1961, pp.164-74.
[40] Thomas W. Shapcott, *A Taste of Salt Water* (Sydney 1967), p.31.

Even the use of the capital leter for "the Chroniclers" whilst denying it to the "his" of Christ carries ironic implications. The crucifixion itself is understated drily, distanced remotely:

> *The cross is raised up, one among many.*
> *Acknowledgment is not easy in our city.*
> *Fact; and specific. The cross is still a poor*
> *untidy death. Three men were nailed that day.*
> *The soldiers were used to the thing, even the jibes*
> *remained half-hearted. What was there to say*
> *at that stage to provoke some final twitch?*
> *They were as good as dead, the prisoners;*
> *useless for sharpening hate as much as wit.*
> *Death had already congested up their eyes.*
> *Death is others, it is never us.*
> *The watchers left, knowing it was no use.*[41]

Here the last line reminds one irresistibly of Lawson's comment as the hard dry Darling River clods rebounded and knocked on the coffin just laid in the grave in "The Union Buries Its Dead": "It didn't matter much—nothing does." In both cases the treatment of death has the dry hardness of the outback clods of earth, whilst Lawson and Shapcott unite in a detachment tanged with a cynical wryness. The title of the section in Shapcott's volume from which the two quotations come is called "The City of Acknowledgment", an ironic title, for the whole point of the poems describing Christ and his miracles is that their significance was *not* acknowledged by the people of Jerusalem. The poems carry, too, I think, the further and profounder implication that acknowledgment in the Christian belief is also not easy in our contemporary city and the strikingly unchristian world of today.

Originally, I have suggested, the Australian irony was caused, not by the social environment, but by the physical one, by the conflict between man and the land, the contrast between good and bad seasons, so that the man on the land, battling through drought, flood, bushfire and pests, swung from prosperity to bankruptcy, and developed, willy-nilly, a cynical acceptance of the ironies of fate. It is the attitude expressed by "Ironbark" in one of his "Nursery Rhymes for Infant Pastoralists":

> *Baa, baa, black sheep,*
> *Have you any wool?*
> *Yes, sir, oh yes, sir! three bales full.*
> *One for the master, who grows so lean and lank;*
> *None for the mistress,*
> *But TWO for the Bank!*[42]

[41] Ibid., p.33.
[42] G. Herbert Gibson ("Ironbark"), *Ironbark Splinters from the Australian Bush* (London, 2nd edn, n.d., first publ. 1912), p.123.

Steele Rudd offers an excellent case of this land-bred irony in the story of the man with the bearskin cap in *On Our Selection*. He was a swagman who took possession of the selection barn, and who wanted to fight Dad for it, until Dad got the gun. The incident was soon forgotten. Then, when church-service was to be held at the selection, and the family dressed up for the rare occasion, Dad's pants, washed and left on the clothes-line all night, had disappeared and could not be found.

As the Rudd family are attending the service, a teamster breaks it up by bringing along a man he found lying on the plain. It was the man with the bearskin cap, dying. As the clergyman gave him a drink, he saw Dad.

He seemed to recognise Dad. He stared for some time at him, then said something in a feeble whisper, which the clergyman interpreted—"He wishes *you*"—looking at Dad—"to get what's in his swag if he dies." Dad nodded, and his thoughts went sadly back to the day he turned the poor devil out of the barn.

They carried the man inside and placed him on the sofa. But soon he took a turn. He sank quickly, and in a few moments he was dead. In a few moments more nearly everyone had gone.

"While you are here," Dad said to the clergyman, in a soft voice, "I'll open the swag." He commenced to unroll it—it was a big blanket—and when he got to the end there were his own trousers—the lost ones, nothing more. Dad's eyes met Mother's; Dave's met Sal's; none of them spoke. But the clergyman drew his own conclusions; and on the following Sunday, at Nobby Nobby, he preached a stirring sermon on that touching bequest of the man with the bear-skin cap.[43]

This deceptively simple story is really a complex of various qualities in our humour. Essentially ironic, it also belongs to the trickster category, exhibits realism and the hardness which gets fun out of the swaggie's death, and is literally sansculottist in depriving Dad of his pants. The terse, evocative style by its understatement leaves the reader to draw the inferences for himself.

This understatement is an integral part of irony, which calls for suggestive rather than descriptive writing, using implication rather than statement. It is seen clearly in the language itself. An Englishman will praise a person as "topping"; an American, as a "swell guy"; but an Australian drawls out that "he's not a bad bloke". Sidney J. Baker has commented:

There is a peculiar meiosal form of humour in our slang, somewhat hard for foreigners to appreciate. Thus we say that a man *performs* when he is indulging in a wild frenzy of anger or vituperation; we call a wild confusion or a particularly difficult task a *picnic;* we say *not so bloody, not so dusty, not so clever* . . . when we mean good or even excellent.

[43] Steele Rudd, *On Our Selection* (Sydney 1901 ed., first publ. 1899), pp.220-1.

In short we are indulging in what is known as meiosis or "lessening"—a form of understatement particularly dear to the Australian humorist.[44]

In all these instances, and in a long list of others given by Baker, the usage is definitely ironic. It is exactly the same kind of irony used by Henry Lawson time and time again, where one thing is said and the exact opposite is meant. The story "Telling Mrs Baker" illustrates this irony perfectly: the whole point of the story lies in the contrast between the kindly story of her husband's death told to Mrs Baker by the drovers Andy and Jack and the harsh truth, which was its complete opposite. So, too, "The Union Buries Its Dead" is essentially a feat of irony: the contrast here is between the expected, usual sentimental treatment of a funeral and the stark facts stated so baldly by Lawson. There are many ironic touches in Lawson, such as the girl who dropped out of Tom Hopkins's life, the taking down of the gentleman sharper by fellow-sharper Steelman, and, perhaps best of all, the sketch "Mitchell on Matrimony". Mitchell expounds his theory of how to treat women to his mate Joe by the camp-fire at the end of the shearing season. He gives details of how to treat a woman with sympathy, understanding, and thoughtful consideration so eloquently that his mate "seemed touched and bothered over something", says he might have made a better husband to his wife, and expresses his determination to try and make up for it when he goes back this time. Then he turns the tables by asking after Mitchell's wife.

"Well, did you put your theory into practice?"
"I did," said Mitchell very deliberately.
Joe waited, but nothing came.
"Well?" he asked impatiently. "How did it act? Did it work well?"
"I don't know," said Mitchell (puff), "she left me."
"What!"
Mitchell jerked the half-smoked pipe from his mouth, and rapped the burning tobacco out against the toe of his boot.
"She left me," he said, standing up and stretching himself. Then, with a vicious jerk of his arm, "She left me for—another kind of a fellow!"[45]

Here we have a triple irony: first, the contrast between Mitchell's theory and its failure in practice; second, the contrast between this failure and Mitchell's success in impressing his mate with his theory; and third, the contrast between the kindly, slightly sentimental character of Mitchell's reflections that induces the reader, like Joe, to feel sympathetic and the dry, cynical realism that ends the story. We might say that Mitchell, his mate, and the reader are all "taken in"

[44] Sidney J. Baker, *The Australian Language* (Sydney 1945), p.263.
[45] Henry Lawson, op. cit., p.242.

and subjected to an ironic twist, Mitchell by his wife, his mate by Mitchell, and the reader by Lawson.

Lawson's irony is usually genial; if occasionally bitter, it has none of the savage anger of Xavier Herbert in *Capricornia*. The story opens right away on this key:

The first white settlement in Capricornia was that of Treachery Bay—afterwards called New Westminster—which was set up on what was perhaps the most fertile and pleasant part of the coast and on the bones of half the Karrapillua Tribe.[46]

It ends with the tragic irony of Norman's discovery of the body of Tocky and the dismal crying of the crows. In between, irony holds a long, violent corroboree. Norman swaggers around thinking he is the son of a Malayan princess until he learns that he is a half-caste, a yeller-feller, his mother an aboriginal gin. Humbolt Lace as deputy protector of aborigines protects Constance Differ by seducing her and then marrying her off to the half-caste rouseabout Yeller Elbert. When he tells Oscar Shillingsworth he is helping the young couple, the unwitting Oscar compliments him, "Very decent of you, very decent". Oscar's wife Jasmine runs away from him to Manila with a Spanish captain, Gomez. Oscar dreams of revenge when he meets Gomez. Finally he meets him only to find that Gomez had been the victim of Jasmine more than he had been, and the two end up drunken friends. The savagery of the irony rises to its height when Joe Ballest sees the railway train strike his mate Mick O'Pick on the line, sending Mick and his tricycle hurtling into the river. The grief-maddened Joe rushes angrily at the train and is killed, horribly mangled, whilst Mick turns up, mud-smothered but unhurt—only to be run over by the mail-train four days later and cut to pieces. And so on. Other instances abound. Throughout *Capricornia* Ossas of irony are piled on ironic Pelions. Such is life in Capricornia as seen by Herbert.

Furphy joins him as another master ironist. The turbulent events in *Capricornia* are linked to one another by a hundred ironic twists; *Such is Life* is designed as one long ironic hoax. Irony is the very basis of its construction—the contrast between its apparent fortuitous-ness and its intricately woven pattern of plot and sub-plot. What seems formless is the subtlest example of fictional form. The device of the diary is ironic, for its so-called casualness masks a deft manipula-tion. The casual and the causal are blended ironically. The whole novel embodies Furphy's philosophy of life as fundamentally ironic: this is its main purpose. Free will has its choice: it can make one option, Collins proclaims, but the rest is a determined "chain of fatalities".

46 Xavier Herbert, op. cit., p.11.

O

In these "fatalities" irony weaves in and out. Tom Collins, for instance, out of a kindly consideration does not speak to the swaggie, and so the latter dies of hunger and exhaustion. Mary O'Halloran, the child of five, when lost in the bush walks nothing less than twenty-two miles, and the search party is out looking for her for seventy-two hours—and she dies less than half an hour before she is found. Collins has no penchant for Mrs Beaudesert but everyone, including her, looks on him as her suitor. When Collins fires the hay-rick, it is he himself who tries to persuade the unsuspecting owner to forego prosecution of the innocent Andy Glover.

It is in the various roles of Tom Collins that Furphy best exploits his ironical vein. For Collins plays three distinct roles: as presumed author, as narrator, and as a character in the story. As author he is supposed to tell his own story about himself, but his name alone betrays the nature of the book, since this was used for a mythical figure who spun idle, baseless rumours—"furphies" we would say today, not after Joseph Furphy but after his brother John who made the Furphy water-carts used in Egypt around which the diggers of the first world war told their rumours: itself an ironic coincidence undreamt of by Furphy. As narrator, Collins stages the farce of the alleged disconnected chronicle. As character he claims a superior insight into men and events, and a great part of the irony of the book lies in the startling contrast between his supposed omniscience and the continual blunders he makes through not seeing significances seen by the more perceptive reader. He reflects eruditely on the problems of race and heredity, for instance, when he observes the Scottish type of Sollicker's child, but never realizes the simple fact that Hungry McIntyre, the Scottish squatter, is the real father. He fails to see that Nosey Alf is really a woman, Warrigal Alf's lost Molly Cooper.

Rigby's Romance, that anabranch subtracted from the original manuscript of the "Murray-meandering" *Such is Life*, is once again a Furphian orgy of irony. Its fishing party assembles in a bend of the Murray River and is eagerly trying to catch the thirty-pounder which had escaped from Steve Thompson, when he makes the "ghastly disclosure" that the cod had got off his hook over ten years ago. When the trapper Furlong actually catches a thirty-pounder and the fishermen tether it in the river—with the chain Tom Collins takes off his dog—in order to keep it fresh for an enjoyable breakfast, there is another ironic contrast between expectation and reality, since the reprobate Pup, now foot-loose, finds the fish and devours it completely. The same contrast emerges frequently in the hapless "love stories" told by the yarning fishermen.

Finally, the romance promised in the book's title turns out to be a double hoax. First, the book is essentially not a love story but

Furphy's sermon on the moral aspects of Socialism as preached to the company by the garrulous Rigby. Second, when Furphy told Miles Franklin that the Socialism was "sugar-coated with the sweetest romance you ever struck"[47] his tongue was in his cheek, since the love story turns out to be the most unromantic ever written. Miss Kate Vanderdecken has adventured all the way from America to the Riverina in search of Rigby, her lover lost twenty-five years before as the result of a quarrel. Two years after the separation Tom Collins as a boy had heard Rigby describe emotionally how the loss of his beautiful and beloved Kate had shattered his life. He is now instrumental in bringing about a meeting of Rigby with Miss Vanderdecken and her friend at the Yooringa hotel, and naturally anticipates —like the reader—a happy reconciliation of two faithful lovers. But Rigby has clean forgotten Kate. Worse still, after he has promised to meet her in the evening, this laggard in love becomes so absorbed in expounding Socialism to the fishing party that he completely forgets his appointments. So, insulted, she retreats early the next morning to Echuca. Learning that Rigby is expected there within a week she waits for him in vain for a fortnight. He has been delayed, and returns the afternoon of the day she finally leaves Echuca in the morning, so that, as the young Sam reports to Collins, he "Just missed her by the skin o' your teeth". Thus irony is piled on irony.

In sketching the story of *Rigby's Romance* to Kate Baker, Furphy said: "I think there's something beautiful—don't you? in the picture of the ever-faithful woman making her long, oversea pilgrimage to find that her demigod has absolutely forgotten that she ever existed."[48] His humour here has the hardness, streaked with the callous touch, of the land which moulded Furphy the teamster into an incorrigible ironist.

[47] Miles Franklin (in association with Kate Baker), *Joseph Furphy: the Legend of a Man and His Book* (Sydney, 1944), p.129.
[48] Ibid., p.165.

IX

The Creed of Mateship

And it came to pass ... that the soul of Jonathan was knit with the soul of David; and Jonathan loved him as his own soul ....

Then Jonathan and David made a covenant, because he loved him as his own soul.

And Jonathan stripped himself of the robe that was upon him, and gave it to David, and his garments, even to his sword, and to his bow, and to his girdle.

THE BIBLE[1]

There is a great deal of this mutual regard and trust engendered by two men working thus together in the otherwise solitary bush; habits of mutual helpfulness arise, and these elicit gratitude, and that leads on to regard. Men under these circumstances often stand by one another through thick and thin; in fact it is a universal feeling that a man ought to be able to trust his own mate in anything.

ALEXANDER HARRIS[2]

"That there dog," said Macquarie to the hospital staff in general, "is a better dog than I'm a man—or you too, it seems—and a better Christian. He's been a better mate to me than I ever was to any man—or any man to me. He's watched over me; kep' me from getting robbed many a time; fought for me; saved my life and took drunken kicks and curses for thanks—and forgave me. He's been a true, straight, honest, and faithful mate to me—and I ain't going to desert him now. I ain't going to kick him out in the road with a broken leg."

HENRY LAWSON[3]

The typical Australian ... was seldom religious in the sense in which the word is generally used. So far as he held a prevailing creed, it was a romantic one inherited from the gold-miner and the bushman, of which the chief article was that a man should at all times and at any cost stand by his mate. That was and is the one law which the good Australian must never break. It is bred in the child and stays with him through life ....

The strongest bond in the Australian Imperial Force was that between a

[1] The Bible, I Samuel, xviii, 1-4.

[2] Alexander Harris, *Settlers and Convicts*, ed. C. M. H. Clark (Melbourne 1953 ed., first publ. 1874), pp.180-1.

[3] Henry Lawson, *Prose Works* (Sydney 1935), pp.42-3, "That There Dog of Mine".

man and his mate . . . . In the foulest French winter, or at Cape Helles when bullets seemed to be raining in sheets, on every occasion when an Australian force went into action there were to be found men who, come what might, regardless of death or wounds, stayed by their fallen friends until they had seen them into safety.

C. E. W. BEAN[4]

The Historical Perspective

Australian mateship offers a new variation on one of the most ancient of tunes—the friendship between man and man, keyed to equality, with loyalty as the refrain. It is a theme running through the literatures of many lands and times.

Henry Lawson was only putting it into true historical perspective in his sketch "Mateship in Shakespeare's Rome", when he examined the relations between Brutus and Cassius in *Julius Caesar*. When he praised the virtues of mateship in various stories and sketches he was in turn only following a long line of distinguished predecessors, from David lamenting the death of Jonathan, whose love to him "was wonderful, passing the love of women", to Spenser celebrating the friendship between Cambel and Triamond and exalting the zeal of friends above the natural affection to kindred and the fire of love to woman kind:

> *For natural affection soone doth cesse,*
> *And quenched is with Cupid's greater flame:*
> *But faithfull friendship doth them both suppresse,*
> *And them with maystring discipline doth tame.*[5]

In Australia this "faithfull friendship" has undoubtedly been a distinctive social pattern which developed, as Alexander Harris noted, early in our history, was expounded by Lawson as a national faith and was described by Dr Bean as the "prevailing creed" of the soldiers in the First A.I.F. It still remains an active force today, as strong as the classic examples of friendship in the past.

For instance, Pythias won fame by risking his life for his friend Damon, but the spirit that moved the Pythagorean philosoper in the fourth century B.C. was displayed no less by the men of the Australian Navy ship *Voyager* when it was sunk by collision with the *Melbourne* in 1964, with the loss of 82 lives. A survivor from the

---

[4] C. E. W. Bean, *The Story of Anzac: the First Phase*, vol. I of *The Official History of Australia in the War of 1914-18* (Sydney 1937), pp.6-7.
[5] Edmund Spenser, *The Faerie Queene*, Cant.IX, 2.

Voyager told me of his experiences during the disaster. When I suggested that it must have been rather terrifying the young stoker replied simply, "Well, no, we were too busy looking after our mates." It was an illuminating remark, revealing how foolish have been some attacks on mateship as a "myth", a "legend" or a "stereotype". For here, today, was the plain fact of mateship as a living reality, an operative creed in action, a practical answer to the danger of death.

The Need for Analysis

Indeed, it is time we looked at mateship, not in vague terms of fanciful mythology, but as an historical truth and a contemporary fact. There is a need, too, to understand and analyze it objectively, since it has been treated too often in a partisan spirit of defence or attack. From Lawson onward its champions have at times, to use an apt phrase of Mark Twain's, "suffered from the panegyrics". Thus J. Le Gay Brereton falls into inflation of mateship when he writes that Lawson "made it the watchword of Australia . . . . In proclaiming the ideal of Australia he announced the living hope of the whole world."[6] In such an exaltation there is no recognition of the limitations of mateship as a code of ethics with one main doctrine—that a man stick by his mate at all costs—and one basic virtue: loyalty. It is an essentially masculine creed confined to certain personal and social relationships, leaving untouched many other worlds of values. Some of its advocates have obscured the genuine meanings of mateship by sentimentalizing it unduly and failing to admit its patent limitations.

In fairness to them, however, we must recognize that a man's sentiment for his mate is like that for his mother, a potent fact in action yet something so intimate and personal that any explicit avowal of it may easily sound uncomfortably sentimental. We tend to suspect "mateship" as sentimentally self-conscious whereas we accept "my mate" or "being mates" as natural and genuine. Thus the explicit Lawson in "Mateship in Shakespeare's Rome" is not as effective as the implicit Lawson in "That There Dog of Mine" and "Telling Mrs. Baker".

It is a natural reaction, therefore, and a healthy sign of our growing critical awareness of national values, when writers subject mateship to a sharp scrutiny as Ray Lawler and Alan Seymour have done in drama and John Morrison has done in a number of his short stories. Thus *Summer of the Seventeenth Doll* shows how the loyalty of mates can break under strain, and though Roo and Barney go off together at the end of the play they leave a battered mateship behind them as well as a broken doll. In Seymour's *The One Day of the*

[6] *Henry Lawson*, by His Mates (Sydney 1931), pp.15-16.

Year the old tradition once again comes through, but its weaknesses have been revealed. Morrison illustrates loyalty and treachery alike operating among mates. The probing of mateship by these three writers is thoughtful and at times penetrating—largely, I feel, because their approach is objective.

On the other hand, a one-sided, hostile approach is less rewarding, as exemplified by Patrick White's unconvincing burlesque of mateship in *Riders in the Chariot*. The "crucifixion" of Himmelfarb is not only incredible but comes incongruously after the brilliant description of his sufferings in Europe in one of the most powerful and moving passages of writing in all our prose. A similar distortion of mateship's meanings comes with some critics biassed by political and religous sentiments. Since the Left has often identified itself with mateship, nationalism, and the bush tradition, anti-nationalist publicists of the Right have attacked mateship with animus and incomprehension. A sectarian intolerance has even crept in when mateship has been resented as a rival religion. Most of such critics, one notes, fail to grasp the significance of mateship because they are also inexperienced in bush life and the fighting services, the two sources of mateship's strongest manifestations, just as academics misunderstand mateship because they cannot appreciate the bond of loyalty between working mates. All could learn much from Morrison's watersiders—or from the *Voyager's* stoker.

If sentimentalism is the chief weakness of mateship's advocates, the main defect of its opponents is simplification. For the first thing to recognize about it is that mateship is not as simple, even primitive, as it is sometimes made to appear. It is a concept with its own complexities. It has a wide variety of meanings, a variety never fully explored. There has been much talk about mateship, for and against, but little solid historical research or objective analysis to reveal its many meanings.

A Complex Pattern

Mateship, in fact, has developed shades of meaning through a double complexity: first, it has received colourations from our other inter-related social patterns, kindred ideas with which it has been associated in our history; second, it is a social pattern which has embodied many forms of thought and behaviour at different times according to the groups that have adopted it.

Looking first at the links between it and other patterns, we find these especially strong in the case of radical democracy and the Great Australian Dream. Mateship went hand in hand with social equality and independence, two basic elements of the democratic tradition. It was also radical in that it operated mainly amongst the workers, who, in Lawson's phrase, "touch their hat to no man". It gave a practical illustration of radical democracy in action.

At the same time it offered a stimulus and example to the idealists of the eighties and nineties in creating their utopian vision, especially those who were socialists or engaged in building up the New Unionism, since it showed how the principle of friendly co-operation worked effectively amongst mates in the bush. It was this principle which leaders like William Lane and W. G. Spence stressed as the basis of their New Order. Thus the familiar concept of mateship was incorporated into the Great Australian Dream as an integral part of it, and widened its popular appeal, especially amongst the bush workers. The simple practice of mateship as a bush custom, as we shall see in detail later, was elevated and extended into an inspiring ideal.

Its association with other social patterns was also intimate. Bush-bred, it gave yet another example of the powerful spell of the bush on the Australian people. If at first it seems opposed to realism as a type of idealism with a romantic touch in its glorification of the virtue of loyalty, a closer examination shows that it linked up with the realistic outlook since it was itself a living, practical reality in the bush world, an efficient and often necessary method of handling the hard facts of that world, such as hardship, danger, and isolation. So, too, it was related closely to the pattern of sombreness, since mateship was the answer made by the bushmen to the challenge of that side of bush life that was harsh, drab, and dispiriting. It was the indigenous antidote to the poison of gloom. Above all, its companionship provided salvation for the soul against the damnation of the over-whelming loneliness of the outback.

Finally, it is associated with earth-vigour in two important respects: it joins it in being a robust affirmation, often an earthy one, of the value of life; its creed is not only non-religious in the ordinary sense of the term, but it also supplies an alternative to religion, as Dr Bean, in the epigraph to this chapter, testified it did for the soldiers of the First A.I.F. In providing its own faith concerned with man's kinship with man, regardless of any god, it makes a distinctive contribution to Australian humanism.

Complex, therefore, in the relations that have given it various colourations of meaning, mateship derives an even more diversified complexity from its different historical manifestations at various times by widely differing social groups. I suggest that ten such groups can be distinguished, each with its special concept of mateship.

The Ecological Types

If we go deeper into these, we find that basically, although not entirely, they resolve themselves into two broad ecological types, the exclusive and the inclusive, the first determined largely by the social environment, the second by the physical environment.

When the response is made to the social environment by four groups composed of convicts, city larrikins, trade unionists, and marxists, the loyalty of mateship presents a form of solidarity directed against other sections of the social structure: with the convicts against the system and, on occasion, against all persons and institutions standing outside the fraternity of the felonry; with the larrikins against other larrikin gangs and society at large; with unionists against employers; with marxists, using the term generally to cover those on the political Left, with communists foremost, we have a group solidarity directed against the capitalist elements of society, particularly its political and industrial establishment. In all cases mates are not merely brothers in loyalty to each other, but also brothers in arms against a human foe. Mateship is used as a weapon in a struggle, and, as in all warfare, there are negative elements of bitterness, narrowness, and intolerance towards the opposing social section and then, with a personal vindictiveness, against any traitor or "scab" guilty of disloyalty. The mateship is definitely exclusive in type.

In contrast, the inclusive type of mateship is directed, not against conflicting or alien groups, but against the hazards or hardships of the physical environment, whether it is the land, the sea, or the air. We find this occurring in three main groups: bushmen; gold-diggers, miners, and seamen, who may be taken together as workers engaged in hazardous occupations; and fighting servicemen—soldiers, sailors, and airmen engaged in active wartime service. All these groups face occupational risks, including the ultimate one of death, which are unknown to the professional or business man, the white-collar brigade or the ordinary factory worker. They join in mateship to fight against an impersonal enemy, brothers in facing fate, with little or no hostility against other groups, no intolerance or bitterness. The bond of loyalty is conceived positively, and is often broadened from the individual or small group to a larger fellowship, as illustrated by the widening of a faith between two bush mates into an inclusive tradition of bush hospitality.

Mateship reaches its apogee of inclusiveness, however, in the group of idealists, socialists, and humanists of the nineties who extended the ideals of bush mateship to all workers, then further to the concept of an Australian utopia in the form of a fraternal socialist society, and finally to the coming brotherhood of all men.

Inclusive, too, is the convivial mateship of drinking practised by the group of contemporary city dwellers, reflected in such novels as Gavin Casey's *The Wits are Out*, Lennie Lower's *Here's Luck*, and

Nino Culotta's *They're a Weird Mob*, as well as by a tenth group in the Australian people in general in its acceptance of a mateship which is, as we shall see, rather a democratic philosophy implicit in the popular usage of the term *mate*.

The complexity of mateship is seen, furthermore, in the fact that these last three of our ten groups, although inclusive in kind, are responses to the social environment, not to the physical one, and thus cut across the broad ecological types as exceptions to the rule. Mateship, in short, is too richly varied to be compressed completely into a single formula. When we try to grasp it we find ourselves with a veritable Proteus in our hands, changing into manifold shapes according to its relations with associated ideas or the particular stamps placed on it by differing groups. Its character goes through contrasting metamorphoses as it appears either savagely exclusive or generously inclusive, a social custom or a deeply felt sentiment, a warm, personal relationship or a utopian ideal, as a practical aid, a convivial convention, an expedient weapon against a conflicting social group, or a vital creed that could fill with its faith the gap created in the lives of men by the discarding of orthodox religion. The story of its development, again, is no simple straightforward text but a true variorum, with variant readings of a diversified script.

Let us now examine the different meanings of mateship illustrated in our historical and fictional literature, taking first the exclusive types and starting with the convict group.

The Proto-mateship of Convicts

I cannot regard the form of mateship practised by the convicts as a true and genuine one. It is rather a proto-mateship, and this for three good reasons: historically it was the earliest form in our history; conceptually it was rudimentary in character; factually it failed too often to fulfil the basic element of loyalty.

The abundant evidence available shows four things indisputably: the fact that the professional criminals who formed such a large proportion of the convicts carried over into the colonies the creed of loyalty to their fellows against their common enemy of the law which they had practised in London, Dublin, and the English provincial cities; that the creed was often honoured more in the breach than the observance, with treachery so frequent that the record tells of dishonour rather than "honour among thieves"; that the punishments meted out by the convicts to those who betrayed them was marked by a savage brutality; and that the combative mateship was thus of a primitive type and only rarely showed the higher elements of generous affection and sacrificial loyalty which were common amongst bushmen, miners, seamen, and fighting servicemen in the fraternal type of mateship.

The derivation of the convict loyalty from that of the professional thieves is clearly indicated by Surgeon Cunningham's description of the convicts on his first voyage to Australia, three-fourths of whom boasted of being thieves whose peculiar code held that

A *good fellow* is one who divides fairly with his companion whatever he thieves in partnership, and who never confesses a theft or gives evidence against an associate . . . while a *great scoundrel* is one who will be *base* enough to acknowledge his crime, or inform upon his partner.[7]

Marcus Clarke, who studied the records before writing *For the Term of His Natural Life*, gives a number of instances showing how strong and widespread was the code of loyalty among the convicts. Thus Dawes refused Captain Frere's offer to make him a constable and explained why to the chaplain: "And betray my mates? I'm not of that sort."[8]

Again, when the giant Gabbett, who had escaped with three other convicts, is recaptured alone, the first question Captain Vickers asks him is, "Where are your mates?" And after Maurice Frere had given him a piece of tobacco to chew: " 'How many mates had he?' asked Maurice, watching the champing jaws as one looks at a strange animal, and asking the question as though a 'mate' was something a convict was born with—like a mole, for instance."[9]

A Fraternity of Self-interest

This "mateship" of the convicts was a fellowship in vice. Thus that doughty critic of the convict system, Dr Ullathorne, when discussing the group loyalty does so by picturing the convicts as unprincipled perjurers when witnessing in the courts:

Let it be borne in mind that each of these men has been true to three hundred shipmates, who were his bosom companions; that, when arrived, he finds various former intimates from the same town or country; that, after a while he probably adds to these some hundred, or two, or three, of chain gang mates; that all these are sworn brothers, prepared, with a true *esprit de corps*, to back each other out of any difficulty.[10]

Such loyalty was in itself a virtue of the unvirtuous, and thus gives the first departure in Australian mateship from the traditional

[7] P. Cunningham, *Two Years in New South Wales*, etc., 2 vols (London 1827), p.249.
[8] Marcus Clarke, *For the Term of His Natural Life* (London 1902 ed., first publ. Melbourne 1874), p.408.
[9] Ibid., p.100.
[10] Cited in Patrick Francis Cardinal Moran, *History of the Catholic Church in Australasia* (Sydney 1896), pp.159-66.

view of the philosophers that friendship was not only, as Aristotle defined it, one of the virtues but also required goodness in friends: "The truest friendship, then, is that of the good."[11] Perfect friendship could only exist between men of goodness, who love the good in each other.

Convict mateship, in contrast, was almost entirely a fraternity of self-interest, and its loyalty was inspired by utility or the profit of self-protection. In standing by their mates, the convicts were primarily following the creed of Fagin, master thief, in "looking after number one". It is hard to find cases of selfless action, although we find it in the narrative written by the convict Surridge in *The Escape of the Notorious Sir William Heans*. First, when he is caught in the great crack in the stables through which he is trying to escape, he is helped by his mates. Then, in pain before dying, he writes his narrative to "do something with my hands for a mate or the prisoner, who...may yet fall upon the secret in these rents."[12] This is a fictional instance of a genuine, benevolent mateship, this provision for others to come, unknown, who might benefit. A selfless spirit is also shown by Maida Gwynnham as an assigned convict when she refuses at risk of severe punishment to get the lad Sam into trouble.[13] The best illustration in convict fiction of a genuine mateship is undoubtedly that of Bill Felix in Warung's story of the Ring, who, doomed by the Ring to kill Harry Reynell, voluntarily sacrifices his own life in order to save his mate.[14]

Dishonour Among Thieves

In general, however, the mateship of the convicts was essentially a selfish one, maintained because of its utility, so that we find frequent instances in Australian literature of thieves or convicts betraying each other. Indeed, it would be a foolish and sentimental romanticism to take the convict "mateship" too literally. It is significant that in "The Liberation of the First Three", the very story in which Price Warung quotes the famous "Convict Oath", the three veteran convicts murder their three "mates" callously as soon as the victims had served their purpose in saving rations for the escape planned. In the following tale, "The Liberation of the Other Three", Hardy murders Tooth, Jones tries to kill Hardy, and in the struggle on the ladder both fall to their death. Thus loyalty to one's mates is turned into a meaningless farce,

---

[11] Aristotle, *Ethica Nichomachea* (London 1940, O.U.P. ed., trans. by W. D. Ross), Book VIII, 5, 25, p.1157b.
[12] William Hay, *The Escape of the Notorious Sir William Heans* (And the Mystery of Mr. Daunt), (London 1918), p.231.
[13] See Oline Keese (Caroline Leakey), *The Broad Arrow* (London 1887), pp.193-229.
[14] See Price Warung (William Astley), *Convict Days* (Sydney 1960), "Secret Society of the Ring", pp.126-77.

and the oft-quoted Convict Oath into a grim mockery. It is worth noting, as an illustration of the false sentimentalism often accorded to the convicts by contemporary writers and historians, that the oath as described by Price Warung is frequently cited approvingly, but its subsequent betrayal by wholesale murdering of the sworn "mates" by each other is never mentioned.

So, too, Frere's questioning of Gabbett about his mates is quoted, with Clarke's comment, but without notice of the fact that this occurs just after Gabbett had not only murdered the three "mates" who had escaped with him but had survived by feasting on their flesh.

If selfless loyalty was rare, the betrayal of mates seems to have been common. Ralph Rashleigh, for instance, was first convicted of crime through his mate Jenkins turning informer on him in order to get his own sentence lightened. Later one of the Foxley bushranging gang, O'Leary, betrays the others to get the reward—just as, in historical fact, Aaron Sherritt betrayed the Kelly gang, including his mate Joe Byrne. Betrayal is pictured by Rashleigh as the common practice in one convict prison:

at the settlement of Newcastle each man feared the other, for Ralph very quickly found out the untruth of the proverb that "there is honour among thieves" . . . .

Thus each prisoner stood in awe of the other, and as traitors . . . were always rewarded with some trifling post of comparative ease and idleness, no man dared to trust his fellow. . . .[15]

The loyalty was often kept only through fear of the consequences of any treachery, and this type of "loyalty" is completely alien to any true mateship. Thus Clarke has Captain Frere tell chaplain Meekin that his policy with convicts is *divide to conquer*, to "set all the dogs spying on each other":

"It's the only way. Why, my dear sir, if the prisoners were as faithful to each other as we are, we couldn't hold the island a week. It's just because no man can trust his neighbour that every mutiny falls to the ground."[16]

The strength of the fear among the convicts caused by untrustworthiness can be measured, no doubt, by the savagery with which it was punished. Literature dealing with the convicts gives frequent examples of the vindictiveness with which they revenged themselves on any informer. Even suspicion of any one "nosing", "pimping", or "peaching" was sufficient, according to the evidence of Cunningham, for him to be subjected to petty annoyances, to be beaten up, and even to be mutilated: "A gang of such desperadoes actually attempted to bite off the nose and ears of one poor fellow in a ship I had charge

---

[15] James Tucker, *Ralph Rashleigh* (Sydney 1953 ed., first publ. London 1929), p.230.
[16] Marcus Clarke, op. cit., p.249.

of, who had merely complained of their annoyances."[17] Dawes was treated as a pariah by his fellow convicts because of his giving warning of a ship mutiny. In *Ralph Rashleigh*, when the escaped convict Foxley and his fellow bushrangers, also "bolters", capture O'Leary, a member of their gang who had betrayed them, they flog him with a belt buckle "until to Rashleigh's sickened sight it appeared as if large pieces of flesh were actually knocked off his back at each of the last blows".[18] After rubbing salt water into their mate's raw wounds, they hang him in prolonged agony. The ruthlessness of convict "mateship" is also shown dramatically by Price Warung in his story "Secret Society of the Ring", which relates in detail how the convict Harry Reynell, because he had responded to Commandant Maconochie's kindly treatment at Norfolk Island, was doomed to death by the Ring and driven to suicide.

City Larrikins

The limitations of the convict gang are repeated in the larrikin push, alike in its intolerant exclusiveness, its ganging up against law and authority, its brutality, and its failure to maintain mateship's fundamental principle of loyalty.

Evolved from the earlier "Cabbagites", described by Lieutenant-Colonel Mundy as "a sort of loafer, known as the Cabbage-tree mob",[19] the larrikins infested Sydney and Melbourne in the last decades of the nineteenth century and the first of the twentieth. One historian contrasts these with the bushmen as showing "a most distinctive social difference.... The bush produced mateship between those who shared its joys and its terrors; the city produced larrikinism".[20]

This larrikinism, however, had its own form of mateship. Louis Stone, who has given in *Jonah* the most authentic account of the Sydney larrikin push, shows Jonah and Chook Fowles as mates in the Cardigan Street Push of Waterloo, "a social wart of a kind familiar to the streets of Sydney .... Their feats ranged from kicking an enemy senseless, and leaving him for dead, to wrecking hotel windows with blue metal .... They were the scum of the streets."[21] Thus Jonah and Chook together in the Push hunt down a bricklayer who had offended it, and kick his struggling body "with silent ferocity". Later Chook helps Jonah to set up his boot-shop. So, too, C. J. Dennis in *The Songs of a Sentimental Bloke* has Bill's mate

[17] P. Cunningham, op. cit., p.229.
[18] James Tucker, op. cit., p.163.
[19] G. C. Mundy, *Our Antipodes*, etc. (London 1855, first publ. 1852), p.17.
[20] R. M. Hartwell, "The Pastoral Ascendancy, 1820-1850" in Gordon Greenwood (ed.), *Australia: a Social and Political History* (Sydney 1955), p.93.
[21] Louis Stone, *Jonah* (Sydney 1933 ed., first publ. 1911), pp.37-8.

Ginger Mick assist him as best man at his wedding with Doreen. Two months later Doreen is not speaking to the Bloke, since he has sinned by drinking and gambling at a two-up school, led astray—like many husbands—by his old mate.

> *'Twus orl becors uv Ginger Mick—the cow!*
> *(I wish't I 'ad 'im 'ere to deal wiv now!*
> *I'd pass 'im one, I would! 'E ain't no man!)*[22]

So Bill, illogically, blames his mate for his own weakness.

Disloyalty also seems to have characterized the larrikin mateship if we may judge from an anonymous ballad published in the *Bulletin* on 9 June 1888 entitled "Uncle Bill: the Larrikin's Lament". In relating the hero's exploits the narrator tells of his behaviour when one Sydney push descended upon another:

> *Who cheered both parties long and loud?*
> *Who heaved blue-metal at the crowd?*
> *And sooled his bull-dog, Fighting Bet,*
> *To bite, haphazard, all she met?*
>
> *And when the mob were lodged in gaol*
> *Who telegraphed to me for bail?*
> *And—here I think he showed his sense—*
> *Who calmly turned Queen's evidence?*[23]

Here Uncle Bill's betrayal of his mates is accepted as an approved larrikin custom.

In the rather scanty literature of larrikinism, moreover, mateship plays only a minor role. The chief reason, I suspect, was woman. Just as the absence of women made mateship between men significant amongst convicts, bushmen, and gold-diggers, so we find larrikins like Jonah and the Bloke deserting the push when they fall into love or get married, whilst their association with their mates Chook and Ginger Mick grows more distant. The larrikin invested his relations with women, furthermore, with such sentimentality that little room could have been left for sentiment about his mate, according to the writers. Dennis has been criticized for giving an over-sentimental picture of the Bloke, but his combination of violence and lovesickness as typical of larrikinism is paralleled by the realistic writers Louis Stone and Edward Dyson. In *Jonah* the types who kick a man almost to death also sing the most sentimental of songs, whilst Chook deserts the Push for love of the red-haired Pinkey. In Dyson's *Factory 'Ands* the characters at Spat's Factory, similar city types to the larrikin, are as sentimental as they are humorous, and display extreme lovesickness.

[22] C. J. Dennis, *The Songs of a Sentimental Bloke* (Sydney 1916), p.86.
[23] Cited by Edgar Waters, "Some Aspects of the Popular Arts in Australia 1880-1915", thesis in the Australian National University Library, pp.203-4.

The stories of Benno and his "push" frequently have love as a theme, but not mateship. Sentimental love is also mingled with violence and humour in the larrikin musical "The Ballad of Angel's Alley", a tuneful and entertaining piece combining the genres of *The Beggar's Opera* and *The Sentimental Bloke* which delighted Melbourne audiences in 1962.

Trade Unionists

A marked development in the quality and scope of mateship comes when we pass from its convict and larrikin forms to the richer, more complex form it takes with trade unionists. This is still chiefly exclusive in type as confined to the unionist group and directed against the employing class in industrial warfare. Yet it has inclusive elements and breadth as well as depth, partly for historical reasons which require some mention.

In the eighties of last century, with the development of the Amalgamated Miners' Association, the Amalgamated Shearers' Union of Australasia, formed in 1886, and the Seamen's Union, industrial unionism became established on a large-scale basis. Thus one historian claims that before 1890

Australian unionism evolved forms of organisation more comprehensive than any others then existing in the world . . . . The Labor Movement of this country had contributed an important chapter to the history of the working class at large. The all-Australian union, whose outlines were clear by the middle 1880's was a model for unions in other lands.[24]

In particular, the organization of the shearers and bush workers in the A.S.U. and the A.W.U. (Australian Workers' Union) was a unique phenomenon at this time, in striking contrast to the backward state of unionism amongst the rural workers of Europe, England, and North America. One cause of this phenomenon was bush mateship, according to the expert testimony of its main dynamic, William Guthrie Spence. His evidence merits fuller mention:

Unionism came to the bushmen as a religion . . . . It had in it that feeling of mateship which he understood already, and which always characterised the action of one "white man" to another. Unionism extended the idea, so that a man's character was gauged by whether he stood true to Union rules or "scabbed" it on his fellows. The man who never went back on his Union is honoured today as no other is honoured or respected. The man who fell once may be forgiven, but he is not fully trusted. The lowest term of reproach is to call a man a "scab".[25]

The part mateship played in the spread of the New Unionism, which went beyond the benefit society or bargaining in wages to a

[24] Brian Fitzpatrick, *A Short History of the Australian Labor Movement* (Melbourne 1944), pp.52-3.
[25] William Guthrie Spence, *Australia's Awakening* (Sydney 1909), p.78.

new deal of collective action for a new social order, can also be seen in the General Secretary's Report to the General Labourers' Union in 1893:

By practising at every opportunity, unity of effort in politics, unity in industrial co-operation, *mateship in all things*, we will have [pave?] the way for the spread of brotherhood and the annihilation of the present competitive, selfish, social warfare.[26] [Italics author's.]

The New Unionism thus adopted the idea of mateship and extended it to cover the loyalty between members of the unions and, more broadly still, between members of the working class. As envisaged by Spence, William Lane, and many fervent advocates of the New Unionism, it became the basis of a workers' solidarity that could produce a wider brotherhood in a socialist, co-operative form of society. This was its positive, idealistic aspect—its inclusive mateship.

One of the best examples of this came in 1894 when the Australian Workers' Union—later to become the largest union in Australia—began the Preface to its Rules with a statement of basic principles in terms of mateship: "Daily, as the various and widespread sections of the human family are being insensibly drawn into closer touch with each other, it becomes clearer that men should become co-operators —mates—instead of antagonists."[27] So, too, the *Hummer*, the official organ of the Associated Riverina Workers, declared in 1892: "the growth of Socialism, true Socialism, will destroy tyranny and make men what men should be—*mates*. ... Socialism is being *mates*."[28] Widely and deeply, therefore, ran the feeling for mateship in the trade union group.

Its exclusive, combative aspect was seen in its general antagonism to "the boss" and, more specifically, in its bitterness against any "scab". Spence gives both aspects in the above quotation, and goes on to say that a man who sells himself to the employer at a time of strike is punished severely, with the girls refusing to dance with him at many a country ball, the barmaids refusing him a drink, and the waitresses a meal. The feeling of the gentler sex is expressed vividly in an old bush song called "The Union Boy", in which a shearer is introduced by his sweetheart to her mother, who protests that four years before he had scabbed it at Forquadee. The girl explains that he is now a reformed character, having joined the union, but warns him:

> *Now, Fred, you've joined the union, so stick to it like glue,*
> *For the scabs that were upon your back, they're now but only few.*

[26] Cited in R.N. Ebbels, *The Australian Labor Movement 1850-1907* (Sydney 1960), p.121.
[27] Cited in C.M.H. Clark, *Select Documents in Australian History, 1851-1900* (Sydney 1955), p.743.
[28] Ibid., pp.587-8.

P

And if ever you go blackleggin' or scabbing likewise,
It's with my long, long fingernails, I'll scratch out both your eyes.

I'll put you to every cruelty, I'll stretch you in a vice,
I'll cut you up in a hay machine and sell you for Chinee rice.[29]

The vindictiveness of the gentle damsel seems a throwback to the convict gang. The bitterness, however, had some historical basis in the series of great strikes between 1890 and 1894—the maritime, miners, and shearers. The bitterness of this class warfare is also reflected by "Banjo" Paterson in his ballad "A Bushman's Song", giving a shearer's view of the use of Chinamen in the shearing shed.

In contemporary writing the best illustration of the two aspects of mateship in unionism is John Morrison's short story called "Going Through", a description of Second Preference men being admitted to the Waterside Workers' Federation of Australia. Morrison himself is a watersider, and his story has the ring of personal conviction. He conveys the delight of being admitted to the union, and what it means, with getting "three thousand mates" in the Federation:

The recruit immediately preceding me turns to give me a happy smile, and we both of us spontaneously salute. We feel suddenly rich. And not because of bigger pay envelopes to come. We've got ourselves three thousand mates. We've come through. We're Federation men. We can wear the little blue button with the clasped hands on it... . My palms tingle. How much more is it than the simple design of a badge![30]

This "warm acclamation of one's fellow-men" is the positive, constructive, sympathetic aspect of union mateship. But John Morrison gives the other aspect, too, in the savage intolerance of the watersiders against a man who had got another job during a strike of the timber-workers in '32, many years before, for the unionist's arm is long against the scab. An angry storm breaks out against him. The narrator sees

...Faces of men I have worked with, eaten with, drunk with. Warm-hearted men who have advised me, helped me, talked to me—about their homes, their wives, their children, their multitudinous interests.

But I know quite positively that a few minutes ago they were also part of the beast that rose up and snarled at the man in the black raincoat. Bitter experience has taught them that they assemble here in defence of all that they have.[31]

"Bitter experience" of the stuggle to live, of the need for complete solidarity of the workers in the class warfare, of the callous greed and ruthless economic power against which they are pitted; this is the

[29] Douglas Stewart and Nancy Keesing (ed.), *Old Bush Songs* (Sydney 1957), p.269, "The Union Boy".
[30] John Morrison, *Black Cargo* (Melbourne 1955), p.21, "Going Through".
[31] Ibid., pp.19-20.

justification of the savagery of "the beast that rose up and snarled at the man in the black raincoat". The same experience resulted in an especially strong bond of loyalty amongst trade unionists, often expressed in the most generous help to fellow workers in cases of necessity, together with deeds of self-sacrifice and courage in the more hazardous occupations such as mining.

Marxists

The same compound of exclusive and inclusive elements is found in the marxist form of mateship, the political aspect of the movement of which unionism represents the industrial side. The term "marxist" is used broadly to cover socialists and communists, and here mateship becomes incorporated into a more conscious, philosophical concept than found among unionists, to whom it is a personal feeling bound up with practical experience and working mates.

The exclusive element is strongest, naturally, among communists, to whom mateship is a handy weapon of the workers in the class war against capitalist society. In contemporary times the Australian Communist Party has directed a shrewd tactical campaign to annex the tradition of mateship for this purpose, along with that of radical democracy and the nationalism of the nineties. The Eureka rebellion, for instance, has been glorified and inflated almost beyond historical recognition. Illustrations of this campaign, which has been skilfully conducted, may be seen in the earlier numbers of the literary magazine *Overland*. Among one of its best contributions was a taut, dramatic, and moving story of mateship in David Forrest's "The Keeper of the Night", the tale of a volunteer ambulance unit in a country sugar town in Queensland. Another issue was made an interesting Henry Lawson Anniversary Number.

The communist capitalizing of mateship has represented it as a radical, nationalist, and proletarian tradition, with a strong exclusivist class bias. In this "take-over" form it has been used as an expedient political device in a literary popular front.

On the other hand, there is a natural affinity between the ideals signified by the two terms "mate" and "comrade". Both have a genuine inclusiveness, especially when the mateship is subsumed in the wider concept and ultimate aim of a final classless society.

This idealism was particularly marked amongst the socialists of the nineties, who will be considered later as one of the inclusive groups. It might be noted here, however, that bush mateship received an effective socialist expansion by William Lane, first into an inter-colonial unionism, and then into an alliance of all workers, Australian and overseas alike. He was, as one historian has stated, "the adviser and friend of the leaders of the trade-union movement and the inspiration of the solidarity action with the London dock workers in 1889. In fact, Lane's role was to wed the labour movement in Queensland to the socialist ideal."[32] We see his application of mateship to this political ideal when he makes his mouthpiece, Geisner, in his novel *The Workingman's Paradise*, explain to Ned, the young bushman:

"Socialism would make men mates to the extent of all sharing up with one another. Each man might have a purse, but he'd put no more into it than his mate who was sick and weak."

"We'd all work together and share together, I take it," said Ned... .

"Co-operation as against competition is the main industrial idea of Socialism."[33]

These were not empty words: in 1889, the year Lane drafted the plan of the Australian Labour Federation by which a socialist objective was adopted by the political labour movement in Queensland, he was also the inspiring force behind the collection and cabling to the dock workers on strike in London of £30,000 from the sympathetic workers of Australia. In 1926 one of the old leaders of the dock workers, "Big Ben" Tillett, told me in London how deeply they were moved by this remarkable generosity—for £30,000 represented a large sum in those days, especially from the pockets of the workers—coming from a land as far away as Australia. It was a striking example of Lane's socialist mateship in action, of men "all sharing up with one another".

Mateship of the Bush

Turning from the exclusive to the inclusive types of mateship, we find that of the bushmen the most significant as well as the earliest form. Indeed, it may be said to have provided a model influencing other forms, just as it set the pattern of thought and behaviour, as we have seen, for the new unionism of the eighties and the idealists of the nineties.

In the bush the mateship has changed its character so radically from the primitive proto-mateship of the convicts and developed so greatly that it seems the very opposite, thus tending to disprove the theory that there was any important convict influence. It must be remembered, at the same time, that the bush life and conditions generally effected, as we have seen earlier, a marked change in the character of the convicts after they had been freed from the disabilities of the penal system.

[32] Robin Gollan, *Radical and Working Class Politics: a Study of Eastern Australia 1850-1910* (Melbourne 1960), p.124.

[33] "John Miller" (William Lane), *The Workingman's Paradise: an Australian Labour Novel* (Sydney 1948 ed., first publ. 1892), p.120.

The main determinant for them, as for all bushmen, was the land, the physical environment invoking certain ecological adaptations. This demanded that a man should have a companion for many purposes: to carry out a job of work which he could not do on his own; to give mutual protection against danger or accident when travelling in isolated areas up country; to help one another in many ways; and to gain companionship in the lonely bush. Self-interest, therefore, and the sheer necessity of the working and living conditions in the bush required that a man should have a mate. The same conditions prescribed that, instead of the group mateship that was inevitable for convicts banded together in chain-gangs, prisons, and settlements, the bush mateship should be confined usually to two men, although it was extended on occasion to three or four for certain occupations. The result was a personal relationship of a new kind.

A Deepened Loyalty

The consequent intimacy between two mates led to a deepening of loyalty to each other. As workmates they shared the trials and rewards of their work, its hazards and its humours, and got to know each other very well. Close knowledge often brought greater understanding and sympathy. An excellent illustration of these developments is given by Alexander Harris in describing his relations with the currency youth he calls R-. A casual encounter leads to their teaming up together on a job of sawing timber. They get on together very happily, and become true mates. R- goes off to get supplies and money for Harris, and returns hungry from his trip, having been at one stage three days and two nights without anything to eat. Harris comments:

Well enough he might be hungry, for the good-hearted fellow had knocked his horse up the night before, full forty miles away, and had come on foot, with nearly fifty pounds weight of one thing and another on his back, all over the mountains; and it must have been so sludgy and wet under foot best part of the way, that an unincumbered foot-man could hardly have taken two steps together without slipping.[34]

Harris is so impressed that he is driven to the thoughtful and penetrating observation:

Looked at in an abstract point of view, it is quite surprising what exertions bushmen of new countries, especially mates, will make for one another, beyond people of the old countries. I suppose want prevailing less in the new countries makes men less selfish, and difficulties prevailing more make them more social and mutually helpful.[35]

[34] Alexander Harris, op. cit., p.176.
[35] Ibid.

Harris, with his usual shrewdness, has put his finger on the relation between bush conditions and the resulting kind of mateship. Later, he goes to the heart of mateship when he analyzes it in the comment already given as an epigraph.

By the 1820s and 1830s, therefore, the period covered by the soi-disant "emigrant mechanic" in his Australian wanderings, mateship had become "universal" in the bush, and its characteristics had been thoroughly developed. Its practice in neighbouring communities, too, is illustrated by Simpson Newland's account in *Paving the Way* of the whalers in Encounter Bay, such as "Harpooner Jack":

Of course, if the temptation to go "on the cross" was too strong he could not help it. By this it must not be understood, however, that he would, under any circumstances, betray his "pal": that, in the rude ethics of the community, was the unpardonable sin—a baseness that could not be condoned.[36]

Lawson's Exposition

It was not until the end of the nineteenth century, however, that bush mateship was fully expounded as a full-fledged doctrine by Henry Lawson. His stories abound in examples of its usages and sentiments. It is especially fitting that in "That There Dog of Mine" the disabled Macquarie refuses aid at the hospital because help is not being given to his dog, suffering from a broken leg, and praises the loyalty of his four-footed mate, since this essential virtue of mateship has also been the traditional prerogative of the dog amongst living things, human or animal. In "Telling Mrs Baker" the two drovers Jack and Andy undertake to look after Bob Baker as their mate, and then, after his death, to comfort his widow by a fictitious account of the manner of his passing.

In "That Pretty Girl in the Army" Lawson tells of some of the ways in which a bushman stands by his mate:

A bushman has always a mate to comfort him and argue with him, and work and tramp and drink with him, and lend him quids when he's hard up, and call him a b—— fool, and fight him sometimes; to abuse him to his face and defend his name behind his back; to bear false witness for him if he's single, and to his wife if he's married; to secure a "pen" for him at a shed when he isn't on the spot, or, if the mate is away in New Zealand or South Africa, to write and tell him if it's any good coming over this way. And each would take the word of the other against all the world, and each believes that the other is the straightest chap that ever lived—"A white man!"[37]

Other elements of mateship appear, too. Thus Lawson gives a graphic, realistic picture of jealousy in "Mateship" when one mate Bob chums up with another man, and Jim is jealous until Bob explains

---

[36] Simpson Newland, *Paving the Way: a Romance of the Australian Bush* (Adelaide 1936 ed., first publ. 1898), p.45.
[37] Henry Lawson, op. cit., pp.388-9.

that the newcomer had been in jail with him, and Jim apologizes. Lawson comments: "The faith of men is as strong as the sympathy between them, and perhaps the hardest thing on earth for a woman to kill."[38] Perhaps the best demonstration of the final remark is to be found, however, not in Australian literature but in American, when Bret Harte tells how after Tennessee's partner on the Californian gold-fields had married, his wife smiled not unkindly when Tennessee made approaches to her, and fled to Marysville where Tennessee followed her "and where they went to housekeeping without the aid of a Justice of the peace".

> Tennessee's Partner took the loss of his wife simply and seriously, as was his fashion. But to everybody's surprise, when Tennessee returned one day from Marysville, without his partner's wife,—she having smiled and retreated with somebody else,—Tennessee's Partner was the first man to shake his hand and greet him with affection. The boys who had gathered in the cañon to see the shooting were naturally indignant.[39]

When Tennessee, gambler and thief, is caught as a highway robber, and brought before Judge Lynch, it is his "partner" (Californian for "mate") who tries vainly to save him by offering all his "pile" of gold, and then buries him beside his cabin, loyal to the last.

Some Defections

In contrast to this, we also find some cynical and realistic reflections on mates who had failed to keep up the high standards expected. The chief cause of defection is the root of all evil, love of money. Thus "Ironbark", G. Herbert Gibson, parodies the sentimental popular song "Ben Bolt" in "A Ballad of Queensland", reprinted by Paterson in his *Old Bush Songs* as "Sam Holt". In this Jim the drover "apostrophiseth his quondam mate, who hath made his pile, and gone home":

> *Say, don't you remember that fiver, Sam Holt,*
>   *You borrowed so frank and so free,*
> *When the publicans landed your fifty-pound cheque*
>   *In Tambo, your very last spree?*
> *Luck changes some nature, and yours, Sammy Holt,*
>   *'Ain't a grand one as ever I see,*
> *And I guess I may whistle a good many tunes,*
>   *'Fore you'll think of that fiver, or me.*[40]

Even Lawson, after telling about the embarrassment of meeting an old mate when you are well off and he is down on his luck and

[38] Henry Lawson, *Mateship, His Mistake and Strangers' Friend* (Melbourne 1930), p.14.
[39] Bret Harte, *Short Stories*, ed. William Macdonald (London 1928, O.U.P. The World's Classics), p.101.
[40] G. Herbert Gibson ("Ironbark"), *Ironbark Splinters from the Australian Bush* (London 1912), pp.74-5.

can't afford to "shout" you and "makes you mad with his beastly pride" so that you cannot give him any money, adds drily:

P.S.—I met an old mate of that description once, and so successfully persuaded him out of his beastly pride that he borrowed two pounds off me till Monday. I never got it back since, and I want it badly at the present moment. In future I'll leave old mates with their pride unimpaired.[41]

If bush mateship had small defections, it seems to have had, however, only a little outright disloyalty.

The Answer to Loneliness

The next aspect of mateship to be considered is one which strikes deep. The bush practice of a man having a mate developed primarily as a practical necessity for sharing work and ensuring safety. But it also gave sanity as well as security, since the company of a mate was the most potent defence against that loneliness in the isolated bush which, if not mitigated by human fellowship, led to eccentricity and even insanity, as we saw earlier in "The Cry of the Crow". In the pioneering solitudes men often had to live only with their own thoughts, and feed upon their own hearts in a way that recalls the shrewd words of Francis Bacon: "The Parable of Pythagoras is darke, but true; *Cor ne edito,—Eat not the Heart*. Certainly, if a Man would give it a hard Phrase, Those that want Friends to open themselves unto are Canniballs of their owne Hearts."[42]

Such was the madness caused by long solitude. It is against such darkness of the mind that we must see bush mateship shining, a redemptive candle of light. We cannot enter into the full meaning of mateship for the bushmen unless we see fully the vast solitudes behind it, the challenge of the loneliness to which it was the fulfilling answer.

Bacon's picture of the lonely heart-eaters wanting friends may be applied not only to the "hatters" of the bush but to familiar literary figures. Richard Mahony's tragedy, for instance, was largely that of an egocentric incapable of any true permanent mateship. He breaks with his early mate Purdy, and he fails to make a true mate of his wife Mary. His madness was the damnation of a self-imposed isolation, the penalty of a mateless loneliness.

So, too, Patrick White creates both Voss and Stan Parker as lonely characters. Voss, like Mahony, was incapable of mateship, and his fanatic journey partakes of madness. Stan Parker never achieved complete understanding with his wife, and he remained without a mate. Indeed, this exceptional remoteness of the settler from his wife,

---

[41] Henry Lawson, op. cit., p.269, in "Meeting Old Mates".
[42] Alfred S. West (ed.), *Bacon's Essays* (Cambridge 1931), p.79, in "Of Friendship".

his neighbours, and any mates makes *The Tree of Man* wear an alien air, so that the Australian reader feels that it is not an authentic rendering of his country and people. The portrait of Stan Parker has to be accepted, rather, as an attempt to abstract the element of loneliness both in pioneering the land and in the human spirit.

Indeed, it is akin to the iconographs showing man as a lonely figure in the isolation of an illimitable solitude of the inland desert which have been painted by contemporary artists exploring the inner truth of the Australian landscape. Drysdale, recurring to the theme of loneliness, presents in his Albury paintings, as Bernard Smith commented, "a landscape alien to man, harsh, weird, spacious and vacant, given over to the oddities and whimsies of nature, fit only for heroes and clowns, saints, exiles, and primitive men".[43]

Looking at the preoccupation with loneliness in our literature and the way Australia as a lonely land has become a dominant motif of our leading artists, I wonder whether one significant reason why mateship has persisted so tenaciously as a social pattern is that it still answers a bush-bred sense of isolation which has entered deep into our collective consciousness and become an integral part of the national imagination.

In one of his 1954 Kelly series, for instance, Nolan pictures Ned Kelly riding away, a centaur-like figure, into a vast emptiness, with the faceless head as only an armoured headpiece, with a slit of blue sky and wisp of white cloud seen through the black rectangle, as if the emptiness of space were even evoked as an element in Kelly's mind. Is this perhaps also an iconograph that symbolizes a lonely solitude existing in the national mind—a solitude against which mateship offers a defence?

A Refined Sensibility

In answering loneliness the bush mateship provided more than a merely protective company. It developed into a special kind of companionship that was close to the intimacy of man and wife in a happy marriage, based on the knowledge, sympathy, and understanding of two persons living and working together in a daily partnership.

It is also probable that often, in compensation for the lack of white women in the outback, the relations between a bushman and his mate connoted, as Russel Ward has suggested discerningly, an unconscious sublimation of the sex instinct.[44] This seems, on the whole, to have been a true sublimation, with no physical element. Earlier, of course, homosexuality was common amongst the convicts,

[43] Bernard Smith, *Australian Painting 1788-1960* (Melbourne 1962), p.251.
[44] Russel Ward, *The Australian Legend* (Melbourne 1958), p.93.

especially the more hardened offenders in the penal settlements in Van Diemen's Land and Norfolk Island, and there is evidence to indicate that it was continued by some convicts when they went "up country". But the bush mateship, in general, seems to have been notably free of it, according to Lawson and other writers of the nineties. Indeed, when D. H. Lawrence as a visiting Englishman introduces a physical attraction as operating between the English Somers and Kangaroo or Jack Callcott in *Kangaroo*, we immediately feel a false note, an English concept quite alien to the Australian *ethos*.

What we do find in the literature of the bush are many instances of a refined sensibility, sometimes feminine in its delicacy of consideration, being practised by bush mates. In Lawson's "Telling Mrs Baker" the two drovers Jack and Andy, after the death of their mate Bob Baker, comfort his widow by a fictitious account of his passing which is full of gentleness as well as irony. A similar touch of the refinement of feeling developed in mateship comes when the swagman Mitchell, waking up in the night by the camp fire, sees the moon's light on the face of Peter, the bush missionary. "Then Mitchell quietly got some boughs and stuck them in the ground at a little distance from Peter's head, to shade his face from the moonlight."[45]

Lawson also expresses this sensibility among mates when he tells, with a characteristic blend of sentiment and humour, how his mates would get small "tokens of mateship" and give them to a mate departing for Maoriland to cheer and comfort him on his uncertain way:

You may battle round with mates for many years, and share and share alike, good times or hard, and find the said mates true and straight through it all; but it is their little thoughtful attentions when you are going away, that go right down to the bottom of your heart, and lift it up and make you feel inclined—as you stand alone by the rail when the sun goes down on the sea— to write or recite poetry and otherwise make a fool of yourself.[46]

The sentiment aroused by mateship among the bushmen was strong and took many forms. It even took the form of tears when a mate was dying or at his death, according to one of the old bush songs, "The Dying Stockman", which begins with the death-bed picture: "His two mates around him were crying". Lawson, too, depicts the same sensibility when he tells of the death of the squatter Jack Denver and the sorrow of his old mate Ben Duggan: "And big Ben Duggan by the bed stood sobbing like a child."[47] Lawson's ballad, although stirring in its way, seems too sentimental, especially

[45] Henry Lawson, op. cit., vol.II, p.284, "The Story of Gentleman Once".
[46] Ibid., vol.I, p.195.
[47] Henry Lawson, *Poetical Works* (Sydney 1956), p.70, "Talbragar".

when Christmas Day is thrown in, gratuitously, for Jack Denver's funeral. More effective is the quiet but moving farewell between the Boss and his dying mate Briglow in Louis Esson's classic one-act play *The Drovers*.

First Place to the Stranger

Accompanying this kindly sensibility is that extension of fellowship called bush hospitality, a natural and even necessary product of the isolation of the inland. For the food and drink and shelter given by the bushman to the traveller today might be needed by himself tomorrow. Without such friendly aid life in the bush would not have been possible. All observers of the New South Wales colony in the early days were struck by this universal hospitality, so that Harris termed it "proverbial". Nor was it in any way merely a class custom of the bush workers. Thus Gerstaecker, after describing the welcome given by squatters at station after station to the traveller on horseback, "a swell", goes on to record:

The traveller on foot is never received with less hospitality, let his appearance be as it may; and mine was not very satisfactory after the shipwreck. But he is very seldom allowed to enter the house, his place is in the kitchen, where he is styled, in the most kind and friendly manner, "mate". In the largest head station, or in the poorest shepherd's hut, the treatment is the same, whatever the cook or the hut-keeper has in his larder he brings forward for the guest, and the "Welcome with all my heart", of the house is not warmer than the "You're welcome to it" in the kitchen.[48]

The term "mate" as used here indicates that the bush hospitality is a widening of the relationship between two mates in the bush to a generous inclusiveness of all men as partners against the hazards of the bush environment.

How closely bush hospitality, as a recognised form of mateship, is linked to personal fellowship, is brought out clearly by Lawson in his "Shearers":

> *No church-bell rings them from the Track,*
> *No pulpit lights their blindness—*
> *'Tis hardship, drought, and homelessness*
> *That teach those Bushmen kindness:*
> *The mateship born, in barren lands,*
> *Of toil and thirst and danger,*
> *The camp-fare for the wanderer set,*
> *The first place to the stranger.*[49]

Self-sacrifice

The unselfish character of bush mateship is shown in many daily,

[48] F. Gerstaecker, *Narrative of a Journey Round the World*, etc., 3 vols (London 1853), vol.3, pp.13-14.
[49] Henry Lawson, *Poetical Works*, p.103.

casual acts, considerate gestures, and sharing of fortunes, but is also shown, if need be, by the sacrifice of life itself. Commenting on this, Lawson writes:

They say that self-preservation is the strongest instinct of mankind; it may come with the last gasp, but I think the preservation of the life or liberty of a mate—man or woman—is the first and strongest. It is the instinct that irresistibly impels a thirsty, parched man, out on the burning sands, to pour the last drop of water down the throat of a dying mate, where none save the sun or moon or stars may see. And the sun, moon and stars do not write to the newspapers.[50]

The bush story is certainly not lacking in such instances. One popular among bushmen was John Farrell's melodramatic, sentimental ballad "How He Died". This told how Nabbage, the boozing, despised drudge of the station, rode desperately at night to the township doctor to save the life of "his little mate" the squatter's boy Freddie, trampled by a rush of steers. Himself dying after his horse had broken his neck at a creek, Nabbage crawls in agony to the doctor. Thinking that the doctor may delay the boy's rescue by attending to himself, Nabbage pretends to be unhurt and drunk, so that the doctor kicks him indignantly and drives off. "So he died."[51]

Far superior in every way is "Banjo" Paterson's ballad "How Gilbert Died". The two bushrangers Gilbert and Dunn, hunted as outlaws with a thousand pounds on their heads, were betrayed. Wakened at night, they heard the command to lay down their arms from the troopers surrounding their mountain hut. Gilbert tried to fire his rifle, but it had been drenched with water, and was useless:

> *Then he dropped the piece with a bitter oath,*
> *And he turned to his comrade Dunn:*
> *"We are sold," he said, "we are dead men both,*
> *But there may be a chance for one;*
> *I'll stop and I'll fight with the pistol here,*
> *You take to your heels and run."*

So Dunn escaped in the darkness whilst Gilbert covered his flight by walking out of the hut and drawing the fire of the troopers, who riddled his body with rifle balls. His bravery and sacrifice were remembered:

> *There's never a stone at the sleeper's head,*
> *There's never a fence beside,*
> *And the wandering stock on the grave may tread*
> *Unnoticed and undenied;*
> *But the smallest child on the Watershed*
> *Can tell you how Gilbert died.*[52]

[50] Henry Lawson, *Mateship, His Mistake and Strangers' Friend* (Melbourne 1930), p.7.
[51] John Farrell, *How He Died and Other Poems* (Melbourne 1907 ed., first publ. 1887), p.23.   [52] A. B. Paterson, *Collected Verse* (Sydney 1921), pp.91-2.

Gold-diggers, Miners and Seamen

Similar to the mateship of bushmen is that of a group of workers, such as gold-diggers, miners, and seamen, whose fellowship is an inclusive one responding to the physical environment, a working partnership in which men shared daily toil, hardships, and dangers. With diggers there was also the additional freemasonry of fortune, with mates sharing ill-luck or a rich strike. They often shared a communal purse, a sharing which recalls how the bush youth Ned explained to Geisner, "mates is them wot's got one purse".[53] In Katharine Prichard's saga of the Western Australian gold-fields, for instance, when Morris Gough is leaving Ma Buggins on Hannans and cannot pay her the fifty pounds he owes her for meals and stores, his mate Frisco immediately planks down payment in gold. When Sally Gough thanks Frisco and says her husband would repay him as soon as possible, " 'Don't worry about that, Mrs. Gough,' Frisco replied easily. 'Morrey'd do the same for me. If you've got gold, up here, and a mate hasn't, it's his if he wants it.' "[54]

On the gold-fields the loyalty of mateship was widely observed. Deviations from it were punished firmly, but justly, without the convict or larrikin violence and vindictiveness, except in the case of the Chinese. At Coolgardie, writes Katharine Prichard:

Men on the rush dealt drastically with any violation of the unwritten law of loyalty between mates. The camp code was scrupulously observed: the most serious crime on the prospector's calendar to hide or steal gold from a mate: betray the mutual interest of the diggers.[55]

A dispute or offence was tried by the diggers fairly at the camp roll-up. If a man was found guilty, the diggers' code "required that the offender should be banished from the camp, with food and water for twenty-four hours. The man became a pariah wherever he went."[56]

There was a strong sentiment felt between mates, often marked by tenderness. Thus Lawson gives the picture of Peter McKenzie, an old Ballarat digger on the Gulgong field, weeping at the funeral of an old Ballarat mate.

The mateship observed, too, was like that of the bushmen in that it was hospitable and generous. A good example is given by Edward Dyson in his story "The Washerwoman of Jacker's Flat". One Sunday, the diggers discovered that Brummy Peters, the amazonian, masculine, pipe-smoking laundress, had adopted the illegitimate

[53] "John Miller" (William Lane), op. cit., pp.119-20.
[54] Katharine Susannah Prichard, *The Roaring Nineties: a Story of the Goldfields of Western Australia* (London 1946), p.103.
[55] Ibid., p.38.
[56] Ibid.

month-old baby of a wretched girl who had committed suicide the night before.

On the Monday evening following Brummy Peters was waited on by a deputation. A very respectful deputation it was, and wished "to signerfy that the fellers all voted her a brick, an' hoped how she'd pocket that trifle to help her with the youngster, an' say nothin'." That trifle was a roll of notes of all sorts and sizes surrounding a five-ounce nugget, the biggest ever found on the rush.[57]

The loyalty of the miners, again, was expressed in many forms of sympathy, understanding, and self-sacrifice. *The Fortunes of Richard Mahony* opens with a lad trying vainly to save a mate on whom the shaft had fallen in at the Ballarat diggings. It goes on to tell of a licence hunt by the Commissioner and the troopers, with the digger Long Jim trying to escape, and his youthful—and equally licenceless —mate saving him by diverting attention at the cost of being captured himself beside a store. As he is being handcuffed by the police, the storekeeper frees him by paying his bail. The young scapegrace laughed and winked at his friend. "I knew you'd go bail."[58] So Richard Mahony rescues his mate Purdy. So Henry Handel Richardson begins her eminent trilogy with two illustrations of mateship on the diggings.

The opening passages of her novel also illustrate the hazards of life and death that created a tradition of self-sacrifice amongst diggers and miners. When men's lives were endangered their mates never hesitated to risk their own lives to save them. A vivid account of such an occasion is given by Dyson in his poem "The Rescue":

The relay hurries in to the rescue, caring not for the danger a straw;
'Tis not toil, but a battle, they're called to, and like Trojans the miners
*   respond,*
For a dead man lies crushed 'neath the timbers, or a live man is choking
*   beyond.*[59]

Akin to the mateship of the miners is that of the seamen and workers on ships as another ecological response to environmental hardships and hazards. Its strength, generosity, and gentleness have been shown movingly by John Morrison in "The Nightshift" and other stories of stevedores.

Fighting Servicemen

The hazard of death present at times for the last group of workers was intensified, of course, to an almost daily risk for the group of

[57] Edward Dyson, *Below and On Top* (Melbourne 1898), p.161.
[58] Henry Handel Richardson, *The Fortunes of Richard Mahony* (Melbourne 1946 ed., first publ. 1930), p.21.
[59] Edward Dyson, *Rhymes from the Mines* (Sydney 1898), p.28.

servicemen in action. The mateship directed against this risk was naturally inclusive, with a loyalty that could be associated with other loyalties to the family, the fighting unit, and the country. Since any betrayal of mates was rare under wartime conditions there was no need for intolerance or vindictiveness. The loyalty was strengthened, again, by two factors notable in stimulating the close fellowship of men in the bush—the relative absence of women and of institutional religion.

Indeed, the parallel between the mateship of the bushmen and that of soldiers was noted by the French critic Emile Saillens in his *Mercure* article on Lawson, where he wrote:

la camaraderie des bushmen . . . rappelle ces fraternités de caserne . . . elle est admirable par son caractère de fidélité aveugle, quasi-religieuse, d'affection formée lentement, mais pour toujours. C'est assurément cet esprit de camaraderie à la vie et à la mort.

(the mateship of the bushmen . . . recalls the brotherhoods of the barracks . . . it is admirable by its character of blind fidelity, almost religious, of affection formed slowly, but for always. It is certainly that spirit of mateship for life and to the death.)[60]

Excellent illustrations of this brotherhood in arms are found in the entertaining, authentic stories of the first world war diggers by Harley Matthews in his *Saints and Soldiers*.

The mateship of the diggers in both world wars applied equally, of course, to their fellow servicemen fighting in the Royal Australian Navy and the Royal Australian Air Force, although examples are here confined, for space reasons, to soldiers. Two important aspects of it extend to all servicemen: its democratic quality and its heroic self-sacrifice.

Officers and men fought side by side, and on many occasions risked their lives to save each other, completely irrespective of rank, especially in platoons and small detachments. The First AIF, which established the national traditions of servicemen in action, differed from the British and European armies as a volunteer force; with general freedom from class distinctions; with officers in the militia, professional men, and wealthy graziers enlisting in the ranks as privates and gunners; and with a system of promotion from the ranks. The Second AIF continued the democratic tradition. When I enlisted in it in 1940 as a gunner, for instance, my gun team was made up at times of a diverse crew from country and city alike—a grazier and sheep breeder whose prize rams had won awards at the Sydney Sheep Show, a partner in a well known country store who was a crack rifle shot, a youthful bush labourer who could quote Burns and Shelley,

[60] Emile Saillens, "Le Bush Australien et Son Poète" in *Mercure de France*, 1 octobre 1910 (Paris), pp.444-5.

a North Coast farmer who was an "old digger" of the First AIF, a bank clerk whose mathematical talent was superior to that of any of the field regiment's officers, a window-cleaner from Redfern who had been a city gamin and S.P. "bookie", and myself, a leader-writer on the *Sydney Morning Herald* and former Professor of English in the Philippines. We were a motley lot, and there was no class distinction whatever. Each man was taken on his own merits, and we were all fellow gunners together, all good mates. Our fellowship was one of the finest things I have known.

It must be remembered too, that Australia's official history of the first world war was as unique as its army, since its editor, that great Australian Dr Bean, revolutionized official war histories by writing the first democratic one, with the emphasis placed, not on G.H.Q. and the generals, but on the actual first-hand experiences of the men in the ranks and the units in action. As Professor K. S. Inglis wrote of Dr Bean in a penetrating article in *Meanjin Quarterly* on "The Anzac Tradition":

For he identifies himself with the man in the front line; and that stand governs his method as an historian. He believed that he was writing about an army which was unusually good because of the character, and in particular the egalitarian comradeship, of its members; and he wrote a history appropriate to this belief.[61]

We have been fortunate that the tradition of democratic history established by Dr Bean has been splendidly maintained by another brilliant historian, Gavin Long, as editor of the official history of the second world war.

Self-sacrifice

So, too, that war brought forth once again the sacrificial courage that marked, above all, the mateship of the servicemen. Examples could be multiplied from the war literature, especially the official history. In the fighting for the capture of Tobruk,

Sergeant Burgess ran forward to one of the tanks and was trying to heave up the lid to drop in a grenade when he was hit by several bullets. "His last effort before he died," wrote one diarist, "was to struggle to put the pin back and throw the grenade clear of his comrades."[62]

In the Muar River battle in Malaya Lieutenant Ben Hackney was one of the wounded left behind at Parit Sulong who fell into the hands of the Japanese. They were tortured and finally burnt alive.

[61] K. S. Inglis, "The Anzac Tradition" in *Meanjin Quarterly*, no. 100, vol.XXIV, no.i, 1965.

[62] *Australia in the War of 1939-1945*, series I (Army), vol.I, Gavin Long, *To Benghazi* (Canberra 1952), p.227. See also p.175.

Hackney, left for dead, crawled away and later was saved by Sergeant Ron Croft:

Weak and nerve-racked, and smaller than Hackney, who weighed fourteen stone, he yet managed to return and stagger off with Hackney across his shoulder.

Sheer strength alone did not enable him to carry his burden. It was something more than that—his wish and willingness to help; courage, guts, and manliness.[63]

Many, many more of such incidents lie memorialized in the war histories, which constitute a superb thesaurus of sacrificial deeds which declare, more eloquently than any words, the enduring gallantry of the human spirit.

It might be considered that they go beyond the theme of mateship. They do. Yet they also form its supreme manifestation. Their inspiring force was linked with the loyalty of mateship, and this simple, but profound link was discerned clearly by the man best fitted to judge, Dr Bean. At the end of *The Story of Anzac* he inquired into the motives that sustained the Australian troops during the fighting at Gallipoli:

What was the dominant motive that impelled them? It lay in the mettle of the men themselves. To be the sort of man who would give way when his mates were trusting to his firmness; to be the sort of man who would fail when the line, the whole force, and the allied cause required his endurance...—that was the prospect which these men could not face. Life was very dear, but life was not worth living unless they could be true to their idea of Australian manhood.[64]

So, at the end of his history, Dr Bean found that loyalty to their mates was an integral part of the Anzacs' idea of manhood, the dominant motive that kept them going, just as in the beginning of his book he had declared that the prevailing creed of these men as typical Australians was that "a man should at all times and at any cost stand by his mate".[65] What was true of the men on Gallipoli was no less true of all servicemen, on land, in the air, and on the sea, throughout two world wars.

The Brotherhood of Man

If the mateship of the servicemen was a concrete, realistic fact of their living and dying, we must turn to the idealists of the nineties to find another mateship that was developed in the form of an abstract, romantic ideal, the all-embracing concept of human

[63] Ibid., vol.IV, Lionel Wigmore, *The Japanese Thrust* (Canberra 1957), pp.247-8. The final comment is quoted from Lt Hackney's own account in typescript.

[64] C.E.W. Bean, op. cit., pp.606-7.

[65] Ibid., p.6.

Q

brotherhood. This was a natural extension of the bush mateship for such warm-hearted dreamers as Lawson, O'Dowd, Furphy, Mary Gilmore, J. Le Gay Brereton, and, a little later, such followers of their tradition as Katharine Prichard, Vance Palmer, and that modest pacifist poet R. H. Long. It was also, to a considerable extent, an extension of the belief in radical democracy and the Great Australian Dream, and it was basic in the socialism, as already noted, of such creators of the New Unionism as W. G. Spence and William Lane.

It is voiced notably in Lawson's verse "For'ard", looking to the time when "the sense of Human Kinship" shall revolutionize the world. It is a constant strain in O'Dowd's poetry, especially explicit in such poems as "Young Democracy", "Love and Sacrifice", and "Alma Venus!". To the isocratic Furphy the fraternity of all men was as basic as their equality, and he declares through Rigby: "This initial brotherhood . . . is not a hypothesis that you are called upon to sift; it is the sternest verity of life."[66]

The same democratic feeling for the brotherhood of all men runs throughout the writings of Mary Gilmore, and finds fit expression in her poem "Nationality", already quoted. She was, above all, a humanist, who went beyond class and nation to humanity. This feeling is also implicit in the universality of that gentle but deep singer Shaw Neilson, the finest of all Australian pure lyrists, to whom "Blood that is good and red is on every soil the same".[67] It is explicit in *The Song of Brotherhood and Other Verses* of Professor J. Le Gay Brereton, an old mate of Lawson and, like him, an apostle of mateship. It was Brereton who, writing in memory of Lawson and the ideal of mateship which he voiced, declared stoutly:

So mateship became the lonely poet's watchword, and he made it the watchword of Australia.

. . . But, let me repeat, it is an ideal that refuses the limitation of class or nationality, and the more Lawson saw of men and women of various classes the more he realized their need of it.

. . . He was not merely an Australian. He looked forward to a day when mateship will prevail on earth, and could see the future in which the nations work together "and there ain't no fore-'n'-aft".[68]

It seems valid, therefore, to accept this ideal of the brotherhood of man as one form of mateship in a legitimate extension of the original concept. Its significance has been brought out percipiently by Manning Clark in a *Meanjin* article on "Tradition in Australian Literature". Discussing the creed of the writers in the nineties, its

---

[66] Tom Collins (Joseph Furphy), *Rigby's Romance* (Sydney 1946 ed., first publ. 1921), p.213.
[67] John Shaw Neilson, *Collected Poems*, ed. by R. H. Croll (Melbourne 1934), p.104, in "Show Me the Song".
[68] His Mates, *Henry Lawson* (Sydney 1931), pp.15-16.

various meanings, and its relation to the egalitarian and utopian aspirations, he concludes:

> One thing, however, is certain. Their emphasis was on "mateship". Here is Lawson's version of it in his poem "Shearers":
>
> > *They tramp in mateship side by side—*
> > *The Protestant and Roman—*
> > *They call no biped lord or sir,*
> > *And touch their hat to no man.*
>
> There it is: social equality, mateship, independence. The meaning of these terms can only be gleaned from reading all their works... in extolling "mateship" the writers were drawing attention to what made life worth while, or, once again, making the workers aware of the faith by which they lived. And, in urging mateship as a universal ideal of behaviour, they were simply asking them to extend their affections from the few they knew to the many who had had their experience.
>
> Mateship is also the key to the messianic note which runs through their works.[69]

Drinking Mates

This idealism has deliquesced when we come to the mateship practised by our ninth group, contemporary city dwellers, since here we have, not the fraternity of mankind, but a beery brotherhood of drinking mates. This is pleasant enough, good as far as it goes, but it does not go very far. It is relatively shallow, since there are no hardships, dangers, or enemies to deepen the feeling between mates or make demands on loyalty. It has no call for self-sacrifice. It contains only good cheer and a friendly, inclusive companionship.

A lively picture of it is given in Nino Culotta's humorous tale of an Italian migrant, *They're a Weird Mob*. Here is a romantic world where class distinctions, strikes, and sectarian strife are all conveniently forgotten whilst old and new Australians meet cheerily as mates:

> Joe said, "Had to pick up yer new mate, mate. 'Ow yer goin' mate orright?"
> "Yeah mate. 'Ow yer goin' orright?"
> "Orright mate. Nino, this is Pat. Pat—Nino."
> Pat extended a hand, and said "Pleased ter meet yer."[70]

Here is mateyness raised to the *nth* sentimental power. It has provoked valid criticism. On the other hand, it has led critics to censure the picture of mateship as the social cement binding this Sydney community of bricklayers and building contractors as false, asserting that mateship, a tradition of the lonely bush, has been made anachronistic in the crowded urban environment of today. *They're a Weird Mob*,

---

[69] Manning Clark, "Tradition in Australian Literature", *Meanjin*, vol.VIII, no.I, autumn 1949.
[70] Nino Culotta (John O'Grady), *They're a Weird Mob* (Sydney 1957), p.33.

however, not only rightly shows that mateship flourishes in its different way as vigorously in Punchbowl as it does the other side of the black stump, but it gives the clue explaining why. For Nino writes of his loneliness at his hotel at the end of his first week in Sydney: "Sydney on Sundays can be a very lonely place for a stranger who has no friends, and I was glad to be back at Punchbowl with Pat, on Monday morning. His ' 'Ow yer goin' mate orright?' was a very pleasant sound."[71] The fact that the great majority of Australians live in the cities is, indeed, one of the main reasons why mateship persists as a main social pattern, since its companionship is needed to answer the loneliness of solitude no less in the modern city than in the isolated bush of last century. The sagacious Bacon pointed this out long ago:

But little doe Men perceive what Solitude is, and how farre it extendeth. For a Crowd is not Company; and Faces are but a Gallery of Pictures; and Talke but a *Tinckling Cymball*, where there is no Love. The Latine Adage meeteth with it a little, *Magna Civitas, Magna Solitudo*; Because in a great Towne, Frends are scattered; So that there is not that Fellowship, for the most Part, which is in lesse Neighbourhoods. But we may goe further and affirme most truly, That it is a meere and miserable Solitude to want true Frends, without which the World is but a Wildernesse.[72]

On these points the judgement of the wise old Bacon still remains valid.

The Australian People

Finally, we come to our last grouping, that of the Australian people in general, to whom mateship is not so much a formulated doctrine as a philosophy and practice implicit in the popular usage of the term "mate", accepted without demur or analysis as a distinctive part of the national tradition.

Significant testimony to this general acceptance is offered by Professor Walter Murdoch in one of his essays where he tells, on his return to Australia from abroad, of a man strolling up to him on the wharf at Fremantle and saying: "Got a match, mate?". He describes his reaction:

Any one who has been away from Australia, and returned, will understand with what enthusiasm I handed out my match-box.... There was no doubt, now, about my being really home again; Australia herself had spoken, in a voice unlike any other voice...in four short words that man said everything. He expressed that casual, free-and-easy, good-humoured mateship which was then Australia's ideal; and I still think that...it was a very fine ideal.[73]

[71] Ibid., p.74.

[72] *Bacon's Essays*, op. cit., pp.76-77. "Meere" means "absolute".

[73] Walter Murdoch, "On Tail-chasing" in *Collected Essays* (Sydney 1940), p.99.

In this connection mateship combines, I feel, two of our social patterns: the equality of radical democracy and the brotherhood of man forming part of our utopian aspiration. Mateship is, of course, necessarily democratic. Men can only be mates when they are equals, partners in the freemasonry of independent men. Equality, at the same time, is a premise leading naturally to the conclusion of fraternity, as it did with the bushmen and the idealists of the nineties.

The reality, it is true, often falls far short of the ideal, just as it does in the case of the Christian faith. The Australian society has shown at times an unbrotherly discrimination and intolerance towards the aborigines, the Chinese, and foreigners. It has been guilty of a crude xenophobia and a blind racial prejudice which have now lessened, but which still persist. Migrants in comfortless hostels could look ironically at this version of Lawson's "first place to the stranger". The bitterness of class war on occasion makes a mockery of Murdoch's "good-humoured mateship".

Yet the ideal, even if often betrayed in practice, still remains held widely and genuinely, especially in the shape of a kindly, hospitable friendliness, as envisaged in Lawson's "Shearers". Furphy, no less than Lawson an apostle of equality and brotherhood, held the creed. In *Such is Life* Tom Collins, standing in a class apart from either squatter or bullock driver, is in many ways a complete individualist, yet he practises the bush matership unfailingly, considerate in aiding others. At some trouble to himself he goes to the help of Alf Morris in time of need. He makes loyal efforts to save the trespassing teamster Priestley from discovery and punishment by the squatter Montgomery. He succours the hapless Rory O'Halloran, and gives him half of his only cash to help him on his way.

Assessment

In conclusion, we have found, in tracing the historical development of mateship and its variations in ten differing groups, that its complexity has embraced a diversity of virtues and defects. It has been both generously inclusive and narrowly exclusive. It has promoted both a fine loyalty and a savage vindictiveness. It has ranged from a superficial convention to a sacrificial faith; from a companionship in vice to a selfless and refined consideration for others; from a weapon of solidarity in industrial and political warfare to a vision of human brotherhood.

Criticism of mateship, as I pointed out at the start of my discussion, has come from political, religious, and literary quarters. It has also come from the anti-nationalist cosmopolite, hostile to an undeniably Australian creed, and from the sophisticated academic who regards it as a crude, bush-bred habit of the *hoi polloi*. Much of this criticism has been biased and ill-informed, revealing scant knowledge of mateship's historical development or understanding of its complexity.

On the other hand, some thinking writers have given honest and penetrating criticism, as did John Morrison in such short stories as "Bo Abbot", "A Man's World", and "Open Your Eyes".

What place has mateship in the world of today? Obviously its practice has diminished, and is likely to continue diminishing, since the contemporary urban world of affluence, technology, and admass culture does not provide an environment with the hardships and dangers to demand an answering mateship. No hazards come from the daily bus and the lawnmower in the suburbia in which the average Australian of today lives, moves, and has his conventional being. In this humdrum world there is no absence of women or religion, two factors operating to stimulate mateship amongst bushmen and servicemen. So, too, the increasing growth of white-collar workers in the civil service and the tertiary industries, together with the increasing movement of skilled workers into a suburban *bourgeoisie*, all tend to reduce the class solidarity of the combative mateship in trade unions. In many respects, therefore, the traditional mateship has become outmoded by changes in the social environment. Like the other social patterns, it has an ecological basis, and is affected by changes in the ecology.

Furthermore, the cultural sophistication of the post-war years has inevitably forced a stronger, more critical realization of the real limitations of mateship, since it can offer no full solution to the political and economic problems of the day, it has no relevance in the marked development of the creative arts and scientific research, and it can give no answer to the threat posed by the debasement of the community's mind by the puerilities of the mass communicators, such as the press, the weekly "glossies", radio, and television. The area of activity covered by mateship as a social force in our contemporary urban world is limited, and criticisms which strip the Nino Culotta gilt off the mateship gingerbread thus do a needed service. In particular, an easy, glib cult of mateship can be harmful if used as a substitute creed to exclude the important values of life and thought which lie outside its special ambit.

Within that ambit, however, mateship as an historical fact has rendered, in its different forms, much excellent service to our society. It still works actively today in many fields, especially amongst bushmen, workers in hazardous occupations, trade unionists, and servicemen, as a living reality and daily practical force for good.

It may be, at bottom, a simple enough creed, with its one fundamental doctrine of loyalty. It has no pantheon, no cosmology, no immortality, no law of *karma*. Essentially humanist, it is a godless religion, which does not even sport such simple luxuries as haloes in heaven and everlasting flames curling around the wicked in hell—futurities, however, which seem curiously remote in times when men fly through space to walk around on the moon. It has, however, its own genuine values of the spirit to offer to us today, values which are not outmoded, but timeless and enduring.

In our materialistic age and an era marked by violence, fear, and hatred, mateship at its best offers valuable spiritual truths: the virtue of a selfless loyalty standing firm in a world of chaos, a loyalty which can reach the supreme heights of self-sacrifice; the democratic equality of all men, with its corollary of human worth and dignity; and an inclusive belief in the brotherhood of man. These are values of the spirit which can be as potent and significant for us today as they were in the days of Lawson and Furphy, O'Dowd and Mary Gilmore.

In its brotherly generosity mateship emerges as a code of ethics like Confucianism. Confucius would have approved wholeheartedly of the Giraffe, Lawson's shearer who sent round his hat to collect for the unfortunate and those in need of help, since such bush mateship embraces much of the essential Confucian doctrine of *jen*—variously translated as benevolence, fellow-feeling, goodness, or sympathy. One disciple of Confucius explained:

"The Master's Way," he said, "is a sense of duty and fellow-feeling"—duty not to individuals only but to society and the social ideal, and fellow-feeling which connotes the power to put oneself in the place of others and govern one's actions accordingly.[74]

Mateship fulfilled much of this definition in the bush: a bushman had a sense of duty not only to his mate but also to the stranger to whom he gave hospitality, and both of these connoted "fellow-feeling".

Mateship was partly Christian, too, as well as Confucian in that its loyalty at best was akin to the charity which, in the words of St Paul, "Beareth all things, believeth all things, hopeth all things, endureth all things".[75] Such was the loyalty of a man to his mate.

Finally, although mateship differed from Christianity in that it abrogated the supernatural, it was alike in the readiness of its loyalty to embrace the ultimate duty of self-sacrifice, believing with Christ that "Greater love hath no man than this, that a man lay down his life for his friends."[76]

[74] E. D. Edwards, *What Did They Teach? Confucius* (London 1940), p.101.
[75] *The Bible*, I Corinthians, xiii, 7.
[76] Ibid., St. John, xv, 13.

X

Radical Democracy

Come, all my hearties, we'll roam the mountains high,
Together we will plunder, together we will die.
We'll wander over valleys, and gallop over plains,
And we'll scorn to live in slavery, bound down with iron chains.

OLD BUSH SONG[1]

I cannot think it is anything worse than a locally-seated and curable ignorance which makes men eager to subvert a human equality, self-evident as human variety, and impregnable as any mathematical axiom.

JOSEPH FURPHY[2]

They teach and live the Golden Rule
  Of Young Democracy:

"That culture, joy and goodliness
  Be th' equal right of all:
That greed no more shall those oppress
  Who by the wayside fall:

That each shall share what all men sow:
  That colour, caste's a lie:
That man is God, however low—
  Is man, however high."

BERNARD O'DOWD[3]

The way Mark put it, you could not help seeing he was right. The wrong of the social system that they were living under was perpetuated because a few people had seized power and persisted in wielding it so that they and their kind might have a super-abundance of food, clothing, homes to live in, ease and leisure, while thousands of men, women and children starved, went in rags, toiled all their days, and even in the karri lived in shacks of bagging and waste timber, as poor as any you saw in a slum. And why should not the worker change all this? Insist on a new deal of the cards?

KATHARINE SUSANNAH PRICHARD[4]

[1] "The Wild Colonial Boy", Douglas Stewart and Nancy Keesing (ed.), *Old Bush Songs* (Sydney 1955), p.39.
[2] Tom Collins, *Such is Life* (Melbourne 1917 ed.), p.87.
[3] Bernard O'Dowd, *Collected Poems* (Melbourne 1941), p.61.
[4] Katharine Susannah Prichard, *Working Bullocks* (London 1926), p.257.

The Democratic Spirit

The Australian society began inauspiciously as an autocracy, and then became an oligarchy in which authority was shared by a few army officers, officials, and pastoralists. Middle-class elements were small and uninfluential. A deep gulf of social inequality divided the free from the bond, the exclusivist from the emancipist, the squatters from the workers.

Democratic forces were working, however, as heady ferments, and the new brew bubbled over politically at the middle of last century. In the fifties the defenders of the superior rights of the propertied classes grew alarmed at the demands of the masses. Thus Wentworth, the Radical turned Whig, fought eloquently against "the democratic and levelling principles" which were rapidly increasing in Sydney. James Macarthur trusted that "Reason and England" would prevail against "Democracy and America". John Fairfax, speaking for Australian colonists to the citizens of Leamington in England, declared:

Your altars are our altars; your God is our God. We carry with us the institutions of Great Britain. We love her people; we venerate and respect her laws; under her government, the most perfect of any in the world, we live; and long may the flag of England wave over our shores—protecting us from the democracy within, and from the enemies without, of our highly-favoured and beautiful colonies.[5]

Perhaps the beautiful colonies were too highly-favoured, however, since the flag of England, Reason and the oratory of Wentworth all failed conspicuously to protect the Fairfaxes and Macarthurs from the turbulent, triumphant democracy within. By the end of the fifties constitutional changes had made the colonies political democracies substantially, if not completely, and the colonies went on "shooting Niagara" cheerfully. Thus Professor R. M. Crawford in his excellent history of Australia heads one chapter "Aggressive Democracy, 1860-1890", and later concludes:

By the end of the century, the Australian colonies had worked out a way of life that was in essentials the same over the whole continent. Its assumptions of democratic independence and equality of consideration might often be at war with economic and social facts; but there was no unquestioning acceptance of hierarchy, of one's stations and its duties. Around the turn of the century, these attitudes were made part of the currency of common belief by a self-consciously Australian generation of writers, painters, and cartoonists, and especially by the men who wrote and drew for the *Bulletin*.[6]

This democratic spirit, as Professor Crawford notes, has not been fully triumphant. The Australian society is far from being an economic democracy. Class warfare is strong, furthered by political

[5] John Fairfax, Esq., *The Colonies of Australia*, etc. (London 1852), p.18.
[6] R. M. Crawford, *Australia* (London 1952), p.145.

interests as well as by the modern industrial set-up. Socially there are class divisions, conflicts, and snobberies of various types. The man who sells the sheep alive ranks above the man who sells it dead: in any country town the local grazier is a cut above the local butcher. There, too, the bank manager and the doctor are socially superior to the schoolteacher, the draper, and the produce merchant. The rich enjoy many privileges over the poor that are not merely pecuniary. The aborigines and the half-castes suffer heavy disabilities as dispossessed groups.

Despite such inequalities and inequities, however, the democratic spirit undoubtedly forms a main pattern of our society.

The Ecological Forces

As with our other social patterns, radical democracy developed through determinants which formed an interlocking set of ecological forces. The land itself, as we have seen, was the primary dynamic shaping the society. Its wealth of resources combined with the small population to produce a demand for labour which promoted the independence of the workers. This was the important economic basis for a democratic order. The new land created conditions of colonial life which tended to dissolve old hierarchies. Class barriers were frequently broken down, for instance, by a social fluidity caused by the vicissitudes of fortune on the land and on the gold-fields.

Strong, too, were the effects of the social environment, which included the people's special composition, cultural traditions brought from the homeland, and indigenous development. Thus the large admixture of Irish and Scottish immigrants, the working class majority, and the independent gold-diggers all helped to develop the democratic spirit.

Politically the Australian society, as we have seen, grew up during the regime of English liberalism, influenced by the faith of the French Revolution, the beliefs of Mill and Bentham, the creed of the English Chartists, and the Reform Bill. In the colonies, moreover, liberal ideas could flourish more easily than in England and be applied more radically, since there was no ancient and powerful establishment of aristocracy and church to hold the conservative fort. The squatters' bid for aristocracy failed. The Anglican Church had neither the official position nor the wealth it had in England; the dissenting churches, such as the Presbyterian and Methodist, were largely democratic in composition and outlook; and the Roman Catholic Church, although it fought aspects of liberalism such as secular education, was made sympathetic to many popular aspirations by its Irish tradition of revolt and the working-class character of its Irish membership.

Indeed, Christianity must be reckoned as one of the cultural forces in the social environment which helped to promote the sentiment of democratic equality. This factor has often been overlooked or ignored by our social historians. Yet both Australian history and literature provide numerous examples showing how a personal Christian faith made immigrant settlers practise a democratic equality irrespective of class, creed, or even of race and colour. We have seen this illustrated in Patsy Durack's treatment of servants and aborigines, Danny Delacey's kindness to the Chinaman Wong Foo, and Stewart of Kooltopa's behaviour to all men as "a (adj.) Christian!"

Again, socialists of the nineties drew upon Christianity to buttress their socialism, and even at times, like William Lane in *The Working Man's Paradise* and Furphy in both *Such is Life* and *Rigby's Romance*, tended to equate the two. The same equation was proclaimed by Victor Daley, to whom Christ was not only the carpenter of Nazareth but also the "Beachcomber of Galilee" and the suffering figure of Labour. Christianity was thus an influence in radicalism as well as in the more general democratic spirit.

Aspects of Radical Democracy

This spirit has been imaged faithfully in Australian literature from the time when it became truly indigenous. It runs through most of the writing—or, rather, it forms not a stream but an atmosphere whose light suffuses the literature as a whole. It is as natural as the air. Any trace of servility would be immediately felt as something wrong, un-Australian, whether it occurred in a character or in the attitude of an author. It is not expressed explicitly so much as implicitly through the natural assumption that men are—or should be—free and equal by virtue of their manhood. This pervasive spirit was felt by Edward Garnett when he wrote that he had never read anything in modern English literature "so absolutely democratic in tone, so much the real thing"[7] as "Joe Wilson's Courtship" and, indeed, all Henry Lawson's tales and sketches.

This spirit is linked so intimately with a national strain of radicalism that the two must be taken together as one complex pattern we may call "Radical Democracy". This social pattern embodies six different aspects that are closely allied and often interdependent: an insistence on freedom as personal independence; an individual rebelliousness, or anti-authoritarian sentiment; a sceptical, irreverent, and critical attitude; an emphasis on equality; a proletarian preference in theme and outlook; and an aggressive demand for social justice.

The special combination of these aspects has given a distinctively

[7] See p. 26.

national tang to our democratic tradition, and thus differentiated its expression in our literature from the expression of the democratic spirit in the literatures of the other British Dominions and the United States, despite a common belief in democracy and a common heritage of British ideas and institutions. Australian writing, for example, contains a stronger emphasis on equality than on freedom, whereas the reverse seems true in American literature. This emphasis also appears more aggressive than in Canadian or New Zealand writing. The proletarian preference, too, is also more marked, one feels, than in these other democratic literatures, more express and more insistent.

Again, whilst these other literatures have their radical strain, it is restricted to particular groups rather than spread generally, as in Australian literature. On the whole, Canadian, New Zealand, and American literatures are more equable and more positive, one feels, than Australian literature, since they do not reflect so strongly the critical, radical, and rebellious elements characteristic of our writing. They have not had behind them, of course, a history of convict, Irish, and working-class forces, a struggle of landless native-born for the land, and a battling of pioneers in a country of capricious droughts.

The Panache of Independence

In our democracy the liberty which was the first principle of the French Revolution triad has commonly been interpreted, not in terms of a general philosophy of freedom as in the United States, but as a personal independence. This is natural since the colonists, unlike the Americans, never had to stage a revolution to secure their independence; they had no need to erect a Statue of Liberty. Nor have the Australians been oppressed, like the Poles, by a foreign rule; there has been no occasion for freedom to shriek when an Australian Kosciusko fell. Self-government came constitutionally from a British Government half indifferent to its progeny in the antipodes, half glad to silence their querulous complaints.

Personal independence, on the other hand, has been one of the most powerful national traditions and a constant element in the national literature. It was the dream of the convicts serving their sentences, and the goal that lured the settlers, of all classes, to the new land. In the utilitarian colonial society this goal was thought of in economic terms: the immigrant gentry aspired to wealth, the immigrant workers aspired to be free as their own bosses. When the workers won such freedom, they wore their new independence with a flourish as a *panache*. It seems likely that into this flourish entered a touch of the "flashness" that characterized the convict thief before he became an emancipist, as well as the jauntiness of the beggar on horseback when the English or Irish worker, hitherto an oppressed peasant, rode his own horse as an independent bushman.

Certainly the *panache* derived, too, from the freedom of the bush. As John Sidney commented, "Bush life has the charm of thorough independence."[8] Haygarth records of the squatting life: "This sensation of absolute freedom, which is one of the chief attractions of this sort of life, some might say its only one, gained a strong hold upon many minds."[9] Alexander Harris, after remarking that "The Australians . . . are growing up a race among themselves",[10] concludes his description of Reuben Kable as a typical bush "Native" by a comment on his self-sufficient, careless independence: "The utter, yet not discourteous, nonchalance of his race, however, would have been regarded by a stranger as his most distinctive characteristic."[11]

Reuben Kable emerges as one of the first of a long line of characters in Australian literature marked by a strong sense of independence. They abound in the ballads of convicts, bushrangers, gold-diggers, shearers, drovers, and swagmen, notably in "Bold Jack Donahoo", "The Wild Colonial Boy", "Look Out Below!", "The Murrumbidgee Shearer", "The Overlander", and "The Ramble-eer". The spirit of them all is summed up in the refrain common to the first two ballads mentioned and Donahoo's defiance to the police sergeant when cornered and called upon to surrender:

> *"Resign to you—you cowardly dogs! a thing I ne'er will do,*
> *For I'll fight this night with all my might," cried bold Jack Donahoo,*
> *I'd rather roam these hills and dales, like wolf or kangaroo*
> *Than work one hour for Government!" cried bold Jack Donahoo.[12]*

The independent spirit of the bushmen is depicted clearly in the Marstons in *Robbery Under Arms*, and in the bush characters of Lawson's stories, as well as in the heroes and heroines of the bush chronicles told by Miles Franklin and her *alter ego*, Brent of Bin Bin. Tom Collins and his teamster friends are all rugged individualists.

So, too, Katharine Prichard stresses the independence of the opal miners on Fallen Star Ridge, in the tradition of the gold miners of whom Westgarth had reported:

An *esprit de corps* still survives . . . which proscribes the employed labour of the capitalists and companies, and summons the patriot digger rather to work

[8] A Bushman, *A Voice from the Far Interior of Australia* (London 1847), p.53.

[9] Henry William Haygarth, *Recollections of Bush Life in Australia During a Residence of Eight Years in the Interior* (London 1850), p.21.

[10] The author of *Settlers and Convicts, The Emigrant Family or The Story of an Australian Settler* (London 1849), p.5.

[11] Ibid., p.6.

[12] Hugh Anderson, *Colonial Ballads* (Ferntree Gully 1955), p.92, "Bold Jack Donahoo". The name is also spelt as Donahoe and Donahue.

on independent account for a precarious few shillings a day, than accept the servile pound of a capitalist master.[13]

So, in the same spirit,

Ridge miners find happiness in the sense of being free men . . . . To a man they have decided against any wealthy man, or body of wealthy men forming themselves into a company to buy up the mines, put the men on a weekly wage, and work them, as the opal blocks at Chalk Cliffs had been worked. There might be more money in it: there would be a steadier means of livelihood; but the Ridge miners would not hear of it.

"No," they say; "we'll put up with less money—and be our own masters."[14]

A similar feeling of the miners is depicted by Katharine Prichard in her gold-fields trilogy and by Vance Palmer in his *Golconda*.

The independence of the later "diggers", the men of the AIF in two world wars, is a constant element in our war fiction, such as the novels and stories of Leonard Mann, William Baylebridge, and Harley Matthews dealing with the first world war, and in such second world war novels as *The Ridge and the River*, *We Were the Rats*, and *The Twenty Thousand Thieves*. The *panache* indicated by Reuben Kable's "utter, yet not discourteous, nonchalance" is illustrated superbly in the drawing by Will Dyson in the Australian War Museum entitled "The Cook".[15]

In our modern fiction many writers relish the depiction of strongly independent characters, such as Patrick White's Voss, Stow's Heriot, Keneally's Maitland, and the eponymous heroes of George Johnston's *My Brother Jack* and Peter Mathers' *Trap*.

So, too, in poetry that contains character sketches FitzGerald draws a strong, defiant Warren Hastings, Slessor a masterful Captain Cook, and Francis Webb an adventurous Ben Boyd. In drama Brumby Innes and Ma Bates, Captain Scott and Ned Kelly are typical.

Writers such as Frank Dalby Davison, Henry G. Lamond, and Erle Wilson have gone to the animals of the wild to celebrate a fierce, proud individualism and the independence of the untamed. Davison's red heifer, for instance, when caught and branded did not settle quietly after her release, like the other cattle, but jumps the high rails of the yard and escapes to freedom:

She went down the slope and out across the flat, flying. Not the lumbering, swag-bellied trot of an old milker, but galloping like a wild thing, her head out and her tail up—the plume flying like a pennant on a lance, and her limbs swinging long and free. She passed out of sight behind a clump of box tree—still travelling.[16]

[13] William Westgarth, *Victoria and the Australian Gold Mines in 1857* (London 1857), p.173.
[14] Katharine Susannah Prichard, *Black Opal* (Sydney 1946), p.48.
[15] Reproduced in A. G. Butler, *The Digger: a Study in Democracy* (Sydney 1945), opposite p.17.   [16] Frank Dalby Davison, *Man-Shy* (Sydney 1931), p.52.

Her plume is a literal *panache* of the free spirit. So, too, in *Man-Shy* the picture of the wild scrubber cattle when yarded in captivity refusing to eat as they walked around the paddock fence seeking escape to the hills becomes a powerful symbol of the deep yearning for freedom which moves in the cattle as well as in man.

The Rebel Note

In *Dusty* Frank Davison goes further to make his hero, the dog who is half kelpie, half dingo, turn a sheep-killer. Here the free spirit emerges as the outlaw dog rebelling against the authority of his master, striking against law and property by destroying valuable sheep. Yet Davison delves deeper to show that Dusty was the symbol of an untamed rebelliousness that struck an answering chord even amongst the sheepmen:

In the days of his legend when he had gone from the scene, as all creatures must, he loomed large in men's minds when their yarns turned on sheep-killing dogs.... He did in fact embody something for which men secretly or openly hunger and in the deepest springs of their being wholly adore.[17]

In general the orderliness of Australian society, imaged in its writing, offers a marked contrast to the violence frequent in contemporary American fiction and drama or seen in a Europe which has known the brutalities and tyrannies associated with communism, nazism, and fascism. In comparison Australian life and literature seem remarkably sane, healthy, and civilized, even Christian. Yet they also contain, within this ordered stability a distinctive strain of rebelliousness. In part, as Davison discerned, this is a normal instinct of man for freedom given a twist of the Old Adam towards an untamed expression of himself. It is the wild, defiant brumby lurking deep down in many Australians. Douglas Stewart voices it in his play *Ned Kelly* through Joe Byrne, the brains of the Kelly gang:

> *Ah, yes, a brilliant man! You see before you*
> *As fine a stallion as ever took to the bush*
> *For a brumby mare called Freedom, to breed from her*
> *The white-eyed bucking colts the Kellys ride.*
> *I could have worn the ribbon at the Show,*
> *I could have won my races, then gone to grass*
> *With the knock-kneed station fillies, too tame to pig-root,*
> *But I jumped the blooming fence. Maybe I hated*
> *The silly way a race-course goes round and round,*
> *Maybe I couldn't stand the bit and the spur*
> *And the dirty dwarf in silk you can't shake off,*
> *Keeping you up with the bunch, inside the rails.*[18]

[17] Frank Dalby Davison, *Dusty* (New York 1946), p.167.
[18] Douglas Stewart, *Ned Kelly* (Sydney 1946), p.55.

Stewart suggests through Gribble the parson and Tarleton the bank manager that this defiant individualism comes from the nature of the country and is bush-bred: "The bushfires start in the mind as well as the mountains."[19] Gribble declares that through knowing the country and its people he understands the Kellys, and Ned Kelly is a legendary symbol of the rebel note.

This rebelliousness, however, is more than a brumby instinct for the untamed, since it is also social in character as a radical aspect of democratic freedom. This fact was perceived by Professor Meredith Atkinson when he wrote:

Of the outstanding characteristics of Australians—namely, independence— much is due to their conscious repudiation of the bad traditions of the old world in favour of the strong idealism of a new Commonwealth, established in the fresh fields and untainted atmosphere of a virgin continent. It is not that the people of Australia dislike Britain or the British, but they hate the old systems of caste and privilege, the devious diplomacy of European chancelleries, the chronic prevalence of destitution, the age-old servility of the poor, the atmosphere of aristocratic condescension, the reluctance to change prevalent amongst all classes in the old world.[20]

Here the sociologist has rightly linked the contumacious independence of the Australian with his national sentiment and his radicalism.

The rebelliousness derived, however, more specifically from three elements which were anti-authoritarian by circumstance and tradition —the convicts, the Irish, and the native-born. All were essentially of the working class, and all had grievances: the convicts against the penal system and society as a whole, the Irish against British rule, and the Currency lads against a social system which usually denied them the lands granted or sold to British immigrants. Ned Kelly combined the heritage of all three.

The rebel note sounds strongly through the popular songs and balladry. It emerged first from the convicts, and came most forcibly in the song "Jim Jones at Botany Bay", where the convict cries defiantly:

> But by and by I'll break my chains: into the bush I'll go,
> And join the brave bushrangers there—Jack Donahoo and Co.;
> And some dark night when everything is silent in the town
> I'll kill the tyrants, one and all, and shoot the floggers down:
> I'll give the Law a little shock: remember what I say,
> They'll yet regret they sent Jim Jones in chains to Botany Bay.[21]

The Irish strain in Australia, with its long tradition of being "agin the government" and its fighting spirit, contributed an important

[19] Ibid., p.49.
[20] Meredith Atkinson (ed.), *Australia: Economic and Political Studies* (Melbourne 1920), p.2.
[21] Douglas Stewart and Nancy Keesing (ed.), *Old Bush Songs*, p.18.

share to the motif of rebelliousness. We have seen already how prominently the Irish figured in the Eureka rebellion, and Peter Lalor probably expressed the spirit animating his countrymen when he stated in a letter to the *Ballarat Star*:

If democracy means Chartism, Communism, or Republicanism, I never was, I am not now, nor do I ever intend to be a democrat. But, if democracy means opposition to a tyrannical press, a tyrannical people or a tyrannical government, then I have ever been, I am still, and I will ever remain a democrat.[22]

The rebel note in "Waltzing Matilda" has exerted a popular appeal, since the swagman, preferring death to capture, echoes the old defiance of Donahoo and Kelly. The song embodies, too, the radical revolt of the native-born bush worker against the squatter and the authority he commands. Sheep-stealing and cattle duffing, as Dick Marston points out in *Robbery Under Arms*, were prevalent customs which the people of the bush accepted. They were the protests of the poor against the rich, the landless against the squatter. The historic struggle for the land offers a second reason why the song of a sheep-stealer has become an unofficial national anthem.

This facet of the class struggle has been stressed, of course, by the writers of the political Left, especially the communists. Thus John Manifold in his Kelly ballad glorifies Ned, not because he was brave, but because "Ned Kelly fought the rich men in country and in town".[23] Even the murderous Morgan is glorified in another Manifold ballad, although the author admits he has "cheated slightly in the Morgan poem in making him sympathetic".[24] But all is fair in love and the class war when "Shot in the back died Morgan the friend of the poor".[25] In cold fact, of course, although the bushrangers kept a code of chivalry to women, there was little of the Robin Hood about them. Ned Kelly and Morgan fought for themselves, not for the poor or any idealistic cause. It is significant that Douglas Stewart, probing the Kelly legend sympathetically, cannot really believe that Ned is truly heroic—as, say, Captain Scott or Oates is in *The Fire on the Snow*—and ends up by making Joe Byrne the real hero of his Kelly drama.

The Irreverent Critic

Our next aspect of radical democracy, a sceptical, critical, and irreverent attitude, is a common feature in the national life and literature. Thus A. G. Stephens remarked discerningly:

[22] Quoted by Dr C. H. Currey in *The Irish at Eureka* (Sydney 1954), p.61.
[23] John Manifold, *Selected Verse* (London 1948), p.15.
[24] Ibid., p.87.
[25] Ibid., p.17. For an account of Morgan as "a cold and callous killer", see the ballad "Morgan" by Edward Harrington in his collection *The Swagless Swaggie* (Melbourne 1957), p.52.

R

We are a nation of critics... . So the Australian, confronted with the universe, makes "a transvaluation of all values", reducing the idols and the ideals of the elder world to their common Australian denomination. Inevitably they lose in the process, and we; mystery goes, and with it charm, and the glamour of the false romance. But what remains is seen in the "dry light" of philosophers, and the romance that is true may persist even here.[26]

Stephens himself represented this typically Australian trait of being radical in the original sense of refusing the orthodox to get at the real root of the matter, to practise a democratic independence of judgement. No doubt this sceptical attitude was developed largely by a land in which the pioneer was harassed by drought and flood, pests and bushfires, as we saw in the dry, ironic disillusionment embittering Lawson's sketch entitled "Going on the Land". This attitude offers a contrast to the pre-depression optimism in America, bred by the success of the frontiersmen pushing West into fertile country. Yet the irreverence of Mark Twain indicates that the critical attitude in Australia was partly derived, as in America, from a new land with strange conditions evolving new sets of values. It also stems from the realism of the working class and the impatience of a youthful people critical of its elders and the dead hand of the past.

The critical attitude runs from the earliest writing to that of today. It permeates the folk balladry. It flashes out in Harpur's sonnet "True and False Glory", which rejects the false glory of the conquerors for the true glory of those who fought tyrants:

> *Compare an Alexander's wild renown*
> *With the immaculate Memories that crown*
> *The Souls of Hampden, Washington, and Tell.*[27]

It is seen in Kendall's bush ballads when he assesses realistically the merits and defects of Bill the Bullock Driver, Jim the Splitter, and Billy Vickers. In the nineties it flourished in the irreverent *Bulletin*, which made a special point of attacking the cant and humbug of the day and mocking at authority or privilege. It emerged strongly in the stories of Lawson and the novels of Furphy.

Miles Franklin has the same iconoclastic way of thought in exuberant measure. In *Pioneers on Parade* she burlesques the Sesquicentenary Anniversary celebrations, whilst in *Up the Country* even the Deity is weighed and found wanting as Mrs Mazere attends to the agonizing childbirth of a settler's wife. Although Mrs Mazere is wife to a leading squatter and a true Christian in both faith and works,

[26] A. G. Stephens, "National Character" in *The Bookfellow*, vol.I, no.26, 27 June 1907.

[27] Marjorie Pizer (ed.), *Freedom on the Wallaby: Poems of the Australian People* (Sydney, n.d.), p.33.

The case inclined her to think that God had no practical knowledge of birth as experienced by women; she further reflected that had God given birth to His son Himself, instead of imposing the task upon a woman, it might have resulted in fundamental reforms.[28]

The discussion of satire has already illustrated how social criticism and the critical, irreverent tradition are increasing notably. Thus in poetry Hope has been joined by McAuley, Buckley, Stow, Dawe, and Beaver. In fiction the critical tone varies from the light mockery of David Martin in *The Hero of Too* to the savagery of Peter Mathers in *Trap*. The criticism ranges widely, too, as Kylie Tennant quizzes numerous aspects of society and Xavier Herbert swings lustily at many heads in *Capricornia*, often with harsh irony. The most thorough-going articulation of sceptical mockery, however, is "Lennie" Lower's extravaganza *Here's Luck*. The tone is set right at the beginning when John Gudgeon, the narrator, discusses his son Stanley:

He is taller and thinner than I but otherwise resembles me as closely as can be expected these days.... Problems innumerable beset the conscientious father, but the greatest problem of all is to know in what trade or profession the boy will be best fitted to support his old father at a later date.[29]

With Lower cynicism goes on an uproarious, sardonic spree.

Martin Boyd, on the other hand, shows its impact in England when Sim Montfort is treated "as a zoological specimen" by his English cousins: "They were irritated by his critical mind, which they thought a colonial eccentricity, and vulgar."[30] In contemporary plays both Beynon and Seymour scrutinize Australian social attitudes trenchantly in *The Shifting Heart* and *The One Day of the Year*.

If there is an undoubted touch of vulgarity in the irreverence, it is socially healthy. It exposes humbug. It cuts down the pompous or the pretentious to true size by applying, as Walter Murdoch does in his essay "Tripe and Onions", a drastic test of realism. It preserves the democratic, independent temper. It also carries, however, as A. G. Stephens noted justly, its defects, withering mystery and romance, and we have already seen how our literature is definitely limited in the theme of romantic love. In destroying idols, the irreverence also smashes ideals. Whilst Americans draw strength from the heroic symbol of Lincoln, many Australians do not rise above such "heroes" as Ned Kelly, Don Bradman, and Phar Lap. To limit a nation's greatness to the bushranger, cricketer, and racehorse is a sign of its spiritual impoverishment. The critical, sceptical irreverence can

[28] Brent of Bin Bin, *Up the Country* (Edinburgh 1928), pp.99-100.
[29] L. W. Lower, *Here's Luck* (Sydney 1955 ed., first publ. 1930), p.2.
[30] Martin Mills (Martin Boyd), *The Montforts* (London 1928), p.75.

degenerate into mere sterility, and neither a people nor an individual can achieve greatness without the dynamic of faith. It is probably the unconscious realization of this that has impelled contemporary Australian poets into the creation of national myths and legends, seeking to make the past a source of the inspiration drawn from tradition.

The Stress on Equality

One article of faith, however, has been held firmly, even uncritically, in the Australian creed—the belief in human equality. Professor Hancock noted this when he declared: "This, then, is the prevailing ideology of Australian democracy—the sentiment of justice, the claim of right, the conception of equality, and the appeal to Government as the instrument of self-realisation."[31] Visiting observers have generally been struck by the universal prevalence of the belief. Mr Hartley Grattan, we saw, was impressed with "The aggressive insistence on the growth and unique importance of the common man", and regarded Australia as "perhaps the last stronghold of egalitarian democracy".[32] Dr Thomas Wood commented that: "Australian society is built up on the principle that a man is as good as the next. As observers have pointed out, he tends to think himself twice as good as the next. This whole-heartedness has effects worth examining."[33]

The stress on equality came remarkably early in our social development, since Alexander Harris noticed it as a social pattern on his arrival in Sydney in the 1820s, when he went into a public-house in George Street and found drinking there a strange assemblage composed of many ex-convicts, Englishmen and Irishmen, with an odd Scotchman, several foreigners, and some youngish men, natives of the colony. He writes:

I could not, however, even at this early period of my acquaintance with this class of people, help observing one remarkable peculiarity common to them all —there was no offensive intrusiveness about their civility; every man seemed to consider himself just on a level with all the rest, and so quite content either to be sociable or not.[34]

The company was of "the very lowest class", and it is perhaps significant that "most had been convicts", since the emancipists would naturally assert themselves as good as the free. Later, in 1851, Gerstaecker noted that there had occurred such an amalgamation of the different classes of ex-convicts and free emigrants that "it would

[31] W. K. Hancock, *Australia* (Sydney 1945 ed., first publ. London 1930), pp.63-4.
[32] C. Hartley Grattan, *Australian Literature* (Seattle 1929), p.29.
[33] Thomas Wood, *Cobbers* (Melbourne 1948 ed., first publ. London 1934), p.204.
[34] Alexander Harris, *Settlers and Convicts* (Melbourne 1953), p.5.

take a 'knowing cove' to tell a former 'government-man' from a gentleman merchant."[35]

A number of ecological factors promoted the stress on equality. Colonial and pioneering conditions tended to blur class distinctions, and the gold diggings provided a strong equalizing factor. Above all, the greatest levelling determinant was the economic opportunity offered to the workers, as Westgarth perceived when he stated that in Victoria there was no poor class, for

any industrious individual is nearly as sure of his daily competence as if he drew it by the most undoubted of rights out of the British Treasury. From this feature derives an equality of consideration for all classes, and by consequence a political and social inclusiveness, that are quite irresistible in colonial society, although not always palatable to minds that are tenacious of the home stamp.[36]

This "equality of consideration for all classes" runs throughout our literature from the time it became indigenous in the nationalist period. Sometimes it is proclaimed explicitly, even clamantly, as a doctrine, notably by Lawson and O'Dowd in verse and by Furphy in prose. In "For'ard" Lawson begins by expressing the angry resentment of the poorer passengers travelling for'ard in the steerage against "the gentlemen and ladies" travelling comfortably aft, but ends with the vision of an egalitarian future:

> But the curse of class distinctions from our shoulders shall be hurled,
> An' the sense of Human Kinship revolutionize the world;
> There'll be higher education for the toilin', starvin' clown,
> An' the rich an' educated shall be educated down;
> Then we all will meet amidships on this stout old earthly craft,
> An' there won't be any friction 'twixt the classes for-'n'-aft.[37]

This poem of Lawson's is representative in indicating two sides of Australian egalitarianism: on the one hand, its democratic humanism which sees men equal in the brotherhood of man; on the other hand, a radical, class-conscious demand that "the rich an' educated shall be educated down", so that "all will meet amidships". Will this mean, however, that all classes will meet amidships in mere mediocrity? O'Dowd, an intellectual taking a wider sweep of thought than Lawson, foresaw this possible danger to our "young democracy" and questioned:

> "Equality!" Will each a king
> Become, a seer, a sage?
> Or will it ruthless all men fling
> In cosmic helotage?

[35] F. Gerstaecker, *Narrative of a Journey Round the World*, etc. 3 vols (London 1853), vol.2, p.270.
[36] William Westgarth, op. cit., p.268.
[37] Henry Lawson, *Poetical Works* (Sydney 1956), p.92.

Will crucibles, wherein, tho' great
With primal vice, we pour
Equalities, precipitate
Napoleons—as before?[38]

This question has been answered by the fact that in the Australian democracy the best men have risen to the top, and commanded respect. Nor can we dub mediocre, either in ability or personality, those Australians who have been outstanding in many varied fields. Furthermore, Cyril Brudenell White, whom Monash described as "far away the ablest soldier Australia has ever turned out",[39] refuted the allegation of the "mediocrity", sometimes alleged, when he wrote of the first A.I.F. in 1919: "This is a deliberate statement, nowhere were there better officers. It is significant, this bent of democracy towards efficient leadership."[40]

The outstanding quality of some leading Australians also comes out interestingly in a story told by Sir Robert Garran about Sir Samuel Griffith, once Premier and Chief Justice of Queensland, translator of Dante, and the chief draftsman of the Commonwealth Constitution:

When Griffith later, as a member of the Privy Council took his seat on the Judicial Committee, his British colleagues were astonished at his learning. Sir John Simon, at a dinner in London, said to me, "Garran, I am not surprised at the excellence of Australia's raw produce—we expect your wool and wheat and butter to be good. But I am sometimes surprised at the excellence of your finished articles." I asked what he had in mind. He ticked off on his fingers: "Nellie Melba, Sam Griffith, Victor Trumper".[41]

In the literature, too, there is no lack of exceptional figures removed from any stigma of mediocrity: in fiction, for example, Starlight, Tom Collins and Dad Rudd, Steelman and Richard Mahony, Mrs Yabsley and Voss. In poetry there has been a strong trend towards creation of exceptional or heroic characters, from the Man from Snowy River, Brennan as his own hero, and McCrae's Joan of Arc to Slessor's Captain Cook, FitzGerald's Tasman, Finau, and Hastings, Stewart's Captain Scott and Ned Kelly, and Webb's Ben Boyd.

The Nietzschean Cross-current

Indeed, any true analysis of the main democratic, egalitarian current must recognize that there has also been among some writers an anti-democratic cross-current of aristocratic inequality, commonly

[38] Bernard O'Dowd, op. cit., p.38, from "Dawnward?".
[39] Cited in H. M. Green, *A History of Australian Literature* (Sydney 1961), 2 vols, p.762.
[40] C. E. W. Bean, *Two Men I Knew* (Sydney 1957), p.185.
[41] Sir Robert Randolph Garran, *Prosper the Commonwealth* (Sydney 1958), p.94.

swirling into Nietzschean eddies. Certain of the original writers, as strong individualists set in the context of an orthodox community, assert their individuality by rebellion against it, stressing the primacy of the personal will, the superiority of the creative artist, and his transcendence of conventional morals and manners. Since Nietzsche has been the eloquent proponent of this aristocracy of art, he has become the chief outside influence upon writers hostile to the main democratic pattern. Thus Nietzscheanism, although confined to a few writers, derives significance as a social pattern because of their outstanding quality and the way they have conflicted with the main egalitarian current.

It is worth noting that these Australian writers—Brennan, Norman and Jack Lindsay, Baylebridge, Henry Handel Richardson, A. D. Hope, and Patrick White—were attracted most by Nietzsche's affirmation of the artist as superman, whereas the American intelligentsia who adopted Nietzsche blithely, such as H. L. Mencken, James Branch Cabell, and Ben Hecht, were iconoclasts who used him as a stick for cudgelling the Puritans, orthodox morals, and democratic values. As one American critic put it: "In Nietzsche's thinking the Philistine is also the bourgeois democrat, a creature who espouses levelling and equalitarianism to protect his own inconsequence. With unexampled fury, Mencken, as a result, fell upon democracy in all his writings."[42]

True, Norman Lindsay attacked – and shocked – Australian wowserism in much the same way as Mencken did American comstockery, and here one can find a parallel between *Vision*, the short-lived magazine edited by Jack Lindsay as inspired by Norman, and the great *American Mercury* which Mencken edited so brilliantly. But he did so with humour and satire, whereas the Lindsays preached their joy-of-life crusade with the unsmiling zeal of evangelists. Indeed, *Creative Effort*, the exposition by Norman of his Nietzschean ideas, is a curious book to have come from the author of entertaining novels, the humorously realistic *Saturdee*, and the exuberant felicities of *The Magic Pudding*. Jack Lindsay has since related how deeply his father was shocked into horror and disgust by the first world war, and suggests that he found isolation and escape from a world of blood and chaos in a transcending Nietzsche:

Hence the scheme of *Creative Effort*, which saw the art-image as autonomous, living in its own unity, its own higher time-space, and which saw the artist as a member of a sort of Apollonian secret-society or blood-brotherhood spread over the ages and redeeming the hungry chaos of matter by the stabilizing Image. A sort of Neoplatonism cast in the focus of all that was most lost and exasperated in Nietzsche.[43]

[42] Oscar Cargill, *Intellectual America: Ideas on the March* (New York 1941), p.492.
[43] Jack Lindsay, *The Roaring Twenties* (London 1960), p.67.

In the hands of the youthful Jack, however, *Vision* was hardly Apollonian, since it stood for a Dionysian delight in beauty, poetry, and love. It was strongly anti-nationalist, excessively romantic, and zestful. Slessor and FitzGerald shared in the fun without becoming disciples of the Lindsay creed, whilst Hugh McCrae, although prominent in *Vision*, maintained his constitutional aversion to all abstractions.

On Brennan the influence of Nietzsche was very slight compared with the other philosophical and literary influences which coloured his poetry, but it appears directly in his line "Out beyond good and evil are we blown",[44] and there may be a trace of Nietzsche as well as Schlegel in his final concept in his *Poems* of a self-shaping towards a personal perfection by the use of the individual will. Certainly, Brennan would have disagreed profoundly with Nietzsche's a-morality. Yet he is, in some ways, a Nietzschean figure: in his assertion of his personal values, his lonely brooding over the search for the creative word "that should become the deed of might", his recurrent use of the warrior image, and his scorn for the conventional hearth-loving people indifferent to the mysteries of the night besetting the human soul.

William Baylebridge, on the other hand, is a direct disciple of Nietzsche as of Bergson, explicitly denouncing democracy for its attempt to attain equality. In his *National Notes* he writes: "Have we not overdone the idea of equality, and lost sight of the idea of leadership? Where all are assumed to be equal there can be no true leadership."[45] For him "Our democracy would be an aristocracy of the efficient".[46] In *The New Life* he demands a Nietzschean transvaluation of values, and castigates modern democracy as

a sword
to smite true-portioned man![47]

Henry Handel Richardson, again, owed an explicit debt to Nietzsche, and she used quotations from his work to introduce some chapters of her autobiographical novel of her schooldays *The Getting of Wisdom*. Her husband, Professor Robertson, has pointed out that the book's theme is the gaining by Laura, the girl heroine, of a Nietzschean "wisdom"—the attainment of the attitude of "the free spirit" of the artist that passes beyond good and evil. Professor Hope has argued with his usual critical acuteness that in the case of Maurice Guest "The starting point of the novel and the key to understanding

[44] C. J. Brennan, *Poems* (Sydney 1913), page unnumbered, from "This is the sea where good and evil merge".
[45] William Baylebridge, *National Notes* (Sydney 1936), p.53.
[46] Ibid., p.57.
[47] William Baylebridge, *This Vital Flesh* (Sydney 1939), p.70.

its theme is, I believe, the philosophy of Nietzsche."[48] Thus of the Leipzig novel's characters Schilsky the musician, Krafft the philosopher, and Louise as a woman with a genius for love, are all seen as belonging to the superior world of artistic genius, a-moral and even *morbid* or degenerate types, but by virtue of their genius beyond the philistine, inartistic types such as Madeleine and Maurice Guest himself. The tragedy of Maurice is not his failure as a lover with Louise but his complete inability as an artist. This interpretation is both sound and illuminating, although the Nietzschean theme still remains, I believe, subordinate to the central theme of Maurice's torturing passion for Louise. In *The Fortunes of Richard Mahony* Richardson shows a slight Nietzschean bias towards Richard as against Mary, since Richard, although he lacks any creative artistic talent, can appreciate it, whereas the practical Mary is often treated unsympathetically as merely one of Nietzsche's common, inartistic herd.

Professor Hope himself in a number of poems adopts the Nietzschean dichotomy of the artistic elite, comprising the uncommon poets and princely wills, and the "servile spirits" of the common herd. In "Pyramis *or* The House of Ascent" he sings of the Pharaohs, builders of pyramids by which the king "Takes, for all men, his apotheosis", and goes on in purely Nietzschean vein to praise the creative artists as similar free spirits with the will to power:

> *I think of other pyramids, not in stone,*
> *The great, incredible monuments of art,*
> *And of their builders, men who put aside*
> *Consideration, dared, and stood alone,*
> *Strengthening those powers that fence the failing heart:*
> *Intemperate will and incorruptible pride.*[49]

In "Invocation" he calls on the poets "who alone defend That darkness out of which our light is won", and proclaims himself as one of the elect, sharing in "that naked act

> *By which the few, the free, the chosen light*
> *Our way, and deeply live and proudly move,*
> *Renew the uncompromising choice of love,*
> *Engender power and beauty on our night.*
> *That breed is in my bones: in me again*
> *The spirit elect works out its mighty plan.*"[50]

The same aristocracy of the artist as superman is also implied in other poems, and the lesser herd is seen as useful only as data for the poet. One critic has criticized it as "a kind of desperate Aestheticism: life

[48] A. D. Hope, "Henry Handel Richardson's *Maurice Guest*" in *Meanjin*, vol.XIV, no.2, winter 1955, p.192.
[49] A. D. Hope, *Poems* (London 1960), pp.12-13.
[50] Ibid., p.29.

for art's sake".[51] Such Nietzscheanism has, indeed, a narrowness about it as well as arrogance, and in later poems, such as "Meditation on a Bone" and "An Epistle: Edward Sackville to Venetia Digby", Hope has passed beyond it to a wider breadth of feeling and a deeper, human compassion. Thus it forms only one aspect of a rich complexity in his work.

Like Hope, Patrick White is another exceptional writer who stands apart from the democratic pattern and in open hostility to some of its manifestations. His Voss is clearly a Nietzschean figure, an exaggerated embodiment of the conquering will to power, a lonely, isolated, arrogant soul. He is not exalted, however, as such, but, on the contrary, is humbled; in humility he finds ultimate salvation. The physical and spiritual journeying of Voss is pictured by Christian symbols and parallels, but these are somewhat misleading, since Voss does not finally achieve the love of God, only the human love between himself and Laura. His humility through suffering is portrayed as virtually an end in itself, whereas in Christian faith it is only a means to salvation.

In *Riders in the Chariot* the Christian parallelism is used again, but this time less successfully than in *Voss*, since the crucifixion of Himmelfarb is an unconvincing blend of realism and fable, just as the sharing of the vision of the chariot—an arbitrary symbol—among the four illuminates passes into fantasy. Rich and powerful in its blend of poetic imagination and satiric realism, this novel, in which White's style flows more easily than ever before without losing its exceptional density, advances beyond *Voss* in proceeding from humility to redemption. Yet the central theme is Nietzschean rather than Christian, since Miss Hare, Himmelfarb, Dubbo and Mrs Godbold form a small aristocracy of the spiritual elect resembling Nietzsche's description of his aristocracy of "Higher Men": "I love him who is of a free spirit and a free heart; I love all those who are like heavy drops falling singly from the dark cloud that hangs over mankind; they prophesy the coming of the lightning and as prophets they perish."[52]

White's initiates are similarly free spirits in respect to the ordinary world. As outcasts, with the exception of Mrs Godbold, they also resemble Nietzsche's "morbid" types of artistic genius. White, again, attacks the common people with the same scorn Nietzsche lavishes on "the mob", "the servile herd". Indeed, White goes even further in making Mrs Jolley and Mrs Flack types of evil. They are shown with the same savagery with which White attacks Australian suburbia

[51] S. L. Goldberg, "The Poet as Hero: A. D. Hope's *The Wandering Islands*" in *Meanjin*, vol.XVI, no.2, winter 1957, p.134.

[52] Nietzsche, *Thus Spake Zarathustra* (Middlesex 1961, Penguin ed.), trans. by R. J. Hollingdale, p.43.

in his play *The Season at Sarsaparilla*. White's attitude, therefore, is un-Christian, anti-democratic, and spiritually aristocratic. Despite the brilliance with which it is conveyed, it suffers, like the belief in the superiority of the artist and poet expressed by Richardson and Hope, from an exclusiveness reducing the great mass of struggling, suffering, and striving humanity to an inferior class in contrast to the broad humanism based on democratic equality usually found in Australian writing.

The Proletarian Preference

Our literature displays, not only creeds of an elect group of artists, poets, and spiritual visionaries, but also the special cult of an aristocracy of the proletariat. The national conviction that, as Walter Murdoch phrased it, "we are all blokes" reveals itself in the dominant preference of writers in choosing working-class themes and adopting working-class attitudes. This phenomenon seems to be confined to Australian literature outside the literatures of the countries in the Soviet bloc. It does not occur in the writing of such democratic peoples as those of Scandinavia or the United States. American writing is concerned with the middle and the working classes alike, whilst English is predominantly middle-class, but Australian literature is essentially a literature of "blokes". Its proletarian preference, if by no means universal, is an outstanding feature. It even emerges in the most unlikely places, such as the poetry of Hugh McCrae. An aristocrat by cultural training, in bearing and the elegance of his style, McCrae was also an Australian, a poet who sang praises of the local pub-keeper, mocked gaily at the aura of aristocracy associated with the historic Camden Park, and declared himself one of the common blokes:

> *Behold the milkman in his cart!*
> *(First cousin to a knight, or bart;)*
> *All people, here, are more or less,*
> *(But mostly more, I'm sure, O yes;)*
> *Related to the—can you guess?*
> *I am the one and only pleb,*
> *Who still conserves the canaille ebb:*
> *And proud of this I am as Punch.*[53]

McCrae's attitude reflects the tradition established in the nationalist period. In the colonial period only the folk ballads and the songs of such popular entertainers as Charles R. Thatcher expressed the workers' point of view. In formal literature the writers, such as Kingsley and Clarke, Gordon and Kendall, Ada Cambridge and Tasma, Mrs Campbell Praed and Rolf Boldrewood, belonged to the

[53] Hugh McCrae, *Poems* (Sydney 1939), p.166, "Camden Town".

middle class and held its values. They naturally assumed that the educated class were superior to the workers, and they regarded the latter, even when sympathetically, from the outside, as can be seen from Kendall's ballads of the bush workers. It is impossible to imagine any of them being proud, like McCrae, of being "the one and only pleb".

The nationalist writers of the eighties and nineties, on the other hand, either came from the working class like Lawson and Furphy, or identified themselves with it like O'Dowd and Daley, Miles Franklin and Mary Gilmore. Most of them were socialists and supporters of the Labour movement. In such journals as the *Bulletin*, the *Boomerang*, Sydney *Worker*, and Melbourne *Tocsin* they created an apotheosis of the bush workers, miners, and men on the land. These writers adopted the proletarian preference almost unanimously, although most of them belonged to the professional middle class. No radical was more fervent than O'Dowd, State Parliamentary Draughtsman. The best exponent in the ballad of the bush worker's values, "Banjo" Paterson, was solicitor, newspaper editor, and squatter. The influence of democratic, radical values of the working class as a social dynamic was strengthened tremendously, further-more, by their identification with the vehement nationalist sentiment.

This proletarian tradition was established so firmly that it has continued, except for the interlude of the individualist and inter-nationalist twenties, ever since in the novel, short story, and drama. It has also given some colouring to our modern poetry. It is true that fiction broadened its range as novelists like Eleanor Dark, Kenneth Mackenzie, and Margaret Trist, followed by such recent writers as Hal Porter, Keneally, and Thea Astley, wrote of the professional and business classes. The heroes of our numerous pastoral chronicles have mostly been squatters and graziers, not bush workers. Henry Handel Richardson, believing in the aristocracy of artistic genius, stands out-side the proletarian tradition, as do Martin Boyd and Patrick White. These three writers, however, are exceptional as expatriates with European attitudes. On the whole, the proletarian preference, if lessened since the days of the simpler and more single-minded nineties, still prevails in the majority of the fiction and drama. Working-class characters have expanded from the bush to the city, from shearers and drovers to wharf labourers, sailors, fishermen, miners of all kinds, fettlers, workers in steel mills and textile factories, aborigines, cane-cutters, barmaids, and New Australians.

As an aspect of radical democracy the proletarian preference has functioned in our literature for both good and ill. On the one hand, it has kept literature close to life, and given it the vitality which comes from a firm hold upon the earth and the fundamentals of living and working. It provides writing with a solid basis of social reality. How etiolated, for instance, despite its urbanity, appears a novel like Martin Boyd's *The Cardboard Crown*, which deals with the aimless life of leisured gentility, alongside a novel like *Capricornia* with its raw, lusty realities of working life in the Northern Territory. With the richness of life goes, too, an intimate understanding of humanity in its daily struggle for bread and butter, a compassion for suffering, and an enlargement of sympathies. At its best the novel of social realism, using the term in its broad sense, which is the most common genre in our contemporary fiction, contains the humanist virtues which characterized the stories of Lawson.

On the other hand, the proletarian preference has undeniable and serious defects. By concentrating on working-class groups it tends to be deficient in intellectual, artistic, and imaginative qualities. There is little room for the novel of ideas, for appreciation of cultural activities, and for the sense of beauty—for many elements of the mind and spirit which we regard as most valuable in any higher civilization. These include, too, the joy of life, since the social realists often stress the drab and sombre in works more earnest than entertaining.

It was a sense of these grave deficiencies in proletarian fiction that produced a revolt amongst many contemporary novelists, who have turned away from the simple reportage of social realism to the complexity of wider intellectual, moral, and spiritual issues. Patrick White, for instance, stating his intentions in writing *The Tree of Man*, attacked "the dreary, dun-coloured offspring of journalistic realism".[54]

The more radical realists, especially the communist writers, have departed, moreover, from the humanism of the nineties by turning fiction into a weapon of class warfare. The poor are always virtuous, the rich inevitably wicked. Humanity is reduced to a Hollywood caricature of Goodies and Baddies. A literary dictatorship of the proletariat is set up whereby the miner or the wharfie is naively assumed to be more valuable to the community than the research scientist, the skilled surgeon, the poet, the artist, the entrepreneur, or the man on the land. The proletarian preference becomes a class bias, a kind of inverted snobbishness by which the working class is considered superior to the middle class. The writing permeated by this attitude is completely undemocratic, since it loses the Australian conviction that we are all blokes, squatter and swagman alike, the boss along with the worker. It is thus a betrayal of the democratic spirit of Lawson and Furphy.

This difference between the class-biassed writers of today and the

[54] Patrick White, "The Prodigal Son", article in *Australian Letters*, vol.I, no.3, April 1958, p.39.

writers of the nineties was discerned by Vance Palmer when he wrote of the latter:

They were more interested in men's significance as human beings than as representatives of their class; they took for granted that the swagman camping in the creek-bend might be as dramatic a figure as the squatter on his station verandah; perhaps they were apt to think the swagman would be richer in the essential stuff of life or more exuberant in his revelation of himself. But this stance was assumed naturally, not in the tendentious spirit of some of the proletarian writing of a later day.[55]

This "tendentious spirit" results in some proletarian novels, such as *Power without Glory*, *The Unbending*, *The Twenty Thousand Thieves*, and *Bobbin Up*, passing from literature to propaganda despite their varying merits. Whilst writers of originality can some-times make propaganda achieve artistic greatness, like Bunyan in *Pilgrim's Progress*, usually the propagandist element distorts reality and narrows vision to a doctrinaire formula, thus reducing the literary value. This reduction can be observed not only in some social realist fiction but also in writers who have written at different times from both the artistic and the propagandist viewpoint. Thus the Lawson preaching proletarian sermons in his verse is a second-rate poet, whilst the prose Lawson, observing life with artistic integrity, attains universality. Katharine Prichard's gold-fields trilogy, impregnated with class propaganda, loses some of the qualities which make her *Coonardoo* a beautiful and moving tragedy, a significant work of art.

The Demand for Social Justice

The radical aspect of Australian democracy appears nowhere more forcibly and more widely than in the demand for social justice which has been a main pattern of our society since its earliest days. This particular manifestation of the democratic spirit has been displayed politically in the progressive legislation of what Professor Crawford called "aggressive democracy" and in the policies of the Labour Party. In the economic sphere it has been represented by the strength of trade unionism—a strength more marked than in any other country in the world—with its militancy of strikes, the acceptance of the basic wage doctrine, and the system of industrial arbitration with its provi-sion for the full expression of the unions' economic claims.

Throughout history every society has had some unjust features, and protests against them have been common to all literatures. Social criticism has usually been made, however, by a few individuals and minority groups, whereas in Australian literature it has been made by the general majority of writers, often with a sharper insistence than in many other literatures. Probably this is due to a combination of

[55] Vance Palmer, *The Legend of the Nineties* (Melbourne 1954), p.170.

historical factors. At the very outset the convicts had ample cause for protest against the brutality of the "system", and they voiced it in the convict songs and ballads. Then the Australian people, as Mr Pringle noted, are "fundamentally working class in origin and in habits of thought",[56] and this class has suffered most from social and economic inequities, especially in the worst days of the master-servant relationship. Its habit of thought was—and is—inevitably critical of society, and it was in turn expressed by the many writers who either belonged to the working class or identified themselves with it, first in the nineties and then in modern times.

Our writers, moreover, have not merely protested against social wrongs, but also made a very positive demand for social justice, largely because they felt with Furphy that the "petrified injustice" of the old world should have no place in the new. The vision of an Australian Utopia gave an added edge to the writers' social criticism. From the eighties onward injustice has been condemned as being unaustralian as well as being undemocratic. Thus various historic forces joined to make radicalism, not a minority movement, but an attitude in "widest commonalty spread" throughout Australian writing.

Criticism of injustice, already vigorous in the folk ballads and old bush songs, was expressed abundantly, as we have seen, in both the prose and verse of the nineties period. Even the genial Paterson grew bitter in "On Kiley's Run", which condemns the absentee owner in England who cut the shearers' wages, underpaid his overseer, and refused any grass to the drovers. Even Brennan, immersed in scholarship and his personal drama of the spirit, was moved by pity for the city crowds in an early poem and called on "red flame or deluge" to cleanse the tormented city, whilst in the final piece in his *Poems* he identifies himself with the evening crowd in one common urge for comfort against the darkness of suffering. Radical sentiment also found expression in two dramas of the nineties, *The Democrat* by Alf. S. Day, which shows the hero in a Melbourne prison cell, and J. W. Wallace's *Social Shadows*, which turns from the London dock strike to satirize the colonial snobocracy in Melbourne.

This radicalism of the nineties was rarely revolutionary in temper and only occasionally doctrinaire. Nor was it intellectual except with such philosophic thinkers as Furphy and O'Dowd, and they were both concerned with democratic principles rather than specific programmes of reform. In general, and notably with such representative figures as Lawson and Mary Gilmore, society was criticized in terms of a simple humanitarian sentiment, with sympathy for those in

[56] John Douglas Pringle, *Australian Accent* (London 1958), p.100.

poverty and misery, with anger at the established system which produced man's inhumanity to man.

Whilst contemporary radicalism has broadly followed the tradition of the nineties, it has been less naively emotional, more intellectual and complex in its attitude, and more specific in its arraignment of social ills. The economic depression of the thirties deepened the social conscience of writers and made them examine capitalist society with a drastic scrutiny. The most penetrating analysis in fiction was made by M. Barnard Eldershaw in *Tomorrow and Tomorrow*.

Leading novelists like Prichard, Palmer, Dark, Mann, Herbert, and Tennant all criticize social injustice from a radical viewpoint. This is particularly true, of course, with those who write from the communist viewpoint, such as Katharine Prichard in her gold-fields trilogy, Frank Hardy, Judah Waten and others, whose novels and stories form calculated campaigns against capitalism. Other novelists and short story writers with radical sympathies, such as Dymphna Cusack, Gavin Casey, Alan Marshall, Frank Dalby Davison, Dal Stivens, F. B. Vickers and Ruth Park, also indict the social and economic system at many points, from the slums, industry, and business to the treatment of aborigines and half-castes. Often the indictment is most effective when it is left implied, as in Jon Cleary's novel *You Can't See Round Corners*. In the latter, a powerful character study of Frankie McCoy, S.P. bookie of Paddington, his rake's progress from theft to army desertion, rape, and murder is presented as the inevitable outcome of the way in which his slum environment had shaped his character.

In our modern drama a considerable number of plays tackle social problems and criticize existing attitudes. Different aspects of the aborigine problem, for example, come under criticism, direct or indirect, in George Landen Dann's *Fountains Beyond*, Henrietta Drake-Brockman's *Men Without Wives*, and Louis Esson's *Andeganora*. Leslie Haylen, Edgar Holt, and Sumner Locke-Elliott deal with the theme of war critically, whilst J. V. Duhig satirizes our gambling habits and Dymphna Cusack attacks defects in our educational system in *Morning Sacrifice*. Richard Beynon's *The Shifting Heart* is both a moving indictment of the brutality with which some Australians treat the migrants, similar to that made by Tom Hungerford in his novel *Riverslake*, and a plea for more sympathetic understanding of our New Australians.

At first sight modern Australian poetry seems to be only slightly concerned with the radical demand for social justice apart from a number of leftist poets. Amongst them the radical note is often most effective when it is struck with the ballad simplicity, as in John Manifold's "The Death of Ned Kelly", "The Last Scab of Hawarth", and "Night Piece" with their incisive bitterness, Dorothy Hewett's lilting "Clancy and Dooley and Don McLeod", or David Martin's "Lament for the Gordons", the Scottish soldiers who fell at Singapore fighting the Japanese for the sake, as the poet sees it, of British vested interests in Malayan tin and rubber:

> *I sing of the Gordons,*
> *Lament to young soldiers,*
> *Who never came back to the land of their kin.*
> *O Lowland and Highland!*
> *On Singapore island*
> *Your sons fell for freedom and Bonny Prince Tin.*[57]

Too often, however, the note in the leftist verse is forced, and it rarely approaches the depth of feeling shown, for instance, in the best poems of Mary Gilmore.

Indeed, a close scrutiny of our modern poetry reveals that the most forceful social criticism, whether explicit or implied, comes from the less tendentious poets, and that it is more widespread than at first appears, often flashing out incidentally. It is deliberate with Frank Wilmot, a disciple of O'Dowd's, who points the tragedies lying behind the old boots in a pawnbroker's window during the depression and attacks the cruelty of war:

> *For we have shown the world a bitter thing,*
> *Men suffering for no end but suffering.*[58]

Mary Gilmore, that indomitable crusader for a better, juster world, sings with deep compassion of suffering—the starving sempstress, the children of the poor with their little wet feet, and the lonely wild aboriginal in prison:

> *Lone, lone, and lone I stand,*
> *With none to hear my cry,*
> *As the black feet of the night*
> *Go walking down the sky.*[59]

In the same spirit Shaw Neilson, the gentle dreamer, cries out against the cruelty in the city, and enters into the feelings of the poor who feed the birds in the park pond on Sunday as the rich go to the church nearby:

> *The rich go out in clattering pomp and dare*
> *In the most holy places to insult*
> *The deep Benevolence there.*

[57] David Martin, *The Poems of David Martin, 1938-1958* (Sydney, undated), p.24.

[58] Furnley Maurice (Frank Wilmot), "To God: From the Warring Nations" in *Poems* (Melbourne 1944), p.31.

[59] Mary Gilmore, "The Myall in Prison" in *Selected Verse* (Sydney 1948), p.136.

But 'tis the poor who make the loving words.
Slowly they stoop; it is a Sacrament:
The poor can feed the birds.[60]

FitzGerald, to quote one more example, also voices the tragedy of the city streets where the multitude fends back the threatening silences "with straws of livelihood", and identifies himself elsewhere with "the ragamuffin army" beating at the city gates. Like Marcus Clarke in his great novel of convict suffering and Mary Gilmore in her poem "Botany Bay", he looks back in pity and understanding at our first radicals, the convicts—the men who had most cause of all to rebel against their social system—and suggests our debt of the present to these sufferers of past cruelty:

That wind blows to your door down all these years.
Have you not known it when some breath you drew
tasted of blood? Your comfort is in arrears
of just thanks to a savagery tamed in you
only as subtler fears may serve in lieu
of thong and noose—old savagery which has built
your world and laws out of the lives it spilt.

For what was jailyard widens and takes in
my country. Fifty paces of stamped earth
stretch; and grey walls retreat and grow so thin
that towns show through and clearings—new raw birth
which burst from handcuffs—and free hands go forth
to win to-morrow's harvest from a vast
ploughland—the fifty paces of that past.[61]

[60] Shaw Neilson, "The Poor Can Feed the Birds" in *Beauty Imposes: Some Recent Verse* (Sydney 1938), p.28.
[61] Robert D. FitzGerald, *The Wind at Your Door* (Cremorne 1959), p.3.

XI

The Great Australian Dream

"You'd be making a new people."
"What a people! A mob of despairing immigrants."
Gursey brushed this aside. "People don't immigrate in despair. They immigrate in hope," he said.

BRIAN PENTON[1]

> And, O Brittania! shouldst thou cease to ride
> Despotic Empress of old Ocean's tide;—
> ... May all thy glories in another sphere
> Relume, and shine more brightly still than here;
> May this, thy last-born infant, then arise,
> To glad thy heart and greet thy parent eyes;
> And Australasia float, with flag unfurled,
> A new Britannia in another world!

W. C. WENTWORTH[2]

High protection, and a devotion, almost one-eyed and absolutely single-hearted, to Australia, will make Australia a lodestone to the best people of other countries. As it is the best land on earth, it must have the best people.... We want, then, the finest people for this, the finest country.

RANDOLPH BEDFORD[3]

> She is our own, unstained, if worthy we,
> By dream, or god, or star we would not see;
> Her crystal beams all but the eagle dazzle;
>   Her wind-wide ways none but the strong-winged sail:
> She is Eutopia, she is Hy-Brasil,
>   The watchers on the towers of morning hail!

BERNARD O'DOWD[4]

[1] Brian Penton, *Landtakers: the Story of an Epoch* (Sydney 1934), p.138.
[2] W. C. Wentworth, *Australasia*. A Poem. Written for the Chancellor's Medal at the Cambridge Commencement, July 1823 (London 1873 ed., first publ. 1823), p.33.
[3] Randolph Bedford, *Naught to Thirty-three* (Sydney 1944), p.273.
[4] Bernard O'Dowd, "The Bush" in *Collected Poems* (Melbourne 1941), p.208.

A Land of Promise

"If only a receptacle for convicts be intended," wrote that judicious observer Captain Tench of Sydney Cove in 1788, "this place stands unequalled from the situation, extent, and nature of the country. When viewed in a commercial light, I fear its insignificance will appear very striking."[5] The indomitable Phillip, however, tackling obstacles that would have daunted a governor of lesser fibre, foresaw a future significance. Writing home to tell of losses in precious live-stock, clashes with the natives, the threat of starvation, sickness among his convict charges, and the alarm of an earthquake, he could yet conclude his despatch on a sanguine note: "Nor do I doubt but that this country will prove the most valuable acquisition Great Britain ever made."[6]

Phillip was, indeed, the first of our optimists. His faith in the future of the country, coeval with the First Settlement, marked the beginning of the dream of a Great Australia that has persisted from the eighteenth to the twentieth century. Moreover, although Phillip was probably conveying to Lord Sydney his hope of a material great-ness, the imaginative may well see in his policy of putting himself on the same ration as that given to the marines and convicts a prophetic intimation of the Dream's widening into the Utopian ideal of demo-cratic equality and social justice.

In more than one way this dream seems curiously contradictory to the usual characteristics of the Australian people, who have been realistic, empirical, and hedonistic. In both action and outlook they have tended to be severely practical, since the land which moulded them forced them to concentrate on hard realities. In general, as many observers have noted, they have cared little for ideas, and still less for ideals. They have torn their living from the country without thought for the morrow. The pioneers developed their lands bravely, yet also greedily and fecklessly. Australians have often lived in the present only, content to savour the pleasures of the moment. There seems to have been justice in the comment made by a visiting Congre-gational minister from Birmingham who wrote in 1887 of the colonial life he was trying to explore and understand:

What strikes me most . . . is the absence in every direction of any clear pre-vision of the policy which these new communities should follow. I have talked with politicians, men who have been in office, men who are in office—and they seem to be living from hand to mouth, and it is the same with the men who are leading our churches. Newman's phrase "one step enough for me" seems to be the law in every case.[7]

[5] Watkin Tench, *A Narrative of the Expedition to Botany Bay*, etc. (London 1789), p.138.
[6] *Historical Records of Australia*, series I, vol.I (Sydney 1914), p.51. Governor Phillip to Lord Sydney, Despatch No.4.
[7] Sir Robert Randolph Garran, *Prosper the Commonwealth* (Sydney 1958), p.54.

If the colonial communities had little pre-vision of policy or planning of action, they entertained, however, their own pictures of coming felicity. Composed of individuals who, being human, were partly irrational, they were moved by impulses which combined happily even if illogically. So the prevailing realism has been crossed by a romantic strain of idealism expressed in two ideals: the creed of mateship and the belief in Australia as a Land of Promise.

This belief has been stronger, perhaps, in the literature than in the life, since writers are naturally more imaginative, more romantic, and more idealistic than the mass of their fellow citizens. In particular the visionary tribe of poets have provided many of our Utopians. A poet like O'Dowd could find portents in the bush beyond the scope of the squatter busied with his sheep, the businessman devising increased profits, or the worker placing his bets on the Saturday races.

Yet the writers in general only articulated aspirations which were widespread enough to form definite social patterns in Australia from the earliest times down to our own day. In their daily actions the convicts, settlers, and gold-diggers might have concentrated on the practical immediacies of the present, but almost all in their inmost thoughts harboured some dream of the future.

Looking Forward

Indeed, the Australians, native-born or immigrant, were forced to be futurists. Like colonists in any new country, they looked forward as they built up their new societies, but the special circumstances of Australian settlement made this futurism gain particular strength. Here the settlers were severed from the past more drastically than those who peopled the United States and Canada owing to the greatness of the isolating distance between the colonies and the mother country. The masses of the people, the working class, were cut off from their roots in the homeland, and could not return to them. Even the settlers who came from the gentry, exiles who for years looked back wistfully from their drought-stricken plains to the green fields of England, gradually, insensibly, became part of the new land they had found so incredibly alien at first.

Brian Penton has illustrated this dissipation of the English past in his portrait of Derek Cabell, showing how there came at last a time when Cabell turned from an Englishman into an Australian:

Cabell shook his head. "Ah, that's a long, long way from here, all that," he said, half to himself.

"The Old Country?" Gursey said.

Wonderingly Cabell repeated the words: "The *Old* Country! . . . Yes, a long way from here," Cabell repeated slowly. In this was none of the bitterness that always sharpened his voice when he spoke of England, none of the jealous longing for precious things taken from him, but just the faintest accent of contempt.[8]

At the beginning, too, of *Landtakers*, Penton also noted the contradictions in the colonies together with the idealism which rejected a tyrannous past for the larger promise of the future. Seeking to understand the roots of the new psyche animating the Australians as a new people, he looked back to the pioneering epoch of Cabell:

> If I could piece together the picture of that epoch as I had inherited it from him—the savage deeds, the crude life, the hatred between men and men and men and country, the homesickness, the loneliness, the despair of inescapable exile in the bush; the strange forms of madness and cruelty; the brooding, inturned characteristics; and, joined with this, an almost fanatic idealism which repudiated the past and the tyranny of the past and looked to the future in a new country for a new heaven and earth, a new justice; on the one hand the social outcasts, men broken by degradation and suffering, on the other the adventurers; blackest pessimism balancing the most radiant optimism—if I could only *see* all this, then I would understand.[9]

Even if Penton characteristically exaggerated the more sombre features of life in the 1840s, he rightly discerned the relation of the convict system to the "almost fanatic idealism" bred in the early pioneering days, since the dominating fact of convictism made the Australian colonies profoundly different from other colonies in America, Canada, and New Zealand. First, it made some bright hope for the future necessary for the convicts to endure their present sufferings. Out of the blackness of the system the promise of freedom glowed with an aura of intenser radiance. Second, when transportation was abolished, the colonies naturally wanted to put such an unpleasant past behind them, to forget it as much as possible, and to look only to the future. The literature imaged this tendency, and so stood in contrast to the literatures of most countries, which show pride in the traditional past.

In the middle of the nineteenth century, for instance, Daniel Deniehy expressed clearly this common sentiment that Australia, because of its inadequate past, was forced to concentrate on its future:

> He himself was a native of the soil, and he was proud of his birthplace. It is true its past was not hallowed in history by the achievements of men whose names reflected a light upon the times in which they lived. They had no long line of poets or statesmen or warriors; in this country Art had done nothing but Nature everything. It was theirs, then, alone to inaugurate the future.[10]

[8] Brian Penton, op. cit., pp.147-9.

[9] Ibid., p.29.

[10] E. A. Martin (ed.), *Life and Speeches of Daniel Henry Deniehy* (Sydney 1884), p.55, "Speech on Mr. Wentworth's Constitution Bill (1854)".

This sentiment still prevailed at the end of the century, when A. G. Stephens expressed it in words that half-echo those of Deniehy:

Horatius fought all the better for the ashes of his fathers because he had a sincere reverence for the temples of his gods.

And here in Australia, we have no temples, no ashes worth the name. We still have to make the history and create the legendary associations that are such a powerful binding force in national life. The Murray to the Australians is still only a geographical label; but think what the Thames means to an Englishman! Think how Nelson was nerved by the thought of Westminster Abbey; of how his sailors were nerved by the signal *"England* expects..."! What a mass of record and tradition, of song and story, of memorable life and love and death, presses behind that *England! Australia* is meaningless by comparison, lacking the inspiration of the past. But is it not possible to catch meaning and inspiration from the future? Is it not better to be of those who make St. Crispin's day worthy remembrance than of those who look back to remember it? This country has still for us few hallowed associations; but if we choose it may have them for our children. If we are not history's legatees, it is because we have the chance to be history's founders and establishers.... Even already, how few Australians would exchange for England's glowing national sunset—or if you will, her splendid noon—our own intimate and fragrant dawn?[11]

In the nineties then, as for four decades after, Australia remained the land, not of inspiration from traditional yesterdays, but of promise in the morrow's dawn. Not until the fifties of this century was there a substantial change as interest in the past quickened, even pride in it, and a people more advanced in national maturity began to look back for its roots in its history, searching for its half-lost folk lore and creating in its poetry or imaginative prose the myths and legends which are the basic stuff of a nation's tradition.

The communal dream of Australia as a Land of Promise took three distinct forms which might be best termed The Vision of Freedom, the Hope of Australia Felix, and The Ideal of an Australian Utopia. The first two both began as essentially individual in the convict hungering for his liberty and the settler struggling towards fortune, but they broadened into a social character as idealists postulated a democratic freedom for the whole community and a prosperous society where wealth was distributed justly and no man went in fear of want. The Utopian ideal, however, was national from its beginning. It embraced the first two forms of the Dream but went beyond them into a more spacious, more spiritual, configuration of a millennial Australia.

The Vision of Freedom

Just as the fact of slavery in the United States made freedom a

[11] A. G. Stephens, "A Word for Australia", the *Bulletin*, 9 December 1899, reprinted in *The Red Pagan* (Sydney 1904), pp.156-7.

fundamental issue there to be fought out in a civil war, so in the Australian colonies the fact of transportation—virtually another form of slavery—made both free settler and convict deeply conscious of freedom and its value. The contrast offered by the bond made the free acutely aware of the advantages of their own state, whilst the convicts sought freedom first as that kingdom of heaven to which all other things should be added. The fortunate ones who drew good masters in the lottery of assignment worked towards tickets of leave and pardons as well as looking forward to the expiration of their sentences. Those who suffered in the chain-gangs or in such places of savage punishment as Norfolk Island, Newcastle, or Port Arthur clung desperately to their vision of freedom. It was the one hope that enabled men with backs bloodied from the cat-o-nine-tails to stand up defiantly to their floggers.

Again and again this note of hope is struck, angrily and passionately, in the literature of the convict period. It comes out strongly, for instance, in the folk ballads, where it is typified by the chorus sung in "The Wild Colonial Boy",[12] with its defiant note: "And we'll scorn to live in slavery, bound down with iron chains."

In fiction *For the Term of His Natural Life* shows vividly how the convicts, made desperate by punishment, would undertake the greatest risks in order to escape to freedom, braving starvation in the inhospitable bush, death at the hands of the aborigines, or even the grisly fate of being murdered and devoured by some cannibalistic Gabbett. So, too, the author of *Ralph Rashleigh* relates how his adventurer, when tortured in the limeburner's settlement at Newcastle, was aroused by the discovery of a boat on the river bank:

Quick as lightning a hope of liberty darted into his brain. The breeze was blowing freshly down the river to seaward, and he hastily returned in quest of some companions. Unperceived by any overseer, he soon collected several of the men, and Ralph having briefly explained his views, they were easily induced to risk one bold attempt for life and freedom, the bare thought of which animated their pallid features with unwonted fires and appeared to nerve their debilitated frames to dare any danger.[13]

With the convicts the vision of freedom was an individual desire, but early in our history it also widened into a social aspiration for the land and its people. Thus Wentworth in his ode written at Cambridge looked forward to the time when his native land would be freed of "slavery's badge" and "the felon's shame":

Land of my hope! soon may this early blot,
Amid thy growing honours, be forgot:—
Soon may a freeman's soul, a freeman's blade,

[12] A. B. Paterson (ed.), *Old Bush Songs* (Sydney 1912), p.33.
[13] James Tucker, *Ralph Rashleigh* (Sydney 1952), p.231.

Nerve ev'ry arm, and gleam thro' ev'ry glade;
No more the outcast convicts' clanking chains
Deform thy wilds, and stigmatize thy plains:—[14]

Later, Charles Harpur, native-born son of a convict father, not only cherished fervently the dream of a great Australia to come but also envisioned freedom as its first fundamental. He cheered the emigrant with such hopes:

In the far sunny South there's a refuge from wrong,
'Tis the Shiloh of freedom expected so long....
Till the future a numberless people shall see,
Eager, and noble, and equal, and free.[15]

In his song "The Tree of Liberty" he also pictures freedom as the means to win a democratic Utopia:

That happiness all men to bless
Out with its growth may grow—
Our Southern Tree of Liberty
Shall flourish even so![16]

A similar emphasis on Freedom as an essential of a future Australian greatness also animated Kendall. In one of his earliest poems he prophesied that Australia, then only a congeries of jealous colonies, would become a united and independent nation in some far future when her flag would fly as "The shelter of Freedom and boast of the world".[17] Despite the debt of gratitude he owed to Henry Parkes for friendly benefits, he attacked the Premier indignantly in bitter satires[18] for sponsoring a bill restricting the freedom of the press to criticize the New South Wales Parliament. Freedom was not only a sacred part of this ideal nation but also a right to be defended in practical politics.

Except for such idealists as Harpur and Kendall, the issue of freedom gradually receded in the colonies after transportation had been abolished and self-government won. By the time of the nineties the emphasis had shifted to the need for equality, social and economic, with the concept of freedom surviving in the ideal of personal independence. The ex-convicts, for instance, stressed their free status, sometimes with surly defiance but more often, it seems, with that "sort of open sturdy manliness" which Harris found so agreeable in an old miller and thought to be characteristic of "most of those who have risen from the ranks of the prison population by

14 W. C. Wentworth, op. cit., p.27.
15 Charles Harpur, *Poems* (Melbourne 1883), p.199, "The Emigrant's Vision".
16 Marjorie Pizer (ed.), *Freedom on the Wallaby* (Sydney 1947), p.34.
17 T. Inglis Moore (ed.), *Selected Poems of Henry Kendall* (Sydney 1957), p.120, "The Far Future".
18 Ibid., pp.161 and 172.

their own efforts".[19] The sense of independence also became common throughout the colonial communities. It lay behind the demand for opening the land to settlement so that workers could enjoy the economic freedom hitherto reserved for the privileged squatters.

The Hope of Australia Felix

So, too, the dream of the emigrants in coming to Australia was the hope of a fortune that would give not only the security and material advantages of wealth but also its independence. Here Rowcroft's emigrant hero William Thornley furnishes a typical example. After settling successfully in Van Diemen's Land, he records in his journal:

Rose early, according to my custom, and surveyed my new dwelling with a particular sort of satisfaction. "No rent to pay for you," said I; "no taxes, that's pleasant; no poor-rates, that's another comfort; and it's my own, thank God, and that's the greatest comfort of all." I cast my eyes on the plain before me, and saw my flock of sheep studding the plain, with my working bullocks at a little distance.... As we sat at breakfast that morning in my rude cottage, with the bare walls of logs of trees and the shingle roof above us, all rough enough, but spacious, and a little too airy, I began to have a foretaste of that feeling of independence and security of home and subsistence which I have so many years enjoyed.[20]

Besides the solid satisfactions of the settler experienced by the hard-headed Thornley, the country also aroused a romantic strain which Rowcroft brought into his vigorous and entertaining narrative. He was accepted by his contemporaries as a second Defoe, and his hero as an Australian Robinson Crusoe whose tale blended romance with realism. If the difficulties of the new country forced the colonists to be severely practical, its waiting possibilities engendered aspirations as spacious as its virgin forests and plains. The changeable nature of the seasons, too, made the pioneers inveterate gamblers, always hoping that fortune would turn up around the corner. The bush bred a race of Micawbers. If it demanded much in endurance and resource, it also promised wonders.

Thus there must have come to many of the emigrants moments of revelation of the kind that Mary Fullerton captured in her poem "Emus" when describing an experience of her pioneer mother:

> My annals have it so:
> A thing my mother saw,
> Nigh eighty years ago,
> With happiness and awe.

[19] A. Harris, *Settlers and Convicts*, ed. C. M. H. Clark (Melbourne 1953 ed., first publ. 1847), p.68.

[20] Charles Rowcroft, *Tales of the Colonies; or, The Adventures of an Emigrant*, 3 vols (London 1850 ed., first publ. 1843), p.90.

Along a level hill
A clearing in wild space,
And Night's last tardy chill
Yet damp on morning's face.

Sight never to forget:
Solemn against the sky
In stately silhouette
Ten emus walking by.

One after one they went
In line, and without haste:
On their unknown intent,
Ten emus grandly paced.

She, used to hedged-in fields
Watched them go filing past
Into the great Bush Wilds
Silent and vast.

Sudden that hour she knew
That this far place was good,
This mighty land and new
For the soul's hardihood.

For hearts that loved the strange,
That carry wonder;
The bush, the hills, the range,
And the dark flats under.[21]

The individual dream of personal fortune naturally became enlarged into a social form with the country seen as Australia Felix, a land of prosperity and material greatness. Indeed, considering that settlement began as a barren jail in a harsh, strange land, it is strange that this hope for the future was held in the very earliest days of our history. It was not only expressed by Phillip but also, in 1788 itself, by Erasmus Darwin in his poem "Visit of Hope to Sydney Cove", in which he looked forward to a great city by the Cove and even prophesied the Harbour Bridge:

Where Sydney Cove her lucid bosom swells,
Courts her young navies, and the storm repels,
High on a rock amid the troubled air
HOPE stood sublime, and wav'd her golden hair...
"There the proud arch, colossus-like, bestride
Yon glittering streams, and bound the chafing tide."[22]

With the discovery of gold it might indeed be claimed that for colonists and immigrant diggers alike "Hope stood sublime, and wav'd

---

[21] "E" (Mary Fullerton), "Emus" in T. Inglis Moore (ed.), *Australian Poetry 1946* (Sydney 1947), pp.11-12.
[22] Preface in *The Voyage of Governor Phillip to Botany Bay* (London 1879), p.v. Also reprinted in Geoffrey C. Ingleton, *True Patriots All* (Sydney 1952), p.5.

her golden hair". Ballarat and Bendigo, Gympie and Mount Morgan, Coolgardie and Kalgoorlie made a Golden Dream come true. The country became envisaged not merely as an Australia Felix but a veritable Eldorado, a miraculous home of great expectations. Is it any wonder that men came to expect developments of many kinds in this place of fabulous riches; that when the mirage of fortune was dissipated for the great mass of unlucky diggers, they should turn to the locked land to stake their claim for justice and equality in a new social order; that O'Dowd should imagine the bush bringing forth an ideal society as "the Eldorado of old dreamers"?

The Utopian Ideal

Extending beyond the Vision of Freedom and the Hope of Australia Felix, the Great Australian Dream also took into itself the third concept I have termed the Ideal of an Australian Utopia. This concept emerged in the early days of the New South Wales settlement, persisted throughout the nineteenth century, found its strongest expression in the nationalist period from 1880 to 1918, and remains a potent force in the national society today. It has inspired an ardent faith in many idealists and patriots, even if its course has been chequered, and its aspirations have often been vague or confused as it attracted to itself diverse and even conflicting dreams. It became a composite heaven in which various felicities were strange bedfellows. During its vicissitudes at different times it has embraced Wentworth's dream of a creative culture, the republicanism of John Dunmore Lang, William Lane and the *Bulletin*, the socialism of W. G. Spence, Lane, and Farrell, the narrow and exclusivist racialism of Lane and the *Bulletin*, the egalitarianism of Furphy, the democratic humanism of Henry Lawson and Mary Gilmore, the spacious visions of O'Dowd, the patriotic ardour of Miles Franklin, Ted Brady, and Randolph Bedford, the ideal of social justice implemented by liberals such as Alfred Deakin and Henry Bournes Higgins, the mystique of the land and the aboriginal culture proclaimed by Rex Ingamells and the Jindyworobak movement, the Nietzschean social philosophy of William Baylebridge, the mateship preached by Lawson and practised by two generations of citizen soldiers in the First and the Second AIF, the Browningesque vitalism of Robert D. FitzGerald, and the radicalism of the leftist poets and novelists.

Whatever the accretions to the Utopian ideal at the circumference, at its centre remained the hard core of the principles described in our discussion of radical democracy. The French Revolution triad of liberty, equality, and fraternity was to be implemented thoroughly in the economic, political, and social spheres. An egalitarian, classless and democratic society was to dispense social justice for all. The common man was at long last to come into his own. With every opportunity of realizing his potentialities, he would soar to the highest achievements in knowledge and power, in literature and the arts. In the great southern continent a commonwealth of happiness was to be established on earth, to serve as an inspiration to the rest of the benighted world. Here, after many ages, would be fulfilled such dreams as those pictured in Plato's *Republic*, Campanella's *City of the Sun*, More's *Utopia*, and Bellamy's *Looking Backward*. Progress was accepted as a social axiom in the nineteenth century, but the more generous spirits carried progress to its ultimate by a hopeful faith in a millennial perfection that could be achieved in what A. G. Stephens called the "ampler ether", the "diviner air" of Australia.

To explore fully the ramifications of this complex Utopian concept in Australian history and literature would require a book in itself, so that one can only give here a few illustrations selected to indicate the continuity of the Utopian strain, some of its more significant expressions, its social determinants, and its strength or weakness.

It is worth noting that a succession of poets voiced the strain from early days throughout the last century, and the limitation of their talents as minor poets does not alter the fact, significant historically, of this continuing faith in the future. Even the very first of our versifiers were moved to expansive prophecies at a time when a lively, optimistic imagination must have been needed to envisage such remote felicities for the unpromising settlement. Thus the stilted couplets of Macquarie's convict poet-laureate Michael Massey Robinson were stirred by the vastness of the "boundless regions" opening to his sight and prophesied that "proud Posterity" should prize this land of British "Culture".

As one of the very first of the native-born, the young audacious Wentworth, fresh from conquering the "mighty ridge" and "rugged steeps" of the Blue Mountains, looked forward with boundless confidence to Australian poets who would not only equal the greatest of the English and classic world but even surpass them:

> *And grant that yet an Austral Milton's song*
> *Pactolus-like flow deep and rich along—*
> *An Austral Shakespeare rise, whose living page*
> *To Nature true may charm in ev'ry age:—*
> *And that an Austral Pindar daring soar*
> *Where not the Theban eagle reached before.*[23]

In the first volume of verse by a native-born poet published in Australia, Charles Tompson saw "proud Australia to an Empire rise" in his "Bacchanalian Ode", and in his Anniversary Day song of 1824

[23] W. C. Wentworth, op. cit., p.33.

praised the glory of "happy Australasia", bursting into a climax of capitals:

> *The little star, once marked by none,*
> *Now shines a bright—A BLAZING SUN!*[24]

The sun, a favourite image throughout Australian poetry, was also used in the same year as Tompson's volume (1826) as a symbol of splendour by that fervent patriot John Dunmore Lang in his "Australian Anthem":

> *Australia's sun*
> *Has risen with orient light*
> *To chase the stars of night.*
> *Aye! and in glory bright*
> *His course to run.*[25]

Meanwhile, the English poets Winthrop Mackworth Praed and Thomas Hervey, like Wentworth, painted Australia in Arcadian terms. Hervey even prophesied the "Utopian mood" of poets in the idyllic land:

> *And poets, in Utopian mood, would stray,*
> *Within its shades to dream an hour away;*
> *Imagination wandered o'er the land,*
> *And roamed its smiling vales and golden sand;*
> *...Hesperian groves that wore an endless spring,*
> *And birds of nameless beauty on the wing.*[26]

Hervey's prophecy was to be fulfilled when Harpur and Kendall saw visions of a national Utopia as they wandered in the coastal shades of Eurobodalla and Camden Haven. Just as Harpur looked forward to the time when Australia would be "the Shiloh of freedom expected so long", so Kendall, with equal passion and conviction as a native-born patriot, saw himself as

> *a singer of the Dawn,*
> *With gaze upturned to where wan summits lie*
> *Against the morning flowing up the sky—*
> *Whose eyes in dreams of many colours see*
> *A glittering vision of the years to be—*[27]

Filled with pride in the achievements here of the past, he also prophesies, twenty-one years before the union of the colonies, the many glories of the nation to be:

> *A strong September flames beyond the lea—*
> *A silver vision on a silver sea.*
> *A new Age "cast in a diviner mould"*
> *Comes crowned with lustre, zoned and shod with gold!*[28]

---

[24] Charles Tompson, *Wild Notes from the Lyre of a Native Minstrel* (Sydney 1826), p.68.   [25] J. D. Lang, *Aurora Australis* (Sydney 1826), p.147.
[26] Thomas Hervey, *Australia* (Cambridge 1824), pp.12-13.
[27] Henry Kendall, op. cit., p.192, "The Sydney International Exhibition".
[28] Ibid., p.196.

His poem "Hy-Brasil"—a word for a paradisal state also adopted later by O'Dowd—led the American critic C. Hartley Grattan to declare of Kendall's poetry:

Two facets are of particular importance, and while as a poet he is "minor", as a precursor he has a perennial interest. The two facets are, first, the valiant effort to assimilate the Australian environment to poetry, and, second, his dream of a Utopia in Australia—in Kendall's term Hy-Brazil [*sic*]. Almost all the important poets in Australia since Kendall's day have, in some measure, been concerned with both problems.[29]

Before the eighties, however, such visions were largely confined to the poets and a few politicians of imagination like Lang, Deniehy, and Parkes. The folk ballads and old bush songs, which rendered the feelings and thoughts of the common people, contained no true Utopianism. They told realistically of their daily troubles and celebrated folk heroes, such as bushrangers, but did not indulge in social pipe-dreams. Aspiration rarely went further than the hope of individual good fortune and economic independence.

From the eighties onward the various ideals held by earlier patriots coalesced in a national dreaming, united by the growing sense of nationalism, furthered by the spread of education, and articulated by the group of indigenous writers clustered around the *Bulletin*. The Utopian ideal for the first time became widespread among the people of the colonies, taking various forms, but in no way restricted to any particular class, even if utopians, of course, were still minority groups in the population as a whole. Thus Lawson depicts even improvident selectors arguing earnestly about the respective merits of Henry George and Bellamy as social prophets. Radicals such as Lane exerted a strong influence on the workers, but when it came to the translation of social justice into action by the new Commonwealth the translators were such middle-class liberals as Deakin and Higgins or moderate Labour leaders like Watson and Fisher. Even a British exile like Douglas Sladen could be moved by the millennial nationalism of the eighties to address Australia as a nation of future greatness, superior to the European nations, who were born in ruder early ages:

> But you are heir and scholar to all the lore of Time;
> You were born in Earth's flower, born in a golden clime;
> You must profit by the errors of all your sisterhood;
> You must purge away the evil and cleave unto good;
> Your reign shall be the first fruits of better years to come,
> And the inauguration of the millennium.[30]

[29] C. Hartley Grattan, *Introducing Australia* (New York 1942), p.167.

[30] Douglas B. W. Sladen, *A Poetry of Exiles* (Sydney and Parramatta 1883), p.5, in the poem "To Australia".

The verse was execrable enough, but it is significant to find an alien patron of Australian literature like Sladen being caught up by local utopianism and basing it on the very assumption that O'Dowd was to develop more eloquently of Australia as "the whole world's legatee". It is worth noting, too, that Sladen, then Professor of History at the University of Sydney, was declaring in the same volume of verse that "Australia has no son more loyal to her than myself"[31] in 1883, eighteen years before the federation of the colonies and almost thirty years before O'Dowd published *The Bush*.

Six years before Sladen's declaration, James Brunton Stephens, forecasting in 1877 the union of the colonies, expressed the collective vision that was to be illustrated later in the choice of the title "Commonwealth" for the new nation:

> *So flows beneath our good and ill*
> *A viewless stream of Common Will,*
> *A gathering force, a present might,*
> *That from its silent depths of gloom*
> *At Wisdom's voice shall leap to light,*
> *And hide our barren feuds in bloom,*
> *Till, all our sundering lines with love o'ergrown,*
> *Our bounds shall be the girdling seas alone.*[32]

It was this ode of Stephens that Sir Henry Parkes was to quote, twelve years later, in his Tenterfield speech that led to the Australasian Convention of 1891, which adopted "Commonwealth" as the term indicating the "viewless stream of Common Will". Sir Keith Hancock has pointed out in his illuminating essay "A Veray and True Comyn Wele" that the word "is current in two meanings which are frequently blended into one: it means the common good, and it means a free community organised on the principle of the common good."[33] Its champions in 1891, Sir Keith suggests,

wanted for their new adventure in brotherly living a word glowing with the magic of England's past and the hope of Australia's future. A true instinct told them that commonwealth was the word for them ... it was a manifesto which the Australians wanted. And, similarly, it was as a manifesto, as a declaration of faith in a way of life, rather than as an accurate description in terms known to political science, that this word commonwealth was later chosen by the free association of self-governing nations under the British Crown. The name Commonwealth is a programme in itself.[34]

Deakin's account of the origin of the Commonwealth's naming is both more prosaic and more complex. The original suggestion for the title of the new union came from Sir Henry Parkes:

[31] Ibid., in preface "To the Reader", n.p.
[32] Brunton Stephens, *Poetical Works* (Sydney 1912), p.3.
[33] W. K. Hancock, *Politics in Pitcairn and Other Essays* (London 1947), p.95.
[34] Ibid., p.97.

He had been accustomed to lecture upon the heroes of the great political convulsion which culminated in the great Civil War, and it was but natural that the name "Commonwealth" should come to him. It was received however with scanty favour by the Committee because of the flavour of Republicanism and the suggestion of Separation that it was considered to convey. After a brief discussion it was rejected.[35]

Deakin himself, however, "became enamoured" of the name, and personally canvassed it, playing upon the republican and separatist sentiments of Adye Douglas and Inglis Clark. "Griffith and Barton accepted it out of friendship for Parkes, and Sir George Grey as the more radical title of those submitted. It was finally carried by one vote, after a heated discussion."[36]

The "Commonwealth" only triumphed, therefore, very narrowly. Yet Sir Keith's suggestion remains a penetrating one. The term, emanating from the English-born Parkes, did indeed link up the new union deliberately with England's past, and with a stage of that past when the middle class and common people had overthrown the divine right of kings in a struggle for democratic liberty. The word attracted Deakin, the radical liberal who was to be the main architect of social democracy for the first decade of the Commonwealth, and it won acceptance throughout the colonies, precisely because it not only appealed to the independent spirit of an aggressive Australian nationalism but also carried the connotation of that "principle of the common good" which was the essence of the Utopian ideal.

After the Commonwealth, but filled with the fire of the nineties, came the most spacious and powerful exposition of the Dream in Bernard O'Dowd's long poem "The Bush". It was over-weighted with allusions from O'Dowd's far-ranging erudition, and cluttered with the polysyllables of abstraction. Often it fell into the old familiar trap into which so much patriotic verse has fallen—the vice of rhetoric. This weakens the poetry of O'Dowd as it does that of Ingamells and Mudie. Yet the rhetoric of "The Bush" rises to eloquence since it conveys not only the sincerity of the patriot and the faith of the idealist but also the passionate vision of the true poet.

O'Dowd is realistic in his sharp criticism of his own society and in his stress that Australia's Utopia can only be realized through the devotion and efforts of her people. Yet joined with this realism is the bold and inspiriting concept that the world ideals of the yesterdays can be projected into a splendid Australia of the morrow:

> ... to her bourn her children still are faring:
> She is a Temple that we are to build:

[35] Alfred Deakin, *The Federal Story* (Melbourne 1944), p.46.
[36] Ibid., p.47.

T

For her the ages have been long preparing:
She is a prophecy to be fulfilled!

All that we love in olden lands and lore
    Was signal of her coming long ago!
Bacon foresaw her, Campanella, More,
    And Plato's eyes were with her truth aglow!
Who toiled for Truth, whate'er their countries were,
Who fought for Liberty, they yearned for her!
No corsair's gathering ground, or tryst for schemers,
    No chapman Carthage to a huckster Tyre,
She is the Eldorado of old dreamers,
    The Sleeping Beauty of the world's desire![37]

Determinants Behind the Dream

What were the ecological forces that made the national Dream appear so bountifully in the 1880s and following decades? How complex were the causes of this phenomenon?

First, perhaps, the Dream embodied democratic and egalitarian ideals which found expression most naturally in political action and progressive legislation. Such ideals were strong in the cities amongst the liberal sections of the commercial and professional middle class as well as amongst the urban workers. Collective organisations and ideas grew more quickly and easily amongst the unionists gathered together in the cities than amongst the scattered nomads of the bush. A basic ecological factor was the nature of the land itself which produced a pastoral instead of an agricultural economy and an urban concentration of the population. The latter, indeed, was considered by a discerning foreign observer, M. Métin, to be the main factor in promoting democratic ideas and working-class legislation:

En Australie et Nouvelle-Zélande la plus grande partie de la population habite les villes. Cette prédominance de l'élément urbain explique les progrès de la démocratie et la développement de la legislation ouvrière qui sont les caractères les plus frappants de l'histoire australasienne à la fin de notre siècle.[38]

Certainly it was in the cities, not in the bush, that liberals and radicals combined to implement by political action the "aggressive democracy" of the second half of the nineteenth century, just as later, in the first decade of the Commonwealth, the Melbourne liberal leader, Deakin, in alliance with the Labour Party, was the strongest force in promoting the Utopian ideal of social justice.

Secondly, the expansion of ideas into a spacious Great Australian Dream certainly corresponded with, and was probably caused largely by, the striking economic expansion of the Australian society from the discovery of gold to the depression of 1890. Analyzing the

[37] Bernard O'Dowd, op. cit., p.208.
[38] Albert Métin, *Le Socialisme sans Doctrines* (Paris 1901), p.21.

rapid and remarkable growth of the Australian economy from 1861 to 1900, Professor N. G. Butlin has calculated that "Gross national product rose from about £50 millions in 1861 (at 1900 prices) to somewhat more than £200 millions—an increase of a little better than 300 per cent in forty years."[39] This rate of growth put Australia second only to the United States amongst the fast-growing countries, and ahead of Canada, Germany, Britain and France. Moreover, of this group of countries, Australia led the way in rates of population growth. During the same period there had been great expansion in agriculture, the building of railways, investments, and the growth of the capital cities, together with substantial political achievements as a result of what one historian has described as the "two bites at political democracy",[40] so that in some respects the colonies were in the vanguard of both economic and political advance throughout the world.

We of today, disillusioned by two world wars and a depression and living uneasily under the threat of an atomic armageddon, find it very hard to project ourselves back into the enthusiastic optimism of the eighties and nineties and to recapture that first, fine, careless rapture, but we must recognize in all fairness that the Great Australian Dream had, after all, some reasonable foundation in the hard facts of a phenomenal expansion and unprecedented political advancement.

Moreover, the particular forms of growth are probably significant in themselves. Professor Butlin found that in the 1861-1900 period "investment decision-making tended to be influenced by long-term considerations, rather than short-run profitability . . . . Public investment revolved around long-term social and economic policy, without great regard for short-term economic conditions."[41] Is there not here a suggestive parallel between these developments and a similar long-term thinking by the utopians, with a corresponding disregard of short-term obstacles to the dream of the future? Again, the most important field of investment was the building industry. In a building era it was natural to suppose that a millennial society could be erected as well as constructions in bricks and mortar. When houses and public buildings were being multiplied so rapidly and plentifully, it was only a step towards erecting castles in the air.

Another important determination of the Dream was certainly the socialist movement, especially as it was spread amongst the workers in both bush and city by the New Unionism—described by Lane as

[39] N. G. Butlin, "The Shape of the Australian Economy, 1861-1900" in *The Economic Record*, vol.XXXIV, no.67, April 1958, p.24.
[40] C. M. H. Clark, *Select Documents in Australian History 1851-1900* (Sydney 1955), pp.316-17. See also R. M. Crawford, *Australia*, pp.125-44.
[41] N. G. Butlin, op. cit., pp.17-18.

"simply the socialistic form of unionism"[42]—and as it influenced the Labour Party. From England, Europe, and America diverse socialist ideas flowed into Australia from influential writers abroad. Behind them, too, lay the general idea of progress sprung from the French Enlightenment and fortified by the theory of evolution and the advances of science. The belief in progress was allied with a belief in human perfectibility, and progress was often regarded as an inevitable historical process. As one sociologist has commented:

Thus, for example, de Tocqueville, for whom progress consisted in the movement towards equality, urged that it was a providential fact, possessing all the characteristics of a Divine decree: "it is universal, it is durable, it eludes all human interference".[43]

So, too, Furphy expressed through Rigby's admonition to Tom Collins a faith in socialism directed towards equality and based on human perfectibility: "The unsophisticated child is human nature *per se*. And of such is the kingdom of heaven, the Divine Commonwealth which we aim at establishing . . . Every child begins as an actual democrat and potential Socialist."[44] Furphy, moreover, was no voice crying in a wilderness, for Dr Lloyd Ross has recorded that when *Rigby's Romance* was published serially in the *Barrier Truth*, the union weekly newspaper at Broken Hill, in 1905-6, it

was read eagerly by the miners, discussed during crib-time, anticipated more enthusiastically than the newspaper's comments on topical affairs. Together with *Looking Backward* by Bellamy, *The Co-operative Commonwealth* by Gronlund, *Socialism* by Tom Mann, and the Verse and Prose of Henry Lawson, *Rigby's Romance* served as a text for many an argument on socialism, free-thought and the coming of the social revolution.[45]

The thinkers of the Labour movement like Hughes and Holman argued the case of socialism cogently, but in general the socialism was emotional rather than logical, so that M. Métin could describe it as one "without doctrines". Yet it taught many to think collectively and attain the vision of a co-operative society organized for the common good and the happiness of all. Just as Spence declared that the New Unionism came to the bushmen as a religion, so it was with a religious fervour that Lane demanded faith in the coming socialist order through his character Geisner in his "labour novel", *The Workingman's Paradise*:

---

[42] "John Miller" (William Lane), *The Workingman's Paradise* (Sydney 1948 ed., first publ. 1892), p.121.

[43] Morris Ginsberg, *The Idea of Progress* (London 1953), pp.3-4.

[44] Tom Collins (Joseph Furphy), *Rigby's Romance* (Sydney 1946 ed., first publ. 1921), pp.206-7.

[45] Ibid., quoted by R. G. Howarth in "Foreword to the New Edition", p.vii.

And year after year the number of men and women who hold Socialism as a religion is growing. And when they are enough you will see this Old Order melt away like a dream and the New Order replace it. That which appears so impregnable will pass away in a moment.... It only needs enough Faith.[46]

So, too, it was with an emotional faith that poets like Victor Daley and Henry Lawson sang such songs as "The Tocsin" and "The Sorrowful One" or "Faces in the Street", "The Army of the Rear", and "For'ard". In these poems the voice of revolt, charged with indignation at social injustice and with sympathy for the suffering, is also vibrant with the faith in a better order of the future "when the people work together, and there ain't no fore-'n'-aft".[47]

Indeed, the body of radical, democratic writing represented by these poems and the writing published in such organs of opinion as the *Bulletin*, the *Boomerang*, and the *Tocsin*, must be accepted in itself as an important determinant of the Great Australian Dream. The *Bulletin*, as we have seen, exercised a shaping power on men's minds throughout the continent. Lane's passionate outpourings influenced many workers, strengthened by other contributors to the *Boomerang* and the *Worker* such as Francis Adams, John Farrell, and Lawson. O'Dowd and Victor Daley spoke through the *Tocsin* as well as the *Bulletin*. Just as Furphy stirred the miners of Broken Hill with *Rigby's Romance*, so Lawson's verses were recited in many a gathering of bushmen, whilst Mary Gilmore's name became a household word through her poems and her articles in the *Worker*. Other writers, like E. J. Brady, Randolph Bedford, and Roderic Quinn were well known, whilst "Banjo" Paterson was the most popular of all. Never before, and probably never since then, have writers in Australia been so close to the people or been so potent in influencing the popular outlook. Even a scholarly, intellectual poet like O'Dowd, who made no concessions to the average reader, inspired the thoughtful: Walter Murdoch praised his "songs of democracy that stirred us like trumpets",[48] whilst Katharine Susannah Prichard has testified how deeply she was affected by his address on Poetry Militant:

Then O'Dowd spoke, his hair flaming to the white-hot intensity of his passion and faith that poetry, and all literary expression should be inspired by love and service to humanity. He made such an impression on those of us who were beginning to think seriously that, upon leaving the meeting, we were almost too exalted and exhilarated to speak. I felt that my eyes had been opened to what I could do, as a writer, to help relieve the woes of the world. O'Dowd had this effect on many other writers of his generation.[49]

[46] John Miller (William Lane), op. cit., p.121.
[47] Henry Lawson, *Poetical Works* (Sydney 1956), p.92, 'For'ard'.
[48] Bernard O'Dowd, op. cit., p.viii, Introduction by Walter Murdoch.
[49] Katharine Susannah Prichard, in "Tributes to Bernard O'Dowd", *Meanjin*, vol.XIV, no.4, 1953, p.419.

No less powerful in its way, if less emotional, was the influence exerted by A. G. Stephens on both readers and fellow writers, not only by his own critical and social writings in the *Bulletin* and the *Bookfellow*, but also by his vital choice of authors for publication by the *Bulletin*.

All of these writers, even the extrovert Paterson, held to some form of the national Dream, and it is difficult to say how far they articulated the sentiments already existing in the people of their time, and how far, in doing so, they also extended and deepened those sentiments.

The democratic activities and political progressiveness of townsmen, economic buoyancy, the religion of socialism, and an indigenous nationalist literature: all of these, then, served as determinants of a Utopian Dream. The force which fused them, however, was the major impulse of nationalism. Looking back to the nineties, E. J. Brady could write later of the authors of that period: "In those vanished days we were all ardent lovers of the Lady Australia who inspired our themes." And the old fervour awakens again as he goes on to praise the spirit which animated the radical, socialist verse of Victor Daley: "It will not perish from the earth wherever Australia takes her place in the forward march of free men, whilst her drums of destiny sound 'Advance'."[50]

Earlier forms of the Dream might be individual or social, but the form it took in Utopian dreaming was nothing if not national in character. It came, above all, from the sentiment which caused men in those days to sign their letters with the flourish "Yours for Australia", the sentiment, felt by socialist and liberal alike, which created the new nation for the common weal. Professor Meredith Atkinson noted this fundamental equating of utopianism with nationalism when he said of Australia:

She has developed a nationalism which is more than ordinary patriotism. It is rooted in a passionate belief that Australian civilization is profoundly different from that of the older world, and that Australia is on the way to become an ideal Commonwealth.[51]

The passion for Australia was the emotional force stirring the esemplastic imagination of the nineties to weld different ideals into the unity shaped as a compelling image of greatness for the country and its people.

[50] Muir Holborn and Marjorie Pizer (ed.), *Creeve Roe: Poetry by Victor Daley* (Sydney 1947), p.12. "Personal Impressions of Victor Daley and His Work" by E. J. Brady.

[51] Meredith Atkinson (ed.), *Australia: Economic and Political Studies* (Sydney 1920), p.1.

The Breaking of the Spell

In the first and second decades of the twentieth century the national feeling persisted, but the romantic ebullience of the nineties evaporated. The spell of the Dream in its more Utopian manifestations was broken. Shorn of its more fantastic illusions, it was cut down to a more practical, workman-like size.

The process of evaporation, of course, was gradual. In literature, for example, *Such is Life* appeared in 1903, *The Bush* in 1912. Both, however, came belatedly. Furphy's mammoth novel, after all, had been written in the nineties, and O'Dowd's poem, the apogee of utopianism, reflected the feeling of the earlier period.

Nor was the hard core of the Dream lost. Rather its central democratic aim of social justice and a better life for the common people was actually achieved in many respects. Despite State jealousies, factional feuds, and the incoherence of party alignments in the early days of the Commonwealth, there was no lack of patriotic ideals in leaders like Barton and Deakin, Watson, Fisher and Hughes. Thus Professor Greenwood, commenting on the progress made from 1901 to 1914, states soundly:

Australia had become a nation before its soldiers set foot on the beaches of Gallipoli, even if full awareness waited on the future. A developing national consciousness, seeking distinct forms of self-expression, and a social regenerative movement, utopian in impulse, inventive in means, equalitarian in conviction, gave shape and individuality to the period.[52]

It was also a constructive period in matters outside Parliamentary enactments: Mr Justice Higgins, for example, by his Harvester judgment of 1907 went beyond conciliation and arbitration to lay down a principle of a fair basic wage which has done far more for the workers than all the messianic eloquence of William Lane.

Yet something of inspiration which had fired the visionary speeches of Lane and the radical verses of Lawson was lost with the breaking of the Utopian spell. As Professor Greenwood has observed: "By the twenties the first generous instinct had spent itself.... Even by 1914 the vision of an ideal society was fading and the formula for its realization was losing something of its magic."[53] This was partly inevitable, since the primary impulse of nationalism, once its upsurge had produced the Commonwealth, ebbed emotionally. The practical problems of working the new constitution demanded practical men, a realistic temper, the compromises of party politics, and the limited gains of expediency. The nationalism which had soared to heaven now had to come down to hard earth and balance its budgets. The

---

[52] Gordon Greenwood (ed.), *Australia: a Social and Political History* (Sydney 1955), pp.253-4.
[53] Ibid., p.254.

industrialized welfare state that emerged was a workable but pedestrian and limited version of the limitless Utopia wooed by the visionary adjurations of Lane and O'Dowd. Furthermore, as the earlier statesmen gave way to professional politicians there was a fall in the standards of national leadership set by Barton and Deakin, so that in the 1920s a discerning visitor, Viscount Bryce, was struck by the low level of attainments among politicians.

National sentiment probably reached the highest point in its history during the first world war, but this development was antipathetic to the Utopian trend, since it replaced the stress on a possible future with the actual achievements of the First AIF in Gallipoli, Palestine, and France.

By the time of the second world war this tradition had rooted itself so strongly that it imbued the Second AIF with a determination to maintain the standards of courage and endurance set in the past. In the 6th Division at Bardia, the official war historian relates, the senior officers had mostly served in the First AIF and "the younger officers had been brought up by such men, and in them, as in the rank and file, the proud traditions of that force were deeply engrained."[54]

From the depression of the 1890s to that of the 1930s, many factors combined to break up the Great Australian Dream. The bank smashes and depression of the nineties cut the ground under the feet of those who confidently expected a material millennium. The fall of the overseas price of wool in the nineties was a reminder of the fact that a Utopian Commonwealth could not be capsulated in a paradisal continent completely isolated from the purgatorial rest of the world. The fallacy of isolationism, which had been a fundamental assumption of the dreaming of the nineties, was ended for ever when Australia was drawn, willy-nilly, into the vortex of the first world war, signed the Versailles Treaty, and became a member of the international organization of the League of Nations.

Various accretions to the Dream were gradually shed in the next few decades without any dramatic struggle. Republicanism, for instance, which had been the first plank in the *Bulletin's* platform, was cast off as meaningless after the colonies had become an independent Commonwealth. The Single Tax Leagues inspired by Henry George faded out, along with the Bellamy Clubs. The painful failure of the New Australia experiment in Paraguay discredited not only Lane, with his inept leadership, but also the whole millennial ideal. So, too, the picture of a cosy classless community living in cheery mateship was shattered, first by the bitter industrial conflicts of the

[54] Gavin Long, *To Benghazi*, series I (Army), vol.I, of *Australia in the War of 1939-1945*, ed. by Gavin Long (Canberra 1952), p.204.

nineties, and again by the class warfare, developed by increasing industrialization and stimulated by Marxian and Communist groups, that followed on the first world war.

During the war the conscription issue not only broke the national unity but also split the Labour movement so disastrously that the body which had supplied so many crusaders for a better social order was rendered politically ineffectual for over a decade. Indeed, even before the war both the Labour Party and the unions had been turning from socialist visions to welfare legislation or to bargaining for improved wages and working conditions.

Time showed up, in fact, a grave weakness in the socialist ideal in that it was emotional rather than intellectual or scientific. It dealt in abstract hopes rather than in concrete programmes, and its attitude was well expressed by Furphy through Rigby when that tireless exponent of socialism explained: "I'm merely an agitator, a voice in the wilderness, preaching preparation for a Palingenesis. The programme is hidden in the order of events, and will be evolved in its own good time. To be fettered by a programme now would be fatal."[55] In fact, one feels, it was this very lack of a definite programme, and its emotionalism—an element naturally evanescent rather than continuous—that led very largely to the waning of socialism. Henry George's *Progress and Poverty* and Bellamy's *Looking Backward* appealed to the hearts, not the heads, of their followers, whilst Lane's *The Working Man's Paradise* and some of Lawson's socialist verse strike us today as sentimental and naive.

There was much naivete, much vagueness, and a lack of realistic hard thinking in the optimism of the socialists and, indeed, of all the Utopian dreamers. They were sometimes as muddle-headed as they were always warm-hearted. One of the reasons why the spell of the Dream was broken was that it had become too remote from realities as well as too vague and amorphous.

In literature the breaking of the Dream's spell was reflected clearly. As the *Bulletin* lost its literary leadership, writers struck out in different directions away from any national focus. Poets such as Brennan, Neilson, and McCrae were individualists, highly personal. In the twenties the international influences were so strong that, as we saw, Frank Wilmot protested against them desperately in his poem "Echoes", feeling that Australia was losing its indigenous sentiment and being swamped by alien currents from overseas. The *Vision* movement provided one instance of the international outlook, hostile to the previous nationalism—even if, paradoxically, its youthful enthusiasm and its utopianism were characteristically Australian. In fiction Richardson became an expatriate following European national-

[55] Tom Collins, op. cit., p.231.

ism, whilst Louis Stone observed his Sydney larrikins with a realistic detachment. Indeed, the difference between the earlier nationalist idealism and the later objective realism is illustrated eloquently by the contrast between such novels as *My Brilliant Career* and *Such is Life*, on the one hand, and on the other, *The Fortunes of Richard Mahony* and *Jonah*.

The Future, Present, and Past

From the 1930s to the 1960s three distinct trends in the Australian society were imaged in its literature. Although these have been mentioned individually in other connections, at this stage they may be summed up and contrasted profitably. Thus a few idealists, such as Miles Franklin, Katharine Prichard, and the Jindyworobaks, continued the old Utopian tradition. But a realistic criticism of the present became the main trend of the post-depression thirties and forties, continuing in strength until today, with a growth of satire in poetry and a radical stimulus from the Left in fiction. The second world war, however, stimulated the third trend, nationalist in temper, which looks to the past to revive folklore and to create historical legends and myths that will serve as viable national traditions.

The realist and mythopoetic writers brought a new depth and complexity to the writing, and the best work was done by them. In comparison the Utopian strain seemed, despite its sincerity, to be a little forced and superficial. After the hard realities of the depression it wore an old-fashioned air. We see this clearly in *All That Swagger*. Miles Franklin created a living and lovable figure in Danny. His dreaming, his dynamic, was made a reality, but this sense of reality evaporated from the novel once his pipe had gone out for the last time. It was replaced by rhetoric as Miles enthused over the future lying before Danny's descendant, Brian the aviator:

Before him lay the destined land of Daniel Brian Robert M. Delacey, in its aura of palpitant silence, enchantment welling from its ageless mystery. From that pregnant oblivion, glittering free of humanity to the Pole, shimmering broadly to the equator, might come the revelation for which man was toiling upward from the abyss. There a man had space to escape from the limitations of his outer shell into the boundless freedom of his inner consciousness. There the sun rose as the promise of God and set as His benediction.[56]

The same Utopian fervour, now communist as well as nationalist, inspires Katharine Prichard when she pictures Sally musing in *Winged Seeds*:

"We must not be satisfied with the myth, and we must work for the reality of a commonwealth," Bill had said. His vision of human deliverance was bound up with the idea of a commonwealth of nations. And why shouldn't the

[56] Miles Franklin, *All That Swagger* (Sydney 1936), p.494.

resources of this country and the labour of the people be used to make it a commonwealth in more than name? A reality which would regard the health and well-being of the people as its greatest asset, stimulating every phase of their development, giving ordinary men and women like herself new pleasures with a knowledge and understanding of the arts and sciences? Wheat and cattle were bred to their utmost usefulness. Why not men and women?

The life force strives towards perfection. What other imperative is there in living?[57]

So the perfectionist Dream lived on. It lived, too, in Rex Ingamells and the verse of his Jindyworobak followers as they try to envision their country in terms of the aboriginal "Dream Time". Often their reach exceeded their grasp, as in the ambitious attempt at an epic by Ingamells in *The Great South Land*, and in Ian Mudie's Whitmanite rhapsody "The Australian Dream", singing of the sons of Australia who will come bravely, heroic:

> *they soon shall wake us to this continent;*
> *the firesticks of their minds will soon relight*
> *the scattered camp-fires of Australia's dream.*[58]

Robust as the poem is, it has a self-conscious forcing of the note that is absent from such lyrics of Mudie's as "This Land" and "Underground" where he sings of his country like a lover of his love, naturally, with warm depth of feeling. Spontaneity of impulse has faded from the Great Australian Dream. Today the ideal is a practical, economic expansion. The younger poets, as we saw in the chapters on realism and irony, are now sceptical in their attitude towards society.

The trend to re-creation of the past stands apart from the Dream of the future and our discussion. On the other hand, the Dream is linked in interesting and significant ways to the main realistic trend of writing since the thirties, with its concentration on the ills of society. This seems to offer a direct contrast to the older dreaming. Its stress is on the present. Its tendentious, critical mood is the very opposite of the dreamers' hopeful confidence. It deals with harsh actualities, not dawnlit visions. Yet the antithesis is by no means complete, since, time and time again, we feel that the realist is, after all, an idealist at heart—an angry, disappointed idealist whose very anger is a measure of his idealism. It is obviously so with Katharine Prichard, a warm-hearted romantic, a humanist with sympathies as wide as deep. Again, no book could be more realistic, more critical of social evils, than *Capricornia*, and here, too, the very savagery of his realism and irony betrays the passionate idealist in Xavier Herbert. Lust is let loose in *Soldiers' Women*, but its orgies are painted by an

[57] Katharine Susannah Prichard, *Winged Seeds* (Sydney 1950), p.379.
[58] Ian Mudie, *The Australian Dream* (Adelaide 1944), p.30.

angry puritan. In *Power Without Glory* Frank Hardy pillories a widespread corruption, a corruption found in the police force, the Roman Catholic Church, business, the press, sport and politics. John West is a ruthless, power-drunk entrepreneur who taints all he touches, and his portrait is drawn powerfully. Yet the indictment comes from a communist writer who gives his ideal in the self-sacrificing Ben Worth and extends his strong sympathies to such idealists as Morrie Blackwell and Frank Ashton—whose originals can be easily identified.

From a completely different angle, that of the generous-hearted but realistic individualist, Kylie Tennant mocks at society in a trenchant, witty realism, but we see her idealism in her sympathetic portraits of such characters as the Apostle, Sorell, and David Aumbry who has a vision of the individual as "part of a purposeful, million-fingered harmony".[59]

So, too, the satirists may pour scorn on their country and country-men, abusing it up hill and down dale, as James McAuley does in "The True Discovery of Australia" and "Envoi" or as A. D. Hope does in his atrabilious "Australia", yet they also indicate an ideal linking them with the land they attack. Thus McAuley confesses he is part of the land and its triumphs are his, and ends his "Envoi" on a positive if slightly grudging note:

> *Beauty is order and good chance in the artesian heart*
> *And does not wholly fail, though we impede;*
> *Though the reluctant and uneasy land resent*
> *The gush of waters, the lean plough, the fretful seed.*[60]

Hope, most savage and cerebral of the satirists, after berating his people with half-truths exaggerated into distortions, ends with an affirmation and a vision to "turn gladly home" from "the lush jungle of modern thought",

> *hoping, if still from deserts the prophets come,*
> *such savage and scarlet as no green hills dare*
> *springs in this waste.*[61]

Thus the Dream, though it may lie dormant for seasons like the wattle seed, has a power of endurance that enables it, after the destructive but quickening fire, to sprout in the blackened earth, rising in phoenix green.

---

[59] Kylie Tennant, *The Joyful Condemned* (London 1953), p.379.
[60] James McAuley, *Under Aldebaran* (Melbourne 1946), p.35.
[61] A. D. Hope, *Poems* (London 1960), p.100.

XII

The Palingenesis of Pan

Let Romanists all at the Confessional kneel,
  Let the Jew with disgust turn from it,
Let the mighty Crown Prelate in Church pander zeal,
  Let the Mussulman worship Mahomet.

From all these I differ—truly wise is my plan,
  With my doctrine, perhaps, you'll agree,
To be upright and downright and act like a man,
  That's the religion for me . . . .

For parsons and preachers are all a mere joke,
  Their hands must be greased for a fee;
But with the poor toiler to share your last "toke",
  That's the religion for me . . . .

But let man unto man like brethren act,
  My doctrine this suits to a T,
The heart that can feel for the woes of another,
  Oh, that's the religion for me.

OLD BUSH SONG[1]

Hither hoary Pan is fled, with His charm and with His dread,
With His honey-fluted stave, with His lore to salve and save,
With His active, sensate hate, planning many a cruel fate,
With His blind, insensate love, joys He filched from Heaven above.
Sharing with His creatures here, whimsical, capricious, queer:
To the very oldest land, product of His prentice hand,
Under tawny Capricorn, cloven hoof and gnarly horn,
Here the living Pan is fled, while the old World mourns Him dead.

          He seeks again His ancient haunts.
A squatter born, a squatter bred, with horns, Himself, upon His head,
His steps outback with glee are bent. He snuffs the saltbush with content,
The deeper for His knowledge sure, His ancient ways and works endure.

PETER HOPEGOOD[2]

---

[1] A. B. Paterson (ed.), *Old Bush Songs* (Sydney 1912), pp.127-8. Anon., "My Religion". "Toke" means a piece of bread.

[2] Peter Hopegood, *Austral Pan* (Perth 1932), p.2, "Austral Pan".

It is not enough
that life should be lived justly, death met quietly;
though that's nobility also. But man's essence
is not nobility, it is man, unrest,
a rushing of wind, distance . . . .

and life's like a wave breaking, not good or ill,
or right or wrong, but action and pressing forward;
a thing tested in the heart which hears and answers;
as when we have men, near-naked and ill armed,
thirteen, half-starved, setting out to conquer kingdoms . . . .

And under longings
man was eternal unrest that no place satisfies,
content never overtakes and no year ends;
for it is earth itself and earth's vitality
working within the bloodstream. We are earth's blood.

ROBERT D. FITZGERALD[3]

We dreamed, we so nearly triumphed, we were defeated
As every man in some great or humble way
Dreams, and nearly triumphs, and is always defeated,
And then, as we did, triumphs again in endurance.
Triumph is nothing, defeat is nothing; life is
Endurance; and, afterwards, death. And whatever death is,
The endurance remains like a fire, a sculpture, a mountain
To hearten our children. I tell you,
Such a struggle as ours is living; it lives after death
Purely, like flame, a thing burning and perfect.

DOUGLAS STEWART[4]

Earth-vigour

Of all the social patterns expressed in Australian literature none
find a clearer and more undeniable embodiment than our two final
patterns: earth-vigour and humanism. "Earth's vitality working
within the bloodstream", as FitzGerald rightly defines it, contains
its own complexity. It appears in the literature in four distinct, if
closely allied, forms: in its purely literary aspect it emerges as an
energy that is characteristic of the writing; on the philosophical side
it is revealed as an emphasis on will, effort, and action; as a positive

[3] Robert D. FitzGerald, *Forty Years' Poems* (Sydney 1965), pp.123, 180, "Between
Two Tides".
[4] Douglas Stewart, *Four Plays* (Sydney 1958), p.30, "The Fire on the Snow".

affirmation of life as worth living and enjoying; and, finally, as a widespread paganism preferring the hedonist and stoic outlooks on life to the faith of orthodox Christian religion.

These activist, life-affirming, and pagan forms have found a fitting literary symbol in Pan, the pastoral earth-god, the emblem of man's primal impulses, who also illustrates the linkage between the earth-vigour and a traditional humanism. Indeed, the two patterns are so closely allied as the pagan element fuses with the humanist one that it seemed best to treat them together in this final chapter.

The earth-vigour is the product, of course, of various ecological forces operating as qualities of the people and the land. One determinant of the social environment in its comparative youthfulness has been indicated by H. M. Green when, as a literary historian searching for distinctive characteristics of Australian literature, he suggested: "Most apparent are the qualities, positive and negative, which one would expect to find in the literary work of any young and comparatively undeveloped country such as vigour and freshness."[5] His argument is sound and still holds good. Our society, in comparison with ancient cultures of Asia and Europe, is a youthful one. It is growing apace, with the confidence engendered by an expanding economy and a developing culture. There has been no period of decadence. Australia may be still an empty land, but so far it has not become a "Waste Land". The national vigour runs too strongly for worlds that go out with a whimper. From the beginning of the society there was also the energizing element of the people, originally toughened convicts and adventurous settlers or gold-diggers.

More important, perhaps, was the character of the pioneer era. Pioneering conditions on the land compelled the facing of hardships, and put a premium of survival value upon qualities of strength, endurance and enterprise. The people attained a pioneering vitality. Toughness has been bred in the character as well as in the bone. Large natural resources of a continent have awaited exploitation by a small population so that, as Danny Delacey put it in *All That Swagger*, the country has had "lashings of opportunity". These in turn have promoted a sturdy confidence, affirming life. The conditions of living have been, on the whole, favourable, owing to a moderate climate despite the threat of drought, the open air life, a country of primary products guaranteeing plenty of wholesome food, and a reasonably wide distribution of wealth. Life has been good and enjoyed. No large-scale poverty and misery, such as exist in some other countries, have sapped the national energy and its expression in literature.

[5] H. M. Green, *An Outline of Australian Literature* (Sydney 1930), p.14.

Literary Vigour

Thus our writing has been marked by strength rather than grace, by a rude energy rather than by subtlety, so that vitality has often atoned for lack of form; freshness for the want of pumiced elegance. In this it resembles, on the whole, the literature of similar societies—the American, Canadian and South African. The prose of the nineties showed this vigour markedly, and it has persisted as characteristic of the best writing of this century. True, Kenneth Mackenzie and Patrick White, Ethel Anderson, Christina Stead and Helen Simpson in prose have created work of delicacy and subtlety. There has been a marked increase in such qualities among contemporary novelists, as we have seen. On the other hand, taking our literature as a whole, we see the characteristic vigour usually expressing itself in simplicity and directness, an honest straightforwardness suitable to men of action rather than of thought.

We can see this directness illustrated if we pick up Henry Lawson, for instance, and read "Brighten's Sister-in-law". Here Joe Wilson, the selector, describes how he and his wife, Mary, found their child Jim having convulsions:

"Jim was bent back like a bow, stiff as a bullock-yoke, in his mother's arms, and his eyeballs were turned up and fixed—a thing I saw twice afterwards and don't ever want to see again.

I was falling over things getting the tub and the hot water when the woman who lived next door rushed in. She called to her husband to run for the doctor, and before the doctor came she and Mary had got Jim into a hot bath and pulled him through.

...You never saw a child in convulsions? Well, you don't want to. It must be only a matter of seconds, but it seems long minutes; and half an hour afterwards the child might be laughing and playing with you, or stretched out dead. It shook me up a lot. I was always pretty high-strung and sensitive. After Jim took the first fit, every time he cried or turned over or stretched out in the night, I'd jump; I was always feeling his forehead in the dark to see if he was feverish, or feeling his limbs to see if he was 'limp' yet. Mary and I often laughed about it—afterwards."[6]

The writing is simple, clean, direct. It brings the whole scene before us in a natural, moving way. And the later description of Joe's ride to save the child when he has another turn is equally vigorous.

Turning to *Capricornia*, we see the graphic strength of Xavier Herbert's description in the passage telling how Oscar Shillingsworth loved his inland station, Red Ochre:

At times he loved it best in Wet season—when the creeks were running and the swamps were full—when the multi-coloured schisty rocks split golden waterfalls—when the scarlet plains were under water, green with wild rice, swarming with Siberian snipe—when the billabongs were brimming and the

[6] Henry Lawson, *Prose Works* (Sydney 1935), vol.2, pp.30-1.

water-lilies blooming and the nuttaguls shouting loudest—when bull-grass towered ten feet high, clothing hills and choking gullies—when every tree was flowering and most were draped with crimson mistletoe and droning with humming-birds and native bees—when cattle wandered a land of plenty, fat and sleek, till the buffalo-flies and marsh-flies came and drove them mad, so that they ran and ran to leanness, often to their death.[7]

A Poetry of Force

In poetry the earth-vigour is again a marked feature. Whatever the artistic defects or limitations of the popular verse in the old bush songs and the bush balladists, there is no doubt that they are vigorous in painting a picture, telling a story, or, as in "My Religion", expressing a point of view. "Jim Jones" and "The Wild Colonial Boy", "The Man from Snowy River" and "The Death of Ben Hall" are characteristic. In poetry Shaw Neilson is exceptional in his delicacy, Victor Daley and Rosemary Dobson have charm and grace, and Hugh McCrae can be delicate as well as robust. In general, however, the poetry is marked by its vigour, from the colonial poets such as Harpur, Gordon and Kendall, through the poets of the nineties like O'Dowd and Brennan, to the leading contemporary poets such as Slessor and FitzGerald, Judith Wright, Mary Gilmore, Douglas Stewart, A. D. Hope, and Francis Webb.

Many examples could be quoted, of course, but it is sufficient here to give just two poems. First, one of Brennan's "The Wanderer" sequence, "O desolate eves":

> *O desolate eves along the way, how oft,*
> *despite your bitterness, was I warm at heart!*
> *not with the glow of remembered hearths, but warm*
> *with the solitary unquenchable fire that burns*
> *a flameless heat deep in the heart who has come*
> *where the formless winds plunge and exult for aye*
> *among the naked spaces of the world,*
> *far past the circle of the ruddy hearths*
> *and all their memories. Desperate eves,*
> *when the wind-bitten hills turn'd violet*
> *along their rims, and the earth huddled her heat*
> *within her niggard bosom, and the dead stones*
> *lay battle-strewn before the iron wind*
> *that, blowing from the chill west, made all its way*
> *a loneliness to yield its triumph room;*
> *yet in that wind a clamour of trumpets rang,*
> *old trumpets, resolute, stark, undauntable,*
> *singing to battle against the eternal foe,*
> *the wronger of this world, and all his powers*
> *in some last fight, foredoom'd disastrous,*
> *upon the final ridges of the world:*
> *a war-worn note, stern fire in the stricken eve,*

[7] Xavier Herbert, *Capricornia* (Sydney 1938), p.88.

U

and fire thro' all my ancient heart, that sprang
towards that last hope of a glory won in defeat,
whence, knowing not sure if such high grace befall
at the end, yet I draw courage to front the way.[8]

Here is a vigour that passes into imaginative power, just as the poet himself ascends from earth into the naked spaces of the universe. Traditional in language and imagery, it is yet deeply personal. Judith Wright's "Woman to Man" is equally personal, but it is modern in tone. Where Brennan's vision is expansive, hers is concentrated to a disciplined intensity. It is, in a sense, a love poem, but one with a difference, since the theme is not the lovers or their love, but its tissue in the child to be born. Both poems are wrought imaginatively by vision, but Brennan is the warrior, with epics stirring in his blood, whilst Judith Wright is the woman writing of the experience reserved to womankind:

The eyeless labourer in the night,
the selfless shapeless seed I hold,
builds for its resurrection day—
silent and swift and deep from sight
foresees the unimagined light.

This is no child with a child's face;
this has no name to name it by;
yet you and I have known it well.
This is our hunter and our chase,
the third who lay in our embrace.

This is the strength that your arm knows,
the arc of flesh that is my breast,
the precise crystals of our eyes.
This is the blood's wild tree that grows
the intricate and folded rose.

This is the maker and the made;
this is the question and reply;
the blind head butting at the dark,
the blaze of light along the blade.
Oh hold me, for I am afraid.[9]

Energy and Power

These poems—and others like them—contain imagination, passion, and universality. Here the vigour becomes power. Often, however, it remains merely as energy precisely because it lacks these three qualities. This is true of much Australian writing in which the accent is on externals, giving the reportage of realism, especially in fiction,

[8] A. R. Chisholm and J. J. Quinn (ed.), *The Verse of Christopher Brennan* (Sydney 1960), p.164.
[9] Judith Wright, *Woman to Man* (Sydney 1949), p.1, "Woman to Man".

glued to the level of partculars, unable to rise to the universal. Vigour is admirable in itself, but it is not enough. It has its limitations if it does not also capture the three qualities mentioned above. It is a general virtue of the Australian writing—as, indeed, of the people it expresses—that it is spirited. Only a small amount, however, is spiritual.

To pass from mere vigour to power, from spirited expression to a moving one, a work must have emotional and spiritual significance. This is found, of course, in the best Australian writing. It exists in *Man-Shy*, for example, because the desire of the scrubber cattle for the hills becomes a symbol of freedom. The red heifer is courage incarnate in hide, hooves and horns. It instances the truth of Carlyle's dictum:

Rightly viewed no meanest object is insignificant; all objects are windows, through which the philosophic eye looks into infinitude itself . . . . All visible things are Emblems; what thou seest is not there on its own account; strictly taken, is not there at all: Matter exists only spiritually, and to represent some Idea, and *body* it forth.[10]

Thus Douglas Stewart takes the Scott expedition in *The Fire on the Snow* and bodies forth the aspiration, gallantry, and endurance of man's spirit in Antarctic wastes. Louis Esson catches his stoic acceptance of fate in "The Drovers", just as Lawson caught it in "The Drover's Wife". In his story "The Double Buggy at Lahey's Creek", Joe Wilson and Mary represent the love of man and wife, and the double buggy, as James drives it casually down the crossing, is a true Carlylean "Emblem". Katharine Prichard raises her Coonardoo to the universal plane. Such poets as O'Dowd, Brennan, Slessor, FitzGerald, Wright, Hope, and Webb, together with many of the younger contemporary poets, have symbolic values, whilst Neilson is deeply symbolist in outlook and expression. In fiction Richardson takes the wilful, sensitive Mahony and makes out of his suffering a monumental tragedy, accumulating power. If the social realists tend to remain on the reportage level, many of the contemporary novelists, especially White, Stead, Stow, Harrower, and Keneally, exercise a vigour marked also by imagination, passion, and a universal vision.

The Activist Tradition

Turning from the literary form of earth-vigour to its various philosophical forms, we might aptly begin with the activist tradition of an emphasis on will, effort, and action, since this has been a continuous characteristic of the society and its writing since the earliest colonial days. It has been linked with the pattern of realism

[10] Carlyle, *Sartor Resartus* (London 1921 ed., first publ. 1838), pp.66-7.

on the one hand, and, on the other, with the utopian aspirations which could only be fulfilled by active effort.

In most cases, of course, the philosophy has been implicit, a natural and underlying assumption, rather than an explicit statement. This is especially true of both the old bush songs and the bush ballads. The two types of balladry were alike in that they generally dealt, freely but unconsciously, with all kinds of actions in a way that implied a strong activist outlook. The emotional element was subordinate, whilst the intellectual one was negligible. The emphasis was all on doing, not on feeling or thinking. Here the chief example would best be the most popular of all the bush ballads: "The Man from Snowy River". The ideal is achievement in action, an achievement determined by the effort of the individual will. This is the essential spirit of the pioneering age, with courage and endurance as the outstanding virtues.

Colonial fiction, no less than the verse, was equally activist in theme and outlook as it dealt with the struggles of the pioneering times. A long line of historical novels and sagas has continued the tradition right up to the present day. The large school of social realists, dominant in fiction until recent writing, was also concerned with action, with actual events in the social scene, whilst many novelists who were reformists also stressed the will and effort needed to make changes in the society. In such cases the activist philosophy became explicit.

It has also been openly avowed and championed in contemporary poetry by the poets who have contributed to the significant series of historical poems centred on the explorers and the voyagers. Figures such as Captain Cook, Columbus, Tasman, Quiros, Leichhardt (first cousin to Patrick White's Voss, the explorer in fiction), and Eyre become symbols of heroic courage and action.

There are many contemporary poems, moreover, which belong to this genre, even if the heroes celebrated are neither strictly explorers nor voyagers. Among those which come to mind out of many are Judith Wright's "Bullocky", Webb's "A Drum for Ben Boyd", Mary Gilmore's "The Ringer" and "Botany Bay", Ian Mudie's "They'll Tell You About Me", John Manifold's "The Tomb of Lieut. John Learmonth, A.I.F.", the "Jervis Bay" of Michael Thwaites, and Thomas Shapcott's "Macquarie, as Father".

The emphasis upon the will has already been seen in such writers as White and Hope in our discussion of the Nietzschean cross-currents in the chapter on Radical Democracy,[11] with an explicit and eloquent statement of the importance of the will in Hope's poem "Pyramis", with its celebration of the "Intemperate will and incor-

[11] See pp.252-7.

ruptible pride" shown by the builders of the great monuments of art.

The greatest activist of our contemporary writers, however, is undoubtedly Robert D. FitzGerald. His *Forty Years' Poems* merits the assessment of an informed American critic, Professor A. Grove Day, when he declared in a letter to the Editor of the *Sydney Morning Herald*: "After studying Australian literature for a quarter of a century I feel qualified to assert that not one of your poets, past or present, fine though many may be, can offer us a volume comparable in lyrical quality and major achievement to *Forty Years' Poems*."[12] Certainly no other collected works can surpass the volume in range and weight of poetic achievement.

It is significant of the importance of the activist aspect of our earth-vigour in our writing that FitzGerald's book as a whole is a testament to its philosophy. Judith Wright rightly perceived this when she wrote: "He is, as it were, the poetic apotheosis of the balladists.... His longer narrative poems...seem like a philosophical translation and re-statement of the attitude behind, say, 'The Man from Snowy River', with its glorification of sheer action and undaunted courage."[13] The attitude of the balladists was, however, a major one of the Australian people, so that FitzGerald emerges as the poet-philosopher who has expressed it most fully and explicitly. Quotation after quotation could be made from his poems which would illustrate this point, but it is summed up adequately in the extracts given as epigraph to this chapter.

The Affirmation of Life

Australian literature as a whole, apart from its social consciousness, has one broad philosophical pattern: its vigour either states or implies a positive affirmation of life. Such an affirmation is part and parcel of the practical pioneering tradition. It is a natural and necessary faith for the bushman. It is integral to our democratic way of life. It is, above all, the lusty product of our good earth. It belongs essentially to an earth-vigour, since we still draw strength, Antaeus-like, from a firm footing on our soil. Despite extension of our factory chimneys, despite our huddling in the cities, we are an open-air people, healthy and affirmative because even our city-dwellers are within easy reach of the bush, the countryside and the beaches. Thus FitzGerald depicts "the untiring Sun" summoning his dancers on Manly surfing sands, where they are "squanderers of mirth". He is no less a Sydneysider when he begins his song by the clarion cry: "I go to meet the sun with singing lips". He calls his first volume *To Meet the Sun*, just as he rightly capitalizes "the untiring Sun" like God to

---

[12] *Sydney Morning Herald*, 14 August 1965.
[13] Judith Wright, *Preoccupations in Australian Poetry* (Melbourne 1965), p.160.

signify that he is a true Australian, a sun-worshipper. It is symbolical, I think, that so many of our writers, especially the poets, invoke the sun in the titles of their books—*Satyrs and Sunlight* (McCrae), *To Meet the Sun* (FitzGerald), *Sun-Freedom* (Ingamells), *Corroboree to the Sun* (Mudie), *Speak with the Sun* (David Campbell), *With the Sun on my Back* (John K. Ewers), *The Sun on the Stubble* (Colin Thiele), and *Surprises of the Sun* (James McAuley). Our poetry is as affirmative as the sunlight.

This affirmation is not unalloyed. The sun causes the desolation of drought as well as the joy of the morning or the content in "the hot, gold hush of noon". We have seen that a distinct note of sombreness runs through both the society and its literature. But we also saw this was a mood, not a metaphysic: that it rarely deepened into an outright pessimism. The major note is the affirmative one, held firmly by the main line of writers. Even Richard Mahony is balanced by the loyal, sturdy Mary. Even Voss wins redemption and Stan Parker, like the Riders in the Chariot, has his moment of vision. Our poets especially unite in a virile faith in life. They accept it joyously; they believe in it in a healthy, even a simple and hearty, fashion. Like Walt Whitman they, too, are "sane and sensual to the core". Paterson leads a chorus of balladists when he sings:

> In my wild erratic fancy visions come to me of Clancy
> Gone a-droving "down the Cooper" where the Western drovers go;
> As the stock are slowly stringing, Clancy rides behind them singing,
> For the drover's life has pleasures that the townsfolk never know.[14]

Hugh McCrae is a lord of life singing:

> Live! Let us live and love each other through,
> Ours is the love of lusty hardihood.[15]

No poets could be more positive than Mary Gilmore and FitzGerald, both holding the ultimate creed of Beauty, both asserting the joy of endeavour and the hard-won achievement. Even Brennan in the midst of his profound gloom triumphs over failure and suffering by throwing defiance to the darkness; his is the old heroic spirit, as we saw in "O desolate eves". Earlier still, moreover, Brennan belonged to the Guild of the Sun:

> What claustral joy today is on the air
> —expanding now and one with the celebrant sun—
> and fills with pointed flame all things aware,
> all flowers and souls that sing—and I am one![16]

The gentle Neilson was another member, an evangel of delight:

[14] A. B. Paterson, *Collected Verse* (Sydney 1921), p.16, "Clancy of the Overflow".
[15] Hugh McCrae, op. cit., p.125, "The Ragged Book".
[16] A. R. Chisholm and J. J. Quinn (ed.), *The Verse of Christopher Brennan* (Sydney 1960), p.70, "Dies Dominica! the sunshine burns".

> Here is the ecstasy
> Of sun-fed wine and song:
> Drink! it is melody
> Under a kurrajong.[17]

and

> Music is of the sunlight, strong and free . . .
> The Sun is up, and Death is far away.[18]

and

> Ever she talks of earth and air
> And sunlit junketing:
> Gaily she says, "I know I shall
> Be dancing in the Spring!"[19]

Kenneth Mackenzie finds joy in love, beauty, and the earth in his long poem *Our Earth*.

Indeed, the affirmation is drawn from earth and air and sun—an earth-vigour. We can see this if we compare Australian poetry with much of modern English poetry, which has been cerebral, cityfied, disillusioned, or rhetorically clamant of social ills and their remedies. T. S. Eliot is the poet representative of his age: weaving vacant shuttles, watching worlds go out in a whimper, venting "thoughts of a dry brain in a dry season", growing old and wearing the bottom of his trousers rolled, stating in "Gerontion":

> I have lost my passion: why should I need to keep it
> Since what is kept must be adulterated.

If Eliot rose to *Murder in the Cathedral* and *Four Quartets*, he also sank to that muddled, flat-rhythmed play *The Cocktail Party*. Earlier Ezra Pound, Eliot's forerunner and teacher, found that "Caliban casts out Ariel" and the men in the first world war died only for "an old bitch gone in the teeth", and "a botched civilization". Louis Mac-Neice mourns that "things draw to an end, the soil is stale", and finds himself left with "endless liabilities, no assets". Auden, Bottrall, Day Lewis all found the times disjoint and immersed themselves, as Stephen Spender has acutely shown, in Conrad's "destructive element". The English poets themselves are right, I think, when they ascribe their malaise to social confusion produced by an industrialized, urbanized society. Auden concludes "That valley is fatal where furnaces burn", MacNeice states there is no salvation from the collapse of "your towns and town-bred thoughts", whilst Spender laments that "The city builds its horrors in my brain". Thus the anaemia from which modern English poetry suffered from the 1920s

---

[17] John Shaw Neilson, *Collected Poems* (Melbourne 1934), p. 66, "Under a Kurrajong".
[18] Ibid., p.10, "The Sun is Up".
[19] Ibid., p.11, "Pale Neighbour".

and 1930s was not just a post-war disillusionment. The continuing vampire drawing the blood from life is the industrialized age, with its megapolis.

In Australia, too, the increasing urban pressure has effected a change in the traditional affirmation since the younger poets, as I have already pointed out elsewhere,[20] have either turned to satirical criticism of our society or cultivated a sceptical, ironic, and realistic detachment. The simple *chanson de joie* of McCrae and Neilson has become alien—perhaps impossible—in the troubled, complex climate of contemporary feeling. Yet the ultimate affirmation of life, as we saw earlier in our discussion of sombreness,[21] is still strong, even if it is now combined with a deeper sense of the tragic and sharper realization of the world's complexities and conflicts.

Austral Pan

Today, again, whilst the poets are finding new interpretations of the classical myths, it is noteworthy that Pan is not one of the gods invoked. Yet nothing indicates more how closely the characteristic vigour is bound with the earth than the prominence given in the past by a number of poets to Pan, the earth-god, the pastoral deity for a pastoral people. This is an attempt to give the environment increased significance by what seemed the most suitable symbol. In his "Poetry in Australia" Professor A. R. Chisholm, discussing how the European landscape had been "humanised", declared: "In Australia the landscape is not yet 'old' enough to have undergone this process of humanisation, and for this reason the Australian poet is destitute of one of the commonest sources of inspiration."[22] Applying this theory to McCrae, he explains his "falling back on the Greek past" and other pasts as forms of escape from Australia—"refuges from a poetically insufficient reality". There was some truth in the theory, but it overlooked the fact that the country had been partly "humanised" by the writers of the colonial period and the nineties, as well as by the old bush songs and the bush balladists. As for the application to McCrae, surely O'Dowd was right when he demanded:

> *Who fenced the nymphs in European vales?*
> *Or Pan tabooed from all but Oxford dreams?*[23]

McCrae has as much right to his nymphs as a European poet. Would we say that Shakespeare was an escapist, "falling back on the Greek past" because he saw Venus bending over Adonis? Was *Venus and*

---

[20] See pp.132-3.
[21] See pp.159-62.
[22] *Australian National Review*, July 1937, p.51.
[23] Bernard O'Dowd, *Collected Poems* (Melbourne 1941), p.205, "The Bush".

Adonis an escapist poem in which Shakespeare was "running away from a poetically insufficient" England? In both cases the poet uses what myths or symbols he wishes as forms of expression, and the only relevant question to be asked is: does his imagination realize the myth so strongly that it becomes alive and significant? We are as much legatees of the past as Europeans, rightful heirs to the myths of all the ages. We can put them to our symbolic use as others have done. McCrae has not used them for mere decoration, but for a vital expression which is Australian in spirit. As Thomas Earp wrote in his preface to the Fanfrolico edition of *Satyrs and Sunlight*:

It is impossible not to feel that the environment of a new land had some share in this magnificent primitive re-creation. . . . Hugh McCrae is essentially an Australian poet. . . . Australia has given him his vitality of word and theme . . . with the figures of mythology and romance whom he delights to invoke. . . . They are lusty, there is blood in their veins; but how sickly they had grown in the North! . . . Under the Australian sun they become real and stretch strong limbs again.[24]

Our writers have tried to acclimatize various myths here. Daley, O'Dowd, H. M. Green, and McKee Wright, for instance, transported the Celtic heroes and fairies to the bush, but the elves and leprechauns refused to hide their crock of gold under the eriostemon. Their gambollings were forced, and they soon fled back to James Stephens. Some writers tried to recreate the mythology of the aboriginals, and the Jindyworobaks in particular endeavoured, with small success, to recall Alcheringa. O'Dowd brought Alma Venus here to behold her "bank of leaf-clad lubras"—but she did not stay. FitzGerald was even audacious enough to invoke Apollo, the god of reason.

Contemporary poets such as Hope, McAuley, and Harold Stewart have issued invitations to the muses, Orpheus, and other Greek mythical figures. But so far only Pan has attracted a strong band of followers amongst our poets. Thus Dorothea Mackellar declared:

> *Of the great gods only Pan walks hourly here—Pan only;*
> *In the warm, dark gullies, in the thin clear upland air,*
> *On the windy sea-cliffs, and the plains apart and lonely,*
> *By the tingling silence you may know that he is there.*[25]

In his poem "The Palingenesis of Pan" Baylebridge paid tribute:

> *Pan shall now returned be,*
> *Past his former majesty—*
> *Healthy, holy, honest Pan,*
> *Broadening out the breath in man . . .*

[24] Hugh McCrae, *Satyrs and Sunlight* (London 1928, Fanfrolico ed.), Introduction by Thomas Earp, pp.xvi, xii, xiii.
[25] Dorothea Mackellar, *The Closed Door and Other Verses* (Melbourne 1911), p.26, "Settlers".

Who hath said that Pan is dead,
And his lieges lapped in lead?
From this breathing foliage round me,
From the vital hills that bound me,
From the earth, the sky, the sea,
A spirit doth commune with me;
It has found the wide and deep
Where the holies dwelling keep![26]

Louis Esson recalled Pan happily in "The Monk and the Faun", whilst Helen Simpson celebrated him in "Pan in Pimlico". Kenneth Slessor discovered him at Lane Cove; announcing:

Now earth is ripe for Pan again,
Barbaric ways and paynim rout,
And revels of old Samian men,
O Chiron, pipe thy centaurs out![27]

Brennan saw Pan alive in his forest, disappearing

with chuckle of laughter in his thicket-beard,
and rustle of scurrying faun-feet.[28]

McCrae treats Pan familiarly as he pictures the centaurs kicking

poor Pan over
The back of his fat spotted leopard
Amid the lush clover.[29]

It is Peter Hopegood, however, who has divined the goat-god best. In his autobiography, *Peter Lecky*, he has described powerfully his experience as a mystic of the Pan-force as a reality in the wild West Australian country, as a spirit perceptible and dynamic, stampeding the cattle—Pan making *panic*, noting that sinister aspect of the earth-god. In his poem "Austral Pan" he has celebrated the original Pan as an elemental force, felt here when disenthroned from his haunts in the old world. Thus the deathless but detached gods of McCrae are given "a local habitation and a name", felt and visioned in Australia. In such a poem Professor Chisholm's need is met and O'Dowd's prophecies are fulfilled, for it effects that "humanisation" and "spiritualisation" of the land which O'Dowd also proclaimed as an event of the future. It puts delight such as Neilson's and the pre-symbolist Brennan's into universal expression through the enduring mythos. It divines that Pan the earth-god, fleshly, primitive, a trinity of the animal, human, and divine; robust; affirming life, sense-delight-

[26] William Baylebridge (as Blocksidge), *Southern Songs* (privately printed 1910), pp.15-16.
[27] Kenneth Slessor, *Poems* (Sydney 1954), p.4, "Pan at Lane Cove".
[28] A. R. Chisholm and J. J. Quinn (ed.), op. cit., p.112.
[29] Hugh McCrae, op. cit., p.7, "Fantasy".

ing yet conscious of the pain and suffering which are part of our life; that such a god, pagan, is the symbol most characteristically Australian.

Paganism

In celebrating Pan the poets did not engage explicitly in the Pan-Christ dialectic imaging the conflict between paganism (or man's natural impulses) and Christianity which was explored last century by many English writers, from Carlyle and the Brownings to Edmund Gosse, R. L. Stevenson, Swinburne and Wilde, and by such writers in Europe as Heine, Gautier, and Clemenceau. Yet the dialectic was sometimes implicit, as was also D. H. Lawrence's interpretation of Pan as the elemental earth force, with the "Pan-power" welling up and establishing a vivid relatedness between man and the universe.

Certainly the cult of Pan illustrates strikingly how earth-vigour has turned to paganism. Australian literature mirrors a society fundamentally irreligious, loosely pagan. True, in its outward form, religion has been an accepted feature of our social life. The colonies, as Trollope observed, built churches and schools even in small villages as a matter of course, as part of the English tradition. Religious toleration has always been practised, despite a certain amount of childish sectarianism. Mark Twain, visiting Adelaide, the city of churches, in the nineties, was entertained by the fact that its small population contained an extraordinary variety of religions according to the census. He even listed them all, discovered "about 64 roads to the other world", and commented sardonically: "You can see how healthy the religious atmosphere is. Anything can live in it."[30] It may be questioned, however, whether Adelaide was typically Australian in this regard.

The great majority of Australians profess Christianity for such purposes as births, deaths, marriage, and the census, with the Church of England leading the field, followed by Roman Catholics, Methodists and Presbyterians. Devoted clergymen and priests have laboured for their faith since the early days, and there have always been, of course, a great many true believers. Religion has been influential, too, in such matters as education, social welfare, customs and morals, and, on occasion, politics. We have seen that it helped to promote democratic equality.

In its special field of faith, however, Christianity has operated with limited success. According to a 1961 Gallup poll only some quarter of the population (27 per cent) attended church regularly. The churches themselves have frequently recognized the prevalence of irreligious or pagan attitudes. In postwar books on our society,

[30] Mark Twain, *Following the Equator* (New York 1897), p.187.

commentators express a consensus to the same effect: Max Harris: "religion exercises little or no influence on Australian behaviour"; A. L. McLeod, explaining why there is no chapter on religion in a symposium on Australian culture: "it cannot be regarded as a cultural force in Australia"; Craig McGregor: "In general the Australian attitude towards religion is one of apathy." In a survey of Australia of 359 pages McGregor spares only two pages to religion. So, too, Christianity is almost entirely disregarded, as K. S. Inglis points out, in the memorials in Sydney, Melbourne, and Canberra commemorating Anzac, our greatest national tradition. In the first two of these monuments, the Shrine of Remembrance and the Anzac Memorial, the architectural inspiration is not Christian but pagan, derived from Greece.[31]

It is natural, therefore, that our writing, reflecting the society, is predominantly pagan, even if there is some truth in the lament of an Anglican spokesman that "Australian literature is impoverished by its lack of the kind of inspiration that is essentially religious."[32] Until recently religious writing of literary quality has been rare. There has been little mysticism, except for a few writers like Peter Hopegood, Max Dunn, and Patrick White. The supernatural only appears as a joke, as in John Arthur Barry's amusing tale, "Steve Brown's Bunyip", or Douglas Stewart's entertaining treatment of our best-known phantom in his "historical comedy", *Fisher's Ghost*. Paul Grano's *Witness to the Stars*, an anthology of verse by Catholic poets, only made manifest the lack of religious inspiration, since the religious verses included were inferior, and the few poems of merit by Roderic Quinn, James Devaney, Martin Haley and Grano himself were hardly religious at all, like John O'Brien's classic "Said Hanrahan".

Religious Writing

There has always been, of course, some poetry with a religious element. In the earlier days of last century there were indifferent verses by such poets as Caroline Leakey and J. D. Lang. Later William Gay pictured the victory of Christianity over the pagan gods in "Christ on Olympus", whilst Ada Cambridge dealt forcefully with her personal conflict between faith and doubt. In this century the Anglican faith has been upheld by the poems of Gilbert White, Bishop of Carpentaria, and Dr Thomas Thornton Reed, Bishop of

[31] Max Harris, "Morals and Manners", in Peter Coleman (ed.), *Australian Civilization* (Melbourne 1962), p.60; A. L. McLeod (ed.), *The Pattern of Australian Culture* (Cornell 1963), p.vi; Craig McGregor, *Profile of Australia* (London 1966), p.344; K. S. Inglis, "The Anzac Tradition", in *Meanjin Quarterly*, no.1, 1965, pp.42-44.
[32] Rev. K. T. Henderson, "Religious Institutions and Aspirations" in George Caiger (ed.), *The Australian Way of Life* (London 1953), pp.119, 127.

Adelaide. In her long dramatic poem "The Lighthouse" Nan McDonald tells with moving simplicity the story of how a lighthouse keeper off the Australian coast, with the corpse of his companion in the store-room, beset by voices tempting him to desert his grim, lonely post but aided by the voices of his mother, dead sweetheart, and a friend, finally finds strength through faith in Christ to remain at his post:

> *Lord, in Thy holy name I kindle*
> *This Lamp, and for Thy sake,*
> *And for all good ships, it shall not dwindle*
> *Till the day break.*[33]

This is a fine poem in which the religious inspiration is fully convincing.

Three Roman Catholic poets have entered the lists for their faith, bringing, at their best, high qualities of intellect, emotion, and craftsmanship to our Catholic poetry. After outstanding lyrics of feeling like "The Incarnation of Sirius" and "Celebration of Love" in his secular stage, James McAuley moved to a classic elegance, sometimes remote, yet sometimes moving, as in "New Guinea" and the beautiful "Pietà".

Vincent Buckley has passed through an eloquent rhetoric to an incisive idiom, whether traditional as in "Good Friday and the Present Crucifixion" or colloquial as in the satirical "Eleven Political Poems" and the Yeatsian "Father and Son", with its forceful drama of

> *Two small, self-wounding, fearful men*
> *Riding on rock, on flint, on knives,*
> *Who travel from their cramping lives.*[34]

It is with the third Catholic poet, Francis Webb, that we have the most powerful and most impassioned of our religious poetry. Its strength is mainly the original genius and high imaginative quality of the poet at his best and clearest, but it is also reinforced by the spontaneity of the religious feeling. This flows pervasively through his poems, and never descends, as often with McAuley and Buckley, to the self-conscious or doctrinaire. Some of Webb's strivings with his inward conflicts make his language and packed imagery difficult or obscure. Yet he can also voice a deep Christian compassion lucidly in such poems as "A Death at Winson Green" and "Harry". The intensity of his faith achieves lyrical beauty in "The Canticle", and his poem celebrating the birth of a child in "Five Days Old" sings with a simple loveliness. It has the fresh magical touch found in mediaeval poems or Blake's *Songs of Innocence*:

[33] Nan McDonald, *The Lighthouse and Other Poems* (Sydney 1959), p.34.
[34] Vincent Buckley, *Masters in Israel* (Sydney 1961), p.36.

Christmas is in the air.
You are given into my hands
Out of quietest, loneliest lands.
My trembling is all my prayer.
To blown straw was given
All the fullness of Heaven . . . .

If this is man, then the danger
And fear are as lights of the inn,
Faint and remote as sin
Out here by the manger.
In the sleeping, weeping weather
We shall all kneel down together.[35]

If we turn from poetry to the novel and short story we find that the religious element is almost entirely absent until Patrick White. Our fiction is almost completely secular and, in a sense, implicitly pagan. There are, of course, scattered instances of scenes and characters exemplifying the Christian faith, but there is no significant novel devoted to a religious theme until Voss appeared in 1957 as an exploration on a double level, actual and spiritual, centred on the salvation of a man's soul. *Riders in the Chariot* again concentrates on a spiritual, religious vision. With Patrick White religion has thus become a dominant feature in contemporary Australian fiction, not only because its domination derives special strength from the fact that the genius of White stands supreme over our contemporary novels, but also because it has deeply influenced other novelists. Randolph Stow's *To the Islands* offers parallel search for the salvation of the soul to *Voss*. Stimulated by White's example and by the horizons he opened up, other novelists have ventured into exploring the inner recesses of the mind and the spirit. Thomas Keneally, for instance, carried out such an exploration in *The Fear*. His *Bring Larks and Heroes* presents an ethical problem of conscience, whilst his *Three Cheers for the Paraclete* is the first significant Australian novel to deal entirely with the problems of institutional religion. In this respect it breaks new ground. It is also of unusual interest in that it criticizes some Catholic attitudes from inside knowledge and yet from a humanist point of view.

Humanism and Its Rejection of Religion

The religious attack on the prevailing paganism has awakened a new consciousness of how strongly this still stands, and how closely it is joined to that traditional concept best defined as humanism. This regards man as the measure of all things, and his goal as happiness on earth, not in heaven. It is the attitude to society which comple-

[35] Francis Webb, *Socrates and Other Poems* (Sydney 1961), pp.33-4.

ments the attitude to earth in earth-vigour. On the negative side, it links up with such social patterns as realism and humour; on the positive side it embraces radical democracy, the spell of the bush, the Great Australian Dream, and mateship.

Taking the negative side first, we see how the facts of history and the environment have produced naturally, almost inevitably, a humanist outlook that begins with a pagan rejection of the orthodox organized religion. In the literature we see this outlook doubly reflected: first as the absence of religious belief or inspiration, and secondly as a substantial strain of anti-religious sentiment, so that the attitude to religion comprises actual hostility as well as a general indifference.

Among the factors that promoted the rejection of religion by the general mass of the people was its relative absence in the early formative days of the New South Wales colony. The first Anglican labourers in the vineyard were few and given little official encouragement. Other Protestant denominations were not recognized officially until 1816, and Roman Catholicism was not allowed until 1821. Clergymen and priests were so scarce that many couples lived as man and wife without benefit of clergy; for instance, Charles Harpur and his elder brother were baptized in 1813, the year of his birth, but it was not until the following year that the Rev. Samuel Marsden baptized his sister of six at the same time as he married Charles Harpur's father and mother. Yet this was at Windsor, close to Sydney, and Joseph Harpur was both the local parish clerk and schoolmaster.

Up country there were generally no clergymen or priests, and bushmen lived in an irreligious state, completely devoid of religious observances and instruction. Generations grew up quite godless. There was heavy drinking, gambling, and swearing. For consolation men used rum, not religion. In *Geoffry Hamlyn* Major Buckley explains to the visiting clergyman, Dean Frank Maberly, how completely irreligious the shepherds were: " 'Then these fellows, Major, are entirely godless, I suppose?' 'Well, I tell you, Dean,' said the Major, stopping short, 'it's about as bad as bad can be! it can't be worse, sir.' "[36]

The majority of the immigrants belonged to the working class, whether bond or free, and this was usually indifferent or hostile to religion. The convicts especially were bitterly anti-religious, since religion was officially part of the hated system. The practice of clergymen serving as magistrates and so becoming "flogging parsons", like Marsden, especially embittered the convicts who saw that the

[36] Henry Kingsley, *The Recollections of Geoffry Hamlyn* (Sydney 1935 ed., first publ. 1859), p.226.

same functionary who on Saturday had been "employed chiefly in sentencing to hard labour on the roads, double irons, and a hundred lashes, was on Sunday transformed into a minister of the gospel of peace, a messenger of mercy, and a herald of salvation!"[37]

Thus not only did pioneering conditions induce indifference to religion but the convict society created hostility to it. Another determinant was what Professor Manning Clark has called "the third force" in addition to Protestantism and Catholicism in our historical development—the force of the Enlightenment, the progressive liberalism which grew so strong that it defeated organized religion by introducing free, secular education. This was naturally anti-clerical. So, too, was the radical movement that comprised, in a sense, its left wing. The socialism that flourished towards the end of the nineteenth century was itself a jealous religion, critical of the orthodox religious institutions bound up with the established social order it was attacking. No better illustration of this anti-clericalism can be found than that of a leader in the *Tocsin*, the first Labour paper in Melbourne, for which O'Dowd and Victor Daley wrote. It is entitled "The Assault on the Education Act. Dogma v Democracy", and was written in 1897:

The guiding spirits of the churches have been for years, and are today more than ever, the enemies of the people.... . The parsons, with a few notable and noble exceptions, have been against political progress, against popular movements, against Socialistic effort, against everything that makes for the Brotherhood of Man.

The leader goes on to denounce roundly "these batteners upon effete superstitions, these cringers to wealth, these despisers of the poor, these prosperous Judases and Peters of the Nineteenth Century who dare to endeavour to despoil a Democracy".[38] This is the voice of pagan humanism, rhetorically indignant with religion because it saw it, rightly or wrongly, as a threat to humanist ideals of radical democracy, the socialist dream for Australia, and the wider mateship of world fraternity. Its rhetoric expresses, however, the same humanist outlook and spirit that we saw, in a more popular expression, in the old bush song entitled "My Religion" that formed an epigraph to this chapter. Whilst the intellectual socialist and the bushman both condemned orthodox religion, where the former abused it with a rival religious zeal, the latter treated it with amused contempt: "For parsons and preachers are all a mere joke." The old bush songs are cheerfully pagan, usually ignoring religion because it was no significant part of early bush life. When parsons and priests come into the bush ballads, they are often presented in a humorous context, as in

[37] J. D. Lang, *Transportation and Colonization*, etc. (London 1837), p.93.
[38] The *Tocsin*, 2 October 1897.

Paterson's "A Bush Christening" and John O'Brien's "Tangmalanga-loo" in which a confirming Bishop is startled to hear from a bush youth his definition of Christmas Day: "It's the day before the races out at Tangmalangaloo".[39] John O'Brien, a parish priest, wrote poems with a strong Catholic sentiment, but he was also a realist who knew the respective values of sport and religion in the bush reckoning. In the novels and short stories the parsons and priests are also presented as figures of fun by such writers as Favenc, Steele Rudd, Lawson, Randolph Bedford, and Dowell O'Reilly.

This irreverence was a natural product of the land itself, the conditions of bush life, and the realistic, sceptical outlook these engendered. The effect of the land itself has been described in *The Boy in the Bush* in a passage quoted earlier, undoubtedly by D. H. Lawrence and not by his collaborator Molly Skinner. Here the English immigrant is impressed by "the weird silent timelessness of the bush", so that "it seemed as if his father and his father's world and his father's gods withered and went to dust at the thought of this bush." One can easily imagine, indeed, how the old gods would wither, and how the narrow beliefs and observances of the old world would become dwarfed and meaningless in the vast spaciousness of the new bush world.

Thus A. G. Stephens, speaking partly as Australian, partly as rationalist, wrote acutely:

And upon religion, as upon everything else, the spirit of Australia—that undefined, indefinable resultant of earth and air, and conditions of climate and life,—had seized; modifying, altering, increasing, or altogether destroying. In the case of religious belief the tendency is clearly to destruction—partly, no doubt, because with the spread of mental enlightenment the tendency is every-where to decay of faith in outworn creeds; but partly also, it seems, because the Australian environment is unfavourable to the growth of religion, and because there is in the developing Australian character a sceptical and utilitarian spirit that values the present hour and refuses to sacrifice the present for any visionary future lacking a rational guarantee.[40]

It is some proof of the soundness of this declaration, made in the *Bulletin* in 1894, that its ideas are echoed over half a century later by the Rev. K. T. Henderson in his discussion of "Religious Institu-tions and Aspirations" in Australia. He finds a "critical, impatient and limited realism" as the most distinctive trait in the Australian character, and states: "A culture without religion would have seemed just as incredible and impossible to our forefathers, primitive or civilized, as a culture fused with religion seems to the 'average, sensual man' in Australia today."[41]

[39] John O'Brien (Father P. J. Hartigan), *Around the Boree Log* (Sydney 1943), p.102.   [40] A. G. Stephens, *The Red Pagan* (Sydney 1904), p.153.
[41] Rev. K. T. Henderson, op. cit., p.136.

v

Earth Versus Hell

This critical realism, especially in Lawrence's bush where the "gods withered and went to dust", looked askance at the threats of hell-fire for the sinful often made by the churches, Protestant and Catholic alike, during the nineteenth century. True there were some. like Alexander Harris, Kendall, Ada Cambridge and Brennan, who went through spiritual struggles, as did some prominent figures in our history depicted so graphically by that devotee of Dostoievsky, Manning Clark. Yet few writers wrote as miserable sinners. Today the Catholic poets mentioned celebrate the joys, not the terrors, of their faith. Indeed, the consciousness of sin has entered into our literature rarely, in contrast to American literature. We have had no Jonathan Edwards fulminating with *Sinners in the Hands of an Angry God* or a powerful Hawthorne showing guilt as "a stain upon the soul". Our society, after all, developed under the eighteenth century enlightenment, whereas in America the earlier Puritanism of New England struck its roots deep. Where there was sombreness here it generally derived, as we have noted, from the outer environment, physical or social, not from an inward sense of sinfulness or of punishment to come.

Certainly the earth-vigour of the poets rejects such gloom and fear. Gordon finds joy in days when the air resembles a long draught of wine; Kendall finds his "higher worship" in the psalm of the winds and the liturgy of the waters; O'Dowd turns to Alma Venus as the creative spirit; Brennan finds his soul moved by the desire "to breathe in one love, song and sun"; Neilson delights in days when "the air was the colour of ale"; McCrae celebrates "clean running wave and sunward soaring flower, The great hot sky"; FitzGerald goes to meet the sun with singing lips, and praises "the struggle to magpie-morning and all life's clamour and lust"; and Judith Wright sings the twilight bell of the wonga vine when "The sunburst day's on fire". Almost one and all, the poets delight in earth, answering the dark despair of hell with an affirmative joy.

Humanism joins with earth-vigour here to reject religion's inferno, shocked and angered by God's alleged inhumanity to man. Thus a long line of Australian poets have not only sung man's pagan joy in earth but have attacked institutional religion in some form or another —Kendall, O'Dowd, Brennan, Daley, Brereton, Baylebridge, Furnley Maurice, Jack Lindsay, Peter Hopegood, FitzGerald, Slessor, and Hope, with many more that could be cited.

In particular, J. Le Gay Brereton and Shaw Neilson tell how religion with its images of sin, its fears, and its terrors of hell oppressed them in childhood and youth, until they were freed from its baleful spell and found salvation through nature, Brereton by the bush and Neilson by the crane's serenity. Thus Brereton in "Buffalo Creek" declares:

> *A timid child with heart oppressed*
> *By images of sin,*
> *I slunk into the bush for rest,*
> *And found my fairy kin....*
> *The sunlight was a golden beer,*
> *I drank a magic draught,*
> *The sky was clear and, void of fear,*
> *I stood erect and laughed....*
>
> *The bay of conscience' bloody hound*
> *That tears the world apart*
> *Has never drowned the silent sound*
> *Within my happy heart.*[42]

Neilson found redemption in the calm beauty of a water-bird:

> *In the far days, when every day was long,*
> *Fear was upon me, and the fear was strong,*
> *Ere I had learned the recompense of song.*
>
> *In the dim days I trembled, for I knew*
> *God was above me, always frowning through,*
> *And God was terrible and thunder-blue.*
>
> *Creeds the discoloured awed my opening mind,*
> *Perils, perplexities—what could I find?—*
> *All the old terror waiting on mankind...*
>
> *There was a lake I loved in gentle rain:*
> *One day there fell a bird, a courtly crane:*
> *Wisely he walked, as one who knows of pain.*
>
> *Gracious he was and lofty as a king:*
> *Silent he was, and yet he seemed to sing*
> *Always of little children and the Spring.*
>
> *God? Did he know him? It was far he flew...*
> *God was not terrible and thunder-blue:*
> *It was a gentle water-bird I knew...*
>
> *As a calm soldier in a cloak of grey*
> *He did commune with me for many a day*
> *Till the dark fear was lifted far away.*[43]

Neilson, a complete humanist, is sometimes bitter against the churches for their coldness, pride, and lack of humanity. Gentle and compassionate poet that he is, he grows indignant at orthodox morality and its hardness in "Maggie Tulliver" and "Child of Tears"; and in

[42] J. Le Gay Brereton, *Swags Up!* (London 1928), p.12.
[43] John Shaw Neilson, *Collected Poems* (Melbourne 1934), pp.176-7.

that humanist lyric "The Poor Can Feed the Birds" he contrasts the pharisaic rich worshippers in the church with the poor feeding the birds in the pond of the near-by park, carrying out the old, old sacrament of the scattering of the bread.

FitzGerald, in turn, seeks the god of light and reason to discover reality,

> *The greater Apollo whose wide reach*
> *Embraces the unguessed-at years*
> *Shaming our ethics, creed, and fears,*
> *Shaming the priests for what they teach,*
> *Shaming the narrow-visioned seers!*[44]

McCrae expresses in his poem "The Ragged Book" the characteristic earth-vigour and humanism both; the joy of life and the independence of man's spirit:

> *The love of God ... The candle-lives of priests*
> *Mumbling obeisance in a stained-glass tomb!*
> *For all their dross, our drinking and our feasts*
> *Were ours by Nature from our mother's womb.*
>
> *Live! Let us live and love each other through,*
> *Ours is the love of lusty hardihood;*
> *True love can never kneel and yet be true;*
> *By standing ye shall prove your love is good.*[45]

This affirmation of humanism, strong as it is amongst the poets, comes even more strongly from a contemporary novelist, Thomas Keneally, trained for the Roman Catholic priesthood, who scarifies a priests' House of Studies in *Three Cheers for the Paraclete* (1968) through the character of Maitland, a priest scholar and historian, who has imbibed liberal ideas from a sojourn in Europe. Above all, he is constantly described, critically, by his fellow priests as that terrible thing, "a humanist".

This accusation is certainly true, since Keneally's hero and mouthpiece, as a genuine humanist, revolts from many fundamental ideas and practices of the Roman Catholic Church. Thus he finds the training of the priests "anti-human". When his fellow priest Costello, promoted as a bishop for his orthodoxy, informed a doctor in the case of a girl who had been attacked and raped, that he could not possibly treat the girl to prevent a possible pregnancy, since this was against the holy teaching of the church, Maitland protests:

I think that it is more than barbarous in a merely human sense to make that girl risk bearing such a child. I think such a thing is *essentially* barbarous. I think that the risk of any minute organism which the doctor might remove

[44] Robert D. FitzGerald, *To Meet the Sun* (Sydney 1929), p.36, "The Greater Apollo".
[45] Hugh McCrae, op. cit., pp.39-40.

being human is ludicrously tiny. And on the basis of such a tiny or non-existent risk I can't see that it's justified to chance the future ruin of both this *real* girl and any child she might bear.[46]

At times Maitland's criticism grows intemperate, suggesting a contrast with James McAuley's "Credo", with its calm confidence in a world of faith where

> *poems are prophecy*
> *Of a new heaven and earth,*
> *A rumour of resurrection.*[47]

Flesh, Mind, and Spirit

Indeed, believers will protest, quite rightly, that the picture of religion drawn by Keneally and the poets is one-sided, incomplete, and hence unjust. It is. But it is simply an historical and literary fact that this is the kind of picture, one of "creeds the discoloured", that the poets and the novelist have actually drawn, proving the strength of the allied social patterns of earth-vigour and humanism as important elements in the Australian society and literature. Its inadequacy is irrelevant to its reality. And it is worth noting that the outstanding mystic, Peter Hopegood, is *sui generis* and no Christian, although he is supported by Max Dunn—a Buddhist.

In dealing with the negative, anti-religious aspect of humanism, we have seen at the same time its positive aspects of man's joy in earth and life, his independent spirit, and his compassionate sympathy with his fellow men. The positive aspects also include the assertion of man's democratic equality, the radical demand for social justice, an attitude of realism towards life and the claims for the supernatural, the aspiration for a better world seen in utopianism and based on the humanist belief that human beings by their own efforts can make some progress towards an ideal of personal and social perfection, and the fellow-feeling for all men that is the wider extension of the mateship concept. All these are combined in the pattern of humanism. Thus our study has now come full circle within the inclusive circumference of humanism.

Despite some minor internal contradictions, such as those between the idealisms of utopianism and mateship, on the one hand, and the sardonic realism and sansculottist humour on the other, or between the sombre strain and the lusty, joyful affirmation of life, there is a strong general coherence amongst the interrelated social patterns. They combine to make a complex which, in its virtues and its faults alike, is distinctively Australian in character.

It only remains, therefore, to clarify two points on which some

[46] Thomas Keneally, *Three Cheers for the Paraclete* (Sydney 1968), p.126.
[47] James McAuley, *Surprises of the Sun* (Sydney 1969), p.30.

critics have shown confusion. Earth-vigour has been charged, under the title of vitalism, as being purely Nietzschean and exclusive, whilst humanism has been libelled as a shallow materialism. Now we have seen that Henry Handel Richardson and Hope hold the exclusive concept of the artist as an elite, and Patrick White advances one of a spiritual elect in the four riders in his coincidental chariot. These restrictive beliefs, however, are exceptional. Narrowly aristocratic, implying forms of artistic or spiritual snobbery, they are in direct opposition to the broad democratic feeling that is absolutely funda-mental in the Australian *ethos*. The main expressions of earth-vigour emerge as the affirmation of life through joy (seen, on the popular level, in the pagan hedonism of the average Australian), and the affirmation of the human will as courage and endurance. I have illustrated these by the poets, who lend themselves most clearly and easily to such illustration, but examples could also be drawn from the majority of the prose-writers, just as no poet is more profoundly humanist than the writers of fiction I have mentioned, from Furphy and Lawson to Christina Stead and Keneally. With the three excep-tions noted, all affirmations of the will as either joy or courage are universal in character, completely inclusive of all men, in full consonance with humanism and the basic sentiment of democratic equality. Demos is stronger than Nietzsche.

Thus the pride turning to humility through suffering as portrayed in *Voss* is exceptional in Australian writing. It stands apart from the usual Australian outlook, as Ian Turner has pointed out in a keenly discerning review of *Voss* in *Overland*: "Pride and humility had little meaning as alternative ways of meeting the Australian situation; con-fidence in one's own ability, founded on a recognition of the real possibilities, held the greater truth."[48] Humility, it may be said, finds scant place in pioneering vitality. So, too, White's use of suffering as redemptive differs from the Australian attitude to it, which is stoic, not Christian, with the emphasis on endurance, as seen typically in Mary Gilmore's brief lyric "Never Admit the Pain":

> *Never admit the pain,*
> *Bury it deep;*
> *Only the weak complain,*
> *Complaint is cheap.*

> *Cover thy wound, fold down*
> *Its curtained place;*
> *Silence is still a crown,*
> *Courage a grace.*[49]

[48] Ian Turner, "The Parable of Voss" in *Overland*, no.12, Winter 1958, p.37.
[49] Mary Gilmore, op. cit., p.103.

This is the same courage in one's troubles that Gordon sang as standing like stone in life's froth and bubble; it is the tough, stoic endurance of Furphy's bullock drivers.

It is a quality of the spirit that forms one of the answers to the charge that Australian humanism is only a crass materialism. This charge is largely based on the assumption that the spiritual must be religious or supernatural. But the objective philosopher might well point out that the spiritual is that which concerns the human spirit deeply, that the pagan tradition in Greece and Rome achieved truth, beauty and goodness as well as Christianity, and such spiritual qualities as loving kindness and compassion, courage and magnanimity, are found in humanity everywhere.

Certainly the Australian people are materialistic—probably no more or less than the great mass of people elsewhere in the world today—or in past ages. There is, indeed, need for a more sufficient growth of activities of the mind and the spirit. Here the society is backward. Yet among the writers the things of the flesh pass into the things of the spirit, conjoined, as Baylebridge imaged in his finest poem, "I worshipped, when my veins were fresh", in which he first worshipped his love's beauty:

> *All the miracle, the power,*
> *Of being had come there to flower.*
> *Each part was perfect in the whole;*
> *The body one was with the soul . . .*
> *I fell before the flesh, and knew*
> *All spirit in terms of that flesh too.*

Then, after her death, her flesh placed in earth, her influence remains so that

> *I fall before the spirit so,*
> *And flesh in terms of spirit know—*
> *The Holy Ghost, the truth that stands*
> *When turned to dust are lips and hands.*[50]

Flesh and spirit thus meet, and the joy of a McCrae or Neilson is spiritual as well as fleshly, passing into ecstasy. So, too, the ideals of our social patterns, such as the independence of the human spirit, the equality of men, the integrity that holds to the truth of realism, the cry for justice, the sense of brotherhood and the self-sacrifice of mateship: all these are things of the mind and the spirit.

More and more, as we have seen, the poets, for instance, are going beyond mere description of nature to seek universal symbols, or creating new worlds of meaning for the mind out of the people's history. Earth-vigour and humanism join in FitzGerald's "Essay on

[50] William Baylebridge, *This Vital Flesh* (Sydney 1939), pp.20-1, "Life's Testament", VI, iii.

Memory", when the pioneering, adventurous spirit is pictured as creative, with men "serving their kind":

> *We'll crash the trestles down*
> *that barricade clear laughter, take the town*
> *on a burst of shouting that through fissures rent*
> *cascades its fervid glee, magnificent.*
> *We'll slit gloom's gullet, oracling defeat,*
> *and crack great barrels of song in open street*
> *free for the drinking. We'll make fabulous*
> *this world, in honour of them who gave it us,*
> *not just the Nelsons, Newtons, of our race,*
> *the Phillips grounding at a landing-place*
> *continent-wide, but all whom violence of mind*
> *violence of action, gave such singleness*
> *that if they did but grow, ambitionless*
> *except to live in the sun, they served their kind*
> *with that straight growth of will which bears for seed*
> *zest to create; which, grasping at blind air*
> *graves flowers from veriest nothing and makes fair*
> *all that we have.*[51]

This is the old tradition of the bush; the pioneer spirit of Australia; the same zest that urged our fathers when, unbaulked by drought and fire and flood, they drove westward beyond Hay and Hell and Booligal. This is the old gusto now swung inwards from this vital flesh, adventuring down Murrays of the mind, setting out to cross the intangible continents of the spirit.

In our literature of the past the discerning eye can see, beyond the material verities of realism, plentiful examples of spiritual grace, such as the courage of the drover's wife, the selfless generosity of Danny Delacey to the stray, frost-bitten Chinaman, or the loyalty of Coonardoo to Youie, enduring until her tragic death. Since the last war, however, poets and novelists have increasingly turned inward, as we have seen, exploring, more explicitly than before, the deeper feelings of man in universal terms.

In this development, where the emphasis has shifted from the physical to the social environment, from the land itself to the psychological complexities of our urban society, the social patterns are inevitably changing and taking on new forms. For the response of the organism to the environment involves evolution as well as mutual interaction. "This mutualism," as one scientist observes, "is the very stuff of ecology; one of two principles, of which the other is change. The web of things and the flow of things."[52]

The web remains, however, along with the flow: there is continuity

---

[51] Robert D. FitzGerald, "Essay on Memory" in *Moonlight Acre* (Melbourne 1938), pp.69-70.

[52] Leslie Reed, *The Sociology of Nature* (London 1962 ed., first publ. 1958), p.26.

as well as change. Here it is significant that a distinguished Canadian scholar, examining Australian writing, finds that Patrick White has deep affinities with Furphy, with both expressing the patterns of realism, sombreness, and "the democratic thrust", both concerned with the land:

Mr White may be said to sustain Furphy's central vision of the land almost as a racial memory; and useful sometimes, too, consciously to fit a novelist's purpose, as in *Voss*. His own vision, building upon the older vision and transcending it, bridges the gap that is the ache at the heart of Furphy's world. Spirit enters matter.[53]

Professor McDougall also states that when he began his investigation into the two writers he had not meant "the land to assume a role of such proportions" as it did when he went deeper into his subject. His experience, in fact, parallels my own exactly, and confirms the basic interpretation of the land as the chief shaping force of the social patterns. The confirmation is especially valuable in that it comes from a penetrating mind and a thinker from another country entering freshly into Australian literature.

Commenting on the fact that Patrick White was born in the year Furphy died, he declares: "I like to think that just as these two lives lie end to end, Mr White's beginning where Furphy's leaves off, so too the worlds of the imagination which they created are subtly led by the land into a kind of continuity."[54] The continuity is indeed there, as is the subtle influence of the land on the people, which is so fundamental and so inescapable a fact that it forced itself on him just as it did on me. After describing the land, Furphy had speculated: "Faithfully and loving interpreted, what is the latent meaning of it all?"[55] I hope that this book, written as a faithful and loving interpretation of it, has suggested some latent meanings through its shaping of the social patterns. By the land, of course, I mean no vague mystique of the soil, no strange eucalyptine magic, but the undeniable, hard realities of the land with its earth, climate, and historical conditions of living, especially in the pioneering days of the pastoral age when the national *ethos* first began to take shape under its powerful impress. The people and the land have interacted on each other, creating an ecological unity in which the various patterns have been integrated. As our Buddhist poet Max Dunn has intimated:

[53] Robert L. McDougall, *The Australian National University, Commonwealth Literary Fund Lecture 1966; Australia Felix: Joseph Furphy and Patrick White* (Canberra 1966), p.8.

[54] Ibid., p.12.

[55] Tom Collins (Joseph Furphy), *Such is Life* (Melbourne 1917 ed., first publ. 1903), p.65.

The country grows
into the image of the people,
and the people grow
into the likeness of the country
till to the soul's geographer
each becomes the symbol of the other.[56]

In this spiritual geography the patterns of our society, our national traditions, imaged in the literature, have been ultimately born of the land.

[56] Max Dunn, *Portrait of a Country* (Melbourne 1962 ed., first publ. 1949), p. 14.

Select Bibliography

The following select list is restricted to authors and works considered or cited in the text and footnotes, together with some background material. Dates are given for the original publication, but in some cases more recent editions are available.

To facilitate reference, the bibliography has been arranged as follows:

I   GENERAL REFERENCE
    A. History and Social Interpretation
    B. Literature

II   SPECIFIC BOOKS AND PAMPHLETS
    A. History and Social Interpretation
    B. Literature
        1. Poetry and Ballads
        2. Novel
        3. Short Story
        4. Drama
        5. Essays, Travel, Letters and Autobiography
        6. Criticism and Biography

III   ARTICLES, THESES, MSS
    A. History and Social Interpretation
    B. Literature

IV   NEWSPAPERS AND PERIODICALS

I GENERAL REFERENCE

A. History and Social Interpretation

Atkinson, Meredith (ed.), *Australia: Economic and Political Studies*, Melbourne, 1920.

Barnard, Marjorie, *A History of Australia*, Sydney, 1962.

Bean, C. E. W., *The Story of Anzac: The First Phase*, vol. I, *Official History of Australia in the War of 1914-1918*, Sydney, 1937.

Benedict, Ruth, *Patterns of Culture*, London, 1935.

Bews, J. W., *Human Ecology*, London, 1953.

Brady, Alexander, *Democracy in the Dominions*, Toronto, 1935.

Chisholm, Alec H. (ed.), *The Australian Encyclopaedia*, 10 vols, Sydney, 1958.

Clark, Manning (ed.), *Select Documents in Australian History 1788-1850*, Sydney, 1950.

— (ed.), *Select Documents in Australian History 1851-1900*, Sydney, 1955.

— *A History of Australia*, vols I, II, Melbourne, 1962, 1968.

Coleman, Peter (ed.), *Australian Civilization*, Melbourne, 1962.

Crawford, R. M., *Australia*, London, 1952.

Davies, A. F. and Encel, S., *Australian Society*, Melbourne, 1965.

Dexter, David, *The New Guinea Offensives*, Series 1, vol.VI, *Australia in the War of 1939-45*, Canberra, 1961.

Fitzpatrick, Brian, *A Short History of the Australian Labor Movement*, Melbourne, 1944.

Froude, J. A., *Oceana*, London, 1896.

Grattan, C. Hartley, *Introducing Australia*, New York, 1942.
 — *The Southwest Pacific to 1900; The Southwest Pacific Since 1900*, 2 vols, Ann Arbor, Michigan, 1963.

Greenwood, Gordon (ed.), *Australia: a Social and Political History*, Sydney, 1955.

Hancock, W. K., *Australia*, London, 1930; Sydney, 1945.

Hasluck, Paul, *The Government and the People*, Series 4, vol.I, *Australia in the War of 1939-45*, Canberra, 1952.

Horne, Donald, *The Lucky Country*, Ringwood, 1964.

Long, Gavin, *To Benghazi*, Series 1 (Army), vol.I, *Australia in the War of 1939-45*, Canberra, 1952.

McGregor, Craig, *Profile of Australia*, London, 1967.

McLeod, A. L. (ed.), *The Pattern of Australian Culture*, Ithaca, N.Y. and Melbourne, 1963.

Madariaga, Salvador de, *Englishmen, Frenchmen, Spaniards*, London, 1931.

Mander, A. E., *The Making of the Australians*, Melbourne, 1958.

Métin, Albert, *Le Socialisme sans Doctrines*, Paris, 1901.

O'Shaughnessy, Peter; Inson, Graeme; and Ward, Russel (eds.), *The Restless Years*, Brisbane, 1968.

Pike, Douglas (ed.), *Australian Dictionary of Biography*, 3 vols, 1966.
 — *Australia: the Quiet Continent*, Cambridge, 1962.

Reed, L., *The Sociology of Nature*, London, 1962.

Schurz, W. L., *Latin America*, New York, 1941.

Scott, Ernest, *A Short History of Australia* (1916). Revised by Burton, Herbert; Melbourne, 1953.

Serle, Percival, *Dictionary of Australian Biography*, 2 vols, Sydney, 1949.

Shaw, A. G. L., *The Story of Australia*, London, 1955.

Taylor, Griffith, *Australia*, London, 1940.

Turner, Ian (ed.), *The Australian Dream*, Melbourne, 1968.

Unamuno, Miguel de, *The Tragic Sense of Life*, London, 1921.

Ward, Russel, *Australia*, Sydney, 1965.
 — and Robertson, John (eds.), *Such Was Life: Select Documents in Australian Social History 1788-1850*, Sydney, 1969.

Wigmore, Lionel, *The Japanese Thrust*, Series 1, vol.IV, *Australia in the War of 1939-45*, Canberra, 1957.

B. Literature

Arciniegas, German, *The Green Continent: a View of Latin America by its Leading Writers*, New York, 1944.

Baker, Sidney J., *The Australian Language*, Sydney, 1945.
 — *The Drum: Australian Character and Slang*, Sydney, 1959.

Barton, G. B., *Literature in New South Wales*, Sydney, 1866.
 — *Poets and Prose Writers of New South Wales*, Sydney, 1866.

Blake, L. J., *Australian Writers*, Adelaide, 1968.

Calverton, V. F., *The Liberation of American Literature*, New York, 1932.

Cargill, Oscar, *Intellectual America: Ideas on the March*, New York, 1941.
Chapman, Robt. and Bennett, Jonathan (eds.), *An Anthology of New Zealand Verse*, London and Wellington, 1956.
Christesen, C. B. (ed.), *Australian Heritage*, Melbourne, 1949.
— (ed.), *On Native Grounds: Australian Writing from Meanjin Quarterly*, Sydney, 1967.
Davin, D. M. (ed.), *New Zealand Short Stories*, Wellington, 1953.
Dutton, Geoffrey (ed.), *The Literature of Australia*, London, 1964.
— (ed.), *Modern Australian Writing*, Manchester, 1966.
— and Harris, Max (eds.), *The Vital Decade: Australian Art and Letters 1957-1967*, Melbourne, 1968.
Ewers, John K., *Creative Writing in Australia*, Melbourne, 1945.
Fellowship of Australian Writers (ed.), *Australian Writers Speak*, Sydney, 1942.
Ferguson, Sir John, *Bibliography of Australia 1784-1900*, 7 vols, Sydney, 1941-69.
Grattan, C. Hartley, *Australian Literature*, Seattle, 1929.
Green, H. M., *An Outline of Australian Literature*, Sydney, 1930.
— *A History of Australian Literature*, 2 vols, Sydney, 1961.
Hadgraft, Cecil, *Australian Literature: a Critical Account to 1955*, London, 1960.
Heseltine, H. P. (ed.), *Australian Idiom*, Melbourne, 1963.
Higham, Charles (ed.), *Australian Writing Today*, Melbourne, 1968.
Jones, Howard Mumford, *The Theory of American Literature*, Ithaca, N.Y., 1948.
Kermode, Frank, *Romantic Image* (1937), London, 1961.
Logan, J. D., *Highways of Canadian Literature*, Toronto, 1924.
Macartney, Frederick T. (ed.), *Australian Literature*, by Morris Miller, extended to 1950, Sydney, 1956.
Matthews, John Pengwerne, *Tradition in Exile*, Melbourne and Toronto, 1962.
Miller, E. Morris, *Australian Literature, from its Beginnings to 1935*, 2 vols, Melbourne, 1940.
Moore, T. Inglis and Stewart, Douglas (eds.), *Poetry in Australia*, 2 vols, Sydney, 1964.
Murdoch, Walter and Mulgan, Alan (eds.), *A Book of Australian and New Zealand Verse*, Oxford, 1950.
Palmer, Vance, *The Legend of the Nineties*, Melbourne, 1954.
Parrington, V. L., *Main Currents in American Thought*, New York, 1927.
Phillips, A. A., *The Australian Tradition*, Melbourne, 1958.
Praz, Mario, *The Romantic Agony* (1933), London, 1960.
Pringle, John Douglas, *Australian Accent*, London, 1958.
Ramson, W. S., *Australian English: an Historical Study of the Vocabulary 1788-1898*, Canberra, 1966.
Reid, J. C., *Creative Writing in New Zealand*, Auckland, 1946.
Semmler, Clement and Whitelock, Derek (eds.), *Literary Australia*, Melbourne, 1966.
Smith, A. J. M. (ed.), *The Book of Canadian Poetry*, Chicago, 1943.
Smith, Bernard, *Australian Painting 1788-1960*, Melbourne, 1965.
Spiller, Robert E., *The Cycle of American Literature*, New York, 1955.
— et al. (eds.), *Literary History of the United States*, New York, 1946.
Stephensen, P. R., *The Foundations of Culture in Australia*, Sydney, 1936.

Taine, H. A., *History of English Literature* (trans. by H. van Laun), Edinburgh, 1873.
Thompson, J., Slessor, K., and Howarth, R. G. (eds.), *The Penguin Book of Australian Verse*, Mitcham, 1958.
Wilkes, G. A., *Australian Literature: a Conspectus*, Sydney, 1969.
Wright, Judith, *A Book of Australian Verse*, 2nd ed., Melbourne, 1968.

II SPECIFIC BOOKS AND PAMPHLETS

A. History and Social Interpretation

Adams, Francis, *The Australians*, London, 1893.
Bigge, J. T., *Report on the State of Agriculture in New South Wales*, London, 1823.
Blainey, Geoffrey, *The Tyranny of Distance*, Melbourne, 1966.
Border, J. T. R., *Church and State in Australia 1788-1872: a Constitutional Study of the Church of England in Australia*, London, 1962.
"A Bushman" (Sidney, John), *A Voice from the Far Interior of Australia*, London, 1847.
Congalton, A. A., *Status and Prestige in Australia*, Melbourne, 1969.
Crawford, R. M., *An Australian Perspective*, Melbourne, 1960.
Cunningham, P., *Two Years in New South Wales*, 2 vols, London, 1827.
Curr, Edward M., *Recollections of Squatting Life in Victoria*, etc., Melbourne, 1883.
Currey, C. H., *The Irish at Eureka*, Sydney, 1954.
Davies, A. F., *Australian Democracy: an Introduction to the Political System*, Melbourne, 1964.
— *Images of Class*, Sydney, 1967.
Deakin, Alfred, *The Federal Story*, Melbourne, 1944.
Durack, Mary, *Kings in Grass Castles*, London, 1959.
Ebbels, R. N., *The Australian Labor Movement 1850-1907*, Sydney, 1960.
Fairfax, John, Esq., *The Colonies of Australia*, etc., London, 1852.
Fitzpatrick, Kathleen (ed.), *Australian Explorers*, London, 1958.
Garran, Sir Robert, *Prosper the Commonwealth*, Sydney, 1958.
Gollan, Robin, *Radical and Working Class Politics*, Melbourne, 1960.
Hancock, W. K., *Politics in Pitcairn and Other Essays*, London, 1947.
Harris, Alexander ("An Emigrant Mechanic"), *Settlers and Convicts*, London, 1847; with Foreword by C. M. H. Clark, Melbourne, 1953.
Joyce, Alfred, *A Homestead History* (ed. G. F. James), Melbourne, 1942.
Keesing, Nancy (ed.), *Gold Fever: the Australian Goldfields 1851 to the 1890s*, Sydney, 1967.
Kiddle, Margaret, *Men of Yesterday: a Social History of the Western District of Victoria 1834-1890*, Melbourne, 1961.
Lang, J. D., *Transportation and Colonization*, etc., London, 1837.
Madgwick, R. B., *Immigration into Eastern Australia*, London, 1937.
Martin, E. A. (ed.), *Life and Speeches of Daniel Henry Deniehy*, Sydney, 1884.
Moran, Patrick Francis Cardinal, *History of the Catholic Church in Australasia*, Sydney, 1896.
Mundy, G. C., *Our Antipodes*, London, 1855.
Murtagh, James G., *Australia: the Catholic Chapter*, New York, 1946.
Nadel, George, *Australia's Colonial Culture*, with Foreword by C. Hartley Grattan, Melbourne, 1957.

O'Brien, E., *The Foundation of Australia 1786-1800*, Sydney, 1950.

O'Farrell, P., *The Catholic Church in Australia*, Melbourne, 1968.

Palmer, Edward, *Early Days in North Queensland*, Sydney, 1903.

Parkes, Henry, *Speeches on Various Occasions Connected with Public Affairs*, Melbourne, 1876.

Roberts, Stephen H., *The Squatting Age in Australia 1835-1847*, Melbourne, 1936.

Robson, L. L., *The Convict Settlers of Australia*, Melbourne, 1965.

Shaw, A. G. L., *Convicts and the Colonies*, London, 1966.

Spence, William Guthrie, *Australia's Awakening*, Sydney and Melbourne, 1909.

Tench, Captain Watkin, *A Narrative of the Expedition to Botany Bay*, London, 1789.

Therry, R., *Reminiscences of Thirty Years' Residence in New South Wales and Victoria*, London, 1863.

Trollope, Anthony, *Australia and New Zealand*, London, 1873.

Wakefield, E. G., *A Letter from Sydney*, London, 1829.

Ward, Russel, *The Australian Legend*, Melbourne, 1958.

Wentworth, W. C., *A Statistical, Historical, and Political Description of the Colony of New South Wales, and its Dependent Settlements in Van Diemen's Land*, London, 1819.

Westgarth, William, *Victoria and the Gold Mines in 1857*, London, 1857.

B. Literature

I. POETRY AND BALLADS

Anderson, Hugh, *Colonial Ballads*, Ferntree Gully, 1955.

Auchterlonie, Dorothy, *The Dolphin*, Melbourne, 1967.

Baylebridge, William, *This Vital Flesh*, Sydney, 1939.

Beaver, Bruce, *Open at Random*, Sydney, 1968.

Blight, John, *My Beachcombing Days*, Sydney, 1968.

Boake, Barcroft, *Where the Dead Men Lie*, Sydney, 1897.

Brennan, C. J., *Poems*, Sydney, 1913.

— *The Verse of Christopher Brennan* (ed. A. R. Chisholm and J. J. Quinn), Sydney, 1960.

Brereton, J. Le Gay, *Swags Up!*, London, 1928.

Buckley, Vincent, *Masters in Israel*, Sydney, 1961.

— *Arcady and Other Places*, Melbourne, 1966.

Campbell, David, *Selected Poems, 1930-1965*, Sydney, 1968.

Daley, Victor, *Creeve Roe: Poetry by Victor Daley* (ed. Muir Holborn and Marjorie Pizer), Sydney, 1947.

Darwin, Erasmus, "Visit of Hope to Sydney Cove", prefaced to *The Voyage of Governor Phillip to Botany Bay*, London, 1879.

Dawe, Bruce, *Beyond the Subdivisions*, Melbourne, 1969.

Dennis, C. J., *The Songs of a Sentimental Bloke*, Sydney, 1916.

Dobson, Rosemary, *Child with a Cockatoo*, Sydney, 1955.

— *Cock Crow*, Sydney, 1965.

Dunn, Max, *Portrait of a Country*, Melbourne, 1962.

Dyson, Edward, *Rhymes from the Mines and Other Lines* (1896), Sydney, 1898.

Farrell, John, *How He Died and Other Poems* (1887), Melbourne, 1907.

Field, Barron, *First Fruits of Australian Poetry*, Sydney, 1819.

FitzGerald, Robert D., *To Meet the Sun*, Sydney, 1929.

— *Moonlight Acre*, Melbourne, 1938.
— *Between Two Tides*, Sydney, 1952.
— *This Night's Orbit*, Melbourne, 1953.
— *The Wind at Your Door*, Cremorne, 1959.
— *Forty Years' Poems*, Sydney, 1965.
Fullerton, Mary ("E"), *Moles Do So Little with Their Privacy*, Sydney, 1942.
Gay, William, *Complete Poetical Works*, Melbourne, 1911.
Gibson, G. Herbert ("Ironbark"), *Ironbark Splinters*, London, 1912.
Gilmore, Mary, *Selected Verse*, Sydney, 1948.
— *Fourteen Men*, Sydney, 1954.
Gordon, Adam Lindsay, *The Poems of Adam Lindsay Gordon* (ed. F. Maldon Robb), London, 1912.
— *Sea Spray and Smoke Drift*, Melbourne, 1876. Preface by Marcus Clarke.
Grano, Paul, *Poems New and Old*, Melbourne, 1945.
Hall, Rodney, *Eyewitness*, Sydney, 1967.
— *Heaven, In a Way*, Brisbane, 1970.
— and Chapcott, Thomas W. (eds.), *New Impulses in Australian Poetry*, St Lucia, 1968.
Harpur, Charles, *Poems*, Melbourne, 1883.
Harwood, Gwen, *Poems*, Sydney, 1963.
— *Poems: Volume Two*, Sydney, 1968.
Higham, Charles, *Noonday Country: Poems 1954-1965*, Sydney, 1966.
Hope, A. D., *The Wandering Islands*, Sydney, 1955.
— *Poems*, London, 1960.
— *Collected Poems 1930-1965*, Sydney, 1966.
— *New Poems 1965-1969*, Sydney, 1969.
Hopegood, Peter, *Austral Pan*, Perth, 1932.
— *Circus at World's End*, Sydney, 1947.
Ingamells, Rex, *The Great South Land*, Melbourne, 1951.
Kendall, Henry, *Selected Poems* (ed. T. Inglis Moore), Sydney, 1957.
— *The Poetical Works* (ed. T. T. Reed), Adelaide, 1966.
Lawson, Henry, *Collected Verse*, 3 vols (ed. Colin Roderick), Sydney, 1967-9.
Mackenzie, Kenneth, *Selected Poems*, Sydney, 1961.
Manifold, John, *Selected Verse*, London, 1948.
Martin, David, *The Poems of David Martin 1938-1958*, Sydney, n.d.
Moll, Ernest G., *Cut from Mulga: Poems*, Sydney, 1940.
Moore, T. Inglis, *Bayonet and Grass*, Sydney, 1957.
Mudie, Ian, *Poems 1934-44*, Melbourne, 1945.
— *The Blue Crane*, Sydney, 1959.
McAuley, James, *Under Aldebaran*, Melbourne, 1946.
— *A Vision of Ceremony*, Sydney, 1956.
— *Captain Quiros*, Sydney, 1964.
— *Surprises of the Sun*, Sydney, 1969.
McCrae, Hugh, *Satyrs and Sunlight*, London, 1928.
— *The Best Poems of Hugh McCrae* (ed. R. G. Howarth), Sydney, 1961.
McCuaig, Ronald, *The Ballad of Bloodthirsty Bessie*, Sydney, 1961.
Neilson, John Shaw, *The Poems of Shaw Neilson* (ed. A. R. Chisholm), Sydney, 1965.
— *Unpublished Poems of Shaw Neilson* (ed. James Devaney), Sydney, 1947.
— *Witnesses of Spring: Unpublished Poems* (ed. Judith Wright), Sydney, 1970.

O'Dowd, Bernard, *Collected Poems*, Melbourne, 1941.
Paterson, A. B. ("Banjo") (ed.), *Old Bush Songs*, Sydney, 1905.
— *Collected Verse*, Sydney, 1921.
Quinn, John, *Battle Stations*, Sydney, 1944.
Robinson, Roland, *Deep Well*, Sydney, 1962.
Shapcott, Thomas W., *A Taste of Salt Water*, Sydney, 1967.
Sladen, Douglas B. W. (ed.), *Australian Ballads and Rhymes*, London, 1888.
Slessor, Kenneth, *Cuckooz Contrey*, Sydney, 1932.
— *Poems*, Sydney, 1944.
Smith, Vivian, *An Island South*, Sydney, 1967.
Stephens, James Brunton, *Poetical Works*, Sydney, 1912.
Stewart, Douglas, *Collected Poems 1936-1967*, Sydney, 1967.
— and Keesing, Nancy (eds.), *Australian Bush Ballads*, Sydney, 1955.
— (eds.), *Old Bush Songs*, Sydney, 1955.
— (eds.), *The Pacific Book of Bush Ballads*, Sydney, 1967.
Stow, Randolph, *A Counterfeit Silence*, Sydney, 1969.
Thompson, John, *Thirty Poems*, Sydney, 1954.
Tompson, Charles, *Wild Notes from the Lyre of a Native Minstrel*, Sydney, 1826.
Wallace-Crabbe, Chris, *The Music of Division*, Sydney, 1959.
Ward, Russel, *The Penguin Book of Australian Ballads*, Melbourne, 1964.
Webb, Francis, *Collected Poems*, Sydney, 1969.
Wentworth, W. C., *Australasia* (1823), London, 1873.
Wilmot, Frank ("Furnley Maurice"), *Poems*, Melbourne, 1944.
Wright, Judith, *The Moving Image*, Melbourne, 1946.
— *Woman to Man*, Sydney, 1949.
— *The Two Fires*, Sydney, 1955.
— *Five Senses*, Sydney, 1963.
— *The Other Half*, Sydney, 1966.

2. NOVEL

Astley, Thea, *The Slow Natives*, Sydney, 1965.
Boldrewood, Rolf (Browne, T. A.), *Robbery Under Arms*, London, 1888.
— *A Sydney-Side Saxon*, London, 1891.
Boyd, Martin, *The Montforts* (written under pseudonym "Martin Mills"), London, 1928.
— *Lucinda Brayford*, London, 1946.
Brent of Bin Bin, *Up the Country*, Edinburgh, 1928.
— *Back to Bool Bool*, Edinburgh, 1931.
Cambridge, Ada, *A Little Minx*, London, 1893.
Clarke, Marcus, *For the Term of His Natural Life*, Melbourne, 1874.
Cleary, Jon, *You Can't See Round Corners*, Sydney, 1948.
Culotta, Nino, *They're a Weird Mob*, Sydney, 1957.
Dark, Eleanor, *The Timeless Land*, London, 1942.
— *Storm of Time*, Sydney, 1948.
— *No Barrier*, London, 1953.
— *Lantana Lane*, London, 1959.
Davison, Frank Dalby, *Man-Shy*, Sydney, 1931; as *Red Heifer*, New York, 1934.
— *Dusty*, Sydney and New York, 1946.
— *The White Thorntree*, Melbourne, 1968.
Durack, Mary, *Keep Him My Country*, London, 1955.
Eldershaw, M. Barnard, *A House is Built*, London, 1929.

W

— *Tomorrow and Tomorrow*, Melbourne, 1947.

Forrest, David, *The Hollow Woodheap*, Brisbane, 1962.

Franklin, Miles, *My Brilliant Career*, Edinburgh, 1901.

— *All That Swagger*, Sydney, 1936.

— and Cusack, Dymphna, *Pioneers on Parade*, Sydney, 1939.

Furphy, Joseph ("Tom Collins"), *Such is Life*, Sydney, 1903; with biographical sketch of author by C. Hartley Grattan, Chicago, 1948.

— *Rigby's Romance* (1905-1906), Sydney, 1946.

— *The Buln-Buln and the Brolga*, Sydney, 1948.

Glassop, Lawson, *We Were the Rats*, Sydney, 1944.

Hardy, Frank, *Power Without Glory*, Melbourne, 1950.

Harris, Alexander, *The Emigrant Family*, London, 1849; as *Martin Beck*, 1852; (ed. W. S. Ramson), Canberra, 1967.

Harrower, Elizabeth, *The Long Prospect*, London, 1958.

Hay, William, *The Escape of the Notorious Sir William Heans*, London, 1918.

Herbert, Xavier, *Capricornia*, Sydney, 1938.

— *Soldiers' Women*, Sydney, 1961.

Hungerford, T. A. G., *The Ridge and the River*, Sydney, 1952.

— *Riverslake*, Sydney, 1953.

Johnston, George, *My Brother Jack*, London, 1964.

— *Clean Straw for Nothing*, London, 1969.

Keneally, Thomas, *The Place at Whitton*, London, 1964.

— *The Fear*, Melbourne, 1965.

— *Bring Larks and Heroes*, Melbourne, 1967.

— *Three Cheers for the Paraclete*, Sydney, 1968.

Kingsley, Henry, *The Recollections of Geoffry Hamlyn*, London, 1859.

Lambert, Eric, *Twenty Thousand Thieves*, London, 1952.

Langley, Eve, *The Pea-pickers*, Sydney, 1942.

Lane, William ("John Miller"), *The Workingman's Paradise*, Sydney and Brisbane, 1892.

Lawrence, D. H., *Kangaroo*, London, 1923.

— and Skinner, Molly, *The Boy in the Bush*, London, 1924.

Leakey, Caroline, *The Broad Arrow*, London, 1887.

Lindsay, Norman, *The Magic Pudding*, Sydney, 1918.

— *Saturdee*, Sydney, 1933.

Little, Cicely, *The Lass with the Delicate Air*, Sydney, 1948.

Lower, L. W., *Here's Luck*, Sydney, 1930.

Mackenzie, (Kenneth) Seaforth, *The Young Desire It*, London, 1937.

Mann, Leonard, *Flesh in Armour*, Melbourne, 1932.

Martin, David, *The Hero of Too*, Melbourne, 1965.

Mathers, Peter, *Trap*, Melbourne, 1966.

Newland, Simpson, *Paving the Way: a Romance of the Australian Bush*, London, 1893.

Palmer, Vance, *The Passage*, London, 1930.

— *Golconda*, Sydney, 1948.

Penton, Brian, *Landtakers: the Story of an Epoch*, Sydney, 1934.

Praed, Mrs Campbell, *Policy and Passion*, London, 1881, reprinted as *Longleat of Kooralbyn*, London, 1887.

Prichard, Katharine Susannah, *Black Opal*, London, 1921.

— *Working Bullocks*, London, 1926.

— *Coonardoo*, London, 1943.

— *The Roaring Nineties: a Story of the Goldfields of Western Australia*, London, 1946.
— *Golden Miles*, London and Sydney, 1948.
— *Winged Seeds*, Sydney, 1950.
Richardson, Henry Handel, *Maurice Guest*, London, 1908.
— *The Getting of Wisdom*, London, 1910.
— *The Fortunes of Richard Mahony*, London, 1930.
Rose, Lyndon, *Country of the Dead*, Sydney, 1959.
Rowcroft, Charles, *Tales of the Colonies*, London, 1843.
Rudd, Steele (Davis, A. H.), *On Our Selection*, Sydney, 1899.
Savery, Henry, *Quintus Servinton: a Tale founded upon Incidents of Real Occurrence*, Hobart Town, 1830-1.
Spence, Catherine, *Clara Morison*, 2 vols, London, 1856.
Stead, Christina, *Seven Poor Men of Sydney*, London, 1934; New York, 1935.
— *The Man Who Loved Children*, New York, 1940.
— *For Love Alone*, London, 1945.
Stivens, Dal, *Jimmy Brockett*, Sydney, 1951.
Stone, Louis, *Jonah*, Sydney and London, 1911.
Stow, Randolph, *To the Islands*, London, 1959.
— *Tourmaline*, London, 1963.
Tasma (Mrs Jessie Couvreur), *Uncle Piper of Piper's Hill*, London, 1889.
Tennant, Kylie, *Tiburon*, Sydney, 1935.
— *Foveaux*, London, 1939.
— *Ride on Stranger*, London, 1943.
— *Tell Morning This*, Sydney, 1967.
Tucker, James, *Ralph Rashleigh*, Introduction by the Earl of Birkenhead, London, 1929; Foreword by Colin Roderick, Sydney, 1952.
Waten, Judah, *The Unbending*, Melbourne, 1954.
White, Patrick, *The Tree of Man*, London, 1955.
— *Voss*, London, 1957.
— *Riders in the Chariot*, London, 1961.
— *The Solid Mandala*, London, 1966.
— *The Vivisector*, London, 1970.

3. SHORT STORY

Anderson, Ethel, *At Parramatta*, Melbourne, 1956.
Baynton, Barbara, *Bush Studies*, London, 1902.
Casey, Gavin, *It's Harder for Girls*, Sydney, 1942.
Clark, Manning, *Disquiet and Other Stories*, Sydney, 1969.
Clarke, Marcus, *Australian Tales and Sketches*, Melbourne, 1897.
Coast to Coast: Australian Short Stories, Sydney; Yearly Issues from 1941 to date, some issues biennial.
Cowan, Peter, *The Unploughed Land*, Sydney, 1958.
Davis, Beatrice (ed.), *Short Stories of Australia: the Moderns*, Sydney, 1967.
Dyson, Edward, *Below and On Top*, Sydney, 1898.
— *Fact'ry 'Ands*, Melbourne, 1906.
Ewers, John K. (ed.), *Modern Australian Short Stories*, Melbourne, 1965.
Hadgraft, Cecil and Wilson, Richard (eds.), *A Century of Australian Short Stories*, Melbourne, 1963.
James, Brian, *Cookabundy Bridge and Other Stories*, Sydney, 1946.
Lawson, Henry, *While the Billy Boils*, Sydney, 1898.
— *Mateship, His Mistake, and the Stranger's Friend*, Melbourne, 1930.

— *Prose Works*, Sydney, 1935.
— *The Stories of Henry Lawson* (ed. Cecil Mann), 3 vols, Sydney, 1964.
McCrae, Hugh, *Story-Book Only*, Sydney, 1948.
Marshall, Alan, *Tell Us About the Turkey, Jo*, Sydney, 1946.
— *How's Andy Going*, Melbourne, 1956.
Matthews, Harley, *Saints and Soldiers*, Sydney, 1918.
Morrison, John, *Black Cargo*, Melbourne, 1955.
— *Twenty-Three*, Sydney, 1962.
O'Reilly, Dowell, *Fivecorners*, Sydney, 1920.
— *Prose and Verse of Dowell O'Reilly*, Sydney, 1924.
Palmer, Nettie (ed.), *An Australian Story Book*, Sydney, 1928.
Palmer, Vance, *Let the Birds Fly*, Sydney, 1955.
— *The Rainbow Bird* (ed. Allan Edwards), Sydney, 1957.
Porter, Hal, *A Bachelor's Children*, Sydney, 1962.
— *The Cats of Venice*, Sydney, 1965.
Prichard, Katharine Susannah, *Happiness: Selected Short Stories*, Sydney, 1967.
Schlunke, E. O., *Stories of the Riverina* (ed. Clement Semmler), Sydney, 1960.
Stewart, Douglas (ed.), *Short Stories of Australia: the Lawson Tradition*, Sydney, 1967.
Stivens, Dal, *The Gambling Ghost*, Sydney, 1953.
— *Selected Stories, 1936-1968* (Introduction by H. P. Heseltine), Sydney, 1969.
Warung, Price (Astley, William), *Convict Days (1892-1898)*, Sydney, 1960.
Waten, Judah, *Alien Son*, Sydney, 1952.
White, Patrick, *The Burnt Ones*, London, 1964.
Wright, Judith, *The Nature of Love*, Melbourne, 1966.

4. DRAMA

Beynon, Richard, *The Shifting Heart*, Sydney, 1960.
Burn, David, *Plays and Fugitive Pieces in Verse*, Hobart, 1842.
Cusack, Dymphna, *Morning Sacrifice*, Sydney, 1943.
Dann, George Landen, *Fountains Beyond*, Sydney, 1944.
Drake-Brockman, Henrietta, *Men Without Wives*, Perth, 1938.
Esson, Louis, *The Southern Cross and Other Plays*, Melbourne, 1946.
Hanger, Eunice (ed.), *Khaki, Bush and Bigotry: Three Australian Plays*, Brisbane, 1968.
— (ed.), *Six One Act Plays*, Brisbane, 1969.
Harpur, Charles, *The Bushrangers: a Play in Five Acts, and other Poems*, Sydney, 1853.
Ireland, David, *Image in the Clay*, Brisbane, 1964.
Kippax, H. G. (ed.), *Three Australian Plays* (Penguin Plays), Mitcham, 1963.
Lawler, Ray, *Summer of the Seventeenth Doll*, Sydney, 1957.
— *Piccadilly Bushman*, Sydney, 1961.
Moore, William and Moore, T. Inglis (eds.), *Best Australian One-act Plays*, Sydney, 1937.
Roland, Betty, *The Touch of Silk*, Melbourne, 1942.
Seymour, Alan, *The One Day of the Year*, Sydney, 1962.
Stewart, Douglas, *Ned Kelly*, Sydney, 1943.
— *The Fire on the Snow and The Golden Lover*, Sydney, 1944.
— *Four Plays*, Sydney, 1958.
— *Fisher's Ghost*, Sydney, 1960.
Throssell, Ric, *The Day Before Tomorrow*, Sydney, 1969.

Tomholt, Sydney, *Bleak Dawn and Other Plays*, Sydney, 1936.
Tucker, James, *Jemmy Green in Australia* (ed. Colin Roderick), Sydney, 1955.
White, Patrick, *Four Plays*, London, 1965.

5. ESSAYS, TRAVEL, LETTERS AND AUTOBIOGRAPHY

Adams, David (ed.), *The Letters of Rachel Henning*, Sydney, 1963.
Bean, C. E. W., *On the Wool Track* (1910), Sydney, 1925.
— *The Dreadnought of the Darling* (1911), Sydney, 1956.
Bedford, Randolph, *Naught to Thirty-three*, Sydney, 1944.
Cambridge, Ada, *Thirty Years in Australia*, London, 1903.
Clarke, Marcus, "Australian Scenery", Preface to A. L. Gordon's *Sea Spray and Smoke Drift*, Melbourne, 1876.
Gerstaecker, F., *Narrative of a Journey Round the World*, etc., 3 vols, London, 1853.
Harris, Alexander, *The Secrets of Alexander Harris* (Intro. by Grant Carr-Harris and Preface by A. H. Chisholm), Sydney, 1961.
Hope, A. D., *The Cave and the Spring*, Adelaide, 1965.
Hopegood, Peter, *Peter Lecky by Himself*, London, 1935.
Lawson, Henry, *The Letters of Henry Lawson* (ed. Colin Roderick), Sydney, 1970.
Lindsay, Jack, *The Roaring Twenties*, London, 1960.
Lower, Lennie, *The Best of Lennie Lower* (ed. Cyril Pearl), Melbourne, 1963.
McAuley, James, *The End of Modernity: Essays on Literature, Art, and Culture*, Sydney, 1959.
McCrae, Hugh, *The Letters of Hugh McCrae* (ed. Robert D. FitzGerald), Sydney, 1970.
Marshall, Alan, *I Can Jump Puddles*, Melbourne, 1955.
Murdoch, Walter, *Collected Essays*, Sydney, 1940.
Palmer, Vance, *Intimate Portraits* (ed. H. P. Heseltine), Melbourne, 1969.
Praed, Mrs Campbell, *My Australian Girlhood*, London, 1902.
Ratcliffe, Francis, *Flying Fox and Drifting Sand*, Sydney, 1947.
Robinson, Ray, *Between Wickets*, London, 1945.
Rodd, L. C. (ed.), *The Australian Essay*, Melbourne, 1968.
Stephens, A. G., *The Red Pagan*, Sydney, 1904.
Twain, Mark, *Following the Equator*, New York, 1917.
Wood, Thomas, *Cobbers*, Melbourne, 1948.

6. CRITICISM AND BIOGRAPHY

Barnes, John (ed.), *The Writer in Australia: a Collection of Literary Documents 1856 to 1964*, Melbourne, 1969.
Buckley, Vincent, *Essays in Poetry Mainly Australian*, Melbourne, 1957.
Burke, Keast, *Thomas Alexander Browne (Rolf Boldrewood): an Annotated Bibliography, Checklist and Chronology*, Sydney, 1956.
Chisholm, A. H., *The Making of a Sentimental Bloke*, Melbourne, 1946.
Chisholm, A. R., *Christopher Brennan*, Sydney, 1946.
Devaney, James, *Shaw Neilson*, Sydney, 1944.
Dutton, G., then Johnston, G. (eds.), *Australian Writers And Their Work* (series of monographs on individual authors), Melbourne, 1961 to date.
Eldershaw, M. Barnard, *Essays in Australian Fiction*, Melbourne, 1938.
Elliott, Brian, *The Landscape of Australian Poetry*, Melbourne, 1967.
— *Marcus Clarke*, Oxford, 1958.
FitzGerald, Robert D., *The Elements of Poetry*, Brisbane, 1963.

Franklin, Miles and Baker, Kate, *Joseph Furphy: the Legend of a Man and His Book*, Sydney, 1944.

Gibson (Kramer), Leonie J., *Henry Handel Richardson and Some of Her Sources*, Melbourne, 1954.

Hasluck, Alexandra, *Portrait with Background*, Oxford, 1955.

Heseltine, Harry, *Vance Palmer*, Brisbane, 1970.

His Mates, *Henry Lawson*, Sydney, 1931.

Johnston, Grahame (ed.), *Australian Literary Criticism*, Melbourne, 1962.

Kellow, H. A., *Queensland Poets*, London, 1930.

Kennedy, Victor and Palmer, Nettie, *Bernard O'Dowd*, Melbourne, 1954.

Macartney, Frederick T., *Furnley Maurice* (Frank Wilmot), Sydney, 1955.

McDougall, Robert L., *Australia Felix: Joseph Furphy and Patrick White*, Canberra, 1966.

Moore, T. Inglis, *Six Australian Poets*, Melbourne, 1942.

Murray-Smith, Stephen, *Henry Lawson*, Melbourne, 1962.

Normington-Rawling, J., *Charles Harpur, An Australian*, Sydney, 1962.

Palmer, Nettie, *Henry Handel Richardson: a Study*, Sydney, 1950.

Palmer, Vance, *A. G. Stephens: His Life and Work*, Melbourne, 1941.

— *Louis Esson and the Australian Theatre*, Melbourne, 1960.

— *Frank Wilmot* (Furnley Maurice), Melbourne, 1942.

Praed, Mrs Campbell, *My Australian Girlhood*, London, 1902.

Prout, Denton, *Henry Lawson: the Grey Dreamer*, Adelaide, 1963.

Reed, Thomas Thornton, *Henry Kendall: a Critical Appreciation*, Adelaide, 1962.

Rees, Leslie, *Towards an Australian Drama*, Sydney, 1953.

Roderick, Colin, *Henry Lawson's Formative Years*, Sydney, 1960.

— *The Later Life of Henry Lawson*, Sydney, 1961.

— *An Introduction to Australian Fiction*, Sydney, 1950.

Semmler, Clement, *The Banjo of the Bush: the Work, Life and Times of A. B. Paterson*, Melbourne, 1966.

— (ed.), *20th Century Australian Literary Criticism*, Melbourne, 1967.

Sinnett, Frederick, *Fiction Fields of Australia* (ed. Cecil Hadgraft) (1856), Brisbane, 1966.

Stephens, A. G., *Chris Brennan: a Monograph*, Sydney, 1933.

Stewart, Douglas, *The Flesh and the Spirit*, Sydney, 1948.

Walker, William, *Australian Literature* (A Lecture Delivered at the Windsor School of Arts, evening of Wednesday, the 30th of July, 1864), Sydney, 1864.

Wilde, W. H., *Three Radicals*, Melbourne, 1969.

Wilkes, G. A., *New Perspectives on Brennan's Poetry*, Sydney, 1953.

Wright, Judith, *Preoccupations in Australian Poetry*, Melbourne, 1965.

III ARTICLES, THESES, MSS

A. History and Social Interpretation

Butlin, N. G., "The Shape of the Australian Economy, 1861-1900" in *The Economic Record*, vol.XXXIV, no. 67, April 1958.

Clark, Manning, "The Origins of the Convicts Transported to Eastern Australia, 1787-1852" in *Historical Studies of Australia and New Zealand*, vol.7, no. 26.

Darling, F. Fraser, "The Ecological Approach to the Social Sciences" in *American Scientist*, 1951, vol.39, p. 254.

Fitzgerald, C. P., "A Chinese Discovery of Australia?" in Moore, T. Inglis (ed.), *Australia Writes*, Melbourne, 1953.

Long, Gavin, "The Case of the Democratic Gold-digger", *The Australian Quarterly*, vol.XXVII, no. 2, 1955.

Stanner, W. E. H., "The Dreaming" in Hungerford, T. A. G. (ed.), *Australian Signpost*, Melbourne, 1956.

Ward, Russel, "The Ethos and Influence of the Australian Pastoral Worker", Ph.D. thesis, the Australian National University, Canberra. (Abridged and published as *The Australian Legend*, Melbourne, 1958.)

B. Literature

Barnard, Marjorie, "Our Literature" in *Australian Writers Speak*, Sydney, 1942.

Clark, Manning, "Tradition in Australian Literature", *Meanjin*, vol.VIII, no. 1, 1949.

Eldershaw, Flora, "The Landscape Writers", *Meanjin*, vol.XI, no. 3, 1952.

Elliott, Brian, "Charmed Circle", *Australian Book Review*, vol.2, no. 7, 1963.

Garnett, Edward, "Henry Lawson and the Democracy", *Friday Nights*, First Series, London, 1922.

Goldberg, S. L., "The Poet as Hero: A. D. Hope's *The Wandering Islands*", *Meanjin*, vol.XVI, no. 2, 1957.

Hope, A. D., "Henry Handel Richardson's *Maurice Guest*", *Meanjin Quarterly*, vol.XIV, no. 2, 1955.

— "Standards in Australian Literature", *Current Affairs Bulletin*, November 1956.

Kramer, Leonie, "James McAuley: Tradition in Australian Poetry", *The Commonwealth Literary Fund Lectures, 1957*, Canberra, 1957.

Lindsay, Jack, "Australian Poetry and Nationalism", *Vision*, no. 1, May 1923.

Miller, E. Morris, "O'Dowd's *The Bush*: an Exposition" in *Diogenes*, University of Tasmania, no. 3, 1957.

Moore, T. Inglis, "Kenneth Slessor", *Southerly*, vol.XIII, no. 4, 1957.

— "The Misfortunes of Henry Handel Richardson", *The Commonwealth Literary Fund Lectures, 1957*, Canberra, 1957.

— "The Tragi-Comedies of Kylie Tennant", *Southerly*, vol.XVIII, no. 1, 1957.

Phillips, A. A., "Criticising the Critics", *Meanjin Quarterly*, vol.XXIII, no. 2, 1963.

Prichard, Katharine Susannah, "Tributes to Bernard O'Dowd", *Meanjin*, vol. XIV, no. 4, 1953.

Richardson, Henry Handel, MS Letters in Moir Collection, Latrobe Library, Melbourne.

Ryan, J. T., "Australasian Character Sketch: an Australian Novelist: Rolf Boldrewood" in *Review of Reviews*, May 1894.

Saillens, Emile, "The Discovery of Australia by France" in *The Lone Hand*, 1 June 1909.

— "Le Bush Australien et Son Poète", *Mercure de France*, Paris, 1 oct., 1910.

Smith, Bernard, "The Interpretation of Australian Nature During the Nineteenth Century", B. A. thesis, University of Sydney.

Stephens, A. G., "Says and Hearsays", *The Bookfellow*, 29 April 1899.

— "National Character", *The Bookfellow*, vol.I, no. 26, June 1907.

— "Under the Gum-tree", *The Bookfellow*, vol.I, no. 12, Nov. 1912.

— "Henry Lawson", *The Bookfellow*, 28 February 1922.

Stephensen, P. R., "Book Publishing in Australia", *The Australian Rhodes Review*, March 1934.

Topp, S. S. ("S.S.T."), "Australian Poetry", *The Melbourne Review*, vol.I, Jan. to Oct. 1876.

Turner, Ian, "The Parable of *Voss*", *Overland*, no. 12, Winter 1958.

Wallace-Crabbe, Chris, "The Habit of Irony? Australian Poets of the Fifties", *Meanjin Quarterly*, vol.XX, no. 2, 1961.

Waters, Edgar, "Some Aspects of the Popular Arts in Australia 1880-1915", unpublished thesis, Australian National University, Canberra, 1962.

White, Patrick, "The Prodigal Son", *Australian Letters*, vol.I, no. 3, April 1958.

Wilkes, G. A., "Brennan and His Literary Affinities", *The Australian Quarterly*, vol.XXXI, no. 2, June 1959.

IV NEWSPAPERS AND PERIODICALS

American Mercury, New York
Atlas, Sydney
Australian Book Review, Adelaide
Australian Letters, Adelaide
Australian Literary Studies, Hobart
Australian National Review, Canberra
Australian Quarterly, Sydney
Australian Rhodes Review, Melbourne
Bookfellow, Sydney
Boomerang, Brisbane
Bulletin, Sydney
Colonial Monthly, Melbourne
Empire, Sydney
Freeman's Journal, Sydney
Hummer, Wagga
Lone Hand, Sydney
Meanjin Quarterly, Melbourne
Mercure de France, Paris
Overland, Melbourne
Poetry Australia, Sydney
Poetry Magazine, Sydney
Quadrant, Sydney
Realist, Sydney
Southerly, Sydney
Sydney Gazette, Sydney
Sydney Morning Herald, Sydney
Times Literary Supplement, London
Tocsin, Melbourne
Vision, Sydney
Worker, Brisbane

Index

Entries for titles of works are given only when the authorship is not indicated in the text.